# TIRYNS

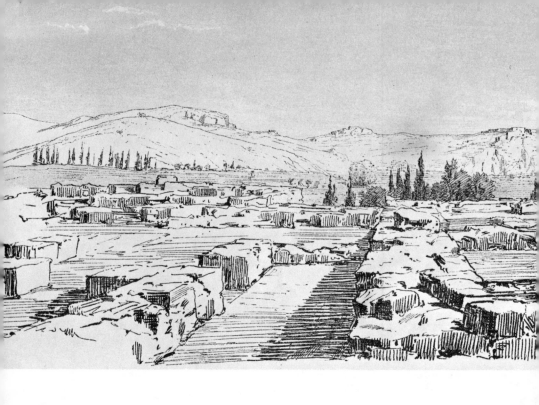

# HEINRICH SCHLIEMANN

# TIRYNS

*The Prehistoric Palace of the*

*Kings of Tiryns*

Arno Press • New York, 1976

First published 1885
Reprint Edition 1967 by Benjamin Blom, Inc.

Reprint Edition 1976 by Arno Press Inc.

LC# 67-14967
ISBN 0-405-09853-7

Manufactured in the United States of America

TO

# JAMES FERGUSSON, Esq.,

C.I.E., D.C.L., LL.D., F.R.S., F.R.I.B.A., M.R.A.S.,
HON. MEM. R.S.L. &c.,

## THE HISTORIAN OF ARCHITECTURE,

EMINENT ALIKE FOR HIS KNOWLEDGE OF THE ART, AND FOR THE
ORIGINAL GENIUS WHICH HE HAS APPLIED TO THE SOLUTION
OF SOME OF ITS MOST INTERESTING PROBLEMS;

### This Work is Dedicated,

IN GRATEFUL ACKNOWLEDGMENT OF HIS INTEREST IN MY LABOURS
AND THE HELP DERIVED FROM HIS SCHOLARSHIP AND
PROFOUND ARCHÆOLOGICAL LEARNING
SINCE THE BEGINNING OF THE DISCOVERIES AT TROY.

### HENRY SCHLIEMANN.

# PREFACE.

—◆◆◆—

WHEN the Author invited me to write a Preface to his work on Tiryns, I declared my readiness to do so without hesitation; for he thus afforded me a welcome opportunity of adding my personal thanks—for the substantial advantages that had accrued to my own studies in the history of architecture—to the universal tribute offered so justly from every side to the indefatigable explorer of the oldest civilisation of Greece and Asia Minor.

I hope to express this feeling most practically by an attempt to gather the results—as regards the technical and artistic aspect of architecture—which follow from Dr. Schliemann's excavations in Troy, Mycenæ, Orchomenos, and Tiryns, and, as far as this is possible to-day, to shape them into a picture of the oldest art of building in Greece and in Asia Minor.

No doubt, there are still great gaps, owing to various causes, and it is certain that our present materials will sooner or later be substantially supplemented. Yet I would justify this essay as a necessary preliminary, which only an architect can supply, to further inquiries as to the development of art in one of the most attractive, though one of the most obscure, regions of classical antiquity. If I have reached beyond Dr. Schliemann's personal work, by utilising the architectural harvest of the latest discoveries in Attica and Argolis, I plead my desire to make my sketch as complete as possible.

Three kinds of architecture have been materially illustrated by the successful work of the spade: (1) Fortresses, (2) Palaces, (3) Tombs. The important branch of Temples is still missing from the list.

True, MM. Schliemann and Dörpfeld had taken two large ruins, lying parallel on the Pergamos (of Priam), to be temples, and supported this view even in *Troja* (pp. 76–86, *seq.*), which appeared in 1884. But they forthwith abandoned this view, when analogous but better-preserved architectural remains at Tiryns proved to be parts of a great palace, plainly discernible as such in its main features. As here, so in Troy, these rooms, superior to the rest in proportion, plan, and strength of walls, were certainly the chief halls of the kingly residence. Hence the fact is to be noted, that no trace has hitherto been found, in any of the three citadels, of buildings for the purpose of worship, dating from the ancient period. The very slight architectural fragments, of Doric style, found at Mycenæ and Tiryns, which may be the remnants of stone temples, are certainly far more recent than the ancient royal palaces, and hence offer no material for the solution of this important problem.

As regards FORTRESSES, the fortifications of Troy, Mycenæ, and Tiryns can alone be considered, since the Acropolis of Orchomenos has not yet been subjected to an accurate investigation. All three are built on an almost identical plan, and show a similarity of situation. For the site, there was always chosen a rocky eminence of more or less height. Tiryns (26 m. over the sea) is the lowest; then comes Troy (40 m.), while Mycenæ lies ten times as high as Tiryns: its summit rises to 277 m. The former are strongholds in the plain. The latter is a proud mountain-fastness.

The scanty room enclosed by the surrounding walls proves that, in the first foundation, only the security of the chieftain was the object aimed at—not the protection of a town-like settlement, or the erection of a great depot for war. Even as in the Middle Ages, huts and houses may somewhat later have sprung up round the citadel. When the increase of population, and the growing wealth, necessitated an enlargement of the existing bulwarks, this extended fortification, even when rationally and skilfully laid out, did not always increase the defensive power of the fortress; nay, it often impaired it.

In the case of Mycenæ, such a combination of town and fortress is certain from the name, from literary evidences, and from architectural remains. The same may be assumed at an early period in the case of Troy, even if we do not regard the evidence of Homer as decisive, because the wells lying to the S.W. were indispensable for a prolonged defence of the fortress, and must therefore soon have been embraced in the fortifications. The town therefore lay certainly S. of the Pergamos. From later times we have also evidence of a town-like settlement beside Tiryns; but its origin is as obscure as the course of its surrounding walls. Probably the town lay not to the west near the sea, but to the east in the plain, protected from pirates by the citadel. This situation seems to be indicated also by a find of coins.

Two citadels, Pergamos and Tiryns, were meant to watch both sea and land. The former commanded the most extensive view, and lay, moreover, on a great highroad of the world's traffic. Mycenæ. on the contrary, is a stronghold thrown forward as an outpost into the mountains, to dominate important passes; hence its natural strength is greatest. Then follows Tiryns; and last of all, Troy. This last only had, at least on its E., W., and S. sides, a dry moat, which was not needed by the others, built, as they were, on steep rocks.

The other indispensable conditions for defence are fulfilled by all alike: with economy of circuit, a minimum of gates and posterns; then, walls of sufficient height and strength, with easily blocked approaches; and finally, a suitable utilising of the inner enclosed ground with a view to dominating the lower parts, *i.e.* a terrace formation of higher and lower citadel. At all times, strongholds have been narrowly girdled, for a small circuit of wall is more quickly built; it diminishes the cost of construction and maintenance, and permanently facilitates the defence. But sometimes the first narrow girdle of defence did not long suffice for the fast growing requirements of the place. Then, on one or more sides, extensions were undertaken. The still existing remains prove this fact in the case of Troy, to the E. and S., as well as at Mycenæ along the S. side. Tiryns, on the other hand, has always preserved the line of its old bounds, and seems certainly a building of uniform plan, though the citadel is not the first, but the second structure on the same site.

The second condition—a minimum of gates and posterns—is obvious in rationally planned fortifications, seeing that every gate, however small, constitutes a weak point, and that every useless postern diminishes the primary intention of safety by enhancing the danger of treason. Hence Tiryns, in addition to two very small apertures in the walls for the purposes of patrolling and getting information, always possessed only one main gate and one postern. The same is the case at Mycenæ; besides the Lions' Gate, there is here only, at the N.E., a postern which, in addition to military purposes, served for getting water from a neighbouring well (Perseia?). So also for the citadel of Troy, two gates sufficed from the beginning— namely, the central gate at the S., and the one leading to the wells, S.W. This number has never been exceeded; for when the extension of the fort made it necessary to plan a new (third) gate S.E., the old central gate was permanently walled up, and the traffic between town and citadel again confined to two gates.

Besides these fundamental points of agreement in ancient fort-building, there are also points of variance, which must not be overlooked. They concern the arrangement of the walls in ground-plan and in section (*tracé* and *profile*).

If we turn first to the ground-plan, we find already in the Pergamos that the ancient walls were flanked by salient, massive, tower-like bastions recurring at pretty regular intervals, from which the intervening wall-sections could be watched and laterally swept by the missiles thrown from the beleaguered stronghold.

This is specially shown in the old central gate—a colossal, massive structure with a narrow, tunnel-like gate-way, which in the first instance was intended to defend the causeway crossing the moat, but which also served to flank the S. side, and therefore assuredly stood out like a great tower over the walls. From the fact that, in the later extension of the fortress, the flanking position of this tower was almost wholly abandoned, we may be certain that its construction must belong to the time of the *second* citadel, the method of fortification in the earliest settlement being unknown. At all events, this structure represents, in its conception, a combination of gate-tower and of salient outwork, which is architecturally of great value.

The flanking system, the application of which, in the heroic age, was even recently still so strangely denied, is absent neither from Mycenæ nor from Tiryns; but, on account of the varying conditions of the ground, it has in neither of these citadels been so thoroughly carried out as at Troy. In the former two cases it was confined to a few very important points. At Troy, it was most fully developed.

To the circuit wall belongs the entrance way into the fort. The final ascent for pedestrians and horsemen was provided for by inclines, which were either simply formed of earth, or paved, and had a moderate incline ($20-25°$) of varying breadth (5–8 m.). At Tiryns and Mycenæ (I speak here of the first foundation of the citadel, before the southern extension was undertaken and the Lions' Gate built) these ramps lay (and still lie) close along the walls, in such a manner that the assailant was forced to expose his unshielded right side to the defenders.  In Troy, on the contrary, where a dry moat had to be crossed, the dam-like ramps lead direct to the gates, and are consequently at right angles with the line of the wall.  Both the ground-plans and the sections of the circuit walls show marked differences.  The variety of the building materials and of the site accounts for that.

The walls of the Pergamos show the simplest structure, because lime quarry-stones of middling size have been used for the substructures, while sun-dried bricks were used for the upper part.  The limestones are laid horizontally in layers without any sort of cement; but the wall is escarped from without (the angle of inclination is at first $45°$, then $60°$), while the inner side rises vertically.  The scarp, or batter, fulfils a twofold object; it makes the undermining of the wall more difficult, and also diminishes the absolute heights for the upper structure.  This latter, built of sun-dried bricks with clay mortar, had an average thickness of $3\frac{1}{2}$–4 m., and within, a similar height.  Its strength was increased by means of inserted beams of wood, which recur at fixed levels and are placed longitudinally in the wall as well as across it—a structure often repeated in stone building.  There must have been a rampart way along the top of the wall with a protecting parapet.  We can also infer from the existing remains an average elevation of 9–10 m.; and thus the wall was externally secure from escalade.  The weakest front was the south side; it was therefore provided with a dry moat, the width of which can be inferred from the flank measurements of the gateway, and may be fixed at 16–17 m.  Its depth cannot have been less than 3 m.

Quite different are the fortifications of Tiryns and Mycenæ.  The escarped substruction of free-stone was omitted, being replaced by the rising rock which could easily, where necessary, be made inaccessible by subsequent chiselling.    Then, as good free-stone was to be found quite close by, the use of sun-dried bricks could be considerably limited, or entirely dispensed with.

The greater part of the walls of Tiryns consists of limestone blocks of large, even colossal size, the interstices being filled up with smaller stones.    Throughout, a horizontal jointing is attempted, as far as possible, with the stones already split in the quarry to obtain an under-surface, and rudely worked with heavy hammers on the other surfaces.    There is no trace of ashlar masonry, or real polygonal bonding; but it is obvious, from mathematical considerations, that at the numerous salient and inverted angles the rude, longish, polyedra must have been wrought into clumsy parallelopipeda to construct these angles.    Hence, upon careful examination, there is clearly to be seen in many places an approach to a horizontal jointing, though rising and falling in crooked lines.

I conjecture that in the construction of all so-called Cyclopean walls a strong mortar of loam, or potter's clay, was used as bedding material, which facilitated the laying, joining, and further piling up of the stones, but dried up afterwards, and, by being gradually washed away, finally disappeared.    Hence there resulted, in many places, both vertical and horizontal joints sufficiently large to make the scaling of the wall possible to experienced climbers, especially if the wall itself was slightly escarped.    As close fitting with oblong or polygonal blocks was not yet usual, this danger was obviated by choosing, for the lowest and middle courses, blocks so large that they could not be surmounted either by upward or oblique climbing.    This view is supported, first, by the circumstance that some stones in the interstices lie there loosely now, because they are no longer held together by pressure, and chiefly by the fact, that the largest blocks are only found in the lower and middle courses on the outside.    Hence I am disposed to attribute the use of the colossal quarry-stones at Tiryns at least as much to this practical reason as to the ambition of the founder of the stronghold. He has indeed, in this latter respect, raised for himself a monument of the first rank. I have myself measured in many instances on the upper citadel, blocks of 2·90–3·20 m. in length, by 1·10–1·50 in height. Their depth was not measurable, but may be taken at 1·20–1·50 m. We thus obtain a weight of from 12–13,000 kgs. for a rudely-prepared block, the transport of which, to its exact place on a high and narrow site, was only possible with the aid of many technical devices —inclined planes and scaffolding—and a host of workmen. Even middle-sized stones, easily measurable in their chief dimensions, weigh 3700–4000 kgs. These figures are important, as proving that the citadel we see before us, and whose gigantic blocks even in antiquity excited astonishment and admiration, cannot have been built in a hurry, in the sight of the enemy, or as the first stronghold of an invasion based on maritime supremacy. If, indeed, the country was here suddenly invaded from the seaside, the first fortress must have consisted of wood and sun-dried bricks; for the colossal walls tell every one able to read the language of stones, that their erection can only have been effected in a long period of peace, by a ruler with unusual resources of power, and who had trained workmen under his permanent control.

In support of the idea, that we have in Tiryns not the first, but the second structure on that site, many additional reasons may be adduced. In the first place, under the foundations of the palace on the upper citadel, occur undoubted traces of older buildings; among them, the substructure of a huge gate-tower, over which the outer Propylæum was afterwards erected. But if the inner part of the citadel was made a good stronghold, the outer must have been so *à fortiori*. This confirms my second observation, that in the wall of the nether citadel there are, in many places, vertical joints coming down, sometimes, to the rock, which show clearly that this part was not built at one and the same time, but in several divisions. Probably the older and cheaper defence of wood and sun-dried bricks was retained here till it could be replaced gradually by a more solid stone structure.

The section of the wall is not uniform, but is generally massive in the nether citadel. Here the depth varies from 7 to 9 m.; the outer height, no longer measurable, may have also been 9 m. The broad rampart way along the top of the wall was contracted closely by massive towers in several places, perhaps even blocked, so that it might be defended in sections. There are deep niches in the wall, covered by rude corbelling out of the blocks, not so much to save material as to gain room. In the upper citadel the thickness of the wall increases to 13, 15, even 17 m., but no longer represents a massive block of wall—*e.g.* in the S.E. corner and along the S. front—but a systematically connected cluster of rooms (stairs, galleries, magazines, cisterns, and casemates), which are all built of large blocks, and are all covered on a system of corbelling, so as to be fireproof. The whole, though partially fallen in, is an astonishing specimen of fortification and construction dating back to hoary antiquity. A huge double tower, with cellars, which perhaps contained prisons, flanked the south part of the W. wall. A second, still greater, in the E. wall, commanded the main entrance. Smaller solid towers were probably here distributed along the wall, as well as in the lower citadel.

The walls of Mycenæ do not possess the general uniformity which marks those at Tiryns; one recognises there various kinds of work, done at periods the succession of which cannot now be determined The construction of the nucleus is, no doubt, almost everywhere the same: it consists of roughly-shaped limestone blocks piled up one upon the other, and bonded by small stones and clay.

But there also appear, outside, large stretches of perfectly horizontal ashlar-masonry; in some spots even the best close-fitting polygonal bonding. It is known from the history of Greek architecture that this last kind of building belongs everywhere to a comparatively late period, and has no connection with the so-called Cyclopean constructions. At Mycenæ this best, but most costly, kind of wall seems to have been applied only where damaged places (breaches, slips) had to be subsequently repaired permanently, or completely renewed.

Considerably older than this patchwork with polygonal blocks is the ashlar masonry, which first occurs here, and which consists of layers of oblong rectangles, with studied variation in the vertical joints. That this does not belong to the earliest building of the fort, is at once clear from the fact, that the northern wall of the approach to the Lions' Gate consists of two parts separated vertically: first, of a thick core of limestone piled up in Cyclopean fashion; and then, of a relatively thin coating of oblong blocks of breccia, in the lower strata of which no bond-stones are to be found. The southern wall of the same approach shows the same oblong ashlar masonry of breccia, not laid on, however, as a mere coating without binding-stones, but joined thoroughly with the core-structure. From both observations it follows with absolute certainty that the oblong ashlar masonry must be more recent than the old Cyclopean limestone building, and is only connected with the extension of the fortress towards the south, and with the erection of the Lions' Gate.

The oldest outer wall of Mycenæ is all of the same stamp; it is built in Cyclopean fashion, like that of Tiryns, but throughout with smaller blocks of stone. It closely surrounded a triangular hill, which is in places very steep, and which could only be terraced with the help of numerous supporting walls, and thereby made fit to bear an upper fortress in the middle, and two lower ones; the

latter lying to the east and west respectively. The old
ascent with its incline was probably at the S. side, above
the well-known pit-graves discovered by Dr. Schliemann;
and the last part of the ascent went from E. to W., so that
the unshielded side of the assailant was here again exposed.
From the first there were two gates here. Besides the
chief gate—in the middle of the old south front—the
position of which cannot be determined without further
excavations, there was the above-mentioned water-gate on
the N.E., which, like the central gate at Troy, had a tower
as a superstructure. The circuit-wall is, generally speaking,
much thinner than that of Tiryns; its average thickness is
5 m. However, in the N. and S.E. there are portions
increasing to the thickness of 14 m. The occurrence, in
one place in the N. wall, of remains of a gallery leads to
the conjecture that, later on, a careful examination of the
masses of ruins which have tumbled down, will bring to
light similar arrangements of stairs, galleries, store-rooms,
and casemates, to those at Tiryns.

At a later period the fortress was enlarged southward;
evidently to gain more room for the increased requirements
of kingly power. Then, not only was a new gate—the
well-known Lions' Gate—added; but the whole N.W.
corner, in order to give it a grander appearance, was
dressed with the above-mentioned thin coat of oblong
square blocks of breccia. Better than this strengthening,
which was only for show, was the erection of the strong
oblong tower of the same material, jutting out at the S.
side like a mole, and destined to defend the approach to
the new gate, and make the western finish to the new
extension wall on the S. It was a very necessary advanced
work for the security of the weak gate. Then, also, the
old ascent to the fort, which came from the S.W. and
swept round, loop-like, towards the W., was given up; and,
as a further consequence, the Castle ramp was carried up
from another direction. It now went straight up from the

Lions' Gate, hence in a favourable position for the assailant ; but the builder could afford to make this apparent error, because the ramp lay now no longer outside, but inside the circuit-wall, and was therefore amply protected.

The gates show differences not less significant than those of the walls. The oldest kind of construction is exhibited in the S. central gate of the Pergamos of Troy, that primitive and massive solid structure of sun-dried bricks, cut through by the narrow gateway. Its roof was constructed, as in the gallery of a mine, by side posts with close timbering above, and it had an upper storey with a platform and breast-work. This rude and simple structure shows that the very old Oriental method of vaulting with sun-dried bricks was unknown at Troy, and that they strove to solve the problem before them in a not very monumental fashion. The covering of the S.W. gate leading to the wells was probably similar ; but trustworthy indications are wanting in the excavated remains.

When the central gate was abandoned in consequence of the enlargement of the fort, the S.W. gate was rebuilt on another plan, suggested by the S.E. gate—viz. in the form of a sluice-chamber with two portals, and with short vestibules bounded by side-walls. This form of gate is also characteristic of Troy, and deserves all the more atten- tion, as we here have the fundamental idea of the later *propugnaculum*. Tiryns and Mycenæ do not, it is true, possess this form of gate ; but in the Propylæa of the palace of Tiryns a similar architectural principle has been applied, and indeed in a more advanced form.

If in the gates of Troy we still find wood largely used, the gates of the other two fortresses show, on the contrary, a perfectly monumental shape. The cases neces- sary for the doors consist here of great and hard stones (breccia), and the lintel is relieved of the superincum- bent weight by obliquely corbelled layers of stone, which close above in triangular form. Thin slabs—one or two,

according to the depth—fill this triangular opening, in
order to prevent climbing over the closed gate.   Such a
structure with two slabs is still preserved in the little N.E.
gate at Mycenæ, while the Lions' Gate probably always
possessed but the one with the famous relief.   The proximity
in situation, as well as the historical connection expressed
in the legends, explain the many points of similarity in the
two fortresses, not only in structure but in detail—to wit:
the identical measurements in the clear, and other technical aids to fortification, such as the construction of the
threshold, the arrangement of the bolting-bar for the gate
wings, &c.   This is also true of the little side gates, posterns
with their modest triangular structures of corbelled layers, to
which, as there were no framing stones, a closing apparatus
could only be applied in a very incomplete manner.   The
most interesting postern is found in the western semicircular structure of the wall of Tiryns.   It is connected
by a flight of sixty-five steps, first, with the middle fortress,
but also by a second flight of steps and by a narrow zigzag
passage with the interior of the palace, as well as with the
upper circuit-wall.   Accordingly, messengers might come
and go—particularly in the direction of the sea—by this
secret way, without using the main entrance; and during a
siege the semicircular structure could at the same time be
used to collect troops for a sortie.   Moreover, the remains
of a chamber, found at a considerable height above it, show
that at this important point a look-out was established.

Next to the outer shell of walls and gates comes
naturally the examination of the core, which was the
dwelling-place of the ruler.   Unfortunately, there is far less
material extant for this *second kind of architecture* than for
the first.   The citadel Pergamos gave but few results,
because the separation of the strata of building was here
very difficult, because in the earlier years of the excavations
much had been inadvertently destroyed.   Nevertheless,
some comparisons are possible.   It is even more to be

deplored that the extensive ruins on the acropolis of
Mycenæ continue to be a book with seven seals, which
every scholar must long to have soon opened by systematic
researches. For even now a surface of 50–60 m., which
fairly corresponds, as the site for a palace, to that at Tiryns,
can be recognised on the highest top. From the graduated
formation of the ground we may conclude that the acropolis
of Mycenæ, with its palace, must have made outwardly a
far more imposing impression than the princely dwelling
at Tiryns, which was half hidden behind its gigantic walls.

Under these circumstances, the results which we owe
to the closer examination of the fortress at Tiryns, are of
all the greater value. This is, so far, the only source
from which we can draw a direct and clear idea of the
architecture of an ancient Greek royal palace.

What first strikes us in examining the ground-plan, is
the orientation, towards the S., of the rooms most used.
This arrangement seems due to two causes. First, the
palace was to be made habitable at all seasons; for the
warmth of the sun was required in winter, the summer heat
being kept off by the national method of building with
thick walls of sun-dried bricks and roofs of wood, covered
with clay. Secondly, it was desirable to keep an eye always
on the neighbouring Nauplia and the broad entrance of
the gulf. An architect's eye is next attracted by the very
skilful distribution of all the portions of the building on
the space afforded by nature and much limited by art.
If, as was obvious, the principal room of the palace—the
Men's Hall—was to occupy the highest place, and, on
account of the outlook on Nauplia, had to be moved as
near as possible to the S. side, then these two requirements could only be satisfied by making the eastern
approach start from the N., ascend in a great sweep, and
end at a suitable distance from that main room. This was
done, and indeed so as to make the first greater section of
the way everywhere still capable of defence. It is only with

the great Propylæum that the huge rampart whose only
aim and object, at first, was security, makes way for a
style of building intended for the purposes of comfortable
human occupation.    The form and grouping of its rooms
had to satisfy the various demands which a princely household has made for itself at all times, both in a real and
an ideal sense.    Proud seclusion towards without; suitable
accommodation for guards and domestics about roomy
courts; dignified approaches up to the reception room;
finally, convenient connection of the dwelling-rooms
proper, both one with another and with the outer rooms—
and all this well lighted, and yet shady and cool : these are
the requirements of a palace in the South.    If with this
basis to go upon we add the aids given us by Homer in his
characteristic descriptions of princely life, we are able, in
spite of sundry gaps, to explain correctly the wonderfully
well-preserved ground-plan in its main features.

There can be no doubt about the central part of the
plan.    The large Men's Hall, distinguished by a stately
ante-room, and the very much smaller Women's Hall,
each lying contiguous to an inner court surrounded with
colonnades, are conspicuous at once; next, the remarkable
bath-room, close to the larger Megaron.    Considering the
custom of the Heroic Age of giving strangers a bath
soon after their arrival, the position of the guest-chambers,
as well as of the servants' rooms, must be sought near the
bath-room—that is, at the W. side of the principal court,
where now, by the fall of the circuit-wall, there is a great
gap.    In the same way, we may set down the small inner
court, lying close beside the Women's Court (XXX on
Plan II.), as a yard devoted to the domestic economy,
and the adjoining rooms to the S. as housewifery rooms;
for it is worthy of remark that this court is not con-
creted, and, doubtless, on account of the continual intercourse with the outside, was in direct communication with
the first great Propylæum.    Finally we have here, and

here only, two separate conduits within the domestic
rooms, which carry off water southward, and point to a
large use of water.   The rooms in the N.E. corner, closely
connected with the women's apartment, were at once, and I
think rightly, designated as the bed-chamber of the married
pair, and the armoury and treasure rooms of the ruler.

Moreover, this handsomely and practically arranged
building was not wanting in an ideal centre-point, where
the ruler, surrounded by his people, thankfully offered
sacrifices to the gods or sought their will; and this was
the altar of Zeus Herkeios, built under the open sky, in
the shape of a circular sacrificial pit.   Like a guardian of
the threshold, it stands in the main court, close to the
inner vestibule; forming, at the same time, the end of the
main axis of the Men's Hall.   It was an admirably chosen
spot for setting up a structure the importance of which
needed no enhancement from art, which was to remind
one of peace, to afford protection, and to hallow the going
in and the coming out.

But although the plan of the inner palace is intelligible
in its main features, it is less easy to tell with certainty the
destination of the buildings about the great fore-court.   In
position and form, it is true, the two pillared vestibules are
at once distinguishable.   Their object, too, is plain; they
were to separate, practically, the inner and the outer parts,
and combine them artistically.   In addition, we may also
regard the rooms between the two gates as very well suited
for guards and servants.   But everything else to the W.
and S. remains doubtful; the fall of the western wall, and
the erection of the Byzantine Church to the S., have
destroyed all useful indications.   Yet this loss must not be
over-estimated.   To the W., not much more than a portico
can have stood, as the course of the upper circuit-wall
leaves but little room; and to the S., the almost immediate
vicinity of the gigantic fortification, with its stairs, galleries,
and magazines, suggests. that with the exception of some

buildings for outer husbandry uses, the majority of rooms once here situated must also have served for defensive purposes.

N. of the palace extends a somewhat lower terrace, with an average breadth of 30 m.—the so-called middle citadel—the excavation of which has scarcely led to any satisfactory results. Neither its connection with the lower citadel, nor its immediate connection with the approach to the Castle, has been established. Yet we may conjecture that here, too, a part of the garrison was posted, because the important way to the W. postern and sally-gate passed through here, and the not less important back-stairs to the palace began here. So momentous a point of the citadel must have been under permanent military guard. Hence it results that the house of the prince was shut in, and carefully guarded on all sides, by gates, walled approaches, watch-posts, and barracks. This main feature in the plan seems to point to Oriental influences.

What kind of buildings the lower citadel once enclosed, is as unknown as their order, form, and size, the spade having only felt its way here, instead of excavating; so that, excepting some graves, nothing important has been as yet discovered. Perhaps the first town settlement stood here.

The ground-plan of the palace shows, in my opinion, a distinct uniformity of design, in spite of some later additions and alterations, and gives us a very favourable idea of the talent and experience of its architect. The principal rooms are arranged in clear order about courts admitting full light and air; they are suitably disposed and easily accessible. They have no want of good and often twofold connection. Particular facility is afforded for the separate home work of serving-men and maids; and the urgent need of secret exit and intercourse with the outside is not forgotten.

We obtain valuable hints also as regards the technical capabilities of the builder. The walls, constructed of sun-

dried bricks with tie-beams, rest on foundations of free-stone
bonded with clay.  The thresholds consist partly of wood,
mostly of stone ; they show us the dimension, arrangement,
and method of fixing of the thick wooden doors.  Astonishment is created by the monolith floor of the bath-room,
weighing 20,000 kg.  What mechanical efforts must its
transport and placing at this elevation have cost!  Its site,
when once chosen, must have been decisive for the
arrangement of all the chief rooms, and so we may infer that
essential changes of the first plan never took place.  Elsewhere, too, the laying of the floors in most of the rooms and
chief courts is carefully considered, and, in connection there-
with, the important question of draining systematically
treated—a sure proof of an advanced state of culture.

The structure shows much variety in the formation of
its rooms : large and small courts ; pillared and unpillared
vestibules ; even a three-aisled state-room, with ante-room.
Like the roofs, all the supports, pillars, pilasters, and door-
posts were of wood.  That the visible wooden surfaces
were even coated with sheet-metal is not impossible, but
scarcely probable, or else some remains of the metal sheets
would have been found in the ruins.  As to the form of
the pillars, nothing certain could be discovered.  But the
still measurable traces of their standing-places, of various
dimensions—together with the heights, which we are taught
by experience can be deduced from the thickness of the
walls—lead us to the sure inference, that the pillars were of
slender proportions : namely, $1 : 7$ or $1 : 8$ ; sometimes even
$1 : 10$.  If, for example, we assume for the side-walls of the
Men's Hall, which are $1 \cdot 32$ m. thick, five times this height—
which is rather too little than too much—we obtain a height
of $6 \cdot 60$ m. up to the lower surface of the two thick girders
which carried the roof, and so with the now measurable
lower diameter of the pillars ($0 \cdot 66$ m.), a proportion of
$1 : 9 \cdot 91$.  A similar result—viz. $1 : 9$—is obtained by a comparison of the corresponding measurements of the great

Prothyron. These are also the minimum proportions commonly employed in wooden structures for supports.

The rotting, dry or wet, of the shafts was obviated by a moderate elevation of the base on flat stone supports. We do not know, however, how the mischief of settlement and splitting of the wooden pillars, caused by their drying, was technically counterbalanced; yet, this point, so important practically for any southern climate, has been well considered in the construction of the pilasters. Both in Troy, and in Tiryns it was preferred to make the *antæ*, throughout, of a number of thin posts rather than of one beam.

As to the construction of the wooden roofs, as well as the form, division, and connection of the roof-beams, we are left to conjecture in the absence of certain indications. From the fact that the widest span does not exceed 5·64 m., we may indeed infer roofs of great weight; but we cannot determine whether they were made in the primæval, simple fashion of a close row of unhewn round beams, such as the Lycian rock-tombs represent, and the Lions' Gate relief and the façade of one of the beehive-tombs at Mycenæ suggest; or of hewn beams set at fixed intervals, with a cover of boards and a coating of clay. Probably both methods were used side by side, the first for the subordinate chambers, the latter for the chief rooms. In no case can we assume an artistic formation of overhanging roofs with architectural members of terra-cotta.

The lighting of separate rooms was certainly, according to southern habits, through the door; the majority, however, probably obtained their light by elevated lateral apertures. I suppose that the triple-naved Men's Hall was also lighted only by an uninterrupted row of side windows treated after the manner of a frieze, between the beam-ends close under the roof. Lighting on the clerestory principle, immediately over the hearth, is too objectionable practically, especially for winter weather, to make it, in my opinion, likely. The construction of a wooden central nave on slender and widely-separated pillars is in itself complicated enough, and as regards the weight produced by the widely-projecting roof, not without danger in the case of violent storms.

Then, the important discovery of the so-called kyanos-frieze of alabaster is to be taken into account. As this architectural member, so remarkable for its original beauty and decorative splendour, must certainly have been intended to be clearly seen, it required a specially good lateral lighting, and it is therefore very possible that it was situated over the place where it was found, on the side wall of the vestibule, close under the roof. With this I connect the further conjecture, that the axes of the upper windows of the great Megaron between the beds of the beams, and also the beams themselves in their main measurements, may have agreed with the corresponding architectural members of the kyanos-frieze, so that these latter may afford us an important basis for the graphic reconstruction of the Megaron roof. The extraordinary simplicity of the system which results therefrom, both for roofing and lighting, recommends this hypothesis.

Lastly, the palace also possessed the important artistic and sympathetic element of coloured decoration—of a decoration which was not confined to the introduction of organic or geometrical ornaments, but even embraced figure-painting. We may expect the complete reproduction and full discussion of this epoch-making find of most archaic wall-painting to form a lasting basis of an important chapter in classical art history. Of great value is, at any rate, the easily recognisable fact that certain decorative designs here painted on the wall, and repeated in chiselled relief on the stone-roof at Orchomenos, undoubtedly come from Egyptian sources.

On the citadel of Troy also stood a palace of similar plan and construction to that at Tiryns; this is now a fact established beyond the possibility of cavil, after the renewed reproduction and discussion of some large structures, formerly regarded as temples.   In the walls, unfortunately much destroyed, certain chief rooms, and particularly characteristic architectural parts, can be forthwith recognised and determined, as soon as the plan of Tiryns is brought into comparison.   I refer to a stately Men's Hall lying S.E. (larger than that at Tiryns), with a hearth and a vestibule; close to it, a smaller hall with vestibule and special back-room—perhaps the women's apartment; and in front of both, separated by a court, a Prothyron of modest dimensions, no doubt, but closely allied in form and structure to the Propylæa of Tiryns.   As regards the construction of walls and *antæ*, there is also so unmistakable an analogy, that missing architectural members, such as pillars, the vestiges of whose standing-places are gone, can be supplemented with great probability.   This point too—the surprising agreement of Tiryns and Troy, both in the artistic and the technical aspects of their style of building—is one of the most important facts for the history of art, which we owe to Dr. Schliemann's latest researches.

*A third kind of architecture*, that of tombs, has also received much elucidation.   Though the number of such monuments has been but little increased, valuable analogies to older and well-known buildings of this kind have turned up, and new forms of graves were discovered.   It was still more important that a methodically conducted inquiry repeatedly came upon still untouched graves, and succeeded in preserving all their contents, with an accurate account of all the facts of the find.   Hence we have before us materials as extensive as they are significant; their thorough scientific treating has only just commenced.   I confine myself to the accentuation of some principal points of view as regards their architectural side.

How comfortably and securely the ruler dwelt in his

castle through his life, the architectural remains of Tiryns
and Troy have proved to us.   How he was laid to rest
at his death, and how gracefully, nay monumentally, his
last abode was adorned, we learn from the sepulchres of
Mycenæ and Orchomenos, especially from the beehive-
tombs of both places.   We are sorry to miss the analogous cases which might have been furnished by Tiryns
and Troy.   The former, apart from some simple earth-
graves in the lower citadel, has yielded us no material;
and of Troy almost the same may be said.   For, the immense barrows which surround Troy at various distances,
were unexpectedly found by the excavations to be ceno-
taphs.   Some of them have indeed a core of stone, circular
and parting walls to secure the earth, but no chambers or
receptacles for bodies.   As, with two exceptions—that of
the tumulus of Besika Tepeh in the Plain of Troy, and
the so-called tomb of Protesilaus in the Chersonesus,
which was excavated, but not architecturally examined—
all these barrows seem to be of more recent date than the
epoch of the walls, gates, and palaces of the Pergamos,
they are beyond the range of our present subject.

Of subordinate value, architecturally, are the rock-
tombs of Nauplia and Spata.   Their ground-plans, consisting of an approach and one or more chambers, are
very simple; the proportions are small, and the technical
arrangement is confined to what is absolutely necessary.
The only ascertained fact of importance is, that these
tombs, though temporarily closed, were still used for a
long time.   Hence the architectural features admit of
no inference as to their date; only the objects found,
which are partly very peculiar, point to an epoch not
far removed from that of the buildings of Tiryns and
Mycenæ.

A distinct contrast to these grotto-tombs is afforded
by the six so-called *pit-graves*, in the southern extension of
the fortress of Mycenæ, which, in the year 1876, yielded

the fortunate discoverer a splendid museum of precious objects of art.    In my opinion the dead were here as elsewhere *buried*; not, however, in quadrangular rock-chambers, but in flat rock-cut graves, which were covered with earth, and marked with unadorned tombstones.    It was only after a little necropolis (seventeen persons in six graves) had gradually arisen,* that it was changed into a sepulchral terrace of moderate height at the foot of the precipitous cliff, by means of a semicircular supporting wall, and with sculptured tomb-*stelæ*.    The forming of a level tomb-terrace in a place where it would have been quite easy to hollow out the adjoining rock-walls into sepulchral chambers, is a fact of great importance.    It proves, I think, that the founder who ordered the building, seeing that he followed a wholly different custom from that of the men who were buried then or a little later at Spata and Nauplia, must have been of different race from them.    We may further see in the choice of the place, as well as in the artistic, though very simple, arrangement of the structure with its marking stones, the deliberate object of maintaining the memory of individual members of the family here buried. This object has been attained.    Even at the critical time when the citadel had to be extended to the S., this terrace, in spite of pressing architectural needs, was spared with pious care.    Nothing proves this plainer than the suddenly and abruptly changed course of the southern circuit-wall, at the S.W. corner, which was made in order to bring the way necessary for communication in its full width along the terrace surrounded by the circular wall. Nay, even more was done.    Finally—either immediately after the building of the Lions' Gate, or even later—the grave-terrace was again raised, surrounded with a boundary of broad stone slabs set upright; and by means of a gate

---

* See my contrary view, at the end of this Preface.—HENRY SCHLIEMANN.

through this boundary towards the N., a direct and solemn entrance was attained from the Lions' Gate.

Considering all this, and moreover the manifold and extremely rich contents of the pit-graves, there can be no doubt that the remarkable necropolis re-discovered by Dr. Schliemann contains the resting-place of the founder of the Castle and his kin. It was for ever held sacrosanct. Originally lying outside, at the old approach to the fortress, and afterwards included in the circuit of the walls, this family sepulchre was at last made into a sacred enclosure with an entrance gate, in order to celebrate solemn rites there. It was therefore no *agora*, but a *temenos*, like the Pelopion or Hippodameion at Olympia, but circular in form, and with far more real contents than those hallowed places. As the legend only recognises one founder of Mycenæ—Perseus,—we are entitled to designate these pit-graves as those of the Persidæ.

It is only with the help of this theory, slowly and carefully elaborated from repeated and careful examination of the place, as regards the original situation and arrangement of the pit-graves, that we can explain two facts, otherwise very puzzling : first, that, against all rules and principles of fortification, a considerable part of the lower citadel was sacrificed to a cemetery which acted as a most inconvenient bar ; and secondly, that the graves lie not only under an artificial accumulation of earth 7–8 m. deep, but are moreover cut into the adjoining rock.

Whilst, therefore, the chief value of the pit-graves—apart from their precious and, in some degree, unique contents— lies for us in the gain for the topography and relative chronology of Mycenæ, the beehive-tombs found there afford the most valuable materials for the history of architecture.

Beehive-tombs, in the strict sense, have hitherto only been found on Greek soil. Asia Minor as yet gives us none ; and similar buildings in Italy are but late derivations from old Greek models.

Beehive-tombs consist of conically erected round chambers of ashlar stones, which in building were already covered externally with small stones bedded in clay-mortar, and when finished, so completely piled over with earth that they appear, outside, like simple barrow-graves. They are, therefore, artificial subterranean chambers, with a central chamber containing only two boundary surfaces; namely, the natural floor, and the artificial wall. As the horizontal layers of stone, on a system of corbelling, form the roof, no separation is visible between wall and roof. Both together form a unity. This simple structural formation points to very ancient models, such as round tents, half-subterranean earth huts, &c.; but it appears here in its monumental and artistic execution, at least in three cases, as a climax which certainly was attained only after many earlier attempts.

The technical execution was not easy, as the sepulchral chamber was to be kept dry, and also to be for a long time accessible in dignified manner, in order to allow of other bodies being entombed after the first interment. A door aperture was therefore required, as well as an approach, the former of which was walled up or closed when a beginning was made with the filling up of the approach. The butment, in the construction, was afforded by the thrust of the earth piled on it from without in connection with the adjoining rock, in which, in spite of the troublesome labour of quarrying it out, the whole building was sometimes embedded up to a certain height. Twice—at Orchomenos and at Mycenæ—the neighbouring rock-wall was even first smoothed down vertically, and then hollowed out, in order to obtain a separate rock-chamber in addition to the beehive-chamber built beside it in the open. The approach (*dromos*), laid out in the form of a trench, but flanked by strong supporting walls, shows, by the expensiveness of these constructive accessories, what stress was laid upon easy access to the tomb for a long space of

time.    The doors, which for reasons of practical use
are remarkably high and correspondingly broad in dimensions, required huge lintels; and these again, to save their
being broken, wanted relief from the weight of the wall
above.    The lintels, therefore, which also acted as tie-
beams, were relieved by a triangular aperture, produced by
corbelled layers of stone, and in the best examples, at all
events, closed within by thin rows of stones; without, by
slabs.    This relieving device never served for lighting;
most beehive-graves were permanently covered up, and
therefore dark.    Only a small minority was kept permanently open, and received what light was necessary for
the beehive-chamber through the door.

As to orientation, there was no fixed rule: doors and
approaches face in all directions.    No doubt, the ground
and its roads often determined the site.    Equally varied is
the quality of the building: it rises from the simplest
structure of necessity to that of monumental splendour,
but is never without a certain solidity, demanded by the
very nature of the construction.    The proportions also
widely differ: the diameter below in the smallest tomb
averages 7·20 m.; in the greatest, 14·62 m.    The altitudes
seem to have been equal to the span in the clear, or at
least approached this proportion.

Down to the present time we know of eleven beehive-
graves in Greece.    Six lie before the citadel of Mycenæ;
single ones near the Heræon of Argos, at Pharis in Laconia,
at Menidi in Attica, at Orchomenos in Bœotia, and at Volo
in Thessaly.    As to the subterranean circular chamber on
the citadel of Pharsalos, it was certainly a cistern.    Four
only have been accurately examined, besides the largest at
Mycenæ: those of the Heræon, of Menidi, and of Orchomenos.    The second largest Tholos at Mycenæ awaits, in
spite of the important indications it has afforded, a yet more
complete excavation.    The tomb of Menidi maintains a
certain pre-eminence, because it was found untouched with

its rich contents, and when excavated was recognised for certain as the common tomb of six persons. Materially as well preserved, but superior in technical and artistic respects, is the largest beehive-tomb of Mycenæ, still erroneously designated as the Treasure-house of Atreus. All the other examples, after the washing away of their cone of earth, have lost their upper part by pulling down, and are filled up with *débris* as high as the lintel of their portals.

According to my investigations, this whole species of graves falls into two classes : (1) tombs where the approach was blocked up with earth, as soon as interments were over ; (2) tombs where the Dromos remained always open. This distinction is based on the existence of peg-holes in the stone lintels and thresholds of the portals. Peg-holes imply the existence of doors turning upon their hinges ; and so the intention of a permanent access to the beehive-chamber is proved.

But if the stately portal was to remain for ever visible, then its framing and crowning, and also the slabs closing the relieving space, as well as the upper parts, must be artistically adorned ; in other words, *such tombs were furnished with a façade.* This was the form and arrangement of the two largest beehive-graves at Mycenæ, of that of Orchomenos, probably also of that of Pharis. On the other hand, the excavations at Menidi and the Heræon have shown, that the portals of all tombs lacking this distinctive feature in their lintels and thresholds, were blocked up with quarry-stones and clay mortar, in order that the approach might be filled up. Besides the two last-named, this also applies to the four smaller tombs at Mycenæ, which lie W. and N.W. of the town-hill ; none of them had a façade.

It is well known that these peculiar buildings were long explained in various ways, sometimes as treasure-houses, sometimes as Chthonian shrines, and, according to vulgar analogies, even as well-chambers. They can never have

served the first or third of these uses, for never has a well
or watercourse been found in them, whilst their number
and scattered position about Mycenæ excludes all possibility of their being treasuries.  No prince ever kept his treasures outside the circuit wall of his fortress, and therefore
the so-called Treasury of Orchomenos, distant 1½ km. from
the Acropolis, cannot, in the ordinary sense of the word,
have been the treasury of Minyas, though in Pausanias'
days this title was already fixed upon it by tradition.  The
origin of the name can be guessed, when we compare the
splendid architectural results of the excavation of Orchomenos with the notice of Pausanias (ix. 38, 2).  Beside the
beehive-chamber, Dr. Schliemann found a richly-decorated
side-chamber cut into the rock, which could be separately
closed.  This circumstance, as well as the splendid decorations of the side chamber, lead us to regard it as the tomb
of the founder of the city (either Minyas or Orchomenos),
the more so as Pausanias mentions the tombs of Minyas and
Hesiod immediately after the Treasury, the structure of
which he characterizes very well.  Hence we may regard
the beehive-chamber as the Heroon of the founder, which,
for the purpose of worship, had always to remain accessible,
and which, from its original or later furnishing with costly
heirlooms or votive gifts, gave rise to the erroneous legend
of a treasury.  The same explanation probably applies to
the Treasury of Hyrieus, to which clung, in the time of
Pausanias, the old Egyptian builder's legend of its having
been plundered by the architects Trophonius and Agamedes.

It is only in this century that the false description has
been further extended to the largest beehive-tomb at
Mycenæ, which has been called the Treasury of Atreus.
Pausanias is innocent of this; his account even contradicts
it.  The traveller comes to the citadel-walls, passes through
the Lions' Gate, and sees under the ruins of the citadel,
besides the artificial well called Perseia, the subterranean
treasuries of Atreus and his sons (II., 16, 6).  It is then

only that his way leads him to the graves of the Atridæ, six of which he mentions by name; adding the express remark, that the last tomb—that of Klytæmnestra and Ægisthus—lay some distance from the city wall, as both were thought unworthy of being buried where Agamemnon and those murdered with him were reposing. From this I draw two conclusions. First, that Pausanias considered his description of the citadel completed when he came to examine the graves of the Atridæ. Secondly, that five of these graves lay within the city walls,—namely, those of Atreus, Agamemnon, Eurymedon, the children of Kassandra, and Elektra. Now, there are still extant, on the slope of the hill adjoining the fortress to the S.W., six *tholoi* (vaulted structures), one of which—the north-western one—lies lowest and furthest outside,* while the two grandest were built close to the citadel on the declivity, and adorned with splendid façades. From this, the obvious conclusion seems to me perfectly justified, that in these six peculiar structures we not only still possess, in their main parts, the tombs of the Atridæ period, which Pausanias saw and described as such, but that we may also designate the two beehive-tombs on the E. slope as the graves of Atreus and Agamemnon, owing to their select position beside the old approach to the fortress, as well as on account of their size and costly building. In accordance with the sequence mentioned by Pausanias, the northern tomb would thus have to be fixed as that of Atreus, the southern as that of Agamemnon. Again, of the remaining three, one surpasses the two others in technical execution, in size, in material, and in select position. This is the Tholos, situated only 100 m. from the Lions' Gate on the N.W. slope of the saddle between the town and fortress hills, and which, even

---

* The city wall certainly included the upper well of Charvati, and therefore probably ran along the west side, following the hill curve pretty closely at a height of 166 m. (above the sea) as far as the northern ravine. Cf. Steffen, *Karten von Mykenai*, Plate 2.

on account of its favoured site, may be set down as being, in all likelihood, that of Electra. This assumption again corresponds accurately to the enumeration of Pausanias. For the tourist coming out of the citadel, it was the most natural course, by using the old approach to the Castle, to pass first round the eastern, and then round the western slope of the town hill, and so to end with the tomb of Electra near the Lions' Gate. The tomb of Ægisthus and Klytæmnestra, lying far away outside the city wall, thus naturally fell into the last place of the peregrination.

Hence we obtain the following series: at the east slope (1) Atreus, (2) Agamemnon; at the west slope, (3) Eurymedon; near it, to the west, (4) the children of Kassandra; (5) Electra; and 540 m. to the west of that grave, (6) Klytæmnestra and Ægisthus. Now, is it mere accident that of the four tombs on the W. slope, No. 4 is by far the poorest in workmanship, and the smallest in size? As a proof of this statement, I adduce the only point which, owing to the blocking up of the tombs, we can at present bring forward, beyond the examination of the material and *technique*. I mean the comparison of the upper width of the portals in ten beehive-tombs. The width in the clear, in them, is as follows:

| | | | |
|---|---|---|---|
| Orchomenos | 2·47 m. | Tomb at the Heræon | 1·65 m. |
| Tomb of Atreus | 2·46 m. | Tomb of Eurymedon | 1·60 m. |
| Tomb of Agamemnon | 2·42 m. | Tomb at Menidi (pro- | |
| Tomb of Electra | 2·33 m. | bably) | 1·53 m.* |
| Tomb at Pharis | 1·83 m. | Tomb of the children: | |
| Tomb of Klytæmnestra | 1·71 m. | only | 1·30 m. |

We see, from this, the close relation of the measurements of the tombs of Atieus, Agamemnon, and Electra, and what a great contrast, as regards measurement, is offered by the children's tomb. Its isolated position, also, is surely not without significance.

Now, although the questions here raised can only be

---

* An exact statement is wanting.

finally settled after the excavation of all the *tholoi* at
Mycenæ, yet so much is already certain, that treasuries are
out of the question, since Tiryns has yielded its evidence—
that is, since the remarkable structures in its circuit walls
(galleries, magazines, cisterns, &c.), described in this book,
have been brought to light. What Pausanias saw in the
ruins of Mycenæ, and admired as the subterranean treasuries of Atreus and his sons, were not the beehive-graves,
but juxta-posited vaulted chambers within the quaintly
massive structure of the walls, similar to those at Tiryns.
And here I may further support my view by bringing the
fact to mind, that the so-called treasure of Priam, as well
as the larger finds of precious metal at Troy, were discovered in like places, namely, close to, or in, the fortress
wall: a striking evidence that people used such fireproof
and concealed places either permanently, or temporarily—
in times of danger—as treasuries. Hence the record of
Pausanias concerning Mycenæ rests on a true basis; but
his brevity, and the misleading analogy of the Treasury
of Minyas, have led to frequent misunderstanding of him.
The substantial distinction between treasuries and beehive-
tombs rendered it necessary for me to discuss again this
much-commented passage.

The beehive-tomb of Menidi has the oldest architectural character, either because it is really the earliest of
those known to us up till now, or because, from want of
means, it was made in a cheap and rude way of rubble limestone. Besides the small dimensions—diameter, $8 \cdot 35$ m.;
width of the approach, 3 m. ; lower width of portal, $1 \cdot 55$ m.
—the first theory would be supported by the absence of
all chiselling, and by the fact that the tomb is embedded,
not in a rocky slope, but in an earth hill; also, that there
is no pavement, and that the requisite external impermeabilisation has been much neglected. Most significant,
moreover, are the different ways in which the relieving of
the lintels has been managed: outside by means of several

slabs laid one over the other, and separated by empty
spaces; inside by a trapezoid gap, closed with stones.
Those outside slabs look like a reminiscence of wooden tie-
beams, from an older manner of building, working with
different materials.

In all these respects the beehive-tomb at the Heræon is
superior, although the *dromos* (approach) is of the same
width, and the diameter not much greater. In particular,
that tomb produces a better effect by the solid stone work
in the *dromos* walls and the portal. Whilst the supporting
walls of the approach are, from the very starting-point,
at first made of small, hard, poros-stones with mortar, we
come, further in, upon carefully cut, oblong, and cubic
blocks, with broadly marked mortar-jointings—just as in
northern granite buildings. The walls themselves slightly
project, from above, towards the interior. The portal,
narrowing a little towards the top, is built of clean-cut
square blocks, with a double fascia in front, and three lintel
stones of breccia, lying one behind the other; the hinder-
most of which attains the considerable weight of 7800 kg.
In the entry there is rude rubble masonry, owing to the
walling-up of the tomb, which was no doubt intended
from the first, and carried out later. But in the circular
chamber the work again improves, although the pointing
is not so carefully done as that of the *dromos*. At the
same time a thorough outer impermeabilisation is obtained
by means of broken stones in clay-mortar, and the floor
paved with pebbles. The whole structure, in spite of its
modest treatment, has a certain air of distinction, as
compared with the coarse, rustic production at Menidi.

A still higher stage is represented by the Atreus-tomb
at Mycenæ, the excavation of which has not been completed. This is all the more regrettable, as probably the
decorative members of the façade are here more fully preserved, than in the neighbouring tomb of Agamemnon,
which was early rifled. Being of almost the same size, and

similarly furnished with a permanent approach, it yet differs
from it by the absence of a side-chamber, and by the
use of smaller stones in the *tholos*.    It is, nevertheless,
a costly and important monumental structure, in which,
for example, are preserved the cleanly cut covering stones
on the supporting wall—a proof, if such were still needed,
that the approach was never meant to be blocked up, and
in itself a valuable help in determining the plane angle of in-
flection of the earth hill.    The façade is built, in exemplary
style, of polished breccia blocks, and simply but artistically
arranged.    The wall strips, slightly projecting at both
sides, joined above by a slab, and crowned by a bipartite
epistyle, form the frame all round.    There are embedded
in it, above, the triangular relieving space; below, the
doubly framed door, which gradually narrows a little.    The
triangular hollow space was closed outside by thick slabs
of red marble, and is still now completely walled up within
by rows of flat square slabs, so that, in presence of this fact,
all notion of an original lighting by means of windows
must be abandoned.    The relieving triangle rests on a
lintel of leek-green marble; while, instead of the head-
moulding of the door, there appears a projecting slab of
blue-grey marble, on which, frieze-like, there is cut, in flat
relief, the front side of a beam-roof made of round poles.
Right and left, this roof is bordered by widely overhanging
abacus-slabs of breccia, which bore some plastic ornament
(a very rude lion-head of grey trachyte, which I saw in the
Museum at Charvati in 1878, might come from here), and
is supported beneath by embedded columns.    Parts of
them have been found, consisting of dark-grey alabaster,
and fluted like Doric work.    Unfortunately, the capitals
have not yet been recovered, and the bases, which are
certainly there, are not yet laid bare.    The embedded
pillars, as the impressions in the walls show, tapered slightly
downward, and were of very slender proportions, reminding
us of wooden buildings.    The lintel of the door is formed

of three stones ; in the centre one are the pivot holes for the door-wings, which opened inwards. The inmost block projects far into the wall on both sides, and joins a stone-course of the same height, running right through, and made of thirteen blocks, which, being provided with several skew-notches, form a real tie-beam. The remaining square blocks are very much lower, and, speaking exactly, cut like slabs. Including that larger stone layer, twenty-five courses are visible ; the upper rows have disappeared, and the lower are not yet uncovered. In the upper courses the depth of the blocks is 1·30 m. ; and behind them comes, as protection from rain-water, a coat of clay mortar mixed with fragments of stone. In the interior there are no nail-holes for a metal-coating. In the front, there are plain traces of the enormous pressure to which the head beams have been exposed, on account of the relieving hollow space. The corbelled stone-courses of the relieving trian-gular space have broken the front upper lintel at both ends, and this break has extended down through almost all the courses of the inner fascia.

The tomb of Agamemnon represents the highest stage of the *tholoi* at Mycenæ, not only in plan, but also in structure and design of façade ; for, despite much similarity to, or even agreement with, the Atreus-tomb, the workman-ship here is very much more solid, and the adornment by far more splendid. Here, the constructive power and rich experience of the architect appear quite a match for the resources of the prince. One point only surprises us : it is the curious plainness of the roomy rock chamber (6·50 m. square), with a hardly indicated plinth, half-smoothed walls, and similarly treated roof. Was this intended as a contrast, or was the builder hindered by sudden death from finishing the tomb ? Two low oblong plinths, like basement stones in profile, are the last enigmatical remains of the former decoration.

The effect of the conical chamber is imposing, in

spite of the absence of all architectural divisions. The
room makes the impression of a natural vault, simply by
its proportions, its disposition, and its texture. Perfect workmanship corresponds to materials of rare excellence ; and
at the same time the enormous inner stone of the lintel
affords documentary proof of the mechanical power at the
architect's command in those days. A clean-cut block,
weighing 122,000 kg., or more than six times as much as
the largest block in the citadel of Tiryns, tells the practised
eye a great deal, and suggests many questions besides.
Where was it quarried ; how dressed on all sides ; by what
means was it brought to this height, and at last safely laid on
its supports? A most extraordinary spending of time and
strength is contained in this mass, which has been lving
firmly in its place for three thousand years. The thirty-four
courses within, including the key-stone, are of various
heights, also divided very differently in square blocks ; yet
they are perfectly joined, and care has been taken to have
neat upright joints everywhere. The chief effect depended
on the perfect smoothness of the wall ; but, as special ornament, there were two frieze-strips of bronze-sheets (probably
gilt), set on the fifth and ninth courses. A complete coating
of metal, such as has often been supposed, was not applied.
Only the little double door leading from the *tholos* to the
rock tomb, had a similar covering ; and thicker bronze
plates seem to have covered the greater threshold, and to
have made a special frame for the principal door. Clear
traces of the same manner of decoration with metal ornament,
are also preserved on the outer side of the lintel.

We have, unfortunately, not sufficient material for a
graphic reconstitution of the stately portal. The front
surface, built of polished breccia blocks, was once coated, in
its upper part, with slabs of red, green, and white marble ;
but the greater portion of this splendid incrustation is gone.
According to technical indications, it was only added after
the completion of the building, and clamped on, so that it

could easily be removed. The greed of subsequent generations did so, and partly dragged it off to neighbouring
churches. Precious fragments are now in London, Athens,
Munich, and Berlin. It remains, therefore, doubtful for
the present, whether the same important façade system, with
pilaster-strips, was here architecturally carried out—that is,
in full plastic existence—as on the tomb of Atreus, or only
indicated by painting on the stone. Double, delicately-
grooved fasciæ surround the lofty portal; while here, too,
the outer frame was formed by two slender, embedded pillars
of dark-grey alabaster, the shafts of which, richly ornamented with sharp zigzags and spirals, were dowelled into
very low, rebated, oblong base stones. That they tapered
downwards—a point which has been much disputed—is
certain. Equally so we can demonstrate, from the identity
of the clamping holes, that the architectural member
known to us since the beginning of this century, which
consists of a leaf-covered cavetto, and an echinus richly
adorned with rhomboid and spiral friezes, together with an
abacus, was not the base, but the capital of these embedded
pillars. On its polished back side it bears a pattern-like
division of clearly-cut, parallel, vertical and horizontal lines,
which reminds us of the like practice of Egyptian sculptors.

It is obvious—and this is a point of special importance
—that the embedded pillars of both tomb façades are closely
related to the pillar of the heraldic relief on the Lions' Gate.
In both of them we find the shafts dowelled in below, and
thickening upwards; and a form of capital, which is the
basis of a distinct variety of the old Doric capital. From a
comparison with the Atreus-tomb, with its indicated roof of
round poles, we can recognise in the little cylinders (not
plates—as appears clearly from looking at them sideways)
over the capital of the Lions' Gate pillar, nothing but a
reduced reproduction of that important, shade-giving,
architectural member of the princely dwelling. In any case,
the close agreement demonstrates that the celebrated Lions'

relief, and consequently the gate and adjoining S. wall, belong to the same epoch as the beehive-graves, and that, therefore, the Atridæ were the extenders and adorners of the citadel, whilst the first foundation was due to the Persidæ.

The last of the tombs which I have to discuss, is that of Orchomenos.* It is only a little smaller than that of Agamemnon, and resembles it in possessing a side chamber for burial purposes, but is distinguished from it both in material and the peculiar construction of the special grave chamber. The structure is composed of moderately-sized blocks of dark-grey marble brought from Lebadeia, and executed in such a manner that not only the *dromos* and *tholos* walls, but also the walls and roof of the moderately large grave chamber are made of it. The founder's evident and manifestly exhibited intention was, that his tomb, by its chisel work, should receive a stamp as thoroughly uniform as it was to be highly artistic. For this object, a wide shaft had to be sunk from above for the proposed Thalamos in the rocky slope, down to its floor, so as to build up in clay mortar, from within, the surrounding walls which would be able to serve as supports for the marble roof slabs, whilst at the same time they could be themselves coated with ornamental marbles. The roof, consisting of four slabs, was treated as a uniform whole; namely, in delicate relief, like a spread-out carpet, with centre pattern and very broad outer bands. The main ornament was of spiral mæanders, with fan-flowers in the corners, while the borders of the centre-piece, as well as of the whole carpet, were formed of rich rosettes. Special precautions were required to prevent any collapse of this splendid ceiling by pressure of the earth from above. How this important supplementary construction was managed, is not yet known. But it is a fact, that it served its purpose

---

* Insufficiency of materials prevents my entering upon a discussion of those of Pharis and Laminospito, near Volo.

for more than three thousand years; the regrettable partial collapse having only taken place a few years ago. The considerable expense of time and trouble demanded by this structure, which for the present must be regarded as a unique one, is doubtless closely connected, in the first place, with the choice of the valuable material, the fine quality of which acted as an inducement for chiselling work. Moreover, there cannot be any doubt that the founder thought no sacrifice too great to leave a monument for posterity, which was to perpetuate his name, and to afford a lasting and speaking evidence of his wealth and artistic taste.

It is, therefore, very probable that later generations at Orchomenos, justly proud of this monument, granted the honour of a tomb in the old royal Thalamos to Hesiod, the great bard of Bœotia; for Pausanias speaks of the graves of Minyas and Hesiod immediately after his description of the Thesauros, and several finds in the beehive-chamber seem to be apt to support this supposition.

There have been found distinct traces of the splendid adornment of the beehive-chamber with bronze plates. We gather from them that this kind of decoration was used more extensively—and at the same time with a greater variety of pattern—than in the *tholos* of Agamemnon. That such a splendid structure had a rich façade like the portal fronts of the Atridæ tombs, may be assumed as certain; but the account of the excavations, so far as it is before us, leaves this important point unexplained. Inside, only the fragments of a small pillar, said to be like the relief pillar on the Lions' Gate, and also several thin marble slabs with spiral ornaments were found; both perhaps remains of an incrustation of the façade.

If it follows with certainty from these observations that the architects of that early time had command of great resources in the matter of structures, architectural members, and ornaments capable of further development, we are still more struck when finding that some of the motives, members, and decorations, adopted and worked by them

on a large scale, were also used in the manufacture of
objects of luxury and ornaments on a much smaller, even
a minute, scale.   Such is the design of the Lions' Gate
relief, which reappears repeatedly, with altered position of
the lions, on an ivory dagger-handle found at Menidi.   So
with a design consisting of a kerbed post and two half-
rosettes leaning against it, which is the fundamental ornament of the so-called kyanos frieze at Tiryns, and which
existed in similar size in the palace of Mycenæ, as is shown
by two fragments from Mycenæ.   So with a cast plate of
glass, which was probably used for the decoration of drapery
—like enamel in modern dress—which turns up at Menidi.
So, also, the peculiar architectural members under the
pillar of the Lions' Gate, which remind us of stone seats,
have served as a model in making fine gold ornaments and
graceful glass plates, as is shown by specimens from Spata
and Menidi.   Finally, the downward-tapering embedded
pillars of the Atridæ tombs, and of the Lions' Gate, were
frequently used as types for furniture and glass ornaments.
There are three ivory specimens, in light and in vigorous
proportions, from Spata ; another of glass, in the form of
a slender pilaster, from Menidi.   A further model, in which
the embedded pillar appears as the separating member
between rows of long-legged sphinxes, is afforded by a
curious ivory plate from Menidi.

Few as these finds, and the results deducible therefrom,
are, they yet deserve careful notice.   Never, in the history
of the art of building, has a new phase in architectonic
development occurred in consequence of new utensils or
ornaments having been brought by trade into a country.
But inversely, when the greater architectonic evolution
was very far advanced, or had completed its course, the
worker of small objects of art-industry or house-implements
appropriated to himself the " language of forms " which had
been gradually elaborated in works carried out on a grand
scale ; adapting it, in a minor degree, and in somewhat
changed manner, to his own ends.   However, as we know

from experience that a long period of time is required before
such a process of gradual adaptation is realised, we may
conclude, that the architecture the striking remains of
which have come down to us partly in the original, partly
in imitations of artistic handicraft, must have gone through
a long course of evolution, and that it cannot have been
confined to a narrow area.

There are but very few places in Greece and Asia
Minor, which, on account of their architectural ruins and
the discoveries made there, could be touched upon here,
rather in a cursory than in an exhaustive way; and yet
they have furnished a rich harvest for the knowledge of the
oldest architecture in those lands.  With astonishment we
see the different epochs opening out, more and more, before
our eyes.  A real primitive architecture is nowhere to be
found; even in Troy the first steps of development are long
passed.  Within certain limits, the materials are already
under full control, and worked variously, according to the
available means and the ends required.  A moderate, but
yet very fruitful, store of detail forms is already gathered,
so as to cover the gradually elaborated shapes of rooms
with significant adornments full of meaning.  In some
peculiarly favoured places, the domain of the higher monumental architecture has already been entered upon with
decisive success.  In the face of such extended and yet
closely connected achievements, which form a consistent
whole, the attempt to search for the roots from which arose
this early bloom of the art of building, is doubly attractive.
Among the architectural monuments here discussed,
the highest stage is represented by the beehive-graves; and
among them, by those with façades.  In my opinion they
are a remarkable, though a too early, attempt to amalgamate
two opposed systems of building, viz. that of wooden roofs
and that of beehive-roofs.  The façade in relief is, in
design, nothing but the schematically reduced type of the
pillared, shady vestibule of the Men's Hall—a type most

clearly recognisable in the Atreus-tomb, and indicated in
closer form—only, sketch-like—by the Lions' Gate relief.
This Prothyron, which certainly was held to be the main
part and feature of the Prince's palace—many allusions in
Greek tragedy point to it—was meant to be combined with
the beehive-chamber, in order *to mark it outwardly as a
royal tomb.*  This was the sum and substance of the architectural program at Mycenæ and Orchomenos.  But still
more important is the information we obtain from an
analysis of the second system.  I think, indeed, I can see in
the *tholos* and its *dromos* the last monumental form of a most
ancient national mode of architecture—that of Phrygia.
Vitruvius reports from Greek sources that the Phrygians
dwelling in valleys were wont to construct their habitations
artificially underground, in that, over an excavated hill of
earth, they set up posts in conical form, which they bound
together at the top.  They covered these posts with reeds
and brushwood, and then put upon the whole the greatest
heap of earth it would bear.  The entrance was made by
cutting in passages from below; and these dwellings, he said,
were very warm in winter and very cool in summer.  The
main features of this construction are repeated by Xenophon
and Diodorus with regard to the Armenians, who were akin,
in race, to the Phrygians; and even to-day we find similar
constructions in the same districts.

Now, the beehive-tomb is composed of a deeply cut-in
approach and a central chamber, afterwards made subterranean by heaping earth upon it.  So striking an agreement
is surely the result, not of accident, but of tradition.  As
men's pretensions advanced, the wooden posts were first
omitted from the primitively simple, conical hut covered
with earth; for they were always perishable and liable to
fire: they were replaced by thick walls of sun-dried bricks,
with wooden tie-beams.  Still later, the bricks were replaced by stone walls: first in rude layers of slabs, as at
Menidi; then in polished blocks, as at Orchomenos and

Mycenæ—so that every reminiscence disappeared of the old earth-and-wood structure which had been the starting-point. The peculiar form of the primitive dwelling only was maintained as the proper tomb type for distinguished families and illustrious princes.

We do not know when and where the important transition took place from wood to brick building. But as it was certainly in a land of bricks, we may at once think of the broad valley of the Hermos, possessing inexhaustible layers of clay, whose natural central point, the magnificent residence, Sardis, still consisted, in the opening of the fifth century B.C., of clay-houses covered with reeds, which could be as easily destroyed as they could be rapidly rebuilt. Now, it is from the Hermos valley, from Sipylos, that the rich princely scion, Pelops, came to Greece—as the ancient tale says. His race attained the highest power and celebrity, then and afterwards: the proverbial riches of the Atridæ are visible even to-day in the Castle and royal graves of Mycenæ. All this, I opine, supports my view, that we have to look upon the beehive-tombs as architectural creations whose fundamental principle has arisen from the national style of building among the Phrygians, and that the transference of this style to Greek soil is connected with the immigration of distinguished Phrygian families. The frequently referred-to relief of the Lions' Gate points to an origin in the same primeval home—now more than ever, since Prof. Ramsay was fortunate enough to find in great rock-façades in Phrygia the older and severer prototypes of well-known later derivations from this kind of composition.

Whilst the kernel structure of the royal tombs has preserved, despite all veiling changes, the still easily discernible building methods of an early Greek race, the influence of the Orient appears distinctly in the architectural system of the splendid façades. It is in particular the pilaster-strips —both in the upper and in the lower part of the Atreus-tomb—as well as their upper connection and crest-work,

which point to such Eastern influence.    How important a
part is played by the system of vertical wall bands in
Oriental architecture, is amply known from Assyrian, Persian, and Old-Syrian monuments.    All the more surprising
is the fact, that its transplanting to Mycenæ led to no
further developments in Greece.    It is still an open question, so far as I know, what was the original home of this
façade system.

The embedded pillars—including that of the Lions'
relief—prove by their slender proportions, and their dowel-
ling into the threshold, their origin from the building with
wood.    The same is true of the ceiling made of round
wooden beams, twice indicated in relief.    We may conclude
therefrom, with some certainty, that such ceilings were
used in every palace of that day—not only as being practical, but as having the sanction of ages.    In this connection, the local legends of Argos deserve special attention,
which record explicitly the close relations between Proitos,
the founder of Tiryns, and early civilised Lycia.    As an
exile, this princely scion from Argos is said to have gained
the hand of the Lycian king's daughter.    Returning with
an army of his father-in-law, he maintained himself in the
land; and by means of the expert Cyclopes whom he
summoned from Lycia, he built the invincibly strong
Castle of Tiryns.    His nephew Perseus is said then to have
employed the same skilled workmen to build Mycenæ.
In both places, men afterwards knew of, and showed, Cyclopean altars, hearths, vestibules, and walls.    Now, Lycia is
that part of Asia Minor, in the innumerable tombs of
which are perpetuated ceilings of round beams, lying close
together, and protruding far out in front.    Nay, the same,
most archaic, feature is still to be seen now in the structure
of their huts.    To Lycia, also—apart from this kind of
ceiling—the undeniable popular legend ascribes the building of walls with immense blocks of stone, which gradually
displaced from fortification architecture the old brick build-

ing, and led to new developments. But if two countries
with kindred populations in Asia Minor transferred to
Greece their ancient national styles of building as well as
newly acquired methods—of course, not all at once, or in
passing, but during a considerable period—there is no
difficulty in understanding, how from such rich sources,
and with the continual stimulus from splendour-loving
courts, there arose a brilliant epoch of architecture which
reached its perfection at Mycenæ, owing to the political
power and greatness of the Atridæ, but which is also to
be presumed as having been in existence at other royal
cities—such as Spata, Orchomenos, Hyriæ, Larissa in
Thessaly, &c.

If the origin of round timber ceilings is thus established,
we still lack the proof of the origin of the embedded
pillars. It is a fact that in no rock-tomb of Lycia have
such pillars yet been found as are seen at Mycenæ, Spata,
and Menidi. Pillars are entirely wanting in the earliest
rock-tombs. Only uprights at the corners and on the
walls, with some cross-bars, form the constructive design
of the tomb, which either stands free, or is constructed in
relief. The embedded columns must, therefore, come from
another home than Lycia, or be the independent creation
of that early epoch.

I consider the latter view all the more probable, as the
most diligent search among our large stock of monumental
materials has led, as yet, to the discovery of no analogy whatever in other styles of architectonic art, and the connection
with the decorative manner of the *stelæ* above the Persidæ
tombs, and with a great many objects discovered in them,
is unmistakable. Their tapering downward remains a
mystery, and its explanation is the more difficult, as free
pillars of that period have not yet been found, and the
embedded pillars may possibly depend on the then accepted
laws of relief style. On mechanical grounds there is no
objection to a moderate tapering downward of wooden

supports; and, practically speaking, some additional room was even gained thereby for thoroughfare—especially if very broad· epistyles were considered necessary for the laying of the roof beams, and hence large diameters were required above.    But perhaps neither of these suggestions hits the real solution.    Perhaps it was a mere temporary vagary of taste, like that which created, within the stiff hieratic art-rules of Egypt, nay, even during a good artistic epoch, in the temple of Karnak, those curious downward tapering stone pillars, with their flower capitals reversed in the same way.*

There are other points of resemblance to Egypt.    The beautifully chiselled ceiling in the grave-chamber at Orchomenos, treated like a carpet, and adorned with spiral mæanders, besides fan-shaped flowers and stripes of rosettes for borders, is clearly derived from Egyptian prototypes— however, as it appears, not directly, but indirectly.    The Palace of Tiryns possessed the same kind of wall-decoration in many places, though applied as a frieze, and worked out in simpler manner in detail—as in rosettes.    Hence this palace, or some other similar one, may easily have served as a model for the ceiling at Orchomenos.

Not less important is the decorative border of the kyanos-frieze with blue smalt at Tiryns, because this *technique*, of which traces have been found at Mycenæ, was familiar in Egypt from the oldest times, and treated with such careful preference, that the materials required for it became precious articles of trade.    As the Phœnicians managed their import, it is possible that this whole decorative style came through that nation to Greece.    But still, Egypt will always have to be looked upon as the starting-point—and not Babylon, where the Egyptian invention of ornamenting with smalt was early adopted—because the kyanos-frieze at Tiryns is connected with stone work and

---

* Cf. Lepsius, *Denkmäler*, I., Pl. 31.

chiselling, not with the special formations of brick architecture.

How are such important relations to be explained?
We may, first of all, think of the early settlements of
Phœnicians at the mouths of the Nile; then, of the continued wars which Libyan tribes, allied with northern coast
and island people, carried on against Egypt since the
14th century before our era. That long-continued peaceful
intercourse, as well as these sudden warlike encounters
which once brought the invaders even as far as Memphis,
surely held out much inducement for becoming acquainted
with Egyptian architecture—both in buildings of sun-
dried bricks and in buildings of quarried stone. But when,
as we know in the case of talented races, the slumbering
instincts for culture are once awakened, then valuable
booty, such as the daggers and swords, the cups and bowls
from the Mycenæan pit-graves—whose Egyptian origin is
beyond doubt, owing to their peculiar and highly-developed
*technique* — would permanently foster and spread this
artistic tendency.

There can, moreover, have been no lack of intermediate
localities and people, to bring about such a slow and long
continuing transference, lasting for generations — now,
according to the favour or disfavour of circumstances, in
an increasing, now in a lessening degree. And this supposition brings us back to Tiryns and its above-mentioned
connection with Lycia, if we remember that, according to
all tradition, the oldest culture of that land came from
Crete—that is to say, from an island lying at the gates of
Egypt and Libya, and therefore destined, before all other
islands, to spread throughout the archipelago the elements
of civilisation of the highly developed kingdom of the
Pharaohs, which Crete had acquired either in war or peace.
Hence this island, though an accurate examination and
classing of its oldest monuments has not yet taken place,
comes within the sphere of our present reflections. Here,

in Crete, it was, that by a wise combination of tribes as
fit for culture as they were competent at sea, the earliest
national power of Greek antiquity was founded.  To Crete
is attached the rare title of fame of "the 100-citied," as
a speaking proof of the early culture and the flourishing wealth of an island  state ruled  by strong  hands.
With  the  venerable  name of  Minos is connected indis-
solubly the name of Dædalos, the oldest hero of Greek
architecture ; and from here, commonwealths were founded,
and cults established.   A structure belonging to that latter
category is, it seems to me, still extant.   The remarkable
grotto  in  Delos,  at  the  foot  of  Kynthos,  which  I  am
inclined to regard as a shrine of Eileithyia, is probably a
branch foundation from Crete in the heyday of its power ;
for the structural system of the very peculiar roof, composed in masterly manner of ten great counterfort stones
certainly  came  from  Egypt,  whose  gigantic  buildings,
with  their  enormous  superincumbent  weight,  compelled
men at an early time to solve that kind of constructive
problem.    This  roof,  which  was  able  to  carry  a  small
mountain, proves what men had seen and learned in Egypt.
It affords another useful support for the theory, started
by others, of a very early influence from Egypt—a theory
derived  from  gems,  as  well  as  from  the  discovery  of
beautiful metal-work, of an ornamented ostrich egg, &c.,
found in the Perseid graves.

Compared with the architecture of Mycenæ, Orchomenos, and Tiryns, that of Troy is distinctly inferior.  Still,
with all its gaps, it is for this reason very instructive, because
the existing remains—looked at as a whole—give us an
older phase of architectural development than the yet
known monuments on Greek soil.  This is true of the
walls and gates, as well as of the palace of the ruler.  At
the same time, however, our judgment must at present rest
rather on the technical than the artistic aspects of Trojan
architecture.  For, as regards the latter, it is much to be

regretted that neither royal graves, nor architectonic details were found in Troy. On the other hand, at the side of the characteristic system of fortifications (with its dry moat, its escarped wall substructions, its flanking towers, &c.), the antique building method of forming all the walls—in citadel and house—of sun-dried bricks with wooden tie-beams, is of very peculiar importance. First, because all these features prevail in Egypt, both in the Delta and in Upper Egypt; secondly, because the walls of the palace at Tiryns still were of a like or a similar structure. This method, then, was widely used, and long maintained from practical as well as economical grounds. Its application at Tiryns, too, is the more easily explained when we remember the fact above mentioned, that the present citadel at Tiryns certainly followed upon an older and simpler one, which can hardly have been very different from that found at Troy.

There was indeed no kind of building so serviceable, as this, for the first provisional securing of any newly occupied point on the coast, as soon as the two materials, clay and wood, could be found in the neighbourhood. Hence we may justify the conjecture, that the numerous, absolutely necessary forts established on the Greek coasts and islands for the protection of Phœnician depots, must have been of an architectural kind not requiring expensive and tedious stone masonry, but that the prompt and cheap building system of sun-dried bricks, with wooden beams, was chosen. From such a foundation, a citadel of a higher class, than that of Troy, might easily be developed.

It will hardly be denied that all these briefly discussed structures must be older than the Trojan war; the most fully developed of them, contemporaneous with it, or very little younger. To go further than this general chronology, the closer determination of which is still in dispute, seems premature in the present state of our researches into the monumental records. The paths, on which we must proceed, are marked out clearly enough. We want continued new discovery of materials, and their methodical and critical sifting. Besides the pressing need of excavating the citadel of Mycenæ, the oldest architectural monuments of Lycia and Crete, especially, must be surveyed, and brought together for comparison, in order to facilitate the solution of the all-important question, how far the Phœnicians were instructors of the Greeks in monumental architecture. I do not deny this influence, but can only admit it to a limited extent for the oldest period, whose architecture had here to be discussed, because hitherto no buildings can be shown anywhere on the Syro-Phœnician coast or the islands, which can compete with the peculiarly severe organism of the beehive-tombs, and the masterly arrangement of the palace at Tiryns. How very far, indeed, does the latter surpass all known ground-plans of Assyrian Royal Palaces in simplicity and clearness! I see in these early creations of architecture, on the soil of Hellas, the conscious expression of the old Greek minu, and evidences, as genuine as they are indelible, of the primitive national connection of the tribes on both shores of the Ægean Sea.

F. ADLER

BERLIN, 31st July, 1885.

---

### POSTSCRIPT.

It is only since reaching this place, after concluding this Preface, that I see, from Dr. Dörpfeld's supplemental accounts, that my conjecture recorded last May, and printed above on p. xi, regarding the use of clay for the bonding of Cyclopean walls, is confirmed by closer investigation. Had this fact been known to me earlier, I should of course have used a different expression.

F. ADLER.

PONTRESINA, 16th August, 1885.

# NOTE.

My honoured friend, the learned author of the Preface, having expressed the opinion (p. xxvii) that the little necropolis in the Citadel of Mycenæ had gradually arisen, I feel it my duty to state that this is an error. I have made the excavations of the royal tombs of Mycenæ in the presence, and with the continual superintendence, of two distinguished archæologists, the Ephoros (the late General Ephoros of Antiquities), Panagiotis Stamatakis, who had been associated with me by the Greek Government to superintend the works, and of Professor Phendiklis, of the University of Athens. The excavations have shown beyond any doubt, that the bodies *could* NOT *possibly have* been buried gradually, but *that all of them must necessarily have been buried simultaneously.* I have proved this in my work *Mycenæ* by a most minute account of the internal arrangement of the graves. All my statements are fully corroborated by the Ephoros Stamatakis in his diary, which is to be published by the Greek Archæological Society. Happily, Professor Phendiklis is still living to confirm them on his part.

HENRY SCHLIEMANN.

# CONTENTS.

————◆◇◆————

# LIST OF ILLUSTRATIONS.

———•◦•———

# LIST OF PLANS AND PLATES.

---

# ARGOLIS.

# TIRYNS.

---

## CHAPTER I.

### THE EXCAVATIONS.

IN the beginning of August 1876, I had worked at Tiryns
for a week with 51 men, had sunk on the high plateau of
the citadel 13 pits and several long trenches down to the
rock, and had also examined by 7 pits the lower plateau of
the citadel and its immediate neighbourhood.* In a
trench dug at the west side of the higher plateau I had
rediscovered the rectangular plinth, together with the
3 pillar-bases, which had been found by Fr. Thiersch and
Al. R. Rangabé, who had dug here for one day in
September 1831.† In seven or eight of the pits on the
higher plateau I had found walls built of large stones
without mortar, which I considered to be the Cyclopean
housewalls of the prehistoric inhabitants of Tiryns. But
afterwards I began to doubt this, and my doubts were
strengthened by the results of my excavations at Mycenæ
and Troy. I was therefore very desirous for years back
to explore Tiryns thoroughly, but was prevented by other
pressing work; for after I had finished in 1876 my very

---

* Cf. my work *Mycenæ* (London, John Murray, 1878). p. 9.

† An account of this is found in Fr. Thiersch's letters to his wife,
published in his *Life* (Leipzig, 1866), by W. J. Thiersch, II. 68. See
also Al. R. Rangabé's communication in the *Mémoires des Savants
Etrangers*, présentés à l'Académie de France, I. Série, Tome V. 1857,
p. 420.

successful excavations at Mycenæ, I was engaged all
through 1877 with the German * and English editions
of my work *Mycenæ*, and with the French † up to the
summer of 1878.  Then I thought it of most importance
to explore Ithaca, and to prosecute the work of exploring
Troy and the so-called heroic tombs of the Troad, which
kept me busy till June 1879.  The concurrent editing in
German ‡ and English § of my book *Ilios* occupied
another year and a half.  Then came the exploration of
the great Minyan treasure-house at Orchomenos, which
took several months.  I then made a journey through
the whole of the Troad, and my writings on these subjects,
*Orchomenos*, ‖ and a *Journey in the Troad*, ¶ together
with other affairs, kept me busy till the end of 1881.
The excavations at Troy (renewed March 1st, 1882) lasted
five months, and my publications on this in German **
and English †† called *Troja*, together with the French
edition of *Ilios* ‡‡ occupied me till the end of 1883.  In
February 1884 I excavated the so-called tomb of the 192
Athenians at Marathon,§§ and it was not till March 1884
that I was able to realise my long-deferred hope of exploring Tiryns.  The necessary permission was readily granted
me by M. Boulpiotes, the learned Minister of Education,
who was constant in helping me to overcome the many

---

* *Mykenæ* (Leipzig, F. A. Brockhaus, 1878).

† *Mycènes* (Paris, Hachette & Co., 1879).

‡ *Ilios* (Leipzig, F. A. Brockhaus, 1881).

§ *Ilios* (London, John Murray, 1880).

‖ *Exploration of the Bœotian Orchomenos* in the Journal of Hellenic
Studies, London, 1881, Vol. II., and in German *Orchomenos* (Leipzig,
F. A. Brockhaus, 1881).

¶ *Reise in der Troas* (Leipzig, F. A. Brockhaus, 1881

** *Troja* (Leipzig, F. A. Brockhaus, 1884).

†† *Troja* (London, John Murray, 1884).

‡‡ *Ilios* (Paris, Firmin-Didot & Co., 1885).

§§ *Zeitschrift für Ethnologie, Organ der Berliner Gesellschaft für
Anthropologie, Ethnologie und Urgeschichte*, 1884, II. Heft, p. 85–88.

obstacles arising during the operations. It is with great pleasure that I here repeat my thanks to this worthy man for the inestimable services he has rendered to science, for without his ready help, it would have been impossible to carry out effectually the exploration of Tiryns.

In order to ensure that none of the information likely to be obtained from architectural fragments should be lost, I again obtained the assistance of the eminent architect of the German Archæological Institute at Athens, Dr. Wilhelm Dörpfeld, who had conducted for four years the architectural department of the German excavations at Olympia, and who had helped me for five months at Troy in 1882. I also re-engaged, as overseer (at 180 frs. per month), G. Basilopoulos from Maguliana in Gortynia, who had served me in the same capacity under the name of *Ilos* at Troy, and now entered on the new campaign under this title; I also engaged Niketas Simigdalas of Thera, for 150 frs. per month. My third overseer was my excellent servant Œdipus Pyromalles. who had also been with me in Troy, and had now much leisure.

The necessary apparatus I brought from Athens, viz. 40 English wheelbarrows with iron wheels; 20 large iron crowbars; one large and two small windlasses; 50 large iron shovels; 50 pickaxes; 25 large hoes, known all through the East by the name of *tschapa*, and used in vineyards; these were again of the greatest use in filling the baskets with *débris*. The baskets necessary, known ever. in Greece by the Turkish name *senbil*, I bought in Nauplia. For the storage of these tools, for the stabling of my horse, and for the lodging of my overseers, I hired rooms (at 50 frs. per month) in the buildings of the model farm started by Capo d'Istria, close to the south wall of Tiryns. It has now decayed into a tumbledown farmhouse.

Dr. Dörpfeld and I found this house too dirty; and as there was near Tiryns only one suitable residence, for which they asked 2000 frs. for three months, we preferred to live in the Hôtel des Etrangers, in Nauplia, where we got for 6 frs. per day a couple of clean rooms, as well as a room for Œdipus, and where the worthy host, Georgios Moschas, did all he could to make us comfortable.

My habit was to rise at 3.45 A.M., swallow 4 grains of quinine as a preservative against fever, and then take a sea bath; a boatman, for 1 fr. daily, awaited me punctually at 4 o'clock, and took me from the quay to the open sea, where I swam for 5 or 10 minutes. I was obliged to climb into the boat again by the oar, but long practice had made this somewhat difficult operation easy and safe. After bathing, I drank in the coffee-house *Agamemnon*, which was always open at that hour, a cup of black coffee without sugar, still to be had for the old sum of 10 Lepta (a penny) though everything had risen enormously in price. A good cob (at 6 frs. daily) stood ready, and took me easily in twenty-five minutes to Tiryns, where I always arrived before sunrise, and at once sent back the horse for Dr. Dörpfeld. Our breakfast was taken regularly at 8 A.M., during the first rest of the workmen, on the floor of the old palace at Tiryns. It consisted of Chicago corned beef, of which a plentiful supply was sent me by my honoured friends Messrs. J. H. Schröder & Co., from London, bread, fresh sheep-cheese, oranges, and white resined wine (*rezinato*), which, on account of its bitter, agrees with quinine, and is more wholesome during heat and hard work than the stronger red wines. During the workmen's second rest, beginning at 12 and lasting at first an hour, in greater heat one hour and three-quarters, we also rested, and two stones of the threshing-floor at the south end of the Acropolis, where we afterwards found the Byzantine Church, served us for pillows. One never rests so well as when thoroughly tired with hard work, and I can assure the reader, that we never enjoyed more refreshing sleep than during this midday hour in the Acropolis of Tiryns, in spite of the hard bed, and the scorching sun, against which we had no other protection than our Indian hats laid flat upon our faces.

Our third and last meal was at our return home in the evening, in the restaurant of the hotel. As my London friends had also supplied me with Liebig's Extract of Meat, we had always excellent soup; this, with fish or mutton, fried in olive-oil, cheese, oranges, and resined wine, completed our menu. Fish and many kinds of vegetables, as potatoes, broad beans, French beans, peas and artichokes, are excellent here, but are so ill-cooked with quantities of olive-oil, that to our taste they are almost useless.

Although wine mixed with resin is not mentioned by any ancient Greek author except Dioscorides, and even Athenaios makes no allusion to it, yet we may assume with high probability that it was in common use in the ancient Greek world, for the fir-cone was sacred to Dionysos, and the thyrsos, a light staff wound with ivy and vine branches, which was carried in processions by the priests of Bacchus, was ornamented at the upper end with a fir-cone. Pliny also, among the various fruits useful for making wine, enumerates the fir-cone, and says that it is dipped and pressed in the must.*

The passage in Dioscorides, which is very characteristic and instructive, runs thus: " Concerning resined wine. Resined wine is prepared by various peoples, but it is most abundant in Galatia, for there, on account of the cold, the grapes do not ripen, and therefore the wine turns sour if it be not tempered with pine resin. The resin is taken off along with the bark, and half a Kotyle (a piece of two ounces) is mixed in an Amphora. Some filter the wine after fermentation, and thus separate the resin; others leave it in. When the wine is long kept it becomes sweet. But

---

* Plinius, *N. H.* XIV. 19, 3–4: " Vinum fit, et e siliqua Syriaca, et e piris, malorumque omnibus generibus. Sed e Punicis, quod rhoiten vocant: et e cornis, mespilis, sorbis, moris siccis, nucleis pineis. Hi musto madidi exprimuntur: superiora per se mitia."

all wines so prepared produce headache and dizziness, yet
promote digestion, are diuretic, and to be recommended
for coughs and colds; also to those suffering from gastric
complaints, dysentery or dropsy, &c., and for internal
ulcers. Also the dark rezinato constipates more than the
white." *

I commenced the excavation on the 17th of March,
with sixty workmen, who were shortly increased to seventy,
and this remained the average number of my labourers
during the two and a half months' campaign at Tiryns in
1884.

The daily wages of my workmen were at first 3 francs;
this, however, increased as the season advanced, and
before Easter rose to 3½ francs. I also employed women,
finding them quite as handy at filling baskets as men; their
wages at first were 1½ francs, and later were increased to
2 francs. At sunrise all the workers came with the tools
and wheelbarrows from the depot to the citadel, where as
soon as I had called over the roll, work began, and lasted
till sundown, when all tools and wheelbarrows were again
returned to the depot. In spite of these precautions, many
tools and a wheelbarrow were stolen from me.

For work with the pickaxe I chose the strongest men,
as it is the heaviest; the others suited for the wheelbarrows,
for filling the rubbish into the baskets, and for clearing

---

* Pedanii Dioscoridis Anazarbei De Materia Medica, V. 43: (Περὶ
ῥητινίτου οἴνου.) Ὁ δὲ ῥητινίτης καὶ κατὰ τὰ ἔθνη σκευάζεται· πλεονάζει δὲ
ἐν Γαλατίᾳ, διὰ τὸ ἀποξύνεσθαι τὸν οἶνον ἀπεπάντου μενούσης τῆς σταφυλῆς,
διὰ τὸ ψύχειν, εἰ μὴ παραπλακῇ πευκίνῃ· κόπτεται δὲ σὺν τῷ φλοιῷ ἡ ῥητίνη,
καὶ τῷ κεραμίῳ μίγνυται ἡμικοτύλιον. καὶ οἱ μὲν ἀπηθοῦσι μετὰ τὸ ἀποζέσαι,
χωρίζοντες τὴν ῥητίνην, οἱ δὲ ἐῶσι. παλαιωθέντες δὲ γίγνονται ἡδεῖς. πάντες
δὲ κεφαλαλγεῖς οἱ τοιοῦτοι καὶ σκοτωματικοί, πεπτικοὶ μέντοι καὶ οὐρητικοί,
καὶ καταρροϊζομένοις καὶ βήσσουσιν ἁρμόζοντες καὶ κοιλιακοῖς, δυσεντερικοῖς,
ὑδρωπικοῖς καὶ ῥοϊκαῖς γυναιξί· τοῖς δὲ ἐν βάθει εἰλκωμένοις ἔγκλυσμα· στυπτι-
κώτερος μέντοι τοῦ λευκοῦ ἐστιν ὁ μελανίζων.— This passage was pointed
out to me by M. Ach. Postolaccas, Director of the National Collection
of Coins at Athens.

them again.   As I desired to provide my people with good drinking-water, I set aside a labourer for the purpose, that he might fetch it in barrels upon a wheelbarrow from the nearest spring.

Another workman, with some knowledge of carpentry, I set aside for the repairs of wheelbarrows and tools ; a third served me as groom.   Unfortunately, I was debarred the pleasure of employing my old servant Nikolaos Zaphyros Giannakis, who since the beginning of 1870 had served me in all my archæological campaigns as comptroller of the household and cashier, for, unhappily, he was drowned in August 1883, in the Skamander, on the east of Yeni Shehr, so I had to manage without him.

The labourers were mostly Albanians from the neighbouring villages of Kophinion, Kutsion, Laluka, and Aria. I had only about fifteen Greeks from the village of Charvati, who had worked with me eight years ago in Mycenæ, and who distinguished themselves by their industry above the Albanians.

The winter, 1883-84, had been very mild, and on our arrival on the 15th of March the trees were already clothed in the richest green and the fields decked with flowers. We saw flocks of cranes only on the 16th of March. These birds do not nest here, but stay only a few hours, and then continue their northward flight. Storks are never seen in Argolis, though often in the marshy plains of the Phthiotis, where they build.

Our first great work was to dig away the rubbish down to the floor made in the manner of mosaic, of lime and small stones, which stretches over the whole higher plateau of the Acropolis, and was covered $1$-$1\frac{1}{2}$ metres deep with *débris* consisting of fragments of brick, tumbled-down masonry of stones bonded with clay and mostly calcined, and of black earth. It then appeared that the walls found by my excavations of 1876, consisting of large stones without mortar, were only the foundation-structure of an immense palace, occupying the whole of the upper citadel. Of its walls, the lower portion, built of smaller stones and clay about 0·50-1 metre high, had been remarkably preserved by the close covering of *débris* over all the building, which came down from the higher walls of the edifice made of unburnt bricks, and from the flat roofs, which consisted probably of clay. This preservation is also due to the conflagration by which the palace was destroyed; for its heat was such, whenever beams of timber fed the flames, that the stones were calcined, the binding clay turned into real brick, and the whole reduced to so hard a mass, that our strongest men had the greatest difficulty in breaking it with pickaxes. Many of these walls thus burnt were visible on the surface, and had misled the best archæologists, as they were assumed to be mediæval, and it had never been imagined that they could be perhaps 2000 years older, and belong to the palace of the mythical Kings of Tiryns. In all guide-books for Greece, therefore, the opinion is expressed that nothing of interest is to be found at Tiryns. As regards the building of this palace and its extant architectural fragments, I refer the reader to Dr. Dörpfeld's full description in the fifth chapter, and his excellent plans at the end of the volume.

Owing to these many remains of walls as hard as stone, reaching to the surface, which the peasants could not break, the upper plateau could never be tilled—a circumstance which may have contributed not a little to the preservation of the remains of the palace. But the lower terrace, as well as the lower Acropolis, and the narrow tract of land around the citadel, and enclosed by the roads (cf. Plan I.), were let to a peasant in Kophinion, who had sowed it with caraway, and sued me at law for the damage done by my excavations. By the friendly intervention of M. J. Mavrikos, in Nauplia, the Director of the Excise, the damage was carefully estimated by experts, and fixed at 275 frs., with which the farmer had to be content. Many other services were kindly rendered me by M. Mavrikos and M. G. Tsakonopoulos, of Nauplia, during my stay at Tiryns ; for which I here again tender them my sincerest thanks.

Our second great work was the clearing of the mid-terrace (Plan I.), where Dr. Dörpfeld thinks badly-built dwelling-houses must have once stood, which required frequent renewing, for we there found at various successive levels thin walls of broken stones and clay, with no plan now recoverable. The accumulation is there about 6 metres.

Our third work was the opening in the lower citadel of two trenches—a wide one along and a smaller across it (cf. Plan I.)—reaching down to the rock, by which it was shown that there also buildings, or at least foundations of buildings, exist. The accumulation of *débris* here reaches a height of 3 metres, though occasionally the rocks penetrate to the surface.

As our fourth work, I may mention the excavation and clearing of the ascent to the palace on the east side of the citadel. This gave us immense trouble, on account of the enormous quantity of huge blocks which had fallen on to it from the walls, and which had to be cleared away or broken up. Further, we cleared a part of the great gallery to the south-east (cf. Plan I.), of which the upper part forms a pointed arch, and it should be remarked that we found therein a floor formed of concrete. We also cleared one of the niches or window openings of this gallery, and partly excavated three other similar galleries (cf. Plans I. and III.).

The trenches which we opened in all directions under the Acropolis, in which we found the same pottery as in the citadel, and much *débris* of burnt bricks, leave no doubt that the lower rown extended round the citadel.

Dr. Dörpfeld and I have carefully cleared, before our departure, all parts of the walls of Tiryns which had been covered up during the excavations, and I can assure the reader that not two stones of the old masonry remain hidden by the *débris* shot by me. This can for the rest be easily proved by Hauptmann Steffen's excellent map,* on which all remnants of the walls of Tiryns are carefully indicated. I have left the *débris* only in those places where the slopes of the Acropolis consist of native rock or of earth covered with sporadic stones, and where, consequently, the clearing away of the newly-shot *débris* was to no purpose.

My excavations in Tiryns had the high honour, in April 1884, of a visit from his Royal Highness the Crown Prince of Saxe-Meiningen, so distinguished by his love of science and learning; also from Herr Eduard Brockhaus, senior of the publishing firm of F. A. Brockhaus, in Leipzig, and his son Herr Arnold Brockhaus. Among other learned visitors to my excavations in April and May, I may further mention the American Ambassador to the Greek Court, Mr. Eugene Schuyler, author of the popular work *Life of Peter the Great,* and Mrs. Schuyler; the well-known historian, Professor J. P. Mahaffy, of Dublin, accompanied by Dr. Panagiotes Kastromenos, from Athens ; also Gymnasial-Director Dr. Schultz, of Charlottenburg, and Professor Püschel, of Berlin, the last of whom unfortunately died of typhus fever at Nauplia. Also Lord and Lady Pembroke; Dr. Ernst Fabricius, from Strassburg, author of a well-known work, *De Architectura Græca ;* Dr. Demetrius Bikellas, the celebrated author of *Loukis Larras* and translator of Homer and Shakespeare; Dr. Meyer, from Pesth ; Messrs. Hugh and James A. Campbell, from St. Louis; Dr. Flemming, from Güstrow; and the architect Karl Siebold, who is conducting the building of the new museum at Olympia.

---

* Hauptmann Steffen und Dr. H. Lolling, *Karten von Mykenæ,* Berlin, 1884.

# CHAPTER II.

## Topography and History of Tiryns.

The plain of Argos was apparently in early prehistoric times a bay running far inland; this was gradually filled up by the deposit of the numerous streams descending from the surrounding hills, which, though now bare and barren, were then covered with forests. These mountains are highest and wildest on the west, where Artemision, 1772 m. high, forms the natural boundary between Arkadia and Argolis, and is the centre point from which the not much lower Κτένια (comb) chain runs towards the south-east, to which again the still lower Parthenion (now 'Ροίνω) unites itself in the south-west, and runs north and south. From the central chain branch many parallel ones, reaching eastward, and divided by deep and narrow valleys; the most northern is the Lyrkeion, from the north-western slopes of which springs the Inachos (now Panitza), and flows round the northern foot of the mountains into the plain. The second mountain chain is the Chaon, with the eastward-stretching Mount Lykone,* which in the days of classical antiquity was clothed with cypress. Close to its eastern foot lies a high, sharp rock (270 m.), on which stood the fortress of Larisa, the Acropolis of Argos  The town itself lies below the hill in the plain.

The third parallel mountain chain is that of Pontinos, of which the base, separated only by a narrow strip of strand from the sea, forms the south-western end of the plain.

---

* Paus. II. 24, 6 : ἐν δεξιᾷ δὲ (τοῦ Ἄργους) ὄρος ἐστὶν ἡ Λυκώνη, δένδρα κυπαρίσσου μάλιστα ἔχουσα.

To the north side of this plain lie the rough and steep
mountains of Treton and Kelossa; in the north-east corner,
to the north and south-east of the Acropolis of Mycenæ,
are the two highest summits of Mount Eubœa,* on the
most northern of which (807 m. high, according to Hauptmann Steffen and Dr. H. Lolling †) stands an open chapel
of the Prophet Elias, with a tree visible far off in the plain.

On the east side the western spurs of the mountains
of Epidaurus slope gently to the plain. In the south, a
broad band of marshy lowland borders the plain towards
the sea. At the south-west corner, at the foot of Mount
Pontinos, numerous springs form the marsh of Lerna,
notorious for malaria, with a small lake 60 m. in depth,
where, according to fable, Hercules slew the nine-headed
Hydra.‡ The myth gives apparently a symbolic account
of an early attempt to drain the marsh and introduce
agriculture.

In the north-east part of the plain, in the neighbourhood of the villages of Chonika and Merbaka, there are
still extensive swamps, used only for the culture of rice
and cotton, but which with careful drainage might be
easily laid dry.

The most important streams are the above-mentioned
Inachos, which runs through the whole length of the plain
of Argos, and its tributary the Charadros (now called
Rema or Xerias), on whose banks, as Thukydides § tells
us, it was the custom of the Argives to assemble their
armies when returning from foreign service, and hold upon
them a court-martial before they were allowed to enter the
city.

Both rivers have for the most part of the year no water
in their broad beds, filled with pebbles and sand, and this

---

* So called by Pausanias, II. 17, 2.

† Hauptmann Steffen und Dr. H. Lolling, *Karten von Mykenæ*,
Berlin, 1884.

‡ Apollod. II. 5, 2.                    § Thukydides, V. 60.

was so in the time of Pausanias, who says* that he found
the sources of the Inachos on Mount Artemision, but that
the flow of water was quite insignificant, and the stream ran
but a short distance; and further,† "neither the Inachos,
or other rivers named (Kephisos and Asterion) have any
water, unless after rain; in summer their beds are dry, except those in the district of Lerna." This would point to
the fact, that even at that time the East-Arcadian mountains were as treeless as now.

As, however, the river Inachos plays an important part
in the myths of Argolis, where he appears as the husband of
Meleia and the father of Phoroneus, the first King of Argos,
and of the Moon-goddess Io, the later Hera, there can be little
doubt that in prehistoric times the Inachos was an important river, and this is only credible on the supposition that
the Arcadian Mountains were at that time covered with
forest. And we possess another proof that during many
thousand years the Inachos must have been a considerable
river, for, as already mentioned, the whole plain of Argos
was formed by the deposit of its rivers and streams, and
especially from that of the Inachos.

The third river of the plain is the Kephisos (Κηφισός)
mentioned by Pausanias,‡ which seems to be indicated by
a narrower river-bed which one passes on the road from
Argos to Mycenæ. I mention also the spring Kynadra,
or the so-called Ἐλευθέριον ὕδωρ, and the rivulet Asterion,
between which, at the foot of Mount Euboea, was situated
the famous Heræon.§ The Kynadra afforded the sacred
water for the Temple, used in religious ceremonies; while
on the banks of the Asterion grew the Asterion plant (a
sort of aster) sacred to Hera, from the leaves of which
crowns were woven for the goddess. And the name of the

---

* Paus. II. 25, 3.        † *Ibid.* II. 15, 5.        ‡ *Ibid.*
§ See Hauptmann Steffen and Dr. H. Lolling, *Karten von Mykenæ*,
p. 40, ff.

hill Euboea appears to point to a time when it furnished a
fair pasture land, whilst now it is bare and sterile as the
banks and beds of the Kynadra and the Asterion.

In conclusion, I mention the river Erasinos, which has
its source at the foot of the mountain chain of Chaon, and
is an important stream, turning many mills, and empty-
ing itself after a short course into the Gulf of Argos.  This
Erasinos was throughout antiquity regarded as identical
with the Stymphalos, which disappears into two subterranean passages beneath Mount Apelauron in Arcadia.  Its
great fountain-head at the foot of Chaon is now called
κεφαλάρι.

In ancient days the plain of Argos was famed for its
breed of horses, and seven times in the *Iliad*\* does Homer
celebrate the most famous pastures of the plain by the
epithet ἱππόβοτος: so also Horace,

> Plurimus in Junonis honorem
> Aptum dicet equis Argos ditesque Mycenas.†

On account of the great dryness of the soil, the vine and
cotton can only be grown on the fruitful lower plains, and
some corn and tobacco are now the only products of the
highlands.  Even at the beginning of the Greek Revolution
(1821) there must have been more moisture, for then the
whole plain and even a large part of the highlands were
covered with mulberry, orange, and olive trees, which are
now only to be seen in the low plains occasionally.

The epithet πολυδίψιον, which Homer gives to the plain
of Argos, suits its present condition well, as does also the
myth related by Pausanias.‡  " Poseidon and Hera quarrelled
for possession of the land (the plain of Argos) and Phoroneus, son of the river Inachos, the Kephisos, the Asterion,
and the Inachos were appointed to decide the claim.  They
allotted the plain to Hera, upon which Poseidon caused the

---

\* *Il.* II. 287 ; III. 75, and 258; VI. 152 ; IX. 246; XV. 30;
XIX. 329.          † Carm. I. 7, 8, 9.          ‡ Paus. II. 15, 5.

water to disappear. On this account neither the Inachos, nor yet any of the rivers named, has any water unless Zeus sends rain (Ζεὺς ὕει). In summer all streams are dry except the Lerna springs."

In the south-eastern corner of the plain of Argos, on the west and lowest and flattest of those rocky heights which here form a group, and rise like islands from the marshy plain, at a distance of 8 stadia, or about 1500 m. from the Gulf of Argos, lay the prehistoric citadel of Tiryns,* now called Palæocastron.

---

* According to Professor Mahaffy, "The etymology of Tiryns is unknown, as is also the language from which it was borrowed, for the form is not Greek—all such endings losing one of the closing consonants. Thus, in Greek, Tirys would have been the necessary form. All the endings in as (αντος) are a proof of this. The few instances in Cretan dialect of the violation of this phonetic law are hardly in point, much more, however, the sister forms Κόρινθος, Ζάκυνθος, Πέρινθος, which show that Τίρυνθος was a possible form, as we actually find it in two places cited below. There seems even to have been an avoidance of the nominative, as if Τίρυνθος had not been generally accepted, while Τίρυνς was felt to be barbarous. The dictionaries cite πείρινς and ἕλμινς, as if such words existed in Greek. In neither case do we find any but oblique cases (πείρινθα, ἕλμισι) in use." Professor Mahaffy is therefore disposed to refer the form Τίρυνς to late grammarians, framing it by analogy from the oblique cases (Τίρυνθα, &c.) occurring in classical writers.

Professor E. Curtius (*Peloponnesos,* II. 567) thinks it related to the Latin *turris.* Professor C. T. Newton considers it the remains of a very ancient form, but refers me to H. L. Ahrens (*De dialecto Dorica,* Gött. 1843, p. 107) who regards Τίρυνς as the Argive (?) or Cretan form; also to Paulus Cauer's *Delectus Inscr. Græc.,* who cites several Cretan words, inserting an ν in the nom. and accus., ex. gr. πάνσαν, ὑπάρχουσαν, καθιστάνσα; also to G. Curtius' *Studien* (Leipzig, 1871, p. 78, and Leipzig, 1875), where we see that the accusative ἄς comes from a primitive ανς, τος from τονς, χαριεις from χαριενς, anima from animans. But all these show precisely the change which Professor Mahaffy postulates. Professor Sayce, of Oxford, thinks also that the probable Τίρυς was a Doric corruption of a prehistoric and pre-Aryan Τίρυνθ, which dates from the days of the older inhabitants of the Peloponnesus, before the Greeks reached it, and he can find neither an Aryan nor a Semitic derivation for it. [The

It was held in the highest veneration as the birthplace of Herakles, and was famed for its Cyclopean walls, which in ancient days were regarded as a miracle. Pausanias indeed places them side by side with the Pyramids of Egypt, saying, " Now the Hellenes have a mania for admiring that which is foreign much more than that which is in their own land, and thus the most eminent writers have agreed to describe the Pyramids with the greatest minute-

---

The earliest occurrence of the actual form Τίρυνς is in the fragments of the so-called Skylax, pp. 19, 49 ; μετὰ δὲ Λακεδαίμονα πόλις ἐστὶν Ἄργος, καὶ ἐν αὐτῇ Ναυπλία πόλις καὶ λιμήν · ἐν μεσογείᾳ δὲ Κλεωναὶ καὶ Μυκῆναι καὶ Τίρυνς. [After Lacedæmon comes the city of Argos, and at it the city and harbour of Nauplia. In the interior are Cleonæ and Mycenæ and Tiryns.] The date of the fragment is very uncertain and may be very late. The form Τίρυνθος occurs in Apollod. II. 7, 18, and in Hesiod's Scutum, 81 : ἦλθε, λιπὼν Τίρυνθον ἐϋκτίμενον πτολίεθρον. Lobeck (Paralip. 167) wishes to read Τίρυνθα here.

The town appears at first to have been called Likymnia, for Strabo (VIII. 373) says that a citadel of this name lay 12 stadia from Nauplia, which agrees exactly with the distance from Nauplia to Tiryns. Strabo does not indeed expressly say that he means Tiryns ; but this appears clearly from a passage in Pindar (Ol. 7, 47) :

καὶ γὰρ Ἀλκμήνας κασίγνητον νόθον σκάπτῳ θένων
σκληρᾶς ἐλαίας ἔκταν' ἐν Τί-
ρυνθι Λικύμνιον, ἐλθόντ' ἐκ θαλάμου Μιδέας
τᾶς δέ ποτε χθονὸς οἰκιστὴρ χολωθείς.

[For he (Tlepolemus) in anger slew with a club of hard olive in Tiryns the bastard brother of Alcmene, Likymnios, sprung from the chamber of Midea (Tlepolemus being) once the founder of the town (Tiryns).] Apollodorus (II. 8, 2) confirms this, saying, however, that he slew him by mistake: Τ. οὖν, κτείνας οὐχ ἑκὼν Λικύμνιον, τῇ βακτηρίᾳ γὰρ αὐτοῦ θεραπεύοντα πλήσσοντος ὑπέδραμε. [T. slew Likymnios by mistake, who ran under his stick as he was striking a servant.] Eustathius says the first name of Tiryns was Halieis or Haleis, as fishermen first settled on that rock. This is repeated by Stephanus Byzantinus, sub voc. Τίρυνς: Ἐκαλεῖτο δὲ πρότερον Ἁλιεῖς διὰ τὸ πολλοὺς Ἑρμιονέας ἁλιευομένους οἰκεῖν αὐτοῦ. (It was first called Haliëis, because many fishermen from Hermione settled there.) E. Curtius, however (Pelop. II. 567), thinks this to be probably a confusion with the later refuge of the Tirynthians in Halike. According to Pausanias II. 25, 7, the town was called after Tiryns, a son of Argos.

ness, whilst they bestow not a word on the treasure-house
of Minyas or the walls of Tiryns, which nevertheless are
fully as deserving of admiration."* Even Homer expresses
his admiration by the epithet τειχιόεσσα, which he bestows
on Thebes—

"For those that held Argos and the walled Tirynth." †

Eustathios remarks on this Homeric passage (*Il.* VI. 559)
τὴν δὲ Τ. τειχιόεσσαν λέγει διὰ τὸ εὖ τετειχίσθαι. Pausanias
says further of the walls of Tiryns, "The surrounding wall,
which is all that remains (of Tiryns) was built by the Cyclopes. It is formed of unhewn stones, each of which is so
large, that a yoke of two mules could not move the smallest
from its place; the interstices are filled with little stones, in
order to fix the great stones more firmly in their beds."‡

The stones of the surrounding wall are on an average
about 2 m. in length and 0·90 m. broad, and to judge
from the existing remains the entire height must have been
about 15 m. Had the blocks been hewn, they would certainly have disappeared centuries since; they would have
been used in building the neighbouring towns of Argos
and Nauplia, but the gigantic size of the blocks and their
roughness protected the walls; for later builders found it
easier and more convenient to hew out their own materials
from the foot of the rock, than to disturb the walls and
break up the colossal stones.

The quarry from which the blocks of the wall of Tiryns

---

* Paus. IX. 36, 5 : Ἕλληνες δὲ ἄρα εἰσὶ δεινοὶ τὰ ὑπερόρια ἐν θαύματι
τίθεσθαι μείζονι ἢ τὰ οἰκεῖα, ὁπότε γε ἀνδράσιν ἐπιφανέσιν ἐς συγγραφὴν
πυραμίδας μὲν τὰς παρὰ Αἰγυπτίοις ἐπῆλθεν ἐξηγήσασθαι πρὸς τὸ ἀκριβέστατον,
θησαυρὸν δὲ τὸν Μινύου καὶ τὰ τείχη τὰ ἐν Τίρυνθι οὐδὲ ἐπὶ βραχὺ ἤγαγον
μνήμης, οὐδὲν ὄντα ἐλάττονος θαύματος.

† *Il.* II. 559 : οἳ δ᾽ Ἄργος τ᾽ εἶχον Τίρυνθα τε τειχιόεσσαν.

‡ Paus. II. 25, 8 : Τὸ δὴ τεῖχος, ὃ δὴ μόνον τῶν ἐρειπίων λείπεται,
κυκλώπων μέν ἐστιν ἔργον, πεποίηται δὲ ἀργῶν λίθων, μέγεθος ἔχων ἕκαστος
λίθος ὡς ἀπ᾽ αὐτῶν μηδ᾽ ἂν ἀρχὴν κινηθῆναι τὸν μικρότατον ὑπὸ ζεύγους ἡμιόνων·
λίθια δὲ ἐνήρμοσται πάλαι ὡς μάλιστα αὐτῶν ἕκαστον ἁρμονίαν τοῖς μεγάλοις
λίθοις εἶναι.

were hewn can be easily recognised at the foot of a rock on the high road between Tiryns and Nauplia, upon the summit of which stands a chapel dedicated to Elias the prophet. Yet this quarry has not formed a ravine like the Latomiæ in Korinth, Baalbek, or Syracuse, for the Cyclopean architects contented themselves with hewing their blocks from the surface.

It may here be not out of place to mention that the name "Cyclopean walls" is frequently misapplied to different kinds of masonry. The name evidently arises from the myth, that the Cyclopes were excellent builders. According to Apollodorus,* Pausanias,† and Strabo,‡ Proitos, King of Tiryns, caused seven of their number to come from Lykia to build for him the walls of Tiryns. By these seven, or by other Cyclopes, were built, according to the myth, many other buildings in Argolis, in particular the walls of Mycenæ, for which reason Euripides calls the whole of Argolis "the Cyclopean land," γᾶ κυκλωπία. § The houses also of Mycenæ are described as Cyclopean.‖ The same poet also calls Mycenæ κυκλώπων θυμέλαι, the altars of the Cyclopes,¶ Μυκῆναι κυκλωπίαι, the Cyclopean Mycenæ,** also,

καλεῖς πόλισμα Περσέως,
κυκλωπίων πόνον χερῶν

(Do you speak of the town of Perseus, the work of Cyclop hands?) ††

Again,

πρὸς τὰς Μυκήνας εἶμι λάζυσθαι χρεών
μοχλοὺς δικέλλας θ' ὡς τὰ κυκλώπων βάθρα
φοίνικι κανόνι καὶ τύκοις ἡρμοσμένα
στρεπτῷ σιδήρῳ συντριαινώσω πόλιν.

---

* Apollod. II. 2, 1.                    † Paus. II. 16, 4.

‡ Strabo, VIII. 372: τῇ μὲν οὖν Τίρυνθι ὁρμητηρίῳ χρήσασθαι δοκεῖ Προῖτος καὶ τειχίσαι διὰ Κυκλώπων, οὓς ἑπτὰ μὲν εἶναι καλεῖσθαι δὲ γαστερό-χειρας τρεφομένους ἐκ τῆς τέχνης, ἥκειν δὲ μεταπέμπτους ἐκ Λυκίας.

§ Euripides, Orestes, 965.

‖ Euripides, Iphig. Taur. 845: κυκλωπίδες ἑστίαι, ὦ πάτρις, Μυκήνα φίλα.          ¶ Euripides, Iphig. Aul. 152.

** Ibid. 265.          †† Ibid. 1500–1.

(I go to Mykenæ; I will take bars and spades, to destroy with worked iron the threshold of the Cyclopes, which is well joined with rule and hammer of stone.*)

Seneca says of the walls of Mycenæ,

> majus mihi
> Bellum Mycenis restat, ut cyclopea
> Eversa manibus saxa nostra concidant.

Again,

> cerno Cyclopum sacras
> Turres, labores majus humano decus ;

And finally: Ulixes ad Ithacæ suæ saxa sic properat, quemadmodum Agamemnon ad Mycenarum nobiles muros.†

We cannot, however, reasonably doubt that walls built of large blocks received the name of Cyclopean walls, *without any historical ground*, from the fabulous Lykian race of the Cyclopes.

Tiryns is also called κυκλώπια πρόθυρα,‡ "Cyclopean court;" we also find Τιρυνθίαν πρὸς κλιτύν § "at the slope of T.," where Herakles casts Iphitos from the top of the towering plateau (ἀπ' ἄκρας πυργώδους πλακός).|| It is specially to be remarked that in Hesychios we hear of Tirynthian brick building (Τιρύνθιον πλίνθευμα), which agrees, as will be seen below, remarkably with the construction of the great palace I excavated there.

The great towers of Tiryns, of which one still stands on the east side, may have occasioned the fame of the Tirynthians as the inventors of tower building (cf. Aristoteles and Theophrastus in Pliny, *H. N.* VII. 56.) ¶

Theophrastus relates that the Tirynthians had an extraordinary inclination to laughter, which made them useless

---

* Euripides, *Herakles furens,* 943–946.
† Seneca, *Epistul. Mor.* Liber VII. Ep. 4 (66).
‡ Pindar, *Fragm.* 642, ed. Böckh.
§ Sophocles, *Trach.* 270, 271.                    || *Ibid.* 273.
¶ The first attributes tower-building to the Cyclopes, the second to the Tirynthians.

for all serious work : he adds, " The Tirynthians desired to overcome their inclination to laughter, and consulted the oracle how they might do so. The god replied that the evil would disappear if they could, without laughing, sacrifice an ox to Poseidon, and cast it into the sea. The Tirynthians, who feared that they should not succeed in obeying the god's commands, ordered that no children should be present at the sacrifice. One child, however, had heard of the affair, and strayed in among the crowd. The child was being driven away and scolded, when he suddenly cried out, ' Are ye then afraid that I should overturn your sacrifice ? ' Hereupon all burst out laughing, and the Tirynthians were convinced that the god desired to teach them that a long-indulged habit is not easily shaken off." *

Although the legend of the Cyclopes points rather to Asia Minor than to the Phœnicians, as Prof. A. H. Sayce remarked to me, yet I must observe, that according to the Odyssey,† the Cyclop Polyphemus is a son of Poseidon, and as Mr. Gladstone has ingeniously argued,‡ a con-

---

* Theophrastos apud Athenæum, VI. 261 : Τιρυνθίους δέ φησι Θεόφραστος ἐν τῷ περὶ κωμῳδίας φιλογέλως ὄντας, ἀχρείους δὲ πρὸς τὰ σπουδαιότερα τῶν πραγμάτων, καταφυγεῖν ἐπὶ τὸ ἐν Δελφοῖς μαντεῖον ἀπαλλαγῆναι βουλομένους τοῦ πάθους, καὶ τὸν θεὸν ἀνελεῖν αὐτοῖς, ἢν θύοντες τῷ Ποσειδῶνι ταῦρον ἀγελαστὶ τοῦτον ἐμβάλωσιν εἰς τὴν θάλατταν, παύσεσθαι. οἳ δὲ δεδιότες μὴ διαμάρτωσι τοῦ λογίου τοὺς παῖδας ἐκώλυσαν παρεῖναι τῇ θυσίᾳ. μαθὼν οὖν εἷς καὶ συγκαταμιχθείς, ἐπείπερ ἐβόων ἀπελαύνοντες αὐτόν, τί δῆτ' ; ἔφη, δεδοίκατε μὴ τὸ σφάγιον ὑμῶν ἀνατρέψω ; γελασάντων δὲ ἔμαθον ἔργῳ τὸν θεὸν δείξαντα ὡς ἄρα τὸ πολυχρόνιον ἦθος ἀμήχανόν ἐστι θεραπευθῆναι.

† Od. IX. 528–530.

‡ Cf. W. E. Gladstone's Preface to my *Mycenæ*, pp. viii. ix. : " The buildings improperly called Cyclopean, and still more improperly endowed with the alternative name of Pelasgian, have long been known, more or less, to exist in Argolis ; but Dr. Schliemann has thrown some light on what I may perhaps be allowed to call their diversity of style. He admits three forms found in this kind of building. I have objected to the current names, the first because it does not inform ; the second because it misleads, for these buildings have no true connection with the Pelasgian tribes. What they indicate is the

nection with this god frequently points to one with the Phœnicians. The connection of Tiryns with this people is specially indicated by the position of the hero Herakles, the Phœnician God Melkarth, who according to myth was born and long dwelt there. And as Karl Victor Müllenhoff has shown beyond all doubt in his *Deutsche Alterthumskunde* \* Herakles is the representative of the Phœnicians. This is also noted by A. H. Sayce, who writes, " The whole circle of myths grouped around the name of Herakles points as clearly to a Semitic source, as do the myths of Aphrodite and Adonis."†

The same friend has also observed to me that the legend of Nauplios, the son of Poseidon ‡, the founder of the seaport Nauplia,§ at a distance of only four km. from

---

handiwork of the great constructing race or races, made up of several elements, who migrated into Greece, and elsewhere on the Mediterranean, from the south and east, and who exhibit an usual, though perhaps not an invariable connection with the Poseidon-worship ; a worship, with which the Cyclopean name is, through the Odyssey, perceptibly associated, and which is one of the main keys, as I have long been persuaded, wherewith in time to unlock, for Hellenic and Homeric regions, the secrets of antiquity. The walls of Troy were built by Poseidon ; that is, by a race who practised the worship of the god. How far those walls conform to any of the minuter points of the descriptions of ' Cyclopean' architecture by Dr. Schliemann (pp. 42, 123), I cannot say. But if he is right, as seems probable, in placing Troy at Hissarlik, it is important to notice that this work of Poseidon had a solidity, which bore it unharmed through the rage of fire, and kept it well together amidst all the changes which have buried it in a hill of rubbish and promiscuous remains. And of course the modes, used by the very same race in the business of building, could not but vary much with the circumstances of each case, and especially with the material at hand. I am tempted, at least until a better name can be found, to call this manner of building Poseidonian. At any rate, whatever it be called, I note it as a point of correspondence between the Poems and the discoveries ; admitting at the same time that the matter is not sufficiently developed to warrant me in laying upon it any considerable stress."

\* W. Christ, *Die Topographie der Troianischen Ebene*, p. 225.

† *Contemporary Review* December 1878.

‡ Apollod. II. 1, 5.        § Paus. II. 38, 2 ; IV. 35, 2.

Tiryns, and of his clever son Palamêdês, show a connection with Phœnicians. He writes on this subject : " I have long since been convinced that the myth of Palamêdês contains a tradition of Phœnician influence on Greece in prehistoric times. It would otherwise be difficult to explain the fact, that to him is ascribed the discovery of the sixteen primitive letters of the alphabet (Euseb. Chr. I. 13). Besides, his name is apparently a ' Volksetymologie '—a play upon the word παλαμάομαι, to describe him as ' the crafty one.' If however his name were of Greek origin, it would be improperly formed ; at all events its relation to Palaimôn, the title under which Melicertes or Melkarth, was worshipped at Corinth, is unmistakeable. But so far I can offer no Semitic etymology for it."

The name of the village near the Heræon, in the Argolic plain, Chónika, seems to be merely a corruption of *Phoinika*, especially as there are remains there of an ancient settlement. As regards other traces of the presence of Phœnicians in the Argolic plain, Dr. H. Lolling has just called my attention to Max Duncker, *Hist. of Greece* (trans. Alleyne ; Bentley & Co., 1883), I. Chap. IV., and also pp. 151 *sq.*, where the names Malea (*malah*, height) and Marathon,* are considered evidence of Phœnician settlements. Along the whole eastern coast of the Morea, from the isthmus to Malea, and also on the coast of Elis there were these settlements.† The name Phoinikaion at the isthmus confirms this.‡ The town of Kyphanta, the ruins of which Curtius places at the citadel of Kyparissi, was a Phœnician settlement; there are further evidences in names: Bay of Tyros, with a promontory Tyru sheltering it to the south, which has a remarkable fort with very ancient polygonal masonry.§ So also the islands Kranæ‖ and

---

* Cf. Marathus = Amrit in Crete, and on the Phœnician coast.
† E. Curtius, *Peloponnesos*, I. 62.
‡ *Ibid.* II. 517.                              § *Ibid.* II. 305, 306, 332.
‖ *Ibid.* II. 269.

Kythera,* Gytheion,† and Patrai,‡ as well as other places in the Gulf of Patras,§ were once flourishing Phœnician settlements. Even in Attica, almost in Athens, there was a Phœnician *deme*, Melite, which was supposed to derive its name from a nymph attached to Herakles, and hence had a famous temple to this hero, where he was worshipped *as a god*.‖ Professor Sayce writes to me: " It is very probable that there was a Phœnician settlement in Athens itself, but so far we have no distinct proof for it." I add that the following facts, not as yet considered, point to the same conclusion : (1) the remains of Cyclopean walls built of great unhewn blocks near the Propylæa, and at other parts of the Acropolis ; (2) the terra-cotta vessels found in the oldest *débris* of the Acropolis, which in form and decoration are identical with those found at Ialysos, and at other ancient Phœnician settlements. By anticipation, I here call attention to the striking likeness of these terra-cottas, and of the eighty-nine rude idols found with them and preserved in the Acropolis Museum, to the idols and pots found at Tiryns, which will be described and drawn in my fourth chapter.

The foundation of Thebes in Bœotia by Kadmos, whose name the Acropolis of the town (Kadmeia) bore through antiquity, points directly to the Phœnicians.

Again, the appearance of Semitic names of places in the immediate neighbourhood of Tiryns, as for example Megara, from מנרה (cave), and Salamis, from שלם (safety),¶

---

* E. Curtius, *Peloponnesos*, II. 299.

† Conrad Bursian, *Geographie von Griechenland*, II. 145.

‡ Ernst Curtius, *op. cit.* I. 439.

§ *Ibid.* I. 456, 476.

‖ Strabo, I. 66, 67 ; Pausanias, I. 23, 11 ; Pliny, IV. 7, 11 ; Schol. Aristoph. *Ranæ*, p. 113. This Phœnician origin of Melite is conclusively proved by Curt. Wachsmuth in his *Stadt Athen*, I. pp. 404–45, where the whole subject is fully discussed.

¶ Kiepert, *Lehrbuch der alten Geographie*, p. 242, note 1 ; p. 273, note 1 ; cf. also Olshausen in the *Rhein. Mus.* VIII. (1853),

can only be explained by the supposition of Semitic colonization.

In like manner the name Ithaka points to a Phœnician settlement, being a Semitic word, of the same root as Utika, and meaning settlement or colony.† I here particularly note the Cyclopean walls, more or less preserved in many parts of Ithaka, which in the old capital of the island, on Mount Ætós, are of enormous dimensions, and very like those of Tiryns.‡ With great probability, therefore, we may assume that these walls, as also the ruins of the ancient capital of the island §, are to be attributed to the Phœnicians. And also the Homeric name for Korfu (Σχερίη) appears to be a Phœnician word and to mean ἀγορά or market-place (compare the Arabic شرى to buy). And it may be that the name of its inhabitants Phæakians (Φαίηκες), is only a corruption of Φοίνικες.¶ Further, the King of

---

pp. 330–332; W. Helbig, *Das Homerische Epos aus den Denkmälern erklärt*, p. 46. (Leipzig, 1884.). The enormous layers of purple-fish shells on the small island of Hagios Georgios, close to Salamis, seem also to point to a Phœnician settlement.

† Bursian, *Geographie von Griechenland* (Leipzig, 1868), II. 368: "The name of the island Ithaka, like that of the larger sister-island, Same, seems to be Semitic, and to point to an ancient mart of the Phœnicians, of which the Greeks had not preserved even a mythical recollection." Ἰθάκη = Ἰτύκη (Utica) = עתיקא "colonia": cf. Olshausen in the *Rhein. Mus.* N. F. VIII. p. 329.

‡ Schliemann, *Ilios*, p. 47–8.

§ Cf. my *Ilios*, p. 48–50.        || *Ibid.* p. 57.

¶ This was the view of Col. Mure (*Hist. Gk. Lit.* I. Appendix E), who thought that the whole picture of the Phæacians was satirical, and intended to paint the foibles of some well-known naval people. Prof. Mahaffy thinks that this application, which is almost suggested by the comic sea-names given to the Phæacian grandees (*Od.* VIII. 111, *sq.*)—

Ὦρτο μὲν Ἀκρόνεώς τε καὶ Ὠκύαλος καὶ Ἐλατρεύς
Ναυτεύς τε Πρυμνεύς τε καὶ Ἀγχίαλος καὶ Ἐρετμεύς
Ποντεύς τε Πρωρεύς τε, Θόων Ἀναβησίνεώς τε
Ἀμφίαλός θ' υἱὸς Πολυνήου Τεκτονίδαο·

cannot be intended for so thoroughly non-Hellenic a people as the Phœnicians, but is perhaps meant for the Phokæans, in early days (7th cent. B.C.), a very adventurous naval state.

the island, Alkinous, was a grandson of Poseidon.* As
other Phœnicians settlement in Greece we may mention the
towns Boulis (Βοῦλις) in Phokis,† and Chalkis‡ in Eubœa;
also Karthaia,§ once the most important town of the island
Keos (Cyclades), and of whose Cyclopean walls, which are
very like those of Tiryns, considerable traces remain. As
similar walls are found in many other parts of Keos,‖ we
may fairly infer that the whole island was once colonized
by Phœnicians. A very rich settlement of the same kind
was also on the island Thasos, which, according to tradition,
was colonized by the Phœnicians under Kadmos, and
called after one of his companions Thasos, the son of
Agenor (or Poseidon, Apollodoros III. 1. 1).¶ I add to
the list the island of Antiparos,** where, as I shall more
fully detail below, Mr. J. Theodore Bent has lately excavated and found very ancient pottery, which has many
analogies with the oldest terra-cottas of Tiryns. So also the
island of Melos,†† which is said to have been called Byblis,
Memblis, or Mimallis.‡‡ Melos and the neighbouring
island Kimolos have large beds of obsidian, the material
from which very ancient arrow-heads and blades are made,
which are found in such masses at Tiryns and Mycenæ,

---

* *Od.* VII. 54–63.

† Conrad Bursian, *Geographie von Griechenland*, I. 185.

‡ *Ibid.* II. 413.

§ *Ibid.* p. 472.

‖ Panagiotes Kastromenos in the Journal Ἑβδομάς, no. 32, 7 Oct.
1884.

¶ Herodot. II. 44; VI. 47; Pausanias, V. 25, 12; Konôn, Narr.
p. 37; Steph. Byz.

** Conrad Bursian, *op. cit.* II. 483.

†† *Ibid. op. cit.* II. 498.

‡‡ Steph. Byz. sub voce Μῆλος; Plin. IV. 12, 70; Hesych. sub voc.
Μεμβλίς and Μιμαλλίς. Euseb. Chron. ad a. Abrah. 590 (ed. Schöne,
p. 35): " Melus et Pafus et Thasus et Callista urbes conditae." Paulus
(ed. Müller, p. 124, 11) makes the Hero-eponymos Melos (cf.
Eustath. ad Dionys. Per. 530) a Phœnician.

but also elsewhere in Greece.* As other Phœnician colonies, I also specify with great probability the Sporad island Amorgos † and Anaphe, ‡ the latter called of old Membliaros, which was the name of one of Kadmos' companions. § The same may be said of Thera, of which Bursian writes : ∥ " Greek tradition tells that Kadmos, seeking his abducted sister Europa, landed on the island then called Kalliste, and built a shrine to Poseidon and Athene, and left there a number of companions under the command of Membliaros, son of Poikiles."¶ These Phœnicians, as the story seems to indicate by the name Poikiles (the variegator), established a branch of industry, which flourished later at Thera—the making of many-coloured stuffs, known to other Greeks from their place of manufacture as *Theræa*.** Eight generations after Membliaros, the story goes on, the Kadmeian Theras, son of Autesion, led a band of Minyans from Laconia to the island, where the descendants of Membliaros gave him the control, and he called it Thera after himself.

On the island of Rhodes there were also flourishing Phœnician colonies. Mr. Sayce writes to me : " Kadmos (i.e. the Phœnicians) seeking Europa, reached the island of Rhodes, and then built a temple to his grandfather, Poseidon

---

* Cf. Finlay, Παρατηρήσεις ἐπὶ τῆς ἐν Ἐλβετίᾳ καὶ Ἑλλάδι προιστορικῆς ἀρχαιολογίας (Athens, 1869), p. 17.

† Conrad Bursian, *op. cit.* II. 513.

‡ *Ibid.* II. 518.

§ Steph. Byz. sub voce Ἀνάφη and Μεμβλίαρος.

∥ Conrad Bursian, *op. cit.* II. 524.

¶ Herodot. IV. 147 ; Theophrast. in schol. Pindar. Pyth. IV. 11 ; schol. *Ibid.* p. 88 ; Pausanias, III. 1, 7 ; Steph. Byz. sub voce Θήρα. Euseb. (ed. Schöne, p. 35) makes the foundation of Kallista contemporary with that of Melos, Paphos, and Thasos in the year of Abraham, 590. Cf. Movers, *Phönizier*, II. 2, p. 266 *et sqq.*

** Poll. VII. 48 and 77 ; Hesych. sub voce Θήραιον πέπλον ; Athen. X. 424 ; cf. H. Blümner, *die gewerbliche Thätigkeit der Völker des klassischen Alterthums*, p. 96.

(*Diodor. Sic.* V. 58). The primitive people of Rhodes
were the Heliades, i.e. the descendants of the Semitic Sun-
god (Konôn in Phot. *Bibl.* 186). But Konôn also says that
the Heliades were conquered by the Phœnicians; these
again by the Karians, and these by the Dorians. On the
other hand two Rhodian authors, Ergias and Polyzêlos,
alleged that when Iphiklos and the Dorians came to
Rhodes, they found the Phœnicians still in possession of
the island, and entrenched in their citadels Kameiros and
Ialysos under their prince Phalas (*Dict. Kret.* I. 15;
IV. 10). Phalas reminds us of Palaimôn and Palamêdês.
According to Diodorus (V. 56), Zeno had seen Kadmeian
inscriptions in the temple of Athene at Lindos; he also
says that the population of Ialysos was partly Greek and
partly Phœnician (V. 58). The excavations of Kameiros
and Ialysos have proved how deep the Phœnician influence
must have been in both places."

I repeat what I shall expound fully in the following
pages, that the pottery of Ialysos has the greatest similarity
to that of Tiryns and Mycenæ.

The greatest and most flourishing settlement of Phœnicians must have been in Crete, as is proved both by the
oldest of the legends, and the Phœnician names still left on
the island.* Cyclopean walls, like those of Tiryns and
Mycenæ, are found in many places in Crete.

The close intercourse of Greece with the Phœnicians in
distant prehistoric days is also proved by the many words of
Semitic origin in the earliest forms of the Greek language.
Thus for example, as W. Helbig concludes,† the name of
the garment χιτών, κιθών, is formed from a word which in

---

* So, for example, the name of the town Käiratos (changed to
Knossos afterwards) suggests the Phœnician *kart*, and the name of the
river Jardanos (Homer, *Od.* III. 292, and Eustathios' note; Pausanias,
VI. 19), the Jordan, &c.

† Wolfgang Helbig, *Das Homerische Epos aus den Denkmälern
erläutert*, p. 131. (Leipzig, 1884.)

Hebrew is *Kuttonet*, in Chaldean *Kittun*,* and also the name of linen raiment, ὀθόνη, from the Semitic word אֵטוּן in Hebrew, which in that language describes thread, or spinning (Proverbs of Solomon, vii. 16).†

Professor Sayce has remarked to me that the Phœnicians' method of building is now well known to us, through the discovery of Phœnician writing on the walls of Mount Eryx (San Giuliano), in Sicily, and that this discovery also shows that the gigantic blocks of the lower walls of the Temple of Baalbek are of Phœnician origin.

We may therefore assume, with great probability, that the gigantic walls of Tiryns were built by Phœnician colonists, and the same is probably the case with the great prehistoric walls in many other parts of Greece.

Pliny says ‡ that there are to be found at Tiryns small snakes which grow out of the earth, and whose bite is harmless to natives, but deadly to strangers. Further, I observe that Tiryns appears as the boundary of Argeia in the oracle quoted by the Schol. ad Theocr. xiv. 48 : οἵ τε μεσηγὺ Τίρυνθος ναίουσι καὶ Ἀρκαδίης πολυμήλου.

Since Tiryns, as already mentioned, is only 1½ km. from the sea, and lies in so flat a plain that the high road at the western foot of the fortress is only 3–4 m. above sea-level,§ it inevitably gives every traveller the impression that within historic times it was situated immediately on the sea, and that the tract of swamp which now separates them is a later growth of the plain. This is, however, a great mistake, of which we have complete proof

---

* Movers, *Die Phönizier*, III. 1, p. 27 ; Hehn, *Die Kulturpflanzen und Hausthiere*, 3rd ed. p. 46.

† Wolfgang Helbig, *op. cit.* p. 128. Cf. Movers in Ersch und Gruber's *Encyklopädie*, 3 Sektion, 24 Thl. p. 358, under the word "Phönizien."

‡ Pliny, *H. N.* 84 : Iam quaedam animalia indigenis innoxia, advenas interimunt : sicut serpentes parvi in Tirynthe : quos terra nasci proditur.

§ Cf. the first-rate map of Hauptmann Steffen (Berlin, 1884).

in the remains of the small port at a distance of about
2 km. south-west of Tiryns, near the chapel of Hagios
Panteleemon, for here the remains of the buildings and
harbour dam are of huge unhewn blocks, pointing to great
antiquity. The ancient harbour is now nearly dried up
and scarcely 30 cm. deep, but the old dam can be traced
in almost its full extent, and 3000 years ago cannot have
stretched above 100 m. further into the sea than it does
to-day. Doubtless the sea-waves once washed the rocks of
Tiryns, but this was probably at a time when our planet
was not yet the home of man.

In fact, the topography of the plain south of Tiryns
appears to have altered very little, if at all, since a time of
high antiquity, for the northern shore of the gulf is occupied chiefly by deep morasses, which still extend far into
the land. For the former existence of these morasses in
the plain of Argos we have the testimony of Aristotle, who
says: " At the time of the Trojan war the land of Argos
was marshy, and could only support few inhabitants; the
land of Mycenæ, on the contrary, was good, and highly
esteemed. Now, however, the opposite is the case, for the
land of Mycenæ is dried up, and therefore lies idle;
while the land of Argos, which was a marsh, and therefore
fallow, is now good and arable land."*

The myth of the birth of Herakles in Tiryns, and of
the twelve labours laid upon him by Eurystheus, the king
of the neighbouring Mycenæ, is, I believe, to be explained by his double nature, as Phœnician Sun-god, and
as Hero.† It is but natural that fable should place the
birth of this mightiest of all heroes within the strongest
walls in the world, which were regarded as the work of

---

* Aristot., *Meteorol.* I. 14 : ἐπὶ μὲν γὰρ τῶν Τρωϊκῶν    μεν Ἀργείων
(χώρα), διὰ τὸ ἑλώδης εἶναι, ὀλίγους ἠδύνατο τρέφειν · ἡ δὲ Μυκηναία καλῶς
εἶχε · διὸ ἐντιμοτέρα ἦν. Νῦν δὲ τοὐναντίον διὰ τὴν εἰρημένην αἰτίαν · ἡ μὲν
γὰρ ἀργὴ γέγονε καὶ ξηρὰ πάμπαν, τῆς δέ, τὰ τότε διὰ τὸ λιμνάζειν ἀργά, νῦν
χρήσιμα γέγονεν.    † Max Müller, *Essays*, II. 79.

supernatural giants, and as Sun-god he must have had many temples in the plain of Argos, and a famous cult in Tiryns, for the marshy lowlands by which the fortress was surrounded, are even at this day in some places barren on account of their moisture, and in ancient days, as at present, produced pestilential fever, and could only be improved by incessant toil and the beneficent influence of the sunshine.

Thus the fable appears quite natural that Herakles as Sun-god had to perform the twelve labours for Eurystheus, king of Mycenæ, to whom the whole plain belonged; these twelve labours being none other than the twelve signs of the Zodiac, through which the sun appears to pass in the annual rotation of the earth.

The German colony which settled fifty years ago immediately west and north-west of Tiryns, never succeeded; almost all the settlers were seized by the deadly fever, and none remain : here and there stand their ruined dwellings.

On account of its great fertility and remarkable situation on the noble gulf, the plain of Argos was the natural central and starting-point of all the political and social development of the land, and thus merited the name given by Sophocles (*Electra*, 4) τὸ παλαιὸν Ἄργος. Here, as the legend tells, Phoroneus, son of Inachos and the Nymph Meleia, with his wife Niobe, first gathered the hitherto scattered inhabitants into a community, and founded a town which he called ἄστυ Φορωνικόν (Pausanias, II. 15, 5; cf. Plato, *Tim.*), which was renamed by his grandson Argos, and formed the nucleus of a great Pelasgic state (cf. Æsch. *Supp.* 250). We find incontrovertible evidence for this Pelasgic settlement in the names Argos and Larissa, which are Pelasgic, the first meaning *plain*, the last *fortress ;* and again in the myth of the old Pelasgic moon- and cow-goddess Io, daughter of Inachos. Argos was succeeded by his son Kriasos, and he again by Gelanor, who surrendered the government to Danaos, who came

from Egypt.*　To these succeeded Lynkeus, followed by
his son by Hypermnestra, daughter of Danaos, Abas, who
again by Okaleia was father of the twin sons Akrisios and
Proitos.†　Akrisios drove out Proitos, and became ruler of
Argos.

The ground of quarrel between the brothers is said to
be that Proitos seduced Danae, the daughter of Akrisios.‡
Proitos fled to Lykia, to King Iobates, and married his
daughter Anteia, § or Stheneboia, ‖ or Antiope. ¶　Iobates
returned with Proitos and an armed force, and subdued
Tiryns.**　The two brothers now divided the rule of the
land; Akrisios retaining Argos, while Proitos took Tiryns,
with control of Mideia and the coast of Argolis. ††

The quarrel between the brothers, however, continued,
and Pausanias saw as he went from Argos to Epidaurus
" on the right hand, a building like a pyramid, and on it
are sculptured shields of Argolic form.　Here took place
the fight between Proitos and Akrisios, who contended for
mastery, and they say that the result of the battle was
not decisive, and so a reconciliation took place, as none
could gain mastery of the other, and they themselves,
together with their armies, are said to have first fought
here armed with shields.　And to those who fell, seeing
they were all fellow-citizens and akin, there was raised in
this place one common tomb." ‡‡

---

* Apollod. II. 1, 3 and 4.　　　　　　† Apollod. II. 2, 1.

‡ Apollod. II. 4, 1 : Ταύτην (τὴν Δανάην), ὡς ἔνιοι λέγουσιν, ἔφθειρε
Προῖτος· ὅθεν αὐτοῖς καὶ ἡ στάσις ἐκινήθη.

§ Apollod. II. 2, 1 ; Homer, *Iliad*, VI. 160 ; Eustathios, 631, 20.

‖ Apollod. II. 2, 1 ; Eustathios, 632, 4.

¶ Serv. on Virgil's *Ecl.* VI. 48.

** Apollod. II. 2, 1 ; Schol. ad Eurip. *Orestes*, 953 ; Paus. II. 16, 2.

†† Paus. II. 16, 2.

‡‡ Paus. II. 25, 6 : Ἐρχομένοις δὲ ἐξ Ἄργους ἐς τὴν Ἐπιδαυρίαν ἔστιν
οἰκοδόμημα ἐν δεξιᾷ πυραμίδι μάλιστα εἰκασμένον, ἔχει δὲ ἀσπίδας σχῆμα
Ἀργολικὰς ἐπειργασμένας· ἐνταῦθα Προίτῳ περὶ τῆς ἀρχῆς πρὸς Ἀκρίσιον
μάχη γίνεται, καὶ τέλος μὲν ἴσον τῷ ἀγῶνι συμβῆναί φασι, καὶ ἀπ᾽ αὐτοῦ

Of this monument no trace remains. Strabo * says: "Proitos seems to have used Tiryns as his basis of operations, and to have had it fortified by Cyclopes, who were seven in number, and were called *belly-hands*, because they lived by their craft, and who were sent for from Lykia; and perhaps the caves about Nauplia, and the work in them is [also] called after them."

The legend of this mythic king in Tiryns, which must be placed about 1400 B.C., is mentioned, among many other ancient writers, by Homer,† according to whom Bellerophon of Corinth, having committed a murder, came to the court of Proitos to seek absolution from him. Here he was met by a fate similar to that of Joseph in Egypt. The Queen Anteia fell in love with the stranger, on whom, as the poet tells, the Immortals had bestowed beauty and strength. As, however, Bellerophon rejected the love of Anteia, and refused her proposals, she, inflamed with passion, complained of him to the King, as though he had offered her violence.‡ According to the legend, Proitos

---

διαλλαγὰς ὕστερον, ὡς οὐδέτεροι βεβαίως κρατεῖν ἐδύναντο· συμβαλεῖν δὲ σφᾶς λέγουσιν ἀσπίσι πρῶτον τότε καὶ αὐτοὺς καὶ τὸ στράτευμα ὡπλισμένους· τοῖς δὲ πεσοῦσιν ἀφ᾽ ἑκατέρων, πολῖται γὰρ καὶ συγγενεῖς ἦσαν, ἐποιήθη ταύτῃ μνῆμα ἐν κοινῷ.

     * Strabo, VIII. 372 : Τῇ μὲν οὖν Τίρυνθι ὁρμητηρίῳ χρήσασθαι δοκεῖ Προῖτος καὶ τειχίσαι διὰ Κυκλώπων, οὓς ἑπτὰ μὲν εἶναι καλεῖσθαι δὲ γαστερό-χειρας τρεφομένους ἐκ τῆς τέχνης, ἥκειν δὲ μεταπέμπτους ἐκ Λυκίας· καὶ ἴσως τὰ σπήλαια τὰ περὶ τὴν Ναυπλίαν καὶ τὰ ἐν αὐτοῖς ἔργα τούτων ἐπώνυμά ἐστιν.

     † *Il.* VI. 155–194. Anteia's love for Bellerophon is also mentioned by Apollodorus, II. 3, 1, and Tzetzes, *Lykophron*, 17.

     ‡ I quote from the prose translation of Messrs. Lang, Leaf, and Myers (Macmillan, 1883). "Then spake she lyingly to King Proitos: 'Die, Proitos, or else slay Bellerophon, that would have converse in love with me against my will.' So spake she, and anger gat hold upon the King at that he heard. To slay him he forbare, for his soul had shame of that; but he sent him to Lykia, and gave him tokens of woe, graving in a folded tablet many deadly things, and bade him show these to Anteia's father, that he might be slain. So fared he to Lykia by the blameless convoy of the gods. Now when he came to Lykia and the stream Xanthos, then did the King of wide Lykia honour him with all

and Antiope, or Stheneboia or Anteia, begat Megapenthes and three daughters, Lysippe, Iphinoë (or Hipponoë), and Iphianassa (or Kyrianassa),* or, as some say † only two, Elege and Keläne. When these maidens grew up, they were punished with madness, because they had laughed at the statue of Hera, in the temple at Argos.‡ They were afterwards cured by Melampous, who caused them to be bathed in a fountain, § or treated them with fumigations of asphalt.‖ Upon this, they married him and his brother Bias.¶ Their dwellings were below the fortress, towards the coast, and were still existing in the time of Pausanias.** There now remains, however, no trace of them. On account of the morass, it is impossible that they could have been subterranean.

King Proitos is also mentioned by Pindar,†† and it was

---

his heart. Nine days he entertained him, and killed nine oxen. And when on the tenth day rosy-fingered dawn appeared, then he questioned him and asked to see what token he bare from his son-in-law, even Proitos. Now when he received of him Proitos' evil token, first he bade him slay Chimaira, the unconquerable. Of divine birth was she, and not of men, in front a lion and behind a serpent, and in the midst a goat; and she breathed dread fierceness of blazing fire. And her he slew, obedient to the signs of heaven.

"Next fought he the famed Solymi; this, said he, was the mightiest battle of warriors wherein he entered. And thirdly, he slew the Amazons, women peers of men. And as he turned back therefrom, the King devised another cunning wile; he picked from wide Lykia the bravest men and set an ambush. But these returned nowise home again; for noble Bellerophon slew them all. So when the King now knew that he was the brave offspring of a god, he kept him there, and plighted him his daughter, and gave him the half of all the honour of his kingdom."

* Serv. I. 1.                                    † Ælian, *V. H.* III. 42.
‡ Apollod. II. 2, 2.
§ Strabo, VIII. 533; Ovid, *Met.* XV. 325; cf. Paus. VIII. 18, 3.
‖ Clemens, Στρωματεῖς, VII. 713; Voss on Virgil, *Ecl.* VIII. 82.
¶ Apollod. II. 2, 2.
** Paus. II. 25, 8 : Καταβάντων δὲ ὡς ἐπὶ θάλασσαν ἐνταῦθα οἱ θάλαμοι τῶν Προίτου θυγατέρων εἰσίν.
†† Pindar, *Nem.* X. 77, 78 :

νικαφορίαις γὰρ ὅσαις Προίτου
τόδ᾽ ἱπποτρόφον ἄστυ θάλησεν.

apparently after him that one of the gates in Bœotian
Thebes was named Proitean * (Πύλαι Προίτου or Πύλαι
Προιτίδες).

As to the name Proitos, which appears to us distinctly
not Greek, Eustathios says (*Iliad* VI. 157), and he is
surely wrong; ὁ δὲ Προῖτος τῇ ἐτυμολογίᾳ προϊτητικὸς
φαίνεται· εἶναι καὶ ὁρμητίας ἀπὸ τοῦ προϊέναι· διὸ καὶ διὰ
διφθόγγου γράφεται.

Proitos was succeeded by his son Megapenthes, who
exchanged his kingdom for that of Perseus, king of Argos,
son of Danae, daughter of Akrisios, and mythical founder
of Mycenæ.† He was followed by his son Elektryon, the
father of Alkmene, mother of Herakles, who, as well as
his father, is said to have dwelt at Mycenæ.‡ Elektryon
resigned the kingdom of Tiryns and Mycenæ to Amphitryon, son of Alkaios, and grandson of Perseus and
Andromeda. § Amphitryon married Alkmene, mother of
Herakles, but was driven out by his uncle Sthenelos, son
of Perseus and Andromeda, || who now became King of
Argos, Tiryns, Mycenæ, Mideia, and Heraion.¶ Sthenelos
and Nikippe, the daughter of Pelops, begat Eurystheus,**
who became King of Mycenæ, and as the myth relates,
laid upon Herakles the twelve labours. The latter conquered Tiryns, and resided there for a long time, in
consequence of which he is commonly called the Tirynthian.††

On the return of the Herakleids, which all ancient
traditions agree in placing about eighty years after the
Trojan war, Tiryns, Mycenæ, Hysiæ, Mideia, and other

---

* Æschyl. *Sept.* 377, 395 ; Euripides, *Phœn.* 1109.
† Paus. II. 16, 3 ; Apollod. II. 4.
‡ Apollod. II. 4 ; Paus. II. 22, 8 ; II. 25, 9.
§ Apollod. II. 4 ; Hesiod. *Scut. Herc.* 86.
|| Homer, *Il.* XIX. 116.                        ¶ Apollod. II. 4.
** Ovid, *Met.* IX. 273 ; cf. *Her.* IX. 25.
†† Pindar, *Ol.* IX. 40 ; Ovid. *Met.* VII. 410 ; Virgil, *Æn.* VII. 662.

towns were obliged to submit to Argos, and lost their independence.    Tiryns remained nevertheless in the hands of its Achaian population, and, together with the town of Mycenæ, sent 400 men to the battle of Platæa.*    Consequently the name of the Tirynthians was inscribed, together with those of all the other Greek citizens who took part in this battle, on the bronze pedestal of the golden tripod, which the Spartans offered as a tenth part of their spoil to the Pythian Apollo at Delphi, and which now ornaments the Maïdan at Constantinople, opposite the Byzantine Hippodrome.    The fame which Tiryns thus acquired is said to have aroused the jealousy of the Argives, who had taken no part in the Persian War, and who besides began to regard the town as a dangerous neighbour, particularly when it fell into the hands of the revolted slaves (Γυμνήσιοι), who for a long time held their own within its Cyclopean walls, and ruled the country around.    At last the insurgents were overcome,† but shortly after (Olympiad 78, 1, or 468 B.C.), the Argives are said to have destroyed the town, ruined a portion of the surrounding Cyclopean wall, and forced the Tirynthians to settle in Argos.‡    According to other accounts they fled to Epidaurus. §

But I cannot here resist quoting the learned dissertation of Professor Mahaffy, ' On the Destruction of Mycenæ by the Argives,' ‖ from which it appears, beyond all doubt, that the destruction of Mycenæ and Tiryns by the Argives should be placed at a very much earlier date.

" No one seems to have found any difficulty in the statement of Diodoros, which Pausanias repeats, that the town of Mycenæ was destroyed by the people of Argos *after the Persian Wars*, though I fancy most scholars, when they first come to attend to it, are surprised that the ancient

---

* Herodot. IX. 28.                          † Herodot. VI. 83.
‡ Paus. II. 17, 5 ; VIII. 27, 1.            § Strabo, VIII. 373.
‖ In the Dublin University Journal, *Hermathena*, V. pp. 60, *sqq.*

city of Mycenæ should have lasted so long in close neighbourhood to Argos, and yet have made so little figure in
Greek history. I suppose any doubt of this kind is allayed
by the recollection that Herodotos mentions eighty Mycenæans as having joined the Greeks at Thermopylæ, and
that he also enumerates both Tirynthians and Mycenæans
among the cities or tribes of Greeks which were inscribed
on the pedestal of the tripod at Delphi as joining in the
repulse of the Persians. The actual pedestal at Constantinople confirms him, for we read in the list Μυκᾶνες and
Τιρύνθιοι, and thus the existence of Mycenæans and
Tirynthians up to the year 470 B.C. is beyond all doubt.

"I have, nevertheless, grave suspicions whether either
historian has given us a true account of the matter, and
therefore propose the following hypothesis, to invite discussion. If I have overlooked any decisive evidence, I
hope it will be put forth in refutation of my conjecture. I
will first quote all Pausanias' statements on the point, but
will group them into two classes, irrespective of their order,
for the sake of more convenient discussion :—

II. 15, 4. "But I shall give the cause of the settlement,
and why the Argives afterwards expelled the Mycenæans.
16, 5. But the Argives destroyed Mycenæ through jealousy;
for when the Argives remained neutral at the invasion of
the Medes, the Mycenæans sent to Thermopylæ eighty
men, who shared with the Lacedæmonians in their deeds
[this is inaccurate]. This ambition brought them destruction, by inciting the Argives."*

"Then follows (Paus. II. 16, 6) the famous passage
about the ruins, and about the tombs of Agamemnon and

---

* Pausanias, II. 15, 4: ἐγὼ δὲ αἰτίαν τε γράψω τοῦ οἰκισμοῦ, καὶ δι᾽
ἥντινα πρόφασιν Ἀργεῖοι Μυκηναίους ὕστερον ἀνέστησαν. II. 16, 5. Μυκήνας
δὲ Ἀργεῖοι καθεῖλον ὑπὸ ζηλοτυπίας· ἡσυχαζόντων γὰρ τῶν Ἀργείων κατὰ
τὴν ἐπιστρατείαν τοῦ Μήδου, Μυκηναῖοι πέμπουσιν εἰς Θερμοπύλας ὀγδοήκοντα
ἄνδρας οἳ Λακεδαιμονίοις μετέσχον τοῦ ἔργου [inaccurate]· τοῦτο ἤνεγκέ
σφισιν ὄλεθρον τὸ φιλοτίμημα παροξῦναι Ἀργείους.

his party, which Dr. Schliemann has brought into such fresh notoriety.

"Pausanias, V. 23, 2. [In the list of cities inscribed on the monument of the victory over the Persians, which Pausanias saw at Olympia, and which appears not to have been an exact duplicate of that of Delphi.] 'But from the Argive country the Tirynthians, and the Platæans alone of the Bœotians, and of the Argives those who dwelt in Mycenæ.' Pausanias, V. 23, 3: 'Of these cities, the following were in our day abandoned: the Mycenæans and Tirynthians were expelled by the Argives after the Median invasion,' &c." *

"For in the case of the Mycenæans their strong fortress could not be taken by storm by the Argives (for it had been fortified in the same way as that of Tiryns [not accurate] by the so-called Cyclopes), but the Mycenæans were forced to abandon their city because food failed them. And some of them retired to Cleonæ. More than half the people fled to Macedonia to that Alexander, to whom Mardonius, the son of Gobryas, entrusted the message to bring to the Athenians. But the rest of them came to Keryneia, and for the future Keryneia became more powerful through the increase of its inhabitants, and more distinguished on account of the settlement of the Mycenæans.†

"Nothing seems more precise than this. Pausanias was

* Pausanias, V. 23, 2 : ἐκ δὲ χώρας τῆς Ἀργείας Τιρύνθιοι, Πλαταιεῖς δὲ μόνοι Βοιωτῶν, καὶ Ἀργείων οἱ Μυκήνας ἔχοντες. Pausanias, V. 23, 3. τούτων τῶν πόλεων τοσαίδε ἦσαν ἐφ' ἡμῶν ἔρημοι. Μυκηναῖοι μὲν καὶ Τιρύνθιοι τῶν Μηδικῶν ὕστερον ἐγένοντο ὑπὸ Ἀργείων ἀνάστατοι.

† Pausanias, VII. 25, 5 : Μυκηναίοις γὰρ τὸ μὲν τεῖχος ἁλῶναι κατὰ τὸ ἰσχυρὸν οὐκ ἐδύνατο ὑπὸ Ἀργείων (ἐτετείχιστο γὰρ κατὰ ταὐτὰ [this is not accurate] τῷ ἐν Τίρυνθι ὑπὸ τῶν Κυκλώπων καλουμένων) κατὰ ἀνάγκην δὲ ἐκλείπουσι Μυκηναῖοι τὴν πόλιν ἐπιλειπόντων σφᾶς τῶν σιτίων, καὶ ἄλλοι μέν τινες ἐς Κλεωνὰς ἀποχωροῦσιν ἐξ αὐτῶν, τοῦ δήμου δὲ πλέον μὲν ἢ ἥμισυ ἐς Μακεδονίαν καταφεύγουσι παρὰ Ἀλέξανδρ ν, ᾧ Μαρδόνιος ὁ Γωβρύου τὴν ἀγγελίαν ἐπίστευσεν ἐς Ἀθηναίους ἀπαγγεῖλαι. ὁ δὲ ἄλλος δῆμος ἀφίκοντο ἐς τὴν Κερύνειαν, καὶ δυνατωτέρα τε ἡ Κερύνεια οἰκητόρων πλήθει καὶ ἐς τὸ ἔπειτα ἐγένετο ἐπιφανεστέρα διὰ τὴν συνοίκησιν τῶν Μυκηναίων.

evidently quite sure of his facts, though one of them—the participation of the Mycenæans in the battle of Thermopylæ —was certainly wrong according to Herodotos. They went there, indeed, but retired with the other Greeks, who left the Spartans and Thespians with Leonidas. Apart from this, it seems, then, that the Argives were so jealous of the fame of Mycenæ on account of this glorious battle (at which Mycenæans never fought), that they undertook the siege of the great Cyclopean fort, and having starved out the population of the place, which they could not storm, they drove them out of the land to Kleonæ, Keryneia, and to Macedonia. The same lot befell the Tirynthians for the same reason, though Pausanias adds no details about the siege of their equally wonderful fort, which excited his loudest admiration.

"Herodotos corroborates the participation of Mycenæans and Tirynthians in the Persian Wars, and says they together furnished four hundred men to the army of the Greeks, which fought at Platæa. He is perfectly silent as to the consequences of this act.

"Let us now examine a very different passage. 'But the Arcadians came together into Megalopolis to gain strength, as being aware that the Argives in olden times were almost every day in danger of war with the Lacedæmonians. But when they increased Argos in its population, abolishing Tiryns and Hysiæ, and Orneæ, and Mycenæ, and Mideia, and whatever other place in Argolis was of no account, their relations towards the Lacedæmonians were more secure, and they gained strength as regards their country dependants (periœci).'*

---

* Pausanias, VIII. 27, 1 : συνῆλθον δὲ ὑπὲρ ἰσχύος ἐς αὐτὴν [sc. τὴν Μεγάλην πόλιν] οἱ Ἀρκάδες, ἅτε καὶ Ἀργείους ἐπιστάμενοι τὰ μὲν ἔτι παλαιότερα μόνον οὐ κατὰ μίαν ἡμέραν ἑκάστην κινδυνεύοντας ὑπὸ Λακεδαι-μονίων παραστῆναι τῷ πολέμῳ, ἐπειδὴ δὲ ἀνθρώπων πλήθει τὸ Ἄργος ἐπηύξησαν καταλύσαντες Τίρυνθα καὶ Ὑσιάς τε καὶ Ὀρνεὰς καὶ Μυκήνας καὶ Μίδειαν καὶ εἰ δή τι ἄλλο πόλισμα οὐκ ἀξιόλογον ἐν τῇ Ἀργολίδι ἦν, τά τε ἀπὸ Λακεδαιμονίων ἀδεέστερα τοῖς Ἀργείοις ὑπάρξοντα καὶ ἅμα ἐς τοὺς περιοίκους ἰσχύν γενομένην αὐτοῖς.

" This passage is corroborated by II. 25, 6 and 8, in which the destruction of Orneæ and of Tiryns is mentioned in the same way. Thus, in § II. 25, 8, ' But the Argives dispossessed the Tirynthians, wishing to have them as fellow-settlers, and to increase the power of Argos.'*

"This account appears not only inconsistent with the former, but contradictory to it.    There the inhabitants of Mycenæ are expelled, and added to the strength of other cities ; here, the special reason of the dispute is to secure more citizens for Argos, and to increase and consolidate its power.    Any one who considers the conditions of the question for one moment will not hesitate to prefer this latter— a sound political view—to the sentimental story about Argive jealousy.    The συνοικισμός of the Argive territory was like that of Thebes, of Athens, and of Megalopolis; and there can be no doubt that the importance of Argos in Greek history was wholly due to its early success in this most difficult and unpopular revolution.

"But is it possible that it took place *after* the Persian Wars?    I think not.    In the face of the patriotic conduct of Tiryns and Mycenæ, and at the moment of Argos' greatest national unpopularity, any such attempt to destroy free Greek cities would have brought down the vengeance of all Greece.    Moreover, early historians are silent about it.    Herodotos and Thucydides never allude to it.    What is still more remarkable, the contemporary Æschylus, though composing plays which ought to have had their scene laid at Mycenæ, never once mentions Mycenæ, and transfers the palace of Agamemnon to Argos.†    If the more

---

* Pausanias, II. 25, 8. ἀνέστησαν δὲ καὶ Τιρυνθίους ᾿Αργεῖοι, συνοίκους προσλαβεῖν καὶ τὸ ᾿Αργος ἐπαυξῆσαι θελήσαντες.

† " This mistake seems to have been noted by critics of an early date, for both Sophocles and Euripides mention and distinguish the two cities, though they seem to confuse the inhabitants.    I was unable, when on the spot, to make out the picture suggested at the opening of Sophocles' *Electra*, which seems, as it were, drawn on the spot, but is more probably

ancient city, whose inhabitants had fought with him in the great Persian struggle, had only lost its independence in his mature age, is such a curious ignorance on his part conceivable? I think, then, that the συνοικισμός of the Argive territory must have taken place long before, and that Pausanias was misled by the monuments of the Persian War to transfer it to an impossible period.

"If we look back into earlier history, and consider at what time Argos was daily expecting an attack from Sparta, and found it necessary to strengthen its power, I think the most natural period will be not immediately after the Persian, but immediately after the Messenian Wars, that is, the second Messenian War, which was concluded in Ol. 29. According to our revised chronology, the development of Pheidon's power at Argos must be placed close to this time, and it was probably the twenty-eighth Ol. which he celebrated with the Pisatans at Olympia to the exclusion of the Eleans. Of course the Spartans were bound to interfere, but the Messenian War must have greatly hampered their vigour. When this war was over, and Sparta had acquired new territory and prestige, the Argives must have expected that they would be the first to suffer. Hence I attribute to Pheidon, and to his policy, the consolidation of all the smaller towns in Argos, and perhaps this may have been the secret of his greatness.

"But how then is the existence of Tirynthians and Mycenæans during the Persian War to be explained? I suppose that these towns, though conquered, and their gods transferred to Argos, nevertheless continued to exist as κῶμαι or villages, but inhabited by Argive citizens, and that accordingly the descendants of the old inhabitants, who took the patriotic side, and had not forgotten their history, joined the Hellenic army under these obsolete names, which the nation was glad to sanction as a slight to

---

a fancy sketch. But Mycenæ is very prominent in it. Sophocles even wrote a play called Μυκηνᾶται."

the neutral Argives.*  The very small number of men they
were able to muster (80 from Mycenæ at Thermopylæ,
400 from Mycenæ and Tiryns together at Platæa) strongly
corroborates this view ; for in that day the smallest Greek
towns had a considerable armed population—Platæa, for
example, had 600.  It is very likely that the Argives were
nettled at this conduct, and determined to efface these
places altogether ; and this change, which was very unimportant, as the real συνοικισμός had been long accomplished,
attracted little notice at the time, but gave rise afterwards
to a distortion of history.

" I will quote, in conclusion, what seems to me a parallel
case.  Pausanias says,† that the Minyæ of Orchomenos
were expelled by the Thebans *after the battle of Leuctra*.
We know very well that the power of Orchomenos was
gone long before, but the increased strength of Thebes,
and some offence on the part of the subject city during
the struggle with Sparta, determined its complete extinction
by the Thebans.  But this was no great siege or subjuga-
tion of a free city.  That had been done by the Thebans
long before.  So I believe the capture of the great fort at
Mycenæ probably occurred long before the Persian Wars.

" The explicit passage in Diodoros,‡ which seems at

---

* " Of course they need not have come directly from Tiryns and
Mycenæ, but *may have been exiles*, who came together under the name of
their old city."

† Pausanias, IV. 27, 10 : Ὀρχομένιοι δὲ οἱ Μινύαι μετὰ τὴν μάχην
τὴν ἐν Λεύκτροις ἐκπεσόντες ὑπὸ Θηβαίων ἐξ Ὀρχομενοῦ κατήχθησαν.

‡ Diodoros Siculos, XI. 65 : Μετὰ δὲ ταῦτα Ἀθήνησι μὲν ἦν ἄρχων
Θεαγενείδης, ἐν Ῥώμῃ δ' ὕπατοι καθειστήκεσαν Λεύκιος Αἰμίλιος Μάμερκος
καὶ Λεύκιος Στούδιος Ἰουλος, ὀλυμπιὰς δ' ἤχθη ἑβδομηκοστὴ καὶ ὀγδόη, καθ' ἣν
ἐνίκα στάδιον Παρμενίδης Ποσειδωνιάτης· ἐπὶ δὲ τούτων Ἀργείοις καὶ
Μυκηναίοις ἐνέστη πόλεμος διὰ τοιαύτας αἰτίας.  Μυκηναῖοι διὰ τὸ παλαιὸν
ἀξίωμα τῆς ἰδίας πατρίδος οὐχ ὑπήκουον τοῖς Ἀργείοις ὥσπερ αἱ λοιπαὶ πόλεις
αἱ κατὰ τὴν Ἀργείαν, ἀλλὰ κατ' ἰδίαν ταττόμενοι τοῖς Ἀργείοις οὐ προσεῖχον·
ἠμφισβήτουν δὲ καὶ περὶ τῶν ἱερῶν τῆς Ἥρας, καὶ τὸν ἀγῶνα τὸν Νεμεαῖον
ἠξίουν ἑαυτοὺς διοικεῖν· πρὸς δὲ τούτοις ὅτι τῶν Ἀργείων ψηφισαμένων μὴ
συμμαχεῖν εἰς Θερμοπύλας τοῖς Λακεδαιμονίοις, ἐὰν μὴ μέρος τῆς ἡγεμονίας

first sight a conclusive corroboration of the ordinary view, only strengthens my conviction that it is wrong. Diodoros is precise about the date. He says that in the 78th Ol. (468-4), while the Spartans were in great trouble on account of a destructive earthquake and rising of the Helots and Messenians, the Argives took the opportunity of attacking Mycenæ. But they did so because Mycenæ *alone of the cities* in their territory would not submit to them. This distinctly asserts that all the other towns, such as Tiryns and Midea, had been formerly subdued, and contradicts Pausanias. Diodoros then enumerates the various claims of Mycenæ to old privileges about the Heraeon and the Nemean Games, and adds what Pausanias says about Mycenæans joining the Greeks at Thermopylæ, alone among the Argive cities. The share taken by Tiryns with Mycenæ at Platæa seems unknown to both authors. But after long waiting for an opportunity, the Argives now collected a considerable force from Argos and the allied cities, and made war upon Mycenæ—upon Mycenæ, which was only able, jointly with Tiryns, to supply 400 men at

---

αὐτοῖς παραδῶσι, μόνοι τῶν τὴν Ἀργείαν κατοικούντων συνεμάχησαν οἱ Μυκηναῖοι τοῖς Λακεδαιμονίοις · τὸ δὲ σύνολον ὑπώπτευον αὐτοὺς μήποτε ἰσχύσαντες ἐπὶ πλέον τῆς ἡγεμονίας ἀμφισβητήσωσι τοῖς Ἀργείοις διὰ τὸ παλαιὸν φρόνημα τῆς πόλεως · διὰ δὴ ταύτας τὰς αἰτίας ἀλλοτρίως διακείμενοι πάλαι μὲν ἔσπευδον ἆραι τὴν πόλιν, τότε δὲ καιρὸν εὔθετον ἔχειν ἐνόμιζον, ὁρῶντες τοὺς Λακεδαιμονίους τεταπεινωμένους καὶ μὴ δυναμένους τοῖς Μυκηναίοις βοηθεῖν · ἀθροίσαντες οὖν ἀξιόλογον δύναμιν ἔκ τε Ἄργους καὶ ἐκ τῶν συμμαχίδων πόλεων ἐστράτευσαν ἐπ᾽ αὐτούς, νικήσαντες δὲ μάχῃ τοὺς Μυκηναίους καὶ συγκλείσαντες ἐντὸς τειχῶν ἐπολιόρκουν τὴν πόλιν · οἱ δὲ Μυκηναῖοι χρόνον μέν τινα τοὺς πολιορκοῦντας εὐτόνως ἠμύνοντο, μετὰ δὲ ταῦτα λειπόμενοι τῷ πολέμῳ καὶ τῶν Λακεδαιμονίων μὴ δυναμένων βοηθῆσαι διὰ τοὺς ἰδίους πολέμους·καὶ τὴν ἐκ τῶν σεισμῶν γενομένην αὐτοῖς συμφοράν, ἄλλων δ᾽ οὐκ ὄντων συμμάχων, ἐρημίᾳ τῶν ἐπικουρούντων κατὰ κράτος ἥλωσαν · οἱ δὲ Ἀργεῖοι τοὺς Μυκηναίους ἀνδραπιδισάμενοι καὶ δεκάτην ἐξ αὐτῶν τῷ θεῷ καθιερώσαντες, τὰς Μυκήνας κατέσκαψαν · αὕτη μὲν οὖν ἡ πόλις εὐδαίμων ἐν τοῖς ἀρχαίοις χρόνοις γενομένη καὶ μεγάλους ἄνδρας ἔχουσα καὶ πράξεις ἀξιολόγους ἐπιτελεσαμένη, τοιαύτην ἔσχε τὴν καταστροφήν, καὶ διέμεινεν ἀοίκητος μέχρι τῶν καθ᾽ ἡμᾶς χρόνων. [This too is false, cf. below, p. 47.]

Platæa, and which, when unaided, sent 80 men to Thermopylæ! The Argives first defeated them in battle, and
then besieged the fortress, which, after some time, through
lack of defenders (which is indeed credible), they *stormed*.
Here again Pausanias is contradicted.   Diodoros concludes with stating that they *enslaved* the Mycenæans, con-
secrating a tenth of the spoil, and levelled the town with
the ground.

  "I think my theory is perfectly consistent with the critical residue which may be extracted from this passage.   It
is probably true that the Argives chose the opportunity of
a Messenian war to make this conquest, but it was the
second, not the third, Messenian war.   It is probably true
—nay, I should say certainly true—that they levelled
the houses of Mycenæ with the ground in the 78th Ol.;
but this was not their first conquest of it.   If they enslaved
the then inhabitants, this harsh measure was probably by
way of punishment for the impertinence of a subject town
in sending an independent contingent to a war in which
the sovereign city had determined to maintain a strict neu-
trality.   That the facts related by Diodoros should have
caused no general comment throughout Greece, or that no
early echo of it should have reached us, seems to me incredible.   There is a possible corroboration of Diodoros'
statement that Mycenæ was the last conquered of the
subject cities in the Homeric Catalogue, where Tiryns is
mentioned as already subject to Argos, while Mycenæ is
the capital of Agamemnon.   But even when that Catalogue
was compiled, Argos had conquered all the seaboard of the
Argolic peninsula, and Mycenæ lies at the extreme south
of the territory (chiefly Corinthian and Sicyonic) which is
assigned to Agamemnon.   Possibly the traditions were still
too strong for the poet to make Mycenæ subject to Argos,
but he plainly denies any hegemony of Mycenæ over the
Argive plain."

  Such is Professor Mahaffy's theory, published before

my excavations at Mycenæ and Tiryns had brought archæological evidence to bear upon it.

Professor A. H. Sayce draws my attention to a passage in Homer, which, in his opinion, appears to support this hypothesis, and categorically to refute the statements which Pausanias and Diodoros have borrowed from Ephoros.* The latter appears to have fallen into error with regard to the era of Pheidon of Argos, for according to Theopompos, and Diodoros apud Syncellum, ' Chronicon,' p. 262, he belongs *to the beginning of the ninth century before Christ, with which also the Parian Chronicle, Ep.* 31, *agrees.* The Homeric passage is as follows :—

"Then Hera, the ox-eyed queen, made answer to him : of a surety three cities are there that be dearest far to me, Argos and Sparta and wide-wayed Mycenæ, these lay thou waste, whene'er they are found hateful to thy heart ; not for them will I stand forth, nor do I grudge thee them. For even if I be jealous, and would forbid thee to overthrow them, yet will my jealousy not avail, seeing thou art far stronger than I." †

According to Professor Sayce, it appears that Homer in this place implies the destruction of at least one of the three towns named by him, and as Argos and Sparta were not destroyed, the destroyed city could be no other than Mycenæ. Sayce concludes from the word διαπέρσαι that the destruction must have been complete. If such is the case, the citation from Homer gives us the highest proof that Mycenæ as well as Tiryns must have been destroyed

---

* Professor Sayce, who has carefully examined the fragments which remain of Ephoros, is of opinion that these fragments, as well as other indications, show that Diodoros had copied some portions of his account, word for word, from Ephoros, and in large part had reproduced the writings of that author

† *Il.* IV. 50–56 :

Τὸν δ' ἠμείβετ' ἔπειτα βοῶπις πότνια "Ηρη·
ἤτοι ἐμοὶ τρεῖς μὲν πολὺ φίλταταί εἰσι πόληες,
"Αργος τε Σπάρτη τε καὶ εὐρυάγυια Μυκήνη·
τὰς διαπέρσαι, ὅτ' ἄν τοι ἀπέχθωνται περὶ κῆρι·
τάων οὔτοι ἐγὼ πρόσθ' ἴσταμαι, οὐδὲ μεγαίρω·
εἴπερ γὰρ φθονέω τε καὶ οὐκ εἰῶ διαπέρσαι,
οὐκ ἀνύω φθονέουσ'· ἐπειὴ πολὺ φέρτερός ἐσσι.

at a very early date, for, as I have already shown, Tiryns
had long before Homer's time lost its independence, and
become a vassal of Argos.

Now this hypothesis finds remarkable confirmation in
the monuments of Mycenæ and Tiryns. I would remind
the reader of what I have written in my work *Mycenæ**
on the destruction of the wall of the Acropolis of Mycenæ.
" On the west side the Cyclopean wall has been nearly
demolished for a distance of 46 feet, and on its interior
side a wall of small stones bound with earth has been built
to sustain its ruins. It must remain mere guesswork when
the Cyclopean wall was destroyed and the small wall built;
but at all events this must have occurred long before the
capture of Mycenæ by the Argives in 468 B.C., because
the small wall was buried deep in the prehistoric *débris*."

Further, I would remark that the following inscription
found in Mycenæ, of which we know with certainty that it

T o B E R o o { ) E M

belongs to the sixth century before Christ, is scratched
upon a fragment of that lustrous black lacquered Hellenic
pottery which must be at least three centuries later in date
than the archaic terra-cottas which are found in Tiryns and
Mycenæ everywhere, on the surface of the ground, and
which must necessarily have been in common use at the
time of the destruction of both towns.

I further recommend to the particular attention of
archæologists the numerous very ancient idols found by me
in Tiryns and Mycenæ, either of simple female figures, or
in the form of a female with horns starting at both sides
of the breast, or in the form of a cow. In Mycenæ I
found these even in the uppermost archaic strata. In

* Pp. 116.

Tiryns I found them everywhere in the rooms of the great prehistoric palace occupying the entire upper citadel. It is therefore to be assumed as certain that these idols were still in universal use at the time of the destruction of the palace of Tiryns as well as at the destruction of Mycenæ. It appears to us, however, incredible that the tutelary goddess of Tiryns and Mycenæ was still in the fifth century before Christ represented in this most ancient form; almost equally improbable does it appear to us that at such a comparatively late period the rude knives and arrowheads of obsidian were still in use, which are found in very large quantities of very primitive form in Mycenæ as well as in the citadel of Tiryns, inside and outside the palace. There can be no doubt that in the Homeric poems Hera is a woman without any of the characteristic marks of a cow, the only remembrance being preserved in the title βοῶπις, hallowed by the use of centuries, which yet in Homer cannot be held to signify more than "large-eyed."

It is to be assumed with certainty that in the time of Homer the habit of representing Juno in cow's form, or with characteristic cow features, had long passed away; and therefore a pre-Homeric date must necessarily be ascribed to the catastrophe of the great destruction of Mycenæ and Tiryns. In fact, when I consider the character of the monuments discovered by me, and the absence of all coins or inscriptions (save that above) of early date, to which Professor Mahaffy has called particular attention, I have no hesitation in ascribing the destruction of both towns, not to 468 B.C., but to the time of the Doric Migration, and the ruin of Mycenæ and Tiryns by the Herakleids would explain to us the remarkable fact that Orestes did not rule in Mycenæ, and that tradition only gives us an account of the very ancient kings of both towns, of whose further fate we know nothing.

In my excavations at Mycenæ I brought the most positive proofs to light that the place was re-settled, probably, as the pottery indicates, from about the beginning of the fourth to the beginning of the second century before Christ *

In the Acropolis of Tiryns, on the other hand, we found even on the surface, numerous sherds of painted *prehistoric* pottery, which during the excavations were brought to light in immense quantities, whilst in spite of most diligent search on the upper and middle terraces we failed to find a single potsherd of Hellenic or Roman time. We found, on the contrary, in the excavations of the gateway on the east side of the Acropolis many potsherds of this kind, as well as broken pieces of roof-tiles, an iron spearhead, and other articles of iron, from which it appears to me certain that this road was roofed over in Greek or Roman times, and served for habitation. At the same period there may have been some small houses on the lowest terrace of the citadel, for there also we found remnants of roof-tiles, as well as occasional late Greek or Roman potsherds.

Though we may assume with certainty that, since the destruction, in far prehistoric days, of the palace of the ancient kings of Tiryns, its site on the upper citadel has never been profaned with human dwellings, it has nevertheless once served for the higher purpose of Divine worship, for on the south end we brought to light the foundations of a little Byzantine church surrounded by many graves. (See Plans I. and II.)

There was, indeed, in classical times a town of Tiryns which stretched around the citadel on the site of the lower town of the more ancient Tiryns. This is proved by the numerous shafts which I sank round the citadel, in which I found near the surface Hellenic potsherds, and, in the lower deposit, painted and monochrome prehistoric terra-cotta fragments, together with knives and arrowheads

---

* Cf. *Mycenæ*, p. 63.

of a very primitive form of obsidian.   This is also shown by
a small treasure of bronze coins discovered some twenty-
five years ago on the east side beneath the citadel, which,
as the Director of the National Collection of Coins at
Athens, M. Achilles Postolaccas maintains, belong mostly
to the fifth [?] century before Christ, and perhaps partly to
the Macedonian period, and have on one side a head of
Apollo, on the other a palm with the legend ΤΙ, ΤΙΡΥΝ or
ΤΙΡΥΝΘΙΩΝ. *

Of the history of this newer Tiryns, we know however,
if possible, even less than of that of ancient Tiryns, for it
is mentioned by no ancient author, and must, to judge
from the Tirynthian coins, of which none is more than a
centimetre in diameter, have been a small poor town.

To the south-east of Tiryns, at the foot and to the east
of a steep rock called Castron, which is 203 m. high and
crowned with a chapel dedicated to St. Elias, lies a small
church, dedicated to St. Taxiarchis.   This stands on the
site of a Cyclopean building, of whose huge unhewn blocks,
many have been built into the church, but the greater part
yet lie without *in situ*.   Many similar blocks, which one
may see south of the church, leave no doubt that many
buildings once stood here.

And I further think that in the village Spaïtziku (cf.
the map of Argolis), which is about three miles south-east
of Tiryns, one may recognize in the rough-hewn limestone
blocks 1 m. 20 long by 1 m. 10 broad, the foundations of
a prehistoric building, which may date from the days of the
glory of Tiryns and Mycenæ, for the neighbouring fields
are strewn with painted prehistoric potsherds.

Of the neighbouring towns, which certainly flourished
contemporaneously, and probably also were destroyed at
the same time as Tiryns and Mycenæ, I must allude to

---

* Cf. A. de Courtois in the *Revue numismatique*, 1864, p. 178 *sqq.*,
and 1866, pp. 153 *sqq.*; Weil in Alfred von Sallet's *Zeitschrift für
Numismatik*, I. pp. 217 *sqq.*

the citadel of the old town of Asine, which lay about eight kilometres to the south-east of Tiryns on the sea-shore (see the map of Argolis), of which the walls, partly built of neatly fitted polygonal blocks and partly of layers of trape- zoids uneven in level, are still better preserved than those at Tiryns. Colossal towers, projecting about 7 m. and 12 m. broad, give the walls an imposing appearance. The terrace of the fortress, where apparently most of the buildings stood, is 37·50 m., the highest point 50 m., above the sea. On the terrace are still evident the foundation walls of numerous chambers, formed of unhewn Cyclopean stones. In the middle of one of these, which is 5·80 m. long and 3·30 wide, may be seen a great rough hewn stone 0·62 m. in diameter, in which is a hollow 0·24 m. long, 0·10 m. broad, and 0·15 m. deep. In many places the rock is skilfully smoothed for building purposes; there is also a large cistern hollowed out in pear shape, whose opening is 1 m. in diameter; there are besides three smaller cisterns. Asine was the old town of the Dryopes, and is mentioned in Homer's Catalogue.* According to Strabo,† Diodorus‡ and Pausanias,§ viz., according to the same authorities who record for us the conquest and destruction of Tiryns and Mycenæ by the Argives, Asine was also destroyed by the Argives, who spared only the sanctuary of Apollo Pythæus, and united the territory of the town to their own. On the Acropolis of Asine are found extra- ordinary masses of potsherds of that painted prehistoric kind peculiar to Mycenæ and Tiryns, and which, though

---

* *Iliad*, II. 559, 560:

Οἱ δ' Ἄργος τ' εἶχον Τίρυνθά τε τειχιόεσσαν,
Ἑρμιόνην, Ἀσίνην τε, βαθὺν κατὰ κόλπον ἐχούσας.

† Strabo, VIII. 373.                    ‡ Diodoros, IV. 37.
§ Paus. II. 36, 4; IV. 34, 9.

exposed to the open air for thousands of years, have lost little or nothing of their freshness, also very many saddle-querns of trachyte, corn-bruisers, &c., rude hammers of diorite or granite, and great masses of knives and arrow-heads of very primitive form, made of obsidian. Together with these is to be found black and red lacquered late Hellenic or Roman pottery, which points to a later settlement. In any case, the fortress must have been occupied in the late Middle Ages, for in many places one sees in the walls and towers considerable repairs dating from the Venetian period.

Only four kilometres south of Tiryns there lay, and still lies, on a small peninsula stretching westward into the bay, and connected by an isthmus with the mountain chain which encloses the Argive plain, the town of Nauplia, now τὸ Ναύπλιον, with an excellent harbour on the north side. As already mentioned, it was founded, according to legend, by Nauplios, a son of Poseidon, and appears, as we have seen by its origin, to point to a connection with the Phœnicians, who may have built the town as an outpost against the inhabitants of the plain.

It is very likely that Nauplia flourished at the time when the King of Tiryns still ruled in his palace, for in the walls of the old Acropolis, now called Itsch-Kale, are to be seen important remains of the old Cyclopean sur-rounding wall, which is built of perfectly fitting polygons, and is therefore probably, like the walls of Asine, of a somewhat later date than those of Tiryns.

The heaps of *débris* which occur in some places in this fortress are not suited for archæological research, for they were brought here from other places to form batteries in the time of the insurrection of 1862, and contain a mixture of pottery from the Roman period, the Middle Ages and modern times. I could not find in them a single prehistoric potsherd.

The son of Nauplios, Palamedes, had a sanctuary on the high steep rock.* The fortress upon it bears his name, which, strange to say, the Frankish conquerors found in use as the name of a mountain. This name also, as Curtius thinks, † was certainly not invented in the Middle Ages, but kept alive by oral tradition from the days when the Heroon of this mythical hero stood there. The old town, which is mentioned by Herodotos ‡ and Skylax,§ was, according to Euripides and Strabo,‖ the haven of the Argives, but of no great importance, partly in consequence of the transference of the inhabitants by the Lacedæmonians to Mothone, at the close of the second Messenian War, about the 29th Olympiad.¶ In the time of Pausanias it was in ruins and deserted.**

Strabo says, "Hard by Nauplia are caves and the labyrinths constructed in them, which are called the Cyclopean."†† However in Nauplia, nothing is known of caves, whether with or without labyrinths. Outside the town, in spite of long search, I have not been able to find any trace of them. I imagine therefore they exist in the western slope of the rock of the old Acropolis, and are concealed by the houses of the modern town of Nauplia. And I venture to conjecture that these caves, with the labyrinths of Cyclopean architecture, may contain the graves of the ancient Kings of Tiryns, for in the immediate neighbourhood of Tiryns there is nothing to point to their existence. I am the more disposed to believe this, because, on the north-east side of Nauplia, at about the distance of a mile, there have been discovered a number of

---

* Ernst Curtius, *Peloponnesos*, II. 390.  † *Ibid.*

‡ Herodotos, VI. 76.  § Skylax, p. 19, ed. Huds.

‖ Euripides, *Orestes*, 54 ; Strabo, VIII 368.

¶ Pausanias, IV. 24, 4 ; 27, 8 ; 35, 2.

** *Ibid.* II. 38, 2.

†† Strabo, VIII. 368 : Ἐφεξῆς δὲ τῇ Ναυπλίᾳ τὰ σπήλαια καὶ οἱ ἐν αὐτοῖς οἰκοδομητοὶ λαβύρινθοι, Κυκλώπεια δ᾽ ὀνομάζουσιν.

small graves of the beehive form, together with a *dromos*, whose construction completely corresponds with that of the so-called treasure-houses of Mycenæ, and the painted terra-cotta vases and idols found in them are also entirely of the same character as those of Mycenæ and Tiryns.*

The panorama which stretches on all sides from the top of the citadel of Tiryns is peculiarly splendid. As I gaze northward, southward, eastward, or westward, I ask myself involuntarily whether I have elsewhere seen aught so beautiful, and mentally recall the ascending peaks of the Himalayas, the luxuriance of the tropical world on the Islands of Sunda, and the Antilles; or, again, I turn to the view from the great Chinese wall, to the glorious valleys of Japan, to the far-famed Yò-Semite Valley in California, or the high peaks of the great Cordilleras, and I confess that the prospect from the citadel of Tiryns far exceeds all of natural beauty which I have elsewhere seen. Indeed the magic of the scene becomes quite overpowering, when in spirit one recalls the mighty deeds of which the theatre was this plain of Argos with its encircling hills.

The view given as frontispiece is taken from the north side of the royal palace explored by me, of which the ruins may be seen in the foreground.

Of the view in the background, Dr. H. Lolling has kindly furnished me the following description, which also completes the panorama on the other side:—

"Looking from the Citadel of Tiryns southward, you see, as appears in our panoramic view (cf. Frontispiece), straight before you the long Palamidi rock with its three tops, of which the westernmost is crowned with the striking Venetian fort, commanding all the surrounding country. Joined to this by a narrow saddle there projects westward into the Argolic Gulf the precipitous cliff of old Nauplia,

---

* Cf. H. Lolling's account of excavations at Palamidi in the *Mittheilungen des Deutschen Archäologischen Instituts*, V. 143, *sqq.*

now called Itsch-Kale, and clothed on the south side with the so-called Frankosykiæ. In the gulf is the small rocky island of Burzi, on which the Venetian fort is now the residence of the public executioner, who is here watched by a picquet of soldiers day and night. On the west side of the gulf are the bleak chains of mountains, through which the way leads southerly over the Zavitza mountains, an arm of the Parthenion, to the district Thyreatis, so long contested by Sparta and Argos; to the westward a good carriage-road goes by Hysiæ (now Achladokampos) and the Byzantine fort of Muchli into the rich Alpine plain of Tegea. As we look, the top of Zavitza lies right beyond the island fort of Burzi. The mountain chains traced in fainter lines, and appearing to join Palamidi to the south in our panorama, belong to the district of Kynuria; they are parts of the Parnon chain (now Malewo), reaching down to Cape Malea. The mountain next Zavitza, on the right (north), which also reaches the Argolic Gulf, is Pontinos, from the point of which, at the 'mills of Nauplia,' the great spring of Lerna bursts a full river from the rock."

"So far our panorama reaches. Let us now, standing on the rock of Tiryns, let our eyes wander northward over the Chaon range, where the already-mentioned great fountain-head of Kephalari rises, to the fine acropolis of Argos, standing out from Lykone into the plain, with its well-preserved mediæval fort. Above the lower hills stretches the long ridge of Artemision, across which two steep paths, the Prinos way and the Klimax way, lead over to Mantinea. Past the fort of Argos, and beyond the large village of Kutzopódi, the eye reaches to Mount Kelossa, on the north of which was the district of Phlius. The hills which here bound the Argive plain to the north-west meet the Treton ridge at Mycenæ. Between them is the principal pass in-land from the plain of Argos, the pass of Dervenaki, which connects the land of Argos with that of Kleonæ, and so with Korinth. Connected with Treton are the mountains in the west near Mycenæ and the Heræon, and further south the western outposts of the gigantic Arachnæon, to the south of which a deep, sheltered valley reaches to the famous shrine of Asklepios in the land of Epidauros. The southern spurs of Arachnæon approach the Palamidi, and so conclude the great circle of mountains which stand like a protecting wall round the Argive plain."

# CHAPTER III.

## THE OBJECTS OF TERRA-COTTA, STONE, ETC., FOUND IN EXCAVATING THE LAYERS OF DÉBRIS OF THE OLDEST SETTLEMENT IN TIRYNS.

As was before mentioned,[*] according to Eustathios and Stephanos Byzantinos the first name of Tiryns was Halieis or Haleis, as fishermen first settled on the rock; and, as a matter of fact, my excavations have discovered on various parts of the hill, especially on the middle terrace (Plan I.), clear traces of a very ancient shabby settlement, which must have anticipated the building of the great Cyclopean walls and the royal palace. We are indeed badly informed about the style of building and plan of these oldest houses of the primitive settlement. Their floors, preserved in many places, were of beaten-down clay, and in this quite different from the floor of the palace, built together with the Cyclopean walls on the upper citadel, for this is always of lime concrete. The most important traces of the oldest settlement we found at the south-west corner of the middle citadel, where we discovered, 3·30 m. under the last step of the communicating staircase (Plan II.), the clay floor, showing deep marks of a conflagration, of a room, two of whose walls made of clay and rough stones remained to a height of 0·75 m. So also the pottery of the oldest settlement (with the single exception of cups) was in form, workmanship, and decoration quite distinct from that used by the inhabitants of the palace, from which we collected many whole vessels and a vast heap of fragments. These latter are, with few exceptions, turned on the wheel, painted, and

---

in general very like those I found at Mycenæ,* and are
also analogous to those found in the deepest strata of the
Acropolis of Athens,† at the foot of the temple of Demeter
at Eleusis, in the bee-hive tomb of Menidi,‡ in the tombs
of Spata § and Aliki‖ near Chasani in Attika, of Nauplia,¶
of Salamis,** of Ialysos at Rhodes,†† in Knossos (Crete).‡‡
This pottery of the primitive settlers at Tiryns belongs to
the stage of the last four prehistoric towns excavated by
me at Troy,§§ as well as to the stage of the settlers on the
site of the tumulus of Protesilaos on the shore of the
Thracian Chersonese,‖‖ and like the very ancient pottery
found in the Necropolis of Antiparos. ¶¶

---

* Cf. Schliemann, *Mycenæ* (London, 1878).

† This pottery is to be seen in the Museum of the Acropolis.

‡ *Das Kuppelgrab bei Menidi, Mittheilungen des Deutschen Archäologischen Instituts in Athen* (1880), p. 5.

§ Cf. Schliemann, *Mycenæ*, XLIII. ; also the ᾿Αθήναιον (1877),
VI. 167–172 ; *Mittheilungen des Deutschen Archäologischen Instituts in
Athen*, II. 82–84 and 261–276; *Bulletin de Correspondance hellénique*,
I. 261–264, II. Pl. XIII–XIX. pp. 185–228 ; A. Milchhöfer, *die Museen
Athens*, pp. 102–104.

‖ Dr. H. Lolling informs me, that the excavations at Aliki and the
pottery discovered therein, will be discussed in the forthcoming continuation of Ad. Furtwängler and G. Löschcke's *Mykenische Thongefässe*.

¶ ᾿Αθήναιον (1878), VII. 183–201 ; (1879) VIII. 517–526 ; *Mittheilungen des Deutschen Archäologischen Instituts in Athen*, V. 143–163.

** These tombs were discovered by Capt. A. Miaoules, Director of
the Arsenal at Salamis, on the N. of the island, and their contents are in
his house near the arsenal.

†† *Archäologische Zeitung* (1873), pp. 104–105 ; Charles T. Newton,
*Essays on Art*, p. 284, *sqq.* ; *Gazette archéologique*, V. (1879), Pl. XXVI.
XXVII. p. 202 ; François Lenormant, *Les Antiquités de la Troade*,
II. 34; Albert Dumont et Jules Chaplain, *Les Céramiques de la Grèce
propre*, Pl. III. pp. 43–46.

‡‡ Albert Dumont et Jules Chaplain, *Les Céramiques de la Grèce
propre* (Paris, 1881), pp. 64, 65.

§§ Cf. Schliemann, *Ilios* (London, 1880) pp. 264–586, and Schliemann, *Troja* (London, 1884), pp. 52–192

‖‖ Schliemann, *Troja*, pp. 254–262.

¶¶ The excavations of the prehistoric Necropolis on the island of
Antiparos were made in the spring of 1884 by Mr. J. Theodore Bent,
and the pottery he found is now provisionally in the British Museum.

The wide contrast of the pottery of the two settlements on the rock of Tiryns in form, *technique*, and decoration are the clearest evidence that they belong to totally different peoples. For, as my friend George Dennis well remarks : * "The several styles of art of the same race at different periods are bound to one another like the links of a chain ; and it is impossible for a people, after having wrought out a style of pottery which had acquired among them a sacred and ritual character, to abandon it on a sudden, and adopt another style of a totally different character. A people may modify, develop, perfect, but can never utterly cast aside its own arts and industry, because in such a case it would deny its own individuality. When we find, therefore, between two styles of art so many and such strongly pronounced discrepancies, that it becomes impossible to perceive the most remote analogy between them, it is not enough to attribute such diversities to a difference of age, or stage of culture ; we can only ascribe them to different races."

If therefore we believe the oldest colonizers of Tiryns to have been the first inhabitants of the land, we may with great probability attribute the later settlement, to which the great palace and the gigantic Cyclopean walls belong, to that great Asiatic people, which about the middle of the second millennium before Christ, covered the whole of the mainland of Greece, as well as the islands of the Ionian and Ægean seas, with settlements, and which had already attained a high level of culture.†

Passing on now to a closer description of the objects discovered, I begin with those belonging to the earliest Tirynthian settlement, and exhibit in No. 1 a small hand-

---

* *The Cities and Cemeteries of Etruria* (2nd ed., London, 1878). This passage is repeated from *Ilios*, p. 279.

† Compare pp. 22, *sqq.*, what is said of the settlements of Phœnicians in Greece. Compare also Max Duncker, *History of Greece* (London, 1884), Vol. I. chap. iv.

made shell-shaped vase, covered with reddish-yellow clay, and more baked than is usual.*   It has on each side of the body an excrescence with two vertical perforations, and brings, therefore, before us exactly the most common type found in the first town at Troy,† but which is also found in the second, or burnt town. ‡

The holes at the sides, which were repeated in a corresponding position in the covers, § served as well for suspension as for closing the vases by means of a string.||

A like arrangement is seen in the vase of green basalt, No. 2, of which the rim is somewhat raised ; the bottom is

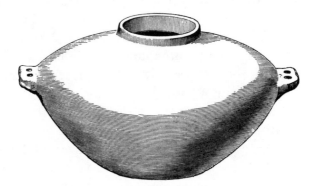

No. 1.—Hand-made terra-cotta vase with double pierced excrescences at the sides.   Half size.
Depth 4 m.

wanting.   Vases of bluish-grey stone appear in the beehive tomb at Menidi,¶ of black granite in Mycenæ,** in Spata,††

---

* The depth at which this and other objects illustrated in this work were found, was always noted on them by the inspectors of the excavations, and I only repeat their statements without vouching personally for their accuracy.

† Compare Schliemann, *Ilios*, pp. 214-5, Nos. 23-5 ; *Troja*, p. 32, No. 3.

‡ *Ibid. Ilios*, p. 363, Nos. 282-3.

§ *Ibid.* p. 215, No. 26.

|| Compare *Ilios*, pp. 356-7, and No. 252.

¶ *Das Kuppelgrab bei Menidi*, published by the Deutsches Archäol. Institut at Athens (Athens, 1880), pp. 20, 23, 25, Pl. IX. Nos. 5, 6, 7.

** Cf. Schliemann, *Mycenæ*, pp. xlvi–xlvii.          †† *Ibid.*

and in the Acropolis at Athens.   The specimens found at
Mycenæ and Spata have holes for suspension at the sides.

A further example, with similar arrangement for suspension and closing, is represented in Plate XXIII., under
Fig. *d.* It was found at a depth of 2 m., and is a hand-
made spherical vase, of well-cleaned green clay, only 3 mm.
thick, covered over with a shining black glaze.   In the
narrow neck, which is only 4 cm. in height, there is on the
right and left side a vertically perforated excrescence for
suspension.

We found, besides, fragments of hand-made bowls, of

No 2.—Vase of green basalt, with double vertically bored excrescences at the sides.   Half size.
Depth 4½ to 5 m.

grey, coarse and slightly baked clay.   They have a broad,
horizontally projecting brim, with two vertical perforations
on each side, which was made separately and joined on
while the clay was yet moist.   The vessel was then polished,
and before baking was repeatedly dipped in a solution of
red clay, by which means it took both on the inner and
outer side a brick-coloured tint.

Vases with similar vertically bored excrescences on both
sides, are rare everywhere, except at Troy, and only a few
are found in the most ancient settlements.   The National
Museum at Athens has but *one* such vase, which was found
in Attica, and is numbered 2185.   The small collection in

the French School at Athens of pottery from the island of Thera (Santorin), found under three layers of pumice and volcanic ashes, contains three hand-made vases provided with the same arrangement for suspension. We see the same on many fragments of hand-made vases which I found in my excavations in Bœotia.*

Several other hand-made vases of the same kind are to be seen in the collection of prehistoric antiquities, provisionally placed in the British Museum, which were dug up by Mr. J. Theodore Bent, from the prehistoric Necropolis on the island of Antiparos.†

In the royal tombs at Mycenæ I found a fragment of a similar vase of terra-cotta, ‡ as well as many perfect examples in gold.§ Fragments of similarly designed terra-cotta vases were found by Dr. Max Ohnefalsch-Richter in his excavations in Cyprus. The Museum of St. Germain-en-Laye contains several fragments of the like hand-made vases, of which one was found in a cave in Andalusia, and three others in dolmens in France; and also the casts of two other such fragments, of which the originals, preserved in the Museum of Vannes, were found in the dolmen of Kerroh, near Locmariaker. The Royal Museum of Northern Antiquities in Copenhagen contains three hand-made vases, closed with lids, and sixteen separate vase lids; ‖ the Royal Museum at Stockholm, three vases on the same plan.

Fragments of similar vessels were found in the caves at Inzighofen, on the Upper Danube.¶ The collection of

---

* Cf. Schliemann, *Orchomenos*, Leipzig, 1881, p. 40, No. 2, and p. 41, No. 3.

† J. Theodore Bent, *Prehistoric Graves at Antiparos*, in the *Athenæum* of May 3rd, 1884. ‡ Cf. Schliemann, *Mycenæ*, p. 158.

§ *Ibid.* p. 205, No. 318; p. 206, No. 319; p. 207, No. 320–2.

‖ J. J. A. Worsaae, *Nordiske Oldsager* (Kjöbenhavn, 1859), Pl. XIX. Nos. 95, 98; Pl. XX. No. 99.

¶ Ludwig Lindenschmit, *Die Vaterländischen Alterthümer der Hohenzollerschen Sammlungen* (Mainz, 1860), Pl. XXVI. Nos. 7, 8.

Babylonian antiquities in the British Museum contains a portion of a hand-made earthen vessel, and the collection of Assyrian antiquities in the same institution three entire hand-made vases of the same system. This design is also to be seen on a hand-made vessel from Cyprus, in the Louvre, on the fragment of a vase in the collection of Count Bela Széchényi in Hungary,* as well as on a hand-made vase found in a cone-shaped grave, called in German *Hünengrab*, at Goldenitz in Mecklenburg, which, under the number 1094, is preserved in the Grand-ducal Museum at Schwerin. Further, the Museum at Parma possesses two hand-made vases, found in the Terramare in Emilia, of which one has a single, and the other two, tubular holes on each side; two similar hand-made vessels of the same origin and construction are in the Museum at Reggio (in Emilia). Two other hand-made vases with this system are in the Museo Preistorico in the Collegio Romano at Rome, of which one was found in the Terramare of Castello, near Bovolone (Province of Verona), and the other in the ancient lake dwellings of the Lake of Garda. A vase, also hand-made and with a similar arrangement, was found in an ancient grave at Corneto (Tarquinii), and may be seen in the museum of that town. The fragment of a similar hand-made vessel found in the Grotto del Farné, near Bologna, is in the prehistoric collection in the Bolognese Museum. † A similar hand-made vessel was found in a Terramare near Campeggine (Province of Reggio di Emilia). ‡ There were also found in ancient graves near Bovolone, which are admittedly of the same period as the

---

* Joseph Hampel, *Catalogue de l'Exposition préhistorique des Musées de province et des collections particulières de la Hongrie* (Budapest, 1876), p. 71, No. 55.

† Edoardo Brizio, *La Grotta del Farné* (Bologna, 1882), p. 20, Pl. III. No. 17.

‡ *Bullettino di Paletnologia Italiana*, 1877, pp. 8, 9, Pl. I. No. 3.

Terramare of Emilia, a pair of hand-made burial-urns, with vertical piercings for suspension at the side.*

A vase with the same arrangement, which was found in Umbria, is in the Prehistoric Museum at Bologna; another from the cave of Trou du Frontal-Furfooz in Belgium, is in the Museum at Brussels. The Prehistoric Museum at Madrid contains five fragments of hand-made vases, with similar vertically perforated excrescences at the sides; these were discovered in caves in Andalusia, inhabited during the Stone Age. Another fragment of similar design, also from an Andalusian cave, is in the Museum at Cassel. A hand-made earthen vessel with vertically perforated excrescences, found in the Landdrostei of Lüneburg, is in the collection of the Historical Society for Niedersachsen in the Museum at Hanover. The splendid private collection of Senator Friedrich Culeman in Hanover likewise contains a hand-made vase of the same kind. A box made in the same way, with vertical perforations on both sides, in the brim and in the lid, was found in the district of Guben, in Prussia.† A hand-made terra-cotta vase, with vertical perforations in the excrescences on the upper edge, as well as in the rim of the foot, was found in Platkow.‡ Several fragments of hand-made vases with vertically perforated excrescences were collected in the excavations of the prehistoric settlement on the mount called "Grosser Brucksberg," near Königsaue.§ Further, in Grone, near Göttingen, a hand-made terra-cotta pitcher, on which at each side are two strong, narrow handles, one above the other, with vertical perforations. ‖ In a megalithic tomb at

---

* *Bullettino di Paletnologia Italiana*, (1880), pp. 182–192, and Pl. XII.

† *Zeitschrift für Ethnologie, Organ der Berliner Gesellschaft für Anthropologie, Ethnologie und Urgeschichte*, 1882, pp. 392–396.

‡ *Verhandlungen der Berliner Gesellschaft für Anthropologie, Ethnologie und Urgeschichte:* Sitzung 20 October, 1883, p. 426.

§ *Ibid.* Sitzung 19 July, 1884, pp. 360–362.

‖ *Ibid.* Sitzung 20 October, 1883, p. 429.

Janischewek in Cujavien,* a hand-made cup-shaped vessel, having on one side two flat excrescences with narrow vertical perforations; in Faliszewo, the rim-fragment of a hand-made terra-cotta vessel, having a broad, flat, vertically per-forated *Ansa lunata* affixed; † in Güssefeld, in the district of Salzwedel, a terra-cotta urn with a vertical and doubly-pierced broad ear. ‡ Further, the prehistoric burying-ground near the tile-yard of Tangermünde has yielded a certain number of similar hand-made vessels for suspension with vertically-pierced ears,§ and several hand-made vases of the same class were discovered in prehistoric graves at Wulfen, in the district of Koethen, ‖ as well as in the oldest graves in a tumulus in Anhalt, in the neighbour-hood of Bernburg.¶ The antiquities from this burial mound are preserved in the collection of the Historical Society of Bernburg. I would also mention a hand-made urn ** found at Dehlitz, near Weissenfels, on the Saale. This specimen has on three sides vertically-bored projec-tions, and indeed on two sides they are double, one above the other, the lowest being close to the bottom; on the third side there is only one.

As in the German graves, which contain pottery of this class, objects of metal are extremely scarce, whilst bone implements and polished stones are characteristic and usual. Professor Rudolf Virchow, with great probability, attri-butes them to the Neolithic Period.†† I may add that the Museum at Breslau, under the direction of Dr. H. Luchs, possesses twelve or fifteen hand-made vessels, with vertically bored excrescences on two sides, which were found

---

* *Verhandlungen der Berliner Gesellschaft für Anthropologie, Ethno-logie und Urgeschichte*, Sitzung 20 October, 1883. pp. 430–432, and Pl. VII. No. 2.                † *Ibid.* p. 434.

‡ *Ibid.* p. 437, note.

§ *Ibid.* pp. 438–442, and Pl. VIII. Nos. 2, 4.

‖ *Ibid.* p. 444.                ¶ *Ibid.* pp. 445. 446.

** *Ibid.* Sitz. 28 November, 1874, p. 7.          †† *Ibid.* p. 448.

together in prehistoric graves in Silesia. And the Museum at Prague, whose director is Herr Vrtiásko Ant. Jaroslav, possesses one vase of the same design found in Bohemia. The Prehistoric Collection in the Museum at Geneva contains some fragments of vases found in France,* which are provided with the same vertical perforations for suspension.

Finally, I mention that the Greek Archeological Society has found a great number of very small and very ancient hand-made terra-cotta vases, only 2–4 cm. high, in the excavations made in Eleusis, at the foot of the Temple of Demeter, of which very many have on two sides vertically pierced excrescences for suspension: also one somewhat larger vessel, with the same arrangement, and many still larger which have but a single perforation for suspension at the foot and rim.

I particularly draw attention to the fact, that I here refer only to those vessels which have *perpendicular* tubular rings or holes for suspending and for shutting up, not of such as have *horizontal* perforations, for these are very common, as well in the Swiss lake-dwellings as in Germany, France, England, Denmark, and particularly in the island of Cyprus.

Are then these vases with vertically perforated excrescences, which, as we have seen, occur frequently in the *débris* of the oldest settlement of Tiryns, commonly in the oldest stratum at Eleusis, by thousands in the prehistoric towns of Troy, often in the neolithic period in Germany, and here and there in settlements of the stone age in Italy, France, Spain, &c., proofs of direct connection ?

" I am not prepared to affirm that these are proofs of a direct connection. That question can only be settled when the countries of the Balkan peninsula shall have been more thoroughly investigated archæologically, a thing which

---

* The locus of the find is not stated.

is urgently to be desired. But even if a real connection should appear, the question will still remain open, whether the current of civilization set from Asia Minor to Eastern Europe, or the reverse way; and since the former is presumably the more probable, little would be gained hence for the chronology of Hissarlik." *

No. 3 represents a hand-made one-handled jug of globular shape, belonging to the first settlement of Tiryns. It is made of rough brick-coloured clay, baked through and through, unpainted, and has an upright neck with

No. 3.—Hand made one-handled jug　Size 1:2.　Depth about 3¼ m.

wide projecting spout, cut in a crescent form; the base is small and flat. Vases with a similar spout are very common in the burnt as well as in the fourth town of Troy.† Another specimen found by Mr. Bent in the prehistoric necropolis on the island of Antiparos, may now be seen in his collection, which has been temporarily placed in the British Museum.

No. 4 represents a hand-made jug, slightly baked, of dark

---

* Rudolf Virchow's Preface to Schliemann's *Ilios*, p. xiii.

† Cf. Schliemann, *Ilios*, p. 384, No. 357 ; p. 387, No. 364 ; p. 388, No. 365 ; p. 551, Nos. 1161. 1162.

brown colour, which before baking was washed over with a
solution of finer clay; it has a handle, the better to secure
which there is at the top a knob-shape projection. Besides
this, there is a larger excrescence on each side of the body
for the purpose of steadying the vessel between two stones

No. 4.—Jug with projections on the sides, and handle. Size 1:2. Depth 5 m.

on the fire. The spout is broken away. Vessels with similar
projections on the body are common in Troy.*

In No. 5 I exhibit a hand-made, slightly baked vessel,
in the shape of two shells laid together. It is formed of
very coarse brown clay, which, previous to baking, was
washed over with a fine brown clay, and ornamented with
white lines stretching irregularly from the neck to the
middle of the body. The vessel had a handle on the back,
but it has been broken off. So far as I know, there have
been in all but six similar vessels found. One by me in
Ilium,† the second also by me in Mycenæ; a third was
discovered on the island of Amorgo. The two last may be

---

* Cf. Schliemann, *Ilios*, p. 388, No. 369.—Schliemann, *Troja*,
p. 183, No. 91.

† Schliemann, *Troja*, p. 216, No. 130.

seen at Athens, one in the Mycenæan Collection, the other in the National Museum. The three other vessels of this kind were found together with hut-urns, under a stratum

No. 5.—Vessel in the form of two shells laid together, with white lines of decoration.
Size 1 : 2.   Depth 4 m.

of peperino at Marino, near Albano, and are in the British Museum.

I also exhibit in No. 6, a hand-made basin of coarse grey clay, 7 mm. thick. It is not painted. The outside,

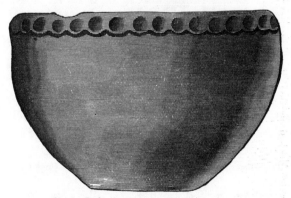

No. 6.—Basin of terra-cotta.   Size 1 : 2.   4·50 m.

which was polished before baking, shows the simple brown colour of the clay. All round the edge, which projects slightly, may be observed an unbroken circle of round, concave impressions, which apparently were made with the finger before baking, while the clay was still soft.

Fragments of vases with an exactly similar decoration have been found in a prehistoric settlement at Imola.*

No. 7.—Terra-cotta vessel with projections right and left.   Size 1 : 2.   Depth 4·50 m.

No. 7 shows a hand-made vessel of coarse grey clay, 6 mm. thick, with projections right and left, not perforated,

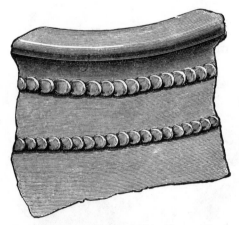

No. 8.—Fragment of brim of a large jar ($\pi\iota\theta$os).   Size 1 : 2.   Depth 4·50 m.

which may have served both as handles, and to steady the vase between the stones on the fire.

In No. 8 is represented the rim fragment of a large

---

* Edoardo Brizio, *Atti e Memorie della R. Deputazione di Storia Patria per le provincie di Romagna*, III. Serie, Vol. II. fasc. 2 (Modena, 1884), p. 19, Tav. III. Nos. 1, 2.

hand-made jar (πίθος), with a projecting rim 52 mm.
wide; it is made of coarse dark-brown clay, 13 mm. thick.
Beneath the rim are two horizontal, parallel clay-bands,
which were made separately, and kneaded on when the clay
was still damp; they are moulded in the surface like small
coins, overlapping each other.    Jars of this form, with
similarly moulded borders, still occur in Peloponnesus.
The cut No. 9 exhibits the fragment of the body of
another large hand-made jar (πίθος) of very coarse grey

No. 9.—Fragment of a large jar (πίθος).  Size 1 : 3.  Depth 3 m.

clay, mixed with small pebbles, badly baked, 14 mm. thick.
Two borders, each 35 mm. wide, pass horizontally round
the body of the vessel.  These are stamped in relief, and
represent spirals, between which are ascending and descending boughs like twigs of pine.  Although this object
was found at a depth of only 2 m., yet I attribute it with
great probability to the earliest settlement.

The first settlers on the rock of Tiryns were, however,
acquainted with the potter's wheel, for the deep plate repre-

sented in No. 10, which was found by Dr. Ernst Fabricius at a depth of 5 m. on the cement floor of a small house of the oldest colonization, is decidedly worked on the wheel. This is of half-baked, rough yellow clay, unglazed, and therefore in every respect similar to the vast number of plates found in Troy.*

Similar very rough, unpolished, wheel-made plates may be seen in the Assyrian, Egyptian, and Cyprian collections of antiquities in the British Museum, and, as I am informed by Professor Joseph Hampel, are found in the excavations at Magyarád, in Hungary. In Germany, Professor Virchow tells me they only occur polished.

I consider it to be in the interest of knowledge that I

No. 10.—Deep plate of terra-cotta.   Size 1: 2.   Depth 5 m.

should here give a description of the remaining characteristic pottery of the most ancient settlement of Tiryns, which is only represented by fragments.

1. Hand-made vessels, of coarse black clay, 5 mm. thick, the outside of which has been coated before baking with a crust nearly 1 mm. thick of fine dark-red clay. These vessels were polished both inside and out, before and after the baking, and thus they have a lustrous red outside and a shining black inside.

2. Large hand-made bowls with a turned-over edge of coarse greyish-yellow clay, which before baking were dipped in a solution of black clay, and are therefore black outside

---

* Cf. Schliemann, *Ilios*, p. 408, Nos. 456–468.

and inside. Others have been dipped in a red solution, and consequently are red. The upper surface of the edge in these last is in many cases painted black. The thickness of the clay of these bowls varies between 12 and 15 mm.

3. Very flat hand-made bowls, in form identical with that of the very numerous black bowls in the first town of Troy.* These are of coarse red clay, and before baking were dipped in a solution of black clay, and well polished on both sides, consequently they have outside a lustrous black, inside a lustrous red colour; their clay-thickness is from 4 to 6 mm.

4. Small hand-made vessels of well-cleaned grey clay, whose thickness is only 2½ mm.; they have been treated like the preceding, and have on the outside a lustrous black colour; on the inside, which is not polished, the original dull grey of the clay.

5. Of the finer vessels of the earliest settlement I must mention the fragments of hand-made, one- or two-handled vases of fine reddish clay, whose thickness in one and the same vessel may vary between 1 and 4 mm.; they are decorated all round with a band of from 15 to 17 incised parallel lines. Before baking they were dipped in a solution of well-cleaned black clay, and several times polished, so that they have on both sides a shining black colour.

6. I mention besides the well-polished, hand-made vessels of coarse reddish clay, 6 to 8 mm. thick, which on the inside have the dull colour of the clay. But, on the outside, they are decorated above and below with broad stripes of a very common red colour; while, in the space between, run parallel horizontal brown lines and a cross line of the same colour.

---

* Cf. Schliemann, *Ilios*, p. 228, No. 62.

7. Further, the fragments of hand-made, well-polished vases of fine clay, 7 mm. thick, outwardly of a rough, crumbling, brown colour; inside, at the rim, runs a zigzag line, and beneath it, on a light-yellow ground, a band of three parallel horizontal brown lines.

8. Also the hand-made vessels, of very coarse red clay, about 6 mm. thick, which are badly polished and unpainted.

9. Then the very numerous large fragments of hand-made vases, of very coarse greyish-yellow clay, about 7½ mm. thick, which had been dipped before baking in a light-yellow solution of clay, superficially glazed on the outside, and decorated by means of a very common dull-black or violet colour (apparently a clay-colour), with linear ornaments of the most varied patterns, and sometimes with spirals. The clay is, however, so coarse, and the polishing so imperfect, that many of the small pebbles in the clay project from the surface.

10. Further, the fragments of larger hand-made vessels of very coarse, ill-polished, unpainted red clay, about 7 mm. thick; they have round the edge a separately made band of clay 30 mm. broad, about 8 mm. thick, which is ornamented with parallel crescent-shaped cuttings.

11. Also the fragments of hand-made vessels of coarse reddish clay, 6 mm. thick, which apparently before baking were filled with a solution of well-cleaned clay; the outside was not, however, dipped in it, for it retains the dull-red natural clay-colour, while the inside is dark red.

12. Again, other hand-made terra-cotta vessels, of grey clay, 5 mm. thick, the outside only of which was dipped in a solution of fine brown clay; the inside has the natural grey clay colour.

13. There are also many fragments of vessels, turned on the potter's wheel, of well-cleaned clay, of which, for example, I may mention the jugs of brownish-yellow clay,

which must have been filled before baking with a solution
of fine grey clay, and then placed in another of fine green,
for inside they are grey, but outside, by polishing before
and after baking, of a lustrous green, and of a beautiful
appearance.

14. I wish particularly to draw attention to the hand-
made goblets of black clay of similar manufacture, which
are little or not at all polished, and therefore have a dull
green colour; fragments of them are frequently found.

They have exactly the form of the goblets, which, in a
broken condition, are found in vast numbers in the Palace
of Tiryns, and of which I represent two in the following
pages (cf. No. 27, and Pl. XXI. Fig. *f*). Strange to say,
this is also in Mycenæ the only existing form of terra-
cotta goblets. In fact, the various examples from Mycenæ
and Tiryns show a variation only in colour and material.
Whilst in the Mycenæan royal tombs, and in the lowest
layers of *débris* outside of them, as well as in the first
settlement at Tiryns, we find these goblets of light-green
colour with black spirals, still, however, hand-made; in
the higher strata of *débris* in Mycenæ, and in the ruins
of the Palace of Tiryns, we see them either of simple
lustrous dark-red colour, of bright yellow with numerous
stripes of various colours, or with no other colour but that
of the light-yellow or white of the clay (No. 27, and
*Mycenæ*, pp. 70–1, Nos. 83, 84, 88). Fragments of goblets
of the latter category are very common in the Palace of
Tiryns; and in Mycenæ they occur in such enormous
quantities, that I could have collected thousands of their
feet or stands. I found also five specimens in gold of this
goblet in the Mycenæan royal tombs.* An exactly similar
goblet, found in one of the most ancient graves in
Nauplia, is in the Mycenæan Museum, and four specimens
found in tombs in Attica, are in the National Museum at

---

* Schliemann, *Mycenæ*, p. 233, No. 343; p. 350, No. 528.

Athens. There are also in the Acropolis Museum four goblets of similar form, and about thirty of the stands, as well as many other fragments of the same kind of goblet, which were found in the most ancient layers of *débris* on the Acropolis at Athens. One, found in a tomb on the island of Salamis by Captain Andreas Miaoules, is in his collection at Salamis. The British Museum possesses fifteen specimens of goblets of this form, of which one was found on the island of Kos, and fourteen (painted) in tombs at Ialysos, in the island of Rhodes. The Museum of the Louvre possesses three painted examples from the island of Rhodes, the exact locality is not stated; the same form of goblet occurs in Knossos in Crete,* as well as in the first town of Troy.†

The Prehistoric Museum at Madrid contains four specimens of similar goblets, but without handles, which were found in caves inhabited during the Stone Age in Andalusia. Of goblets of similar form found elsewhere, I can only mention one from Zaborowo, in the collection of Professor Rudolf Virchow, and one from Pilin;‡ yet the handles of both these goblets are longer, and they have not the broad foot which is peculiar to all the other goblets here mentioned.

15. I also mention the fragments of hand-made vessels of very rough, greyish-red, slightly baked clay, 12 mm. thick, mixed with small stones, which before baking were placed in a solution of blackish clay, and therefore have a dull black colour. They are ornamented with horizontal and vertical white lines from 5 to 10 mm. wide.

---

* As Dr. Ernst Fabricius informs me, many examples of this goblet form have been dug up by Mr. Minos Kalokairinos on the site of Knossos.

† Schliemann, *Ilios*, p. 224, No. 51.

‡ Joseph Hampel, *Antiquités préhistoriques de la Hongrie*, Pl. XIX. No. 3.

16. I must also mention the rudely-made ladles, about 25 cm. long, of coarse reddish clay, which I at first supposed to be the feet of large tripod vases, and only after long deliberation thought to be really ladles. My conjecture was turned into certainty, however, when Dr. Max Ohne-falsch-Richter showed me a photograph of an analogous ladle, found by him at Soli in Cyprus, the handle of which is pierced through near the end.

17. Finally, I must call attention to vase-feet constantly recurring in the *débris* of the most ancient settlement of Tiryns, which show that there terra-cotta vessels with three feet were in common use. Such tripods of terra-cotta appear by hundreds in the five prehistoric towns of Troy,* in fact most terra-cotta vessels have three feet.

Professor Rudolf Virchow, to whom I sent some potsherds from the oldest settlement of Tiryns for examination, writes to me thus: " The yellow colour of the pottery is only produced by baking. When the clay is black, the baking has had less effect. But all these pieces have been enveloped in smoke and impregnated with charcoal."

The famous chemist, Dr. Theodor Schuchardt of Görlitz, to whom I sent four potsherds, Nos. I.–IV., of the oldest settlement, and No. V. a portion of the wall plaster of the palace, also Nos. VI. and VII., two fragments of terra-cotta vessels found in the palace, kindly analysed them and sent me the following information :—

I. Potsherd; red: contains mainly silicic acid, clay, iron, lime, as well as small quantities of magnesia, and the faintest traces of kali. The same ingredients are

---

* Cf. Schliemann, *Ilios*, p. 220, No. 44; p. 227, No. 59; p. 295, No. 163; pp. 354-63, Nos. 251–281; pp. 529–545; Nos. 1018, 1019, 1022, 1025, 1026–1044, 1048, 1049, 1053, 1056, 1069, 1076, 1107, 1110, 1111, 1130, 1131; pp. 578–9, Nos. 1308, 1310: and Schliemann, *Troja*, p. 131, No. 55; p. 140, Nos. 68, 69; p. 144, Nos. 74, 75.

contained in VI. and VII., which are labelled " pottery of
the palace." The analysis gave—

|  | I. | | VI. | | VII. | |
|---|---|---|---|---|---|---|
|  | Per cent. | Per cent. | Per cent. | Per cent. | Per cent. | Per cent. |
| Silicic acid   . | 50·7 | 50·60 | 53·80 | 53·75 | 53·3 | 53·15 |
| Clay   .   .   . | 27·0 | 27·10 | 28·10 | 28·20 | 28·2 | 28·15 |
| Lime   .   .   . | 19·3 | 19·25 | 13·0c | 12·85 | 13·1 | 13·05 |
| Oxide of iron   . | 2·7 | 2·75 | 2·45 | 2.50 | 2·7 | 2·75 |
|  | 99·7 | 99·7 | 97·35 | 97·30 | 97·3 | 97·1 |

II. Potsherd; black: silicic acid, clay, iron, traces of
lime and magnesia.

III. Potsherd; grey with brown stripes; silicic acid,
lime, magnesia, carbonic acid, and traces of iron.

IV. Potsherd; light yellow with black stripes—same
as III., but more iron.

V. Wall-plaster of palace; silicic acid, lime, carbonic
acid, and small quantities of clay.

Dr. Schuchardt writes to me on the subject: " With
regard to the analysis, I have to announce to you that I
have conducted the qualitative analyses of all the seven
specimens personally, with repetition, as is necessary, in
important matters. Of three of your specimens, two complete analyses give a perfectly satisfactory uniformity of
result. Dr. Richter conducted them with the most scru-
pulous accuracy. The quantitative analysis of II., III., IV.,
V., could not, on account of insufficiency of materials,
be completed. Some substance containing carbonic acid
must be present in considerable quantity; this is the case
with III., IV., and V. It is quite surprising that III. contains carbonic acid, whether as limestone pebble containing
carbonic acid, or as carbonic magnesia, I do not venture to
decide; at all events the well-cleaned material effervesced
strongly on pouring in acids.",

Some idols of terra-cotta, of form similar to that repre-

sented on Plate XXV., Fig *d*, occur in the *débris* of the most
ancient settlement; and also the object No. 11, which I
also regard as a fragment of an idol. It is 60 mm. long,
quite flat, and made of badly polished brown clay. The
upper part of the body and feet are wanting. I conjecture
that, like an idol found by me in Mycenæ and preserved
in the Mycenæan Museum at Athens, it had no head, but
only two erect horn-like excrescences, of which I fancy we
see the stumps. If this is so, then the two spirals attached

No. 11.—Fragment of an idol of terra-cotta. Almost     No. 12.—Object of black stone.
actual size.  Depth 4 m.                               Actual size.  Depth about 3 m.

to it on the right and left may represent the breasts, and
the central one the *vulva*.

Although no object of metal has been found which I
could with certainty attribute to this oldest settlement of
Tiryns, yet I have no grounds to suppose that bronze and
copper were unknown or unused; on the contrary, I do
not believe that the beautifully polished polishers and
other objects of very hard stone, which I am going to
describe, could be perfected without bronze tools. We
may, however, assume with certainty that iron did not
exist, for even in the upper palace of Tiryns I found
none, and neither in the prehistoric ruins of Mycenæ

nor in those of Orchomenos or Troy have I ever discovered a trace of it.

Of silex or chalcedony I found only a couple of knives or saws similar to those which I discovered at Troy ;* on the other hand, there are numerous knives and arrow-heads of obsidian, like those represented under Nos. 104–111. The obsidian knives, of 1–6 cm. long and upwards, almost always two-edged and symmetrically formed, are quite similar to the Trojan knives of the same stone.† The arrow-heads (see Nos. 108–111) however, are rudely made, in fact, as rudely as the arrow-heads of silex found in the cave-dwellings of the age of the mammoth and the reindeer in the Dordogne in France, and to be seen in numbers in the Prehistoric Museum at St. Germain-en-Laye. I found, however, just such roughly finished arrow-heads of obsidian in my excavations in the prehistoric tumulus on the plain of Marathon, which previously had been wrongly regarded as the tomb of the 192 Athenians who fell in the battle of Marathon, 490 B.C.‡ But the most remarkable thing is that obsidian knives and arrow-heads, equally rude in form, are found in enormous quantities under the ruins of the royal palace in the upper citadel of Tiryns, and that obsidian knives of the same kind are found in equally great numbers in Mycenæ.§

The many obsidian flakes and the nuclei which one finds in Tiryns and Mycenæ, appear to show that these objects were manufactured on the spot. Most probably the obsidian was imported from the Cyclades islands of Milo or Antiparos,|| for, as far as I know, this kind of stone does not occur elsewhere in Greece.

---

* Schliemann, *Ilios*, p. 246, Nos. 94–7.

† *Ibid.* p. 445, Nos. 658–63.

‡ *Zeitschrift für Ethnologie, Organ der Berliner Gesellschaft für Anthropologie, Ethnologie and Urgeschichte,* Jahrg. XVI. (1884), Heft II., pp. 85–88.        § Schliemann. *Mycenæ,* p. 158.

|| J. Theodore Bent, *Researches amongst the Cyclades,* in the *Journal of Hellenic Studies,* Vol. V. ; April and October, 1884, p. 52 : "In the

In the engraving No. 12, I represent an object of black stone, in form much resembling the Trojan idols.*

Two different kinds of stone polishers for pottery were found. Of one kind only one specimen was discovered; it is of very hard, fine, yellow stone, and extremely like the Trojan polishing stones.† The same form of polishing stone occurs in Mycenæ, where I found six specimens of it. The other kind, of which I represent two specimens (Nos. 13 and 14), is in the form of a cylinder, with the centre contracted. The former (No. 13) is of black marble,

  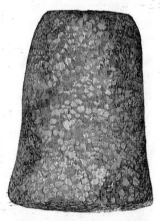

No. 13. — Polishing stone of black marble, speck'ed red and white. Actual size. Depth 4 m.

No. 14.—Polishing stone of fine reddish marble. Size 2 : 3. Depth 4¼ m.

No. 15.—Polishing or grindstone of fine black granite, with white grains. Size 2 : 3. Depth 4·50 m.

speckled red and white, 37 mm. long, 27 mm. in diameter; the latter (No. 14) is of fine reddish marble, 40 mm. long by 25 in diameter. Four exactly similar polishers, found in the lowest *débris* of the Acropolis of Athens, are in the Acropolis Museum.

---

richer tombs on Antiparos, knives and flakes of obsidian are very common. In Antiparos the inhabitants had their obsidian close at hand, for a hill about a mile from the south-eastern graveyard is covered with it."

* Schliemann, *Ilios*, pp. 334–6, Nos. 204–222.

† *Ibid.* p. 443, Nos. 645, 647.

Polishing and grinding stones of this kind of speckled marble, and black granite with white grains, in the form of a flat cone, or bell shape, were also found. The most remarkable is represented in No. 15; this is 75 mm. long, and at the lower end has a thickness of 53 mm. Saddle-querns of trachyte, in the form of a longitudinally divided egg, are occasionally found. These are common at Mycenæ,* and abound in prehistoric Troy.† I found them also in the Tumulus of Protesilaus on the Thracian Chersonesus.‡ They are also often found in the Terramare of Emilia, and many may be seen in the Museum of Reggio and Parma; others, found in the "Caverna delle Arene Candide" near Genoa, are in the Prehistoric Museum of the Collegio Romano at Rome. The Museum of St. Germain-en-Laye contains six similar hand-mills of sandstone, containing iron; and the Prehistoric Museum at Geneva, four from the Swiss lake-dwellings. Many similar hand-mills of trachyte have lately been found in the lowest *débris* of the Acropolis of Athens.

I have already repeatedly shown,§ that by pounding corn between the flat sides of two such stones, only a kind of groats, and not flour, could be obtained. With regard to the use of pounded corn, which could not be used for baking bread, I refer the reader to a long exposition in my last work, *Troja*. ‖

Roughly cut, but sometimes fairly-well polished, almost globular stone tools, which are called corn-bruisers, were found in numbers both in the *débris* of the most ancient settlement and under the ruins of the palace. They consist of granite, quartz, porphyry, or diorite. In Mycenæ I collected fifty similar tools : three specimens found in the

* Schliemann, *Mycenæ*, p. 77.
† Schliemann, *Ilios*, pp. 234, 447, Nos. 74, 75, 678.
‡ Schliemann, *Troja*, p. 257.
§ Schliemann, *Ilios*, p. 234.
‖ Schliemann, *Troja*, pp. 44–46.

*débris* of the Acropolis at Athens may be seen in the Acropolis Museum.   These appear by thousands in the prehistoric towns of Troy,* and are very common in the prehistoric sites of Germany, France, Hungary, and Italy; others found in the most ancient ruins of Chaldea are in the small Chaldean collection in the Museum of the Louvre.

There were also found in the earliest settlement about a dozen hammers of primitive rudeness, made of diorite, silicious stone, or granite, the size and weight of which lead us to suppose that they were grasped by the hand, and not fixed in a wooden handle.   In Troy such large stone hammers are so numerous, † that I could have collected thousands.

Two similar rough stone hammers, found in the lowest *débris* of the Acropolis of Athens, are in the Acropolis Museum; others of the same kind, collected among the prehistoric remains in Chaldea, are in the Louvre Museum; such rough stone hammers are also common in the Terra-mare of Emilia, and many specimens of them are shown in the Museums of Parma and Reggio.

I must not omit to mention a well-polished axe of very hard red stone, of the same form as the bronze battle-axes found in Troy.‡

There were also found in the primitive settlement of Tiryns several cone-shaped spinning-whorls, of blue stone or steatite, of which, in my excavations at Mycenæ, I have collected about 350 specimens. §   Similar spinning-whorls of steatite occur in Troy, but are there so rare, that during my excavations there, extending over many years, I probably found no more than seventy; whilst of cone-shaped spinning whorls of terra-cotta, I was able to collect more than 22,000.

---

* Schliemann, *Ilios*, pp. 236, 442, Nos. 80, 81, 638, 639.
† *Ibid.*, pp. 237, 441, Nos. 83, 634.
‡ *Ibid.*, p. 476, Nos. 806–809 ; p. 486, No. 828.
§ Schliemann, *Mycenæ*, p. 18, No. 15 ; p. 76, No. 126.

Of spinning-whorls of blue stone, several were found in the prehistoric graves of Nauplia, and 157 specimens were collected from the lowest *débris* of the Acropolis of Athens ; * similar stone whorls, found in the graves at Kameiros in Rhodes, are in the British Museum.

Of bone, only a few bodkins and one embroidering-needle, 65 mm. long, with four encircling furrows at the thick end, were found; the latter is represented under No. 16.

I found a similar needle at Mycenæ, † and many hundreds of specimens in Troy; others of the same kind were found in the lowest *débris* of the Acropolis of Athens, and are now in the Acropolis Museum.

No. 16.—Embroidering needle of bone. Actual size. Depth 3 m

The above Tirynthian needle (No. 16) lay by a human skeleton in the longitudinal trench of the lower terrace (see Plan I.). From the same trench were taken three other skeletons, all lying actually on the rock. Beside one of them I found a perforated bead of blue painted glass, which I represent under No. 17.

No. 17.—Pierced bead of blue-painted glass. Actual size. Depth 3 m.

Exactly similar objects were found in numbers in the graves of Spata.‡ In the beehive-tomb at Menidi § over a hundred specimens were collected. An object of the same kind, found in a grave at Kameiros in Rhodes, is in the British Museum.

The investigations of Professor Xavier Landerer show

---

* The stone spinning-whorls found in the Acropolis are to be seen in the Acropolis Museum.

† Schliemann, *Mycenæ*, p. 153, No. 229.

‡ *Ibid.* p. xliv.

§ *Das Kuppelgrab bei Menidi*, published by the Deutsches Archäol Institut in Athen (Athens, 1880), p. 28, Pl. III. Nos. 4, 5, 8, 9.

that these beads consist of glass, alloyed with much
protoxide of lead, which has the property of breaking the
rays of light, and which also imparts to these glass objects
a kind of silvery mirror-like glimmer.  As Landerer remarks, it is soda-glass, and has the peculiarity of dividing
into little leaves or splinters.  In Mycenæ I found but one
similar object, of yellowish glass.  Besides this, there was
found in the *débris* of the primitive settlement of Tiryns
but one bead of blue cobalt glass.

Besides the glass bead there were only some fragments
of monochrome pottery of the first settlement found with
the skeleton.

The second skeleton had no accompaniments; nor
had the third, but it, however, presented this peculiarity,
that the head was separated from the trunk, and lay near
the feet.

In many places in the *débris* of the earliest settlement
were found great masses of burnt grains, of which I sent
specimens to Professor Virchow in Berlin.  This friend
submitted them to the examination of Professor Witmack,
who declared them to be grape-stones of unusual size.

# CHAPTER IV.

## The Objects found in the Débris of the Second Settlement of Tiryns.

I HAVE already pointed out (pp. 49, 56) the close connection of the pottery collected in the Palace of Tiryns with that found in Mycenæ, Asine, Nauplia, the Acropolis of Athens, Eleusis, the beehive tomb of Menidi, the tombs at Spata and Aliki,* the island of Salamis, Ialysos in Rhodes, and in Knossos on the island of Crete; and Dr. Lolling observes to me that I may add to this list the island of Ægina. He has witnessed the discovery there of several tombs, which have yielded pottery similar to that of Tiryns and Mycenæ. Professor Rhousopoulos of Athens also assures me that he collected in the Acropolis of Megara fragments of pottery and idols of the Mycenæan type. I may add, that the analogy of the pottery of all these places is made still more obvious by the absence of the varnished Hellenic vases.† In fact, in spite of the most careful

---

* Aliki is situated near Cape Kolias in Attica. Dr. Lolling informs me, that several rows of tombs have been discovered there close to the shore. They consist of a *dromos* and a circular sepulchral chamber, and have been found to contain terra-cotta vases and other things very similar to those of Tiryns and Mycenæ.

† In the Acropolis of Athens, where the *débris* has been more or less mixed, most ancient pottery occurs in company with the black polished Hellenic pottery of a much later period.

I must in this respect state, that four terra-cotta vessels, which in form, fabric, and decoration closely resemble those of Mycenæ and Tiryns, have been found in a beehive grave near the ancient Ortygia, the Syracuse of to-day, which once had a Phœnician settlement.

W. Helbig writes thus in *Das Homerische Epos aus den Denkmälern*

search during the whole time of the excavations, neither
Dr. Dörpfeld nor I have been able to find in the *débris*
of the palace any trace of such lacquered ware, and yet
the fragment of a well-varnished, lustrous black Hellenic
terra-cotta, found by me in the upper layer of *débris* in the
citadel of Mycenæ, on which is an inscription of the 6th
century B.C. (cf. p. 45), proves with perfect certainty that
this pottery was in common use in the middle of the
first millennium before Christ. The above fragment is of

---

*erläutert* (Leipzig, 1884) pp. 66, 67 : " A most remarkable and quite
peculiar occurrence is a tomb discovered at Matrensa, about 6 km.
from Syracuse (*Annali dell'Instituto*, 1877, Tav. d' agg. E. pp. 56–58).
The beehive-shape of the rock-hewn chamber, and of the dromos
leading into it (*Annali dell' Instituto*, 1877, Tav. d' agg. E. p. 3)
remind us of the ancient beehive graves. In the chamber were found
two terra-cotta vessels, adorned with brownish ornaments, parallel lines
below, and above a design of tendrils, on a polished yellowish ground
(*Annali dell' Instituto*, 1877, Tav. d' agg. E. pp. 6, 7). They show in
form, in fabric, and in decoration a near relation to the examples found
in the pit graves of Mycenæ, and other similar strata (Furtwängler and
Löschcke, *Mykenische Thongefässe*, T. III. 9, 11 ; nearest to the Sicilian
specimens comes a terra-cotta vessel found in Crete, at present in the
Berlin Museum). Besides these, the burial-chamber contained two
vases of black clay (*Annali dell' Instituto*, 1877, Tav. d'agg. E. pp. 4, 5),
which, as Löschcke informs me, appear to be also closely allied to the
Mycenæan pottery. But Syracuse was far from being the oldest of the
Greek settlements in the west, and the Greek remains found in other
parts of Sicily and Italy belong evidently to a later time. I therefore
do not know whether this grave should be attributed to the Corinthian
colonists, or to a more distant pre-Hellenic period. It is known that
before the arrival of the Greeks, Phœnicians had settled on some
islands on the coast of Sicily and the peninsulæ which could be easily
defended, in order to traffic with the natives, and to gather the purple
murex (Thukyd. VI. 2, 6 ; Movers, *Die Phönikier*, II. 2, p. 309, *sqq.* ;
Olshausen, in the *Rheinisches Museum*, VIII. (1853 p. 328 ; Kiepert,
*Lehrbuch der Alten Geographie*, pp. 464, 465), and distinct traces point
to the existence of a Phœnician settlement at Ortygia (Movers, *op. cit.*
II. 2, pp. 325–328). The question then arises, whether the grave
at Matrensa does not belong to the Phœnicians settled at Ortygia, or
to the Siculi who had been influenced by them, and received from
them these vases."

as good quality as any terra-cotta of the same kind in later times.

It is impossible that the art of making such excellent polished black pottery could have been suddenly discovered; it can only occur in a school of pottery which has by the labour of centuries attained to such perfection in the art. I have therefore without hesitation attributed the tumuli of Achilles, of Patroklos, and of Antilochos, excavated by me in the plain of Troy, to the ninth century B.C., although the monochrome terra-cotta collected therein, which by all archæological experience must be referred at least to that date, is mixed with fragments of primitive mono-chrome black polished pottery.* But as this last is wholly wanting in the palace of Tiryns, and the terra-cotta found there must necessarily have been in use by the inhabitants to their last hour, we may unhesitatingly place the great catastrophe, by which the building was destroyed by fire, in the eleventh century B.C., especially as we have found nothing to contradict this assumption. On the contrary, the unmixed prehistoric pottery found in the palace, and particularly the numerous idols of most primitive forms, as well as the immense number of knives and arrow-heads of obsidian of the most ancient type, compel us to accept this date, which is, if possible, still more fully confirmed by the absence of any trace of iron. This chronology would also show a remarkable agreement with the tragic end of the old citadel of Mycenæ, which, as my excava-tions have shown (cf. p. 46), must also have taken place in a remote pre-Homeric age. We may indeed admit, with the highest probability, that both Tiryns and Mycenæ were destroyed at the time of some great revolution, a revolution so destructive in its effect, so terrible in its consequences, that the civilization of Greece was com-pletely overthrown, and upon its ruins arose a new and

---

* Schliemann, *Troja*, pp. 248, 249.

wholly different culture, in all the branches of human industry. And in fact we possess the most trustworthy historical information concerning this fearful revolution. It was brought about by the Doric invasion, or the so-called Return of the Heracleidæ, which the tradition of all antiquity with wonderful agreement places eighty years after the Trojan War, or about the year 1100 B.C.

The inhabitants of the land were either massacred or enslaved, or obliged to emigrate in masses, and thus arose the so-called Æolic migration to Asia Minor.

By this great historical event is explained in the most natural manner the sudden and complete disappearance of the flourishing but quite peculiar civilization of which we have the remains in the antiquities of Tiryns and Mycenæ. There can, however, remain no doubt that this great revolution was not limited, as has been supposed, to the Peloponnesus. It must have extended to North-eastern Greece, and at least, though possibly in a less degree, to Attica, for those remains of culture which we find in the beehive tomb of Menidi, on the Acropolis of Athens and Megara, in Eleusis, in the graves of Spata and Aliki, as well as in the islands of Salamis and Ægina, and which show such close connection with those of Tiryns and Mycenæ, likewise disappear suddenly and leave no trace.

There exist, however, in Tiryns, as well as in Mycenæ, numerous fragments of pottery with geometrical patterns,[*] which, in point of manufacture, form, and decoration, are closely allied to those found in Athens in the graves near the Dipylon.[†]

These vases with geometrical patterns, of which many fragments occur in the lowest stratum of *débris* on the Acropolis of Athens, were commonly held to be the most

---

[*] Schliemann, *Mycenæ*, p. 103, Nos. 157, 158.

[†] G. Hirschfeld, *Vasi Arcaici Ateniesi. Estratto dagli Annali dell' Instituto di Correspondenza archeologica* (Roma, 1872).

ancient pottery in Greece, until my discoveries in Mycenæ
came to be known—about the end of the year 1876. When
it was recognized that Mycenæan pottery was of a higher
antiquity, it was also found that the Dipylon graves must
belong to a later time, and Helbig writes on the subject : *
" It is now universally acknowledged that these graves belong to a later time. †   It is sufficient to recall the fact
that in them the later habit of burning the dead pre-
vails, ‡ and that in Athens during the seventh, § and even
apparently during the sixth century, B.C.‖ pottery corresponding to that obtained from these graves was in use.   As
the objects in metal found with them are not sufficiently
known, ¶ search is principally directed to the painted vases,
of which a considerable number has been found.   Their
painted decoration shows a peculiar employment of geometrical ornament, an arrangement which from these vases has
been distinguished as the Dipylon style.   Yet vases of this
kind have been found, not in Attica alone, but in many other
places of Eastern Greece, as well as in the islands of the
Ægean Sea, particularly in those of Melos and Thera, and,
it would appear, also in Asia Minor and Northern Africa. **
From this it is to be supposed that they were not made in
Attica, whose industry and trade at the period in which we
must place the graves of Dipylon were still unimportant,

---

* W. Helbig, *Das Homerische Epos, aus den Denkmälern erläutert*
(Leipzig, 1884), p. 54.

† Cf. also Furtwängler, *Die Bronzefunde aus Olympia*, p. 10.

‡ G. Hirschfeld, *op. cit.*

§ *Annali dell' Instituto*, 1880, p. 133 ; Transactions of the German
Archæological Institute in Athens, VI. p. 112.

‖ *Annali dell' Instituto*, 1878, pp. 311, 312.   In Olympia the habit
of decorating bronze articles with engraved patterns of this geometrical
character may be observed to the end of the sixth or beginning of the
fifth century B.C.   Furtwängler, *Die Bronzefunde aus Olympia*, p. 12.

¶ *Annali dell'Instituto*, 1872, pp. 136, 154, 155.

** *Ibid.* 1872, pp. 140, 151, 174 ; Furtwängler, *Die Bronzefunde aus
Olympia*, p. 19.

but rather further east, either among the islands of the Ægean, or in Asia Minor."

That the vases with geometrical designs reach back to the remotest antiquity, and owe their origin to the Phœnicians, was shown beyond doubt, ten years ago, by Helbig.*

In fact, we find these geometrical patterns on vases which were brought in the reign of Thuthmes III., king of Egypt (*circa* 1600 B.C.), as tribute from Rutenu, *i.e.* Southern Syria, from Kaft, *i.e.* Phœnicia, and the Isles of the Sea, to Egypt, and of these many show those forms which were usual later in Greece.† Pottery with geometrical ornaments occurs also at Nineveh, in Cyprus, and in Rhodes.‡ Eduard Meyer supports the idea of an Asiatic, *i.e.* a Syrian origin, for the geometrical style, and adds, "In Egypt also, in the New Kingdom, the geometrical style is much used; all objects on which it occurs declare themselves at the first glance to be imitations of a foreign style, and not the product of native art." §

We may therefore assume, with very great probability, that the vases found at Mycenæ and Tiryns with geometrical patterns were imported. For not only are the objects of large size, and their form, their painted ornamentation, and the whole art of their manufacture different in every way from all else found in Tiryns and Mycenæ, but even the kind of clay from which they are made, and the peculiar manner in which they are baked, are found in no other vases. These vases with geometrical patterns must therefore have been imported to the Peloponnesus long before the Doric invasion, and consequently their occurrence in Attica in the later centuries does not come under consideration in our investigations concerning the period of the destruction of Tiryns and Mycenæ.

---

* *Annali dell' Instituto,* 1875, p. 221, *sqq.*

† Eduard Meyer, *Geschichte des Alterthums* (Stuttgart, 1884), p. 245.

‡ *Ibid.*                              § *Ibid.*

### 1. VASE PAINTINGS WITH GEOMETRICAL PATTERNS.

I now pass on to a more particular account of the terra-cottas found in the palace of Tiryns, and as I have just spoken of vases with geometrical designs, I shall first more closely examine these, and commence with two fragments (found at a depth of only 60–70 cm. under the surface) of the upper rim of a large vessel of red clay, with a wide mouth, of which a representation will be found on Plate XV., Fig. a.*

On the outside, the painting is in a reddish-brown tint on a light-yellow ground; its colouring varies in proportion to the thickness with which it is laid on. Above this tint is a decoration in white. On the upper rim is a broad band, and underneath part of a chariot, in which stands a man, who drives the horse attached to it. The movement is from the left to the right. The man has a kind of helmet on his head, which, however, for want of room could not be drawn entirely. In one hand he holds the double reins, in the other a staff. The drawing of the horse is very primitive and unskilful; the mane and ears are, indeed, represented with a childlike naïveté. But on the fragment of another vase the mane, neck and ears are represented precisely in the same manner (cf. Plate XXI., Fig. b). On the extreme right, we see traces of the red border which surrounded the handle.

With regard to the painting of the horse with little dots and crosses of white on the red and brown ground, I would point to the representation Plate XV., Fig. c, which shows a further fragment of the same or a similar vessel, found at a depth of 1 m. from the surface. On this may be seen, under the red border, the upper body of a man;

---

* In the descriptions of the pottery in this chapter, Dr. Ernst Fabricius has been my fellow-worker, and I here renew to him my warmest thanks for the valuable aid he has given me.

further to the right the head of another, both in profile to the right; to the left is a broken-off handle.

The colour of this fragment is somewhat more red; the fabric and decoration are, however, identical with those of the two former fragments.

Another fragment, Plate XV., Fig. *b*, which was also found 1 m. below the surface, gives us the hind leg of a horse and the end of his tail; on the left hand, one sees a part of the chariot. The ground is represented by a streak. Perhaps this fragment belongs to the two on Plate XV., Fig. *a*. Another fragment, Plate XXI., Fig. *a*, which comes from the same depth, is a portion of a vase of red clay; on it is drawn, with red on a light-red ground, a horse, of which the lower part is preserved. The fabric is the same as on Plate XV., Figs. *a*, *b*, *c*; the execution is somewhat less careful. The ground is represented by two horizontal lines.

All the above fragments are coloured on the inside: on Plate XV., Figs. *a*, *b*, dark-brown; Plate XV., Fig. *c*, red; Plate XXI., Fig. *a*, light-red. This last fragment, and Plate XV., Fig. *c*, appear from fabric and colour to be parts of the same vessel. The ground colour of Plate XV., Fig. *b*, is more reddish than on Plate XV., Fig. *a*. I show on Plate XVII., Fig. *b*, a fragment of a similar large vessel found at a depth of 1·50 m.; it was turned on the potter's wheel and is of light-red clay; the painting is blackish-brown with white touches. On the upper edge one sees a broad stripe, and below, two men in profile to the right. The man on the left, the upper part of whose body is preserved, has his right hand on his hip, and holds the left extended in a line with his shoulder to the right. The man on the right, of whom only the lower half remains, stood upon the chariot, as we may see from the preserved rim (ἄντυξ) of the chariot, and from the smaller proportions of the figure (cf. the chariot-driver on Plate XV., Fig. *a*).

The outlines of the bodies are filled in with a network

of finely-crossed lines; on all the black lines of the drawing white dots and lines are laid on. The inner side of the vessel is monochrome black.

Further, at Plate XVII., Fig. *a*, another fragment found at the depth of 1·50 m. of a large wheel-made vase of reddish clay, with red painting. The thickness of the clay is 12 mm. A portion of a girth is visible, with conventionalized women's figures, the heads of which are covered with a cloth, and the profile turned to the right. The hands are stretched out from the shoulders on both sides, in such a manner, that the hands of the neighbouring figures touch each other and appear to hold a branch in common.

The waists are represented as unnaturally narrow, and raise a suspicion that even at the early date of those vases ladies wore some kind of stays, in order to appear more slender and to cause the breasts to project more. Yet in classical antiquity nothing of the kind seems to have been used, for in no ancient writer do we find reference to the use of stays, and there is no name for them in Greek, for στηθόδεσμος* and the diminutive στηθοδεσμίς† and στηθο-δ´σμιον ‡ mean nothing more than a breast-band which caught the nipple and held it back. The folds of the garments are on the right side, indicated by vertical lines. The background around the upper bodies of the women is filled with dots, while beneath the branches the figures are separated by horizontal waving lines. The figure on the right represents the commencement of the row of women.

Professor Charles Newton, of the British Museum, draws my attention to a fragment, preserved in that museum, of a similar geometrical vase found in a grave at Kameiros

---

* Poll. 7, 66 ; Antonio Cocchi, *Græcorum chirurgici libri*, p. 11. Professor Mahaffy asks me : " Was not the στηθόδεσμος a band *under* the breast, which helped to make it stand out? so often in pictures?"

† Jerem. ii 32 ; Isaiah iii. 24 ; Galenus, T. 18, 1, p. 823 ; 17, 824, 2 ; Phlegon. *Mirabil.*, p. 118, 26.

‡ *Etym. Mag.*, p. 749, 40.

in Rhodes, on which an almost identical female figure is drawn with red colour; but in this the size of the waist is natural, and the whole style of the painting seems to point to a later period.

In the cloth, with which the heads of the women are covered, we may recognize the καλύπτρη or the κρήδεμνον, concerning which Helbig writes as follows:— *

" Besides this, there belonged to female clothing a sort of mantle-like head-cloth, the καλύπτρη or the κρήδεμνον. The first,† as well as the last, ‡ was usually drawn over the back of the head, and hung down over the shoulders and back. When Penelope appears before the suitors, she draws the κρήδεμνον modestly over her cheeks. § Even so also sorrowing Demeter screens her face with the καλύπτρη. ‖ As, according to these quotations, the καλύπτρη and the κρήδεμνον were used in the same way, there is no reason why the words should not be considered synonymous. At most they must be but slightly differing types of the same piece of clothing. The archaic sculptures very often represent this head-cloth,¶ and show us women, who, like Penelope in the presence of the suitors, hold it before their faces."**

---

* W. Helbig, *Das Homerische Epos aus den Denkmälern erläutert* (Leipzig, 1884), pp. 123, 124.

† *Il.* XXII. 406; *Od.* V. 232 X. 545.

‡ *Il.* XIV. 184; XXII. 470; *Od.* I. 334; V. 346, 351, 373, 459; VI. 100; XVI. 416; XVIII. 210; XXI. 65. Κρήδεμνα, Hymn. V. (*in Cerer.*) 41.

§ *Od.* I. 334; XVI. 416; XVIII. 210: XXI. 65: ἄντα παρειάων σχομένη λιπαρὰ κρήδεμνα.

‖ Hymn. V. (in Cerer.', 197.

¶ Helbig, *op. cit.* p. 124. Fig. 24. Two women appear on vases from Melos (Conze, *Melische Thongefässe*, vol. 3, Vignette, p. V.); Helen on the Spartan base (*Annali dell' Instituto*, 1861, Tav. d' agg. C. 2; Löschcke, *De basi quadam prope Spartam reperta*, n. 1, p. 7, and fol.; Helbig, *op. cit.* Fig. 24, p. 124. The three goddesses on the cup of Xenokles (Raoul-Rochette, *Mon. inéd.* T. 49. 1; Overbeck, Gal. T. 9, 2).

** Thus, for example, women on Spartan tombstones (*Transactions of the Arch. Inst. in Athens*, II., Pl. XX., XXII.–XXIV.), Thetis as

On four other fragments (Plate XVI., Figs. *b* and *c*), of a wheel-made vase, with red painting, we see (Fig. *b*) a well-preserved female figure in profile to the right. It is the last of a row of four somewhat more naturally represented women. To the right is seen a portion of the lower body and of the head of the following woman, further the complete head of the third, and then finally the middle part of the fourth woman. As in the vase picture, Plate XVII., Fig. *a*, the hands of the four women are raised on both sides to the level of their shoulders, in such a way, that the hands of two neighbouring women touch each other, and appear to hold a branch in common. The first branch on the left is perfect, the other two are only partly preserved. The height of the complete figure, *b*, is 92 mm. She, like the two following women, has no cloth upon her head, and has, as well as the last figure (*c*) on the right, a much wider waist, although still apparently laced.

While the folds of the raiment of the women on Plate XVII., Fig. *a*, are represented by three straight lines, those on the vase we are now considering are given by a single vertical zigzag line. To the right and left of the row of women are bands of vertical, and above these a band of twelve horizontal zigzag lines.

Between the latter band and the very low neck of the vase, which appears above, are two stripes, the lower of which is formed of two parallel horizontal and the upper of horizontal and waved lines. With the vertical band already mentioned, on the right of the women, composed of twelve zigzag lines, is connected, on the right, a field with a chequer ornament. Below is a broad stripe, which in Fig. *b* is composed of three red, and in Fig. *c* of six dark-brown horizontal, parallel bands.

---

bride on the François-Vase (Helbig, *op. cit.* p. 2, note 1). Helen opposite to Menelaus on dark-figured vases (Overbeck, Gal. Pl. 26, 1–3; Mus. Gregorian, II. Plate 49, 2; Helbig, *op. cit.* p. 125, Fig. 25; cf. Löschcke, *op. cit.* p. 7.

The thickness of the clay, which is of a red colour, is 10 mm. The inside is not carefully glazed. Of the same vase there are also preserved some pieces which show alternate straight and waved lines.

We find the same kind of decoration, with female figures, on a fragment found at a depth of 1·20 m.; it is the upper part of a large wheel-made vase, of reddish clay with yellow ground. I represent it here under No. 18. The painting is black, the clay 8 mm. thick.

The upper side of the rim shows alternately slanting

No. 18.—Fragment of Vase with female figures and geometrical patterns.   Size 1 : 2.   Depth 1·20 m.

crosses and ten straight lines. The whole of the narrow neck is decorated with a row of dots between horizontal lines. Then follows a broad band of alternate horizontal and vertical divisions, marked off below with five strong horizontal stripes; the belt itself shows a mixture of horizontal and perpendicular, waved, straight, and zigzag lines. On the extreme right commences a procession of conventionalized women in profile to the left, who, with the exception that they are only half the size (50 mm.), exactly resemble the other women, and hold the branch in common; but they have no cloth on their heads, like the women on Plate XVI., Fig. *b, c.*  The folds of the garments are this time represented by three perpendicular lines.

On Plate XIX., Fig *b*, I give a large fragment of a very large vessel made on the wheel, of which the clay-thickness is not less than 18 mm.  The painting is brown, on a reddish ground; one may distinguish four horizontal stripes or bands, one above the other, separated in each case by three well-marked lines.  Whilst the two lower stripes are simply filled with colour, in the upper one we see

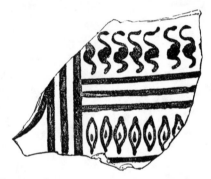

No. 19.—Fragment of a vase with cranes and shells.  Size 1 : 2.  Depth 1 m.

a row of shells, and in the second conventional cranes in profile to the right.

In quite the same manner of decoration is the small fragment of another wheel-made vessel (No. 19), except that in this the row of conventionalized cranes is above and that of the shells below.  To the left are three vertical lines.  The clay as well as the ground are reddish, the painting black.  The inside is red, the thickness is 12 mm.  Very like this is the piece of the upper part of a large wheel-turned vessel (7 mm. thick), which has red-brown paintings on a reddish ground.  On the neck are three horizontal lines; after that, two bands separated by four lines.

The upper band is decorated with a row of conventionalized cranes in profile to the right; the lower is ornamented
with alternate stripes of six perpendicular lines. These
stripes enclose, like triglyphs, square fields, which are filled
in, each with two horizontal zigzag lines. The inside of
the vase is brown. Similarly decorated is a fragment of the
body of a large wheel-made vase of reddish clay, 12 mm.
thick; the painting is brown on reddish ground, and represents three stripes, of which the upper one is the lower
part of a mæander ornament, the second consists of three
broad lines, and the third of a row of conventionalized
cranes. Fragments of vases with geometrical patterns very
like these were also found in Mycenæ.*

On Plate XVIII. I give a drawing of four fragments,
found at an average depth of 1·50 m., which apparently
belong to the upper part of a similar large wheel-turned
vase of reddish clay, which also has a brown painting on a
reddish ground. The thickness of the clay is 12–13 mm.
Beneath the edge, decorated with a zigzag line, we see
seven bands, of which four are formed of three lines each;
from the broken condition one can only see two lines in
the lowest band, but we may reasonably suppose that here,
as in the upper borders, there were three lines. In the
second band there are one horizontal and two upright
mæanders between four vertical bands of seven lines each;
further to the right are six horizontal zigzag-lines. Then
comes on the body a very broad zone, in which to the
right, enclosed by two bands, each of six vertical lines, is a
large rosette, between each leaf of which may be seen a 卐.
Above and below the rosette are two horizontal bands of
four lines each, as well as a horizontal mæander; below
we see a row of shells. To the right of this group is seen
a horse in profile to the left, then a man in profile to the
right; further on, a second horse in profile to the right.

---

* Schliemann, *Mycenæ*, p. 103, Nos. 157, 158.

Between the horses' legs fishes are represented.  The background is filled everywhere with mæanders, Svastikas (卍)
and shells.  Above the backs of the horses are compartments filled with horizontal zigzag-lines, and framed by
straight lines in the form of windows.  Between the fifth
and seventh bands is a row of very rudely drawn cranes, in
profile to the right.  On the inner border of the fragment,
Plate XVIII., are five brown parallel bands ; beneath this
the colour is a monochrome red.

The sign 卍, as well as the equally frequent 卐, I have
discussed *in extenso* in my works *Ilios*, pp. 345–354, and
*Troja*, pp. 122–129, and I have shown that it occurs in
countless instances in Mycenæ, in the four upper prehistoric towns of Troy ; also in India (among other instances
four times in the Footprints of Buddha, cf. *Ilios*, p. 349,
No. 244) ; in Bactria, in China, in Ashantee, in the interior
of the Gold Coast of Africa, among the ancient Hebrews
(cf. Ezekiel ix. 4, 6, where the sign 卐, in the form of the
ancient Hebrew letter Tau, like the corresponding Indian
symbol as the sign of life, is written on the forehead) ; in
Gaza, on Hittite antiquities, in Lapland, and on the antiquities of all the other nations of Europe ; in Yucatan,
in Paraguay ; I have shown that these two symbols are
an unsolved riddle, like the Nile-key or *crux ansata*, which
in hieroglyphics is read as " ankh," the Living One, that
in countless inscriptions of the Nile valley comes before
us in the same form as on a tomb stelé in northern Asia
Minor.*

I therefore refer the reader to that ample treatise and
I especially invite his attention to the learned and important discussion of 卐 and 卍 from the pen of my learned
friend the famous Orientalist, Professor Max Müller of
Oxford, which he will find in *Ilios*, p. 346 *sq.* ; and also to

---

* Guillaume et Perrot, *Exploration archéologique de la Galatie et de la
Bithynie*, Atlas, Plate IX.

the excellent work of Robert Philips Greg, *On the Meaning and Origin of the Fylfot and Swastika* (Westminster, 1884).

I would mention a portion of the border of a large wheel-made vase of reddish clay, 7 mm. thick, found at a depth of 1 m.; it is painted with red geometrical patterns on a yellow ground. The cylinder-shaped edge is painted. Below are seen four strong lines, and above alternate groups of ten vertical straight lines, ten vertical zigzags, and a row

No. 20.—Fragment of a vase, with a man, a horse, and a fish.   Size 1 : 2.   Depth 1·50 m.

of ten upright shells. Below the rim the space is divided by groups of ten vertical lines into twenty fields, ten of which are filled with zigzag lines and inclined waving lines. The inside is plain red.

I must not omit to mention a fragment, found at the same depth, of a wheel-made, wide-bellied vessel of reddish clay, 13 mm. thick, with red paintings on reddish ground. Above three horizontal and parallel bands are the remains of an upright band of straight and waved lines, as well as of a fish-bone pattern. On the inside are traces of colour.

Further, I refer to the fragment found at a depth of

1·50 m. of a wheel-made vase, 14 mm. thick, of red-brown clay, on which one observes in brown paint zigzag-lines close together over horizontal bands. Next, a small fragment of a large wheel-turned vase of reddish clay, 9 mm. thick; the painting is reddish-brown; below we see a band of five horizontal lines; above are three compartments, of which the two outer ones are incomplete. The field to the right is decorated with a chess-board pattern; the middle with upright, and the left with waving lines.

The engraving, No. 20, represents a fragment of a large wheel-turned vase of yellow clay, 9 mm. thick, found at a depth of 1·50 m.. The painting is black on a yellow ground. The subject is analogous to that on Plate XVIII. We see a horse with a bushy tail, in profile to the left. Between the legs of this animal is a fish standing upright, and a shell (?), and on the left a man facing left; he holds up his arms, and seems to have a whip in the right hand; the space is filled up with a mæander, with shells and a ⊐⊔. Here, as in all the vases with geometrical decoration, we observe the *horror vacui* of the primitive artist. The drawing is surrounded with straight lines; above is seen the attachment of the neck of the vase; the inside is dark brown.

A similar representation is found on a fragment of a smaller wheel-made vase of yellow clay, 6 mm. thick. The painting is dark-brown on a yellow ground, and shows a horse in profile to the right. Between his legs is an upright fish, and on the right a large star in outline and a bird. Over the back of the horse may be seen the angle of a compartment, which is bordered by straight and filled with zigzag lines. The inside is monochrome black. This fragment is said to have been found at a depth of from 1·20 to 1·50 m.

I give on Plate XIX., Fig. *a*, a fragment found at the same depth of a smaller wheel-made vase of yellow clay, only 3 mm. thick, with brown painting on yellow ground. We see the hinder part of a horse, in profile to the left.

I give on Plate XVI., Fig. *a*, another fragment from the same depth of a large wheel-made vase (11 mm. thick) of pure yellow clay. The painting is brown on yellow ground. Above, to the right, is part of the frame of a large circular ornament, such as is also seen on the following pieces, consisting of concentric circles, the intermediate spaces of which are filled, in the two upper ones with zig-zag lines, in the following, with pyramids. To the left, one sees the hinder part of a horse with a huge bushy tail.

No. 21.—Fragment of vase with concentric circles and crosses. Size 1 . 2. Depth 1·20 m.

Under the legs of the horse appears a fish-tail, and perhaps a snake. In the interstices are various ornaments, difficult to describe.

The woodcut, No. 21, represents a fragment of a large wheel-made vessel (16 mm. thick), of very clean red clay, of which the painting is brown on a yellow ground. Below a band of three lines, we see, to the left, part of concentric circles and a circular zigzag-line. Further to the right, a

cross framed with straight lines, and still further on, five
concentric circles, of which one is in zigzags. The inner
circle is filled with a cross and twelve points. At the right-
hand top-corner is a star. I may remark here, that I found
another fragment with a similar cross and points.

I present on Plate XX., Fig. *b*, a fragment found at a
depth of 1·50, of a large wheel-made vase of reddish clay,
with brown painting on reddish ground. We see below a
star in the centre of a circle, round which is drawn a
broad mæander. Then follow within three concentric
bands, of which one is formed of three lines and two of
two lines, a circle of two intersecting zigzag lines, and one
simple zigzag-line. This circular ornament appears to
have occupied the centre of an oblong field, of the framing
of which three horizontal lines remain above. The corners
of the quadrangular field were filled with fantastic decorations, of which some small remains may still be seen. The
inside is rough and unpainted.

On Plate XX., Fig. *a*, is represented another fragment
from the same depth of a somewhat smaller wheel-made
vase of yellow clay, 7 mm. thick. The painting is black on
yellow ground. We see on a field, formed by three
horizontal lines on the border and four on the body, two
vertical stripes, of which the left-hand one is composed of
at least seven waved lines, and the right-hand one of
straight lines. Between the two are four concentric circles,
of which the outmost is surrounded by slanting strokes.
Above and below are two pyramidal ornaments, whose
points are connected by waving lines. Below is a narrower
band with upright waving lines ; the decoration terminates
below by a band of four horizontal lines, and uniform
black paint; the inside is brown.

Though the group of vases with geometrical designs
differs in its general style from that of the peculiarly
Tirynthian and Mycenæan group of pottery, which I shall
describe in the following pages, there is yet, as Sophus

Müller very rightly remarks,* no want of connection between these groups, for the straight-line system of ornament
stands in certain relation to the spiral system. The one
system, for instance, expresses in the straight lines of the
mæander what the other puts into curves as spirals, and
while but a small step was made in this way from the
original *motif*, a wholly new system of ornament was the
result.

At the same time let me repeat, that the pottery with
geometrical designs is, as regards form, material and fabric,
quite distinct from the vases of the peculiar Tirynthian and
Mycenæan groups.

## 2. VASES PAINTED WITH GLOSSY WHITE COLOUR.

Plate XIV. places before us seven fragments, which belong together, of the upper part of a wheel-made vessel of
yellowish clay, 7 mm. thick. The outside has on a smooth
yellowish ground, a painting in red, with glossy white
colour laid on. The inside is unpainted. To the right we
see the remains of the handle. Beneath the brim, which
is marked out by a line, is a broad frieze, which is
bordered below by three broad lines. To the right is represented a curious object, in which Professor Newton, of
the British Museum, recognizes the prow of a ship. After
this appear two warriors with helmets on their heads ; a
round shield in the left, and the lance held for hurling in
the right hand. Between the extended legs of the warriors
hangs a long tail, and Dr. Ernst Fabricius believes that
it may be the tail of an animal's skin, which is cast over
the back of the men. And his idea appears to be just,
for in an Egyptian wall-painting from Beit-el-Walli in the
British Museum, which represents the capture of Cush

---

* Sophus Müller, *Ursprung und erste Entwickelung der Europäischen
Bronzecultur* (1882). German translation by Miss J. Mestorf.

or Æthiopia by Ramses II., there are many Æthiopes, with their loins girded with panthers' skins, of which the tips of the legs depend in a similar way to the long tail of the Tirynthian warriors. Behind the warriors the front part of a horse may be seen in profile to the right, to which probably further back the chariot was attached. The horizontal lines, over the back of the horse, are no doubt to be regarded as reins. The spirals above and the arches beneath serve to fill up the space. Between the legs of the horse, a dog leaps towards the right, with its tail well lifted up. Over the red ground colour of the drawing of the men and horse are drawn parallel waving lines of glossy white colour. The contours and fine strokes are all accentuated by dotted lines also of glossy white. The horse wears at the corner of the neck a large disc. The eyes are given by a dot within a rather large circle. The edge of the shield, which is covered with the ground colour, is brought out by two concentric circles of white dots, and in the same manner the Omphalos is marked in white. The high fluttering manes are again remarkably executed in white colour. It is interesting to observe that the figure of the warrior is here represented twice without any variation, and must therefore be regarded as conventionalized.

On Plate XXII., Fig. *e*, I show a fragment found at the same depth of another wheel-made vase of red clay, 7 mm. thick. On this is seen the hinder part of a horse, as well as a portion of a chariot. The technical manipulation of the painting entirely agrees witn that last described; the dimensions are somewhat smaller.

I show further on Plate XXIII., Fig. *a*, a fragment found at a depth of about 50 cm. of a perfectly flat hand-made plate, of which two other portions, not exhibited, were found. As these show, the edge of the plate was bent over. The clay is of reddish colour, and 10 mm. thick. Both sides are finely polished, and painted in brownish-red. The border of the upper side is decorated with mæanders in glossy white colour, on the red varnished ground, which are followed by two concentric circles extending to the edge.

The centre was filled with figures, but the remains do not afford sufficient detail for a complete representation. On the fragment (Plate XXIII., Fig. *a*) we see the lower half of a man, stepping to the left. The lines round the feet no doubt show the straps of the sandals. The naked leg steps from under the richly-ornamented chiton, and Dr. Ernst Fabricius reminds me that the same kind of decoration of clothing is seen on the oldest vases. The man seems to place his foot on the naked thigh of his conquered enemy, of whom part remains to the left. We can still recognize his richly-decorated coat of mail. The filling-in of the space is, as on the other pieces, effected by parallel triangles. To the left we see probably the point of a helmet. On one of the two other fragments we recognize the legs of an upright-standing warrior turned towards the right, with a part of the coat of mail with mæander stripes. On the under side of the fragment (Plate XXIII., Fig. *a*) we observe indistinct remains of painting in red lacquer, with glossy white laid on.

We observe in the free and life-like drawing of the leg in these fragments (Plate XXIII., Fig. *a*), the painting of which in a technical point of view does not differ perceptibly from that of Plate XIV. with the armed warriors, an important advance in an artistic point of view; for the representation, as compared with the others, is no longer conventionalized, but natural.

On Plate XXVII., Fig. *d*, I give a drawing of a wheel-made pitcher from the lower ditch, found at a depth of 1·50 m.; it is of rather fine yellow clay, with a handle. The height is 7 cm., the width of the mouth 6½ cm., and the thickness of the clay 3 mm. The ground is dark blue. Besides a broad violet band round the neck, on which white leaves are drawn, and another narrower one near the

foot, the painting is in glossy white, and consists of a band
on the upper rim, a narrower one below the upper violet
band, pretty spirals on the body and a narrow border
round the foot. The inside is not painted. The handle is
restored.

I remark here, that among the prehistoric pottery found
at Thera, under three strata of pumice-stone and volcanic
ashes, and which are now preserved in the French School at
Athens, there may also be seen several vases, of which the

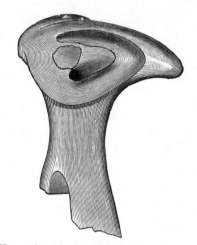

No. 22.—Ram's head in clay.   Size 2 : 3.   Depth 1 m.

ornamentation is executed in white on a dark ground.
Fragments of vases with spirals are exceedingly common,
at Tiryns as well as in Mycenæ.*

I give further on Plate XXVI., Fig. *d*, the representation of a fragment from the same depth of a wheel-made
vase of coarse yellow clay, 6–7 mm. thick. The painting
is also in violet colour, and glossy white on dark-blue
ground. The inside is not painted.

---

* Schliemann, *Mycenæ*, p. 71, No. 86; Pl. VIII. Nos. 30, 34;
Pl. XII. No. 58; Pl. XIII. No. 64; Pl. XIV. No. 70; Pl. XV.,
Nos. 73, 75.

I would further mention the rim-fragment of a wheel-made bowl, found at a depth of 1·50 m. of fine reddish clay, 5 mm. thick. The inside is painted in red, the outside in dark brown on a bright-red ground. On the rim is a narrow, and beneath this, on the inside, a wider band, on which two interlacing serpentine lines are drawn in glossy white.

The accompanying woodcut, No. 22, shows an object found about 1 m. deep, of brown clay, in the form of a ram's head, of which the eye has been made separately and attached when the clay was still soft

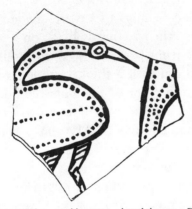

No. 23.—Fragment of a vase with a swan.   Actual size 2 : 3.   Depth 1·50 m.

This object is apparently the fragment of a handle, and seems to have been first painted with black and afterwards with glossy white colour.

### 3. VASE PAINTINGS, WITH REPRESENTATIONS OF BIRDS OR STAGS.

The fragment depicted on Plate XX., Fig. *d*, was found 2 m. deep, and is from the upper part of a large wheel-made vase of light-yellow clay, 11 mm. thick. The painting is dull black on light-yellow ground; the rim is quite covered with colour. Below this there was a row of

water-birds in profile to the right. To the left is the
head of a bird with a broad bill; to the right, the tail
and head of another. The inside is monochromed in
black.

On Plate XXIII., Fig. *b*, is a fragment from the same
depth of a smaller wheel-made vase of red clay, 6 mm.
thick. The painting is executed with brown lacquer on
a red ground. Under a broad band is seen a row of
swans; to the right the upper part of one in profile to
the right, and to the left the head of another looking
back.

On another fragment shown in No. 23, found at a depth
of 1·50 m., which belongs to a wheel-made vase of reddish
clay, 4 mm. thick, the painting is black on a yellow ground;
to the left is the front part of a swan in profile to the right.
The figure is drawn with a thick outline, inside which is a
row of dots; another dotted line cuts the body across. To
the right we observe the tail of another bird in front. I
may observe that I found at Mycenæ a piece of pottery
with a very similar drawing of a swan,* which is placed in
the Mycenæan Museum at Athens.

The same museum contains a fragment of a prehistoric
vase found in a grave at Spata, with a representation of a
swan, but of somewhat different form.

On another fragment of a wheel-made vessel found at a
depth of 1·50 m., made of greyish-yellow clay, 8 mm. thick,
may be seen the hind parts and the feet of a bird turned to
the right.

The fragment on Plate XX., Fig. *c*, is of a wheel-
turned vessel of light-yellow clay, 7 mm. thick. On the
inside it is red, outside on the light-yellow ground the
painting is in red-brown; below a broad band is represented a stag in profile to the right, with his head turned
back, and with huge horns, the ends terminating in spirals.

---

* Schliemann's *Mycenæ*, Pl. VIII. No. 33.

## 4. VASE PAINTINGS, REPRESENTING MARINE ANIMALS.

The representation on Plate XXII., Fig. *b*, shows a fragment of the upper part of a wheel-made vessel of medium size, found at a depth of 1 m., made of reddish-clay, 6 mm. thick.

The painting is dark brown, on a reddish ground. Beneath the coloured rim runs a wide zone, which is bordered below with a brown band. In the intervening space we see a fantastic ornament, apparently designed from a sea-animal, which must have been a great favourite of the

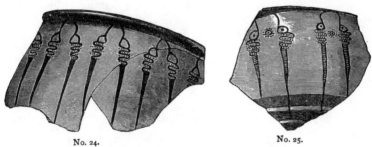

No. 24.                    No. 25.

Vase fragments, with representation of the purple shell (murex) very common in Mycenæ, and often found in Tiryns.

ancient Tirynthians and Mycenæans, since it is frequently found among the ruins of both these towns. The inside is monochrome black.

In the annexed woodcuts, Nos. 24 and 25, reprinted from *Mycenæ*, p. 138, I represent two fragments of vases, with this decoration, which is extremely common on Mycenæan pottery, and also frequent in Tiryns. Vases ornamented with this pattern are always wheel-made, and usually of yellow clay, about 5 mm. thick.

The painting, in red colour on yellow ground, shows a very slender ornament, much like that shown on Plate XXII., Fig. *b*. It represents the purple shell (murex); it likewise is very common at Ialysos,* Spata,† and Knossos.‡ The same ornament is to be seen on a vase-fragment from Eleusis,§ and on another from a grave at Nauplia.‖ It is also found on the vases No. 2078 and No. 2081 in the National Museum at Athens, which were discovered in Attica, the exact place not specified.

## 5. Vase Paintings, with Spiral Ornamentation.

As Sophus Müller remarks,¶ the spiral pattern may have been borrowed from a rolled-up wire. "The drawing was then carried out on a flat surface, and developed itself in various ways. But the fact, that the spirals are often formed of double lines, and are carried on unbroken from the centre of the spiral roll, suggests to us the origin of the pattern. The circular ornamentation, on the other hand, may have arisen from works in bone, wood, and similar soft metals.

"The central point in the circle reminds us that it arose from the use of the compasses, and the further development of the motive rests on its connection with semicircles, lines, and bands."

The spiral ornament so abundantly used in Tiryns and Mycenæ, "appears," as Sophus Müller says,** "also very commonly in Egypt, both in the ornamentation of pottery and other objects,†† which were, in many cases, booty from

---

* Albert Dumont et Jules Chaplain, *Les Céramiques de la Grèce propre* (Paris, 1881), Pl. III. 5, 6.            † *Op. cit.* p. 66.

‡ *Op. cit.* p. 66.            § *Gazette archéologique*, 1879, p. 202.

‖ This last fragment is in the Mycenæan Museum at Athens.

¶ Sophus Müller, *Ursprung und erste Entwickelung der europäischen Bronzecultur.* German translation by Miss J. Mestorf, 1882, p. 338.

** *Ibid.*, p. 333.

†† *E.g.* Rosellini, *op. cit.* I. 100, 102, 158, 159; II. 70, 87; III. 17; Lepsius, *Denkmäler*, VII. Pl. 187 *d*; Prisse d'Avennes, *Histoire de l'art égyptien, op. cit.*

the Phœnicians and other Oriental people; it also occurs in architectural decoration, for instance, in the Necropolis at Thebes, from the last half of the second millennium before Christ.

"Here, exactly as in Mycenæ, the spirals are occasionally free and at other times connected in the centre, or they wind about a circular *cartouche* or a rosette; sometimes, as in the ceiling-ornament of Orchomenos,* a flower is set in at the point where the line diverges from the spiral." Sophus Müller † further remarks: "In Phœnicia the spiral ornament is universal on a certain class of antiquities,‡ and we also find it on those Greek islands which were colonized by Phœnicians. § The origin of the spiral ornament must, therefore, be sought for far from Greece, in the Egypto-Phœnician domains. And, further, we find the spiral ornament on the monuments at almost all points which were touched by Phœnician influence,—on the island of Gozo, near Malta, in South Italy, in Sardinia, and in the East, in the Caucasus, and everywhere in circumstances indicating great antiquity, and yet never with objects which can be attributed with certainty to the Bronze Age proper. We are therefore obliged to conclude, that in all these places the appearance of the spiral ornament points to Phœnician influence."

I may remark that we find the spiral ornament very commonly in the island of Malta, which for many centuries

---

* Schliemann, *Orchomenos* (Leipzig, 1881).

† Sophus Müller, *op. cit.* p. 339.

‡ *E.g.* Renan, *op. cit.* p. 161; *Description de l'Egypte*, V., Pl. 79–83 and 89; Leemanns, *Aegyptische Monumente*, I., Pl. 30.

§ Very characteristic is the appearance of the spiral ornament on pottery at Rhodes (Salzmann, *Camirus*, Plates 25, 26). The Greeks first occupied this island sixty years after the Doric invasion, but we cannot admit that, at that remote antiquity, the spiral ornament belonged to the Greek style. There is therefore no other alternative but to ascribe these vessels to a still more distant age, and to attribute them to the Phœnicians, who then owned colonies in Rhodes.

was settled by Phœnicians ; for instance, on a stelé in the Cesnola Collection at New York,* on a capital from Kition,† on a vase-handle from Amathus,‡ and on two shields.§ Also, in the province of Carthage, on a capital of Djezza,|| and on stelæ from Carthage itself. ¶

The most interesting and remarkable fact is, however, that we very often meet the spirals on the gold-work of the second, or burnt town of Troy.** This fact proves to us that, already while Troy flourished, the Phœnician merchants navigated the Ægean Sea and carried merchandise to the shores of the Hellespont, and that therefore the ruins of Troy can hardly claim the extreme antiquity which many of the learned attribute to them. Thus, for example, Helbig †† thinks that the ruins of Hissarlik should be placed considerably before the fourteenth century B.C., whilst Dumont ‡‡ considers them even much older than the sixteenth century B.C. In fact, the Trojan treasures of gold ornaments, which are now universally supposed to be of Phœnician origin, will hardly allow us to attribute the catastrophe of the second, or burnt city of Troy, to a remoter age than about 1200 B.C., and this date is confirmed by all traditions of antiquity.

In the first place, I would draw the reader's attention to the border fragment of a large wheel-made vase

---

* Georges Perrot et Charles Chipiez, *Histoire de l'Art dans l'Antiquité*, (Paris, 1881), III , p. 217, No. 152.

† *Ibid.* p. 264, No. 198.　　　　　　‡ *Ibid.* p. 282, No. 213.

§ *Ibid.* pp. 870, 871, Nos. 638, 639.

|| *Ibid.* p. 312, No. 235.

¶ *Ibid.* p. 52, No 14; p. 54, No. 16.

** Schliemann, *Ilios*, p. 460, Nos. 694–704 ; p. 462, Nos 752–764 ; p. 488, Nos. 834, 835 ; p. 489, Nos. 836–838, 845, 848–850 ; p. 490, No. 853 , p. 495, Nos. 873, 874 ; p. 501, Nos. 906, 907, 909.

†† W. Helbig, *Das Homerische Epos aus den Denkmälern erläutert*, p. 37.

‡‡ Albert Dumont et Jules Chaplain, *Les Céramiques de la Grèce propre* (Paris, 1881), p. 75.

(Plate XXII., Fig. *d* ) of fine grey clay, 6 mm. thick, with brown painting on a light-yellow ground. Between the somewhat projecting rim, and three parallel horizontal lines round the body of the vessel, there is a broad band of figures like the Greek letter lambda, which run out on the left side into spirals. The inside is monochrome black : found at a depth of 1 m.

Further, I mention a hand-made vessel of green clay, 7 mm. thick, found at a depth of 2 m. The painting is executed with very common black colour, and consists of a band at the rim and two lines on the body, of which the upper one forms three roughly-drawn spirals; the back side is broken, and the form of the vessel can, therefore, not well be determined. It had two handles.

Also a fragment found 1·50 m. deep, of a wheel-made vase, of reddish clay, 3 mm. thick, coated with brownish-yellow, and painted in red. Above a band of eight fine lines we see a large spiral, in the centre of which is a rosette.

Plate XXVI., Fig. *c*, represents a fragment, from about the same depth, of the upper part and handle of a small basin of reddish clay, 3 mm. thick. The painting is red on a light-yellow ground. The rim is finely coloured, and we see below this a band of interlacing and spiral lines.

I further mention a fragment of the shoulder of a wheel-turned vase of reddish clay, 6 mm. thick, with black painting on a light ground; depth 1 m. The neck is all coloured, and surrounded by a broad line; beneath are large spirals.

Similar spirals are to be seen on two fragments of smaller bowls in red and black colours.

Next, I wish to mention a fragment, found 1·50 m. deep, of a deep, wheel-turned bowl of fine yellow clay, 3 mm. thick. The painting is dark brown on a yellow ground; the rim is brought out by a line. Beneath there is a broad border marked off by one broad line and several paler-coloured ones, and decorated with spirals twisting to the left. In the centre of each spiral is a large circle, filled up by parallel lines which cross each other. Each spiral is joined to the next by three waved lines.

Again, the fragment, found 1·50 m. deep, of a wheel-made vase of light-brown somewhat coarse clay, 4 mm. thick, with brown painting on a paler ground. On the inside we see several concentric circles, and a broad band below the rim. On the outside a broad frieze-like zone is marked off by three lines, and within it is repeated a peculiar spiral ornament winding to the left.

I give on Plate XXVI., Fig. *f*, the fragment of the upper part of a small hand-made vessel, found 1 m. deep, of reddish clay, 3 mm. thick, with dark-brown painting. Beneath the rim, which is coloured over, ran a band of spirals, in which a *horizontally pierced excrescence* is fixed.

I mention further a fragment from the same depth of a wheel-made globular vessel of reddish clay, 3 mm. thick, with dark-brown painting, which likewise has a *horizontally perforated excrescence* in an ornament of scales. These are the only two pieces of pottery found in the palace of Tiryns in which the horizontally pierced excrescences occur.

In the oldest settlement of Tiryns,* as also in Troy,† there appear only vases with *perpendicularly perforated excrescences. Horizontally perforated excrescences* occur, on the other hand, on a vase of the Stone Age found in the lake-dwellings at Estavayer ;‡ on four vessels found in French dolmens, and preserved in the Museum of Saint-Germain-en-Laye ; on some fragments of vases in the same Museum; on vessels in the Egyptian collection

---

* Cf. above, pp 58-9, Nos. 1, 2.

† Schliemann, *Ilios*, pp. 214, 215, Nos. 23–25 ; pp. 220, 222, Nos. 44·46; pp. 354–369, Nos. 251–306.

‡ Ferd. Keller, *Etablissements lacustres* (Zurich, 1866), Pl. XVIII. No. 5 ; described by Dr. Victor Gross.

in the British Museum; on two vases of the Stone Age, in the museum at Copenhagen; * on various vases of the collection of old German antiquities in the British Museum; on one from Cyprus, in the South Kensington Museum; on some vases found in the prehistoric necropolis on the island of Antiparos; † on several vases from the excavations at Pilin,‡ in Hungary; and on many vases in the Museum at Schwerin.

The Märkische Provinzial Museum, in Berlin, contains a number of such vases, with horizontal ridges for suspension. Some beautiful examples are also to be seen in the collection of Professor Rudolf Virchow, at Berlin. Moreover Consul Frank Calvert and I in our joint excavations made in the tumulus of Hanai Tepeh,§ in the plains of Troy, found vessels with horizontal tubular holes only.

### 6. POTTERY OF VARIOUS KINDS.

Plate XXII., Fig. *a*, represents a fragment, found only 0·30 m. deep, of the upper part of a wheel-made small bowl, made of reddish clay, 3 mm. thick, with a shining yellow surface and brown painting. Round the rim we see a fine line, and on the outside a fantastic ornament, of which the lower half reminds us of an Ionic pillar. On terra-cotta goblets in Attica we see a similar ornament, together with the purple-fish (murex). We see it also

---

* J. J. A. Worsaae, *Nordiske Oldsager* (1859), Pl. XIX. Nos. 95, 98; Pl. XX. No. 99.

† J. Theodore Bent, "Researches among the Cyclades," in *The Journal of Hellenic Studies*, V., 1884, p. 55, No. 11.

‡ Joseph Hampel, *Catalogue de l'Exposition préhistorique des Musées de province et des collections particulières de la Hongrie* (Budapest, 1876), p. 130, Fig. 130, and p. 41, Fig. 28; *Antiquités préhistoriques de la Hongrie* (Gran, 1877), Pl. XVIII. Figs. 2, 5, 8, 9, 11, 12; Pl. XIX. Fig. 11; Pl. XX. Figs. 4, 8, 19; Pl. XXI. Fig. 9; Pl. XXII. Figs. 2, 3.

§ Schliemann, *Ilios*, p. 710, Nos. 1546, 1547; p. 715, No. 1560.

on two sepulchral stelæ of Carthage,* and on a Phœnician vase. †

At a depth of about ½ m. from the surface were found several fragments of a large unpainted hand-made vessel, of red clay, 10 mm. thick. The accompanying woodcut (No. 26) shows these fragments united. The vessel is of cylindrical form, about 40 cm. in diameter; the rim of the bottom projects 13 mm., the upper rim 25 mm. The outside is badly polished. On the surface of the bottom, from the edge to the central point, we see concentric circles of holes, 6–7 mm. deep and 6–10 mm. apart, shaped like inverted cones, which were made while the

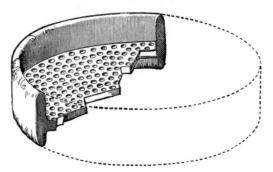

No. 26.—Vessel for baking cakes.   Size 1:6.   Depth 0·50 m.

clay was still soft. None of these holes penetrates the thickness of the clay. On the bottom, outside, we see strong marks of burning. Beyond all doubt, therefore, tne vessel was used as a pan, probably for baking cakes, on which the shape of the holes would then be produced in relief. Of similar but somewhat smaller terra-cotta pans, with holes of the same form, many fragments were found. The same kind of pan is very common in Mycenæ, but, as far as I know, it does not occur elsewhere.

---

* Georges Perrot et Charles Chipiez, *Histoire de l'Art dans l'antiquité* (Paris, 1884), Vol. III. p. 52, No. 14 ; p. 54, No. 16.
 † *Ibid.* Vol. III. p. 74.

In the following woodcut, No. 27, and Plate XXI., Fig. *f*, I give a representation of a form of terra-cotta goblet, very commonly used in Tiryns and Mycenæ.

Most goblets of this kind are of light-yellow, badly-cleaned clay, made on the wheel, unpolished and unpainted; in many cases, however, they are well polished and covered with a lustrous varnish, generally red, but in a few cases black. Very numerous, too, are those with a lustrous light-yellow ground, painted with brown parallel horizontal bands. As before stated (p. 73), there are found in the

No. 27.—Goblet.   Size 1:2.

deepest layers of *débris* fragments of unpainted and un-polished goblets of greenish clay, which appear to be the oldest.

All have one handle, in rare cases two. In the commonest form the foot is flat, in those of better workmanship it is concave. There are often found, too, fragments of such goblets, of finely cleaned yellow clay, well polished, of which the outside is not painted, while on the inside there are parallel bands of red. I have already (pp. 73, 74) given a list of those places where goblets of a similar form have hitherto been found, and refer the reader to it.

No. 28 represents a large vase found near the surface.

It is wheel-made, of red clay, 9 mm. thick, and has two handles. The height of it is 23½ cm.; the width of the orifice 20 cm. It is painted inside and outside uniformly red, only on the rim, between two white lines, we see two violet parallel lines. This form of vase does not again appear, and has never been found elsewhere.

Further, on Plate XXIV., Fig. c, is represented a wheel-made vase, found at a depth of 1·50 m. It has two handles, and a curved rim. It is made of fine, well-polished grey clay, 4 mm. thick. Its height is 9, the width of its

No. 28.—Large vase, Size 1:6. Depth circa 0·50 m.

orifice 15 cm. The painting, which is in lustrous yellow varnish, consists of a line on the external rim, a second round the neck, a band of three lines round the body, and a broad line round the foot. The shining yellow colour gives it an appearance as though it were gilded.

On Plate XXVI., Fig. e, I represent the fragment of a wheel-made mug, of finely cleaned grey clay, 6 mm. thick. The painting is brown, on a light-yellow ground. Between two stripes on the edge there is an ornament of crossing lines. The whole of the lower part is uniformly coloured. The inside is of monochrome grey colour.

Further, in the accompanying woodcut (No. 29) I show a small wheel-made jug, with a broken handle over the orifice, which is 4½ cm. wide. It was found close to the surface. Its height, without the handle, is 10 cm., the thickness of the clay 3 mm.

The jug is of fine bluish-grey clay, well polished, and has a spout projecting from the body. The painting is black, and consists of two broad bands round the body and thirteen lines round the neck. Jugs of precisely the same form frequently occur in Mycenæ and Troy.* Six similar jugs found in graves at Ialysos are in the British Museum; another specimen, which was found in the lowest layers of

No. 29.—Jug with spout.  Size 1 : 2.  Depth about 0·50 m.

*débris* in the Acropolis of Athens, is in the Acropolis Museum; but this latter has the handle on the neck.

No. 30 represents a wheel-made jug, found at a depth of 1·50 m., of fine greyish-yellow clay, 3 mm. thick, without painting. It has a sieve-like spout; a piece is broken from the neck. Three similar jugs, which come from Thera,† are to be seen in the small collection of the French School at Athens.

---

* Schliemann, *Ilios*, p. 407, No. 446.

† Albert Dumont et Jules Chaplain, *Les Céramiques de la Grèce propre*, pp. 33-4.

The British Museum possesses ten similar jugs, having spouts with strainers, of which nine come from tombs at Ialysos, and one from a tomb in Kameiros; eight of the former are tripods.

The next woodcut, No. 31, exhibits a small hand-made jug, found 1 m. deep, of finely cleaned yellow clay, 5 mm. thick, with black painting on a pale under-ground. Round the neck is a horizontal stripe, from which three bands—two of six and one of five vertical lines—run down the sides. The handle is broken off.

No. 30.—Jug with sieve-like spout.        No. 31.—Jug. Size 2 : 3. Depth 1 m.
Size 1 : 2. Depth 1·50 m.

Jugs of similar form and decoration are found both in Mycenæ * and in the tombs at Nauplia, and may be seen in the Mycenæan Museum at Athens. Jugs of the same form were also found in the lowest layers of *débris* on the Acropolis of Athens, and are exhibited in the Acropolis Museum.

No. 32 is a small hand-made one-handled mug, with

---

* Schliemann, *Mycenæ*, p. 66, No. 27.

a convex bottom.  It was found close to the surface, and consists of fine yellow clay.  The painting is black in places, where it is laid on thick, and dark brown, where it is thinner.  The rim is decorated with a stripe, which is continued on each side of the handle; round the neck and body of the vase are three horizontal bands.

I would further mention a rim-fragment found at a depth of 1·50 m.; it belongs to a wheel-made vase of reddish clay, 3 mm. thick, with brown painting on light-red ground.  The straight projecting edge is covered by a

No. 32.—Mug.  Almost actual size.  Depth 0·50 m.

band of two parallel lines, the space between them being filled with zigzag lines, which cross each other.  The body of the vase as well as the inside seem to have been brown.  There was found, besides, another fragment of a similar vase.

The accompanying cut, No. 33, shows a fragment, found 2 m. deep, of the hollow brim of a wheel-made vessel of reddish clay, 4 mm. thick, with reddish-brown painting on a light-red ground.  On the upper surface there are groups each of eight oblique lines.  Outside is a checker ornament.

The next woodcut, No. 34, shows the neck of a wheel-made vase, found 1·50 m. deep, of finely-cleaned reddish clay, 3 mm. thick. The painting is dark red on a light-red ground. The rim is bent out, the mouth is trefoil-

No. 33.—Fragment of a vessel. Size 1:2.
Depth 2 mm.

No. 34.—Neck of vase. Size 1:3.
Depth about 1·50 m.

shaped. To the broad band round the rim succeed four parallel horizontal bands; and next a broad stripe, in which we see a circle of figures resembling the letter Z. Beneath this come six horizontal parallel lines, and then a band

No. 35.—Upper part of a pitcher. Size 1:2. Depth 1·50 m.

decorated with straight and oblique lines, of which only a small part is preserved. The inside is not painted.

The next woodcut, No. 35, represents the upper portion of a wheel-made pitcher, found at a depth of 1·50 m., of reddish clay, 3 mm. thick. It has a yellow coating and is painted brown. There is a band on the rim and two below the neck, the lowest of which consists of a series of signs like **W** and **N** in form.

I further mention the fragment, found at a depth of 1 m., of a wheel-made bowl of red clay, 4 mm. thick, with red painting on light-red ground. The brim is coloured over. Below, we see a band of six lines, of which the upper and lower are strongly marked. In the middle is a band composed of signs resembling the letter **N**. Rows of exactly similar signs often occur on pottery found by me at Mycenæ.* The same signs are seen on fragments of vases from the prehistoric tombs at Nauplia, which are in the Mycenæan Museum, as well as on two fragments found in the lowest layers of *débris* on the Acropolis of Athens, which are in the Acropolis Museum.

I show on Plate XXVI., Fig. *b*, the lower part of a wheel-made vessel of cylindrical form of reddish-yellow clay, 3 mm. thick, found at a depth of 1·50 m. Six bands follow each other on pale-yellow ground. The lowest shows small ascending triangles in red colour; then follows a band of five fine red lines, and above this a broad violet band; the fourth band has two rows of dots between two double lines in red. Above, is a second violet band, succeeded by a stripe of red lines. The inside is red-brown. This fragment is remarkable for its fine painting.

On Plate XXVII., Fig. *a*, I place before the reader the remains, collected from a depth of 1·50 m., of a large wheel-made vase of red clay, 6 mm. thick. There are thirty fragments which fit together. The painting is shining red on a yellow ground. The rim of the vessel as well as the handle are covered with colour; on the broad face of the handle are club-shaped marks. The whole outside is covered with a network of twisted double lines, and the

---

* Schliemann, *Mycenæ*, Pl. IX. No. 38 ; Pl. XIII. No. 62.

interstices are filled with a fish-bone ornament. The inside
is not painted. This is, beyond doubt, the most beautiful of all the vase decorations found by me, whether at
Mycenæ or Tiryns. There was found, however, in the
prehistoric graves of Nauplia another specimen of a similar
decoration, which may be seen in the Mycenæan Museum.
Dr. Fabricius reminds me that on an ivory disc from Spata,
in the Mycenæan Museum, the same double-curved lines
occur, twisted together and superposed in a similar manner,
and that the same kind of ornament may also be seen
on a terra-cotta vessel dug up by Minos Kalokairinos at
Knossos in Crete.

No. 36.—Fragment of vase.        No. 37.—Fragment of vase.  Size 1 : 3.  Depth 1·50 m.
Size 1 : 2.  Depth not given.

The next woodcut, No. 36, represents a fragment of a
very similar wheel-made vase, of red clay, 6 mm. thick,
which on a yellow ground has an ornament like the Greek
letter Є.

The subject of the following woodcut, No. 37, also
deserves mention ; a fragment of a wheel-made vase, from
the depth 1·50 m., of yellow clay, 6 mm. thick, with
brown painting on yellow ground. One can see on this,
above three broad bands, an ornament of arched lines, with
stars between.

On Plate XXII., Fig. c, I show a fragment from the
same depth of a wheel-made vase of red clay, 5 mm. thick,

with dark-brown painting on light-yellow ground. Round the rim is a broad band, to which two bands round the body correspond. The space between is filled with sweeping lines and concentric circles. The inside is monochrome black. Of this vase many fragments were found.

At Plate XIX., Fig. *c*, I show the side fragment of a wheel-made vase of reddish clay, 4 mm. thick, which is remarkable for its *vertically perforated* excrescence in the form of a nipple, on which I lay particular stress. Doubtless the vase had a similar vertically pierced excrescence on the other side of the body. The painting is brown, on a

No. 38.—Fragment of vase. Size 2 : 3. Depth 1 m.

light-red ground. Beneath the nipple are two broad bands, edged on each side by bands of small arches, in each of which is a dot. Round the nipple, the point of which was coloured, are three concentric circles of dotted lines. To the left, the commencement of two intersecting zigzag lines with dots. A vase with similarly painted nipples occurred in the fifth grave at Mycenæ.*

In the next woodcut, No. 38, I represent a border piece of a large wheel-made bowl of reddish clay, finely cleaned, 4 mm. thick. The painting is dark red on light-red ground. The projecting rim is painted. Between

---

* Schliemann, *Mycenæ*, p. 293.

a horizontal band just below the rim, and another round the
body, consisting of three strongly marked and four finer
lines, we see above and below a connected ornament of
four concentric semicircles, joined by a vertical line of
twelve dots. To the right and left are fish-bone ornaments,
to which a decoration, apparently of concentric semicircles,
was opposed below. The inside is painted light red.
Found 1 m. deep.

On Plate XVII., Fig. c, I represent the border of a
wheel-made vase, found near the surface, of greyish-yellow
clay, badly cleaned, 9 mm. thick. The more developed
decoration of this example is much rubbed; however, the
outlines, which were partly scratched in, are still recog-
nizable. On the cylinder-shaped edge there was represented
a footrace of armed warriors moving to the left. One figure
is completely preserved; of a second, the back leg and the
right hand remain. Of the complete figure the left leg is
boldly advanced, while the right is raised in the air behind.
On the left arm the warrior carries the great round shield;
on his head, the helmet with a large crest. The right hand
is stretched far behind. The whole body seems to have
been painted brown. The shield was violet, with a white
circle on the edge, and white rays, like the spokes of a
wheel. To the right of the running warrior the upper part
of a woman's body remains, unfortunately much injured,
yet apparently we can distinguish the face, as turned
towards the running warrior. In any case, the woman
was clothed. On the shoulder of the vase, beneath the
rim, there was a band of fishes. The whole decoration
testifies to considerable artistic power. The impetuosity
of the race could scarcely be rendered more faithfully to
nature, with such simple means. It is, in fact, very remarkable that we find this fragment among very primitive
pottery, and it must have been in some way brought here
from some other place. M. Achilles Postolaccas calls my
attention to the likeness between the heads of Pallas, on

the Athenian tetradrachmæ of the pre-Periclean age, and that of the racing warrior.

I show further, in the woodcut above, No. 39, the fragment found 1·50 m. deep, of a large hand-made jug with handle, of light-coloured clay, 5 mm. thick. The shoulder-piece is varnished black, the body is decorated with narrow brown horizontal stripes on a yellowish ground. Between the second and third stripes from above is a horizontal band of wedge-shaped black marks. The ridged handle is ornamented with four bands of horizontal lines. The inside is roughly painted black.

No. 39.—Fragment of vase.  Size 1 : 3.
Depth 1·50 m.

No. 40.—Fragment of vase.  Size 1 : 3.
Depth 1·50 m.

The next woodcut (No. 40) represents a fragment with a handle, from about the same depth, of a wheel-made vase, of light-yellow clay, 4 mm. thick. The outer edge is black ; beneath this we see, on a yellow ground, a horizontal border of squares standing on one of their angles, and filled in with crossed hatchings, and with wedges between. Below are two black bands. The inside is painted black.

## 7. POTTERY WITH ARCHITECTURAL DESIGNS.

We come now to a peculiar group of pottery, which includes only vessels with wide orifices. The decoration

of the outside has a peculiar style, which we may call architectural. Round the body of the vases go two horizontal
stripes, to which a third on the upper border corresponds.

The space between these bands is filled with a system
of ornaments, consisting of vertical, that is supporting, and
of rounded, that is of filling in members, corresponding to
the metopes and triglyphs of the Doric style of architecture; and in like manner may be seen the division of the
ornaments on the friezes. Of this kind I found numerous
specimens among the pottery of Tiryns. I shall content

No. 41.—Fragment of vase.  Size 1:2.          No. 42.— Fragment of vase.  Size 1:3.
Found near the surface.                                  Found close to the surface.

myself with representing a few. I wish particularly to
observe, that also on the Mycenæan vases the division of
the zones by a supporting decoration (*triglyph*) and a
filling in decoration (*metope*), as above mentioned, frequently occurs (cf *e.g. Mycenæ*, Plate XI., No. 53;
Plate XII., No. 59; Plate XIV., Nos. 68, 69; and page 71,
No. 86).

The woodcut No. 41 shows a fragment of a large
wheel-made vessel, found near the surface, of reddish-
yellow clay, 7 mm. thick, with red-brown painting, which,
where the colour is laid on thick, looks black. Round

the rim is one, round the body, two horizontal bands, between which we see alternate vertical stripes and spiral ornaments. The vertical bands contain two rows each of six lines, bound together by horizontal zigzag-lines. The inside is painted plain black. The next picture, No. 42, shows a piece, found close to the surface, of a large wheel-made vase of finely cleaned, light-yellow clay, 7 mm. thick. The painting is reddish-brown on light-yellow ground. Below the painted rim we see two vertical stripes of seven lines each, and between them a vertical row of squares standing on one of their angles, filled in with crossed lines. Attached to the outside are four concentric semicircles surrounded with a line of dots.

I must not omit a fragment found at a depth of 1·50 m. of a wheel-made vase with a handle, of greyish-yellow clay, 5 mm. thick. The painting is black on a light ground; round the rim there is a broad horizontal band, which is connected with the two horizontal bands round the body by vertical stripes of ten lines each, with stripes of small arches on the outside. The inside is plain black. We see a similar decoration on a fragment from the same depth of a wheel-made vase of finely cleaned reddish clay, 5 mm. thick, with brown painting. Round the rim and body are broad horizontal stripes, connected by perpendicular bands of six or five lines each, to the outer borders of which zigzag lines are appended. The inside is varnished dark brown.

We recognize a similar ornament in the following engraving, No. 43, of a fragment from the same depth, of a wheel-made vase, of light-yellow clay, 6 mm. thick, with dark-brown painting. Round the rim is one, on the body are two, horizontal bands connected by a vertical one. The latter consists of two bands of three lines each; the space between them is filled with five vertical rows of pear-shaped marks; on the outer border of each of the two bands is appended a sort of grape ornament. In the field

to the left is a rosette.    An exactly similar pattern is seen
on another fragment, and we see it repeated identically on
two vase fragments from the lowest strata of the Acropolis

No. 43.—Fragment of Vase.   Size about 2 : 3.   Depth 1·50 m.

of Athens, which are exhibited in the Acropolis Museum.

In the next cut, No. 44, I show a fragment from a depth
of 1 m. under the surface of the ground, of a wheel-made

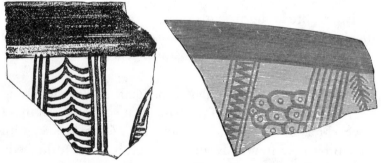

No. 44.—Fragment of vase.   Size about 2 : 3.          No. 45.—Fragment of vase.   Size about 1 : 2.
Depth 1 m.                                    Depth 1 m.

vase of fine reddish clay, 4 mm. thick, with dark-brown
painting.   It has a broad marginal border, from which
descend two vertical stripes, each of three lines; the space

between them is filled up by a fish-bone ornament. The inside is painted brown.

The engraving, No. 45, represents a fragment of a wheel-made vase of fine clay, 4 mm. thick. The painting is red on a reddish ground. Round the rim is a broad horizontal red stripe. Beneath this, two vertical bands, of which one is formed of two stripes, each of two lines, joined by a zigzag ornament, the other of seven lines. These two vertical stripes are connected by a grape ornament. On the right is represented a pine-branch. The inside is simple red.

I also found a fragment of a wheel-made vase, from a depth of 1·50 m., of fine yellow clay, 4 mm. thick. The painting is black on yellow ground. The ornamentation consists of perpendicular bands of two double lines, the internal border of which is decorated with a row of little arches. The outer border is ornamented on each side with a bow-shaped decoration. The inside is varnished black.

Further, a fragment of a wheel-made vessel of coarse yellow clay, 4 mm. thick, with black painting on yellow ground, found at the same depth. The ornamentation again consists of two vertical bands, the middle part of which is filled with an ornament of flexuous lines. The external borders of the bands are decorated with rows of little arches. I mention finally a fragment from the same depth of a wheel-made vase of fine red clay with brown painting on light-yellow ground. Here, too, we see two vertical bands, between which the space is filled with horizontal rows of arched lines. The outside borders of the bands are again ornamented with rows of little arches. The inside is painted plain black.

## 8. Vases with Various Ornamentation.

The next woodcut, No. 46, shows two pieces from a depth of 1·50 m. of a large wheel-made vase with a wide orifice. The clay is yellow and 8 mm. thick ; the painting reddish-brown on a yellow ground. Below the rim of the vessel we see a horizontal band, and parallel to this, three on the body. The intervening space is filled with alternate upright and depending grape ornaments, each of which has ten rows of berries. The inside is painted yellow. A similar ornamentation we see on two vases, one of which was found in Cyprus,* the other in Ialysos on Rhodes.†

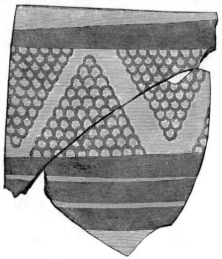

No. 46.—Fragment of vase.   Size about 1 : 2.   Depth 1·50 m.

In the following woodcut, No. 47, I show a fragment from the same depth of a small wheel-made vase of pale-yellow clay, 4 mm. thick. The opening is large, the painting reddish-brown on light ground. The brim is decorated with one, the body with two horizontal stripes, between which are upright painted semicircles, with a straight line on the side of their span. The inside is coloured simply brown.

---

* Louis Palma di Cesnola ; *Cyprus*, London, 1877, p. 247.

† Albert Dumont et Jules Chaplain, *Les Céramiques de la Grèce propre*, Pl. III. No. 15.

In the Fig. No. 48, I show a small perfect wheel-made vase, found at a depth of 1 m. It has two handles, and is of fine yellow clay, with red painting. The whole vessel is ornamented on the outside with horizontal rings. On the shoulder is a band of eleven lines. The lower border of

No. 47.—Fragment of vase. Size about 1 : 2. Depth 1 m.     No. 48.—Vase. Size about 1 : 2.
Depth 1 m.

this band is lined with a row of little arches, to which corresponds a row of inverted arches on the upper border of the broad band round the body; the inside is mono-chrome red.

The following woodcut, No. 49, represents a vase of

No. 49.—Vase. Size about 1 : 3. Depth 1 m.

very fine reddish clay, which was originally intended for suspension by its three upright shoulder-handles. In the neck there is a small breakage. The decoration is red on light-red ground. The rim is ornamented with four bands of sixteen strokes each. The outside has six horizontal bands. Between the second and third of these bands is a stripe of upright zigzag lines; between the fourth and fifth, and the fifth and sixth, are two bands, each of six parallel horizontal lines. The foot is comparatively small; the inside red.

The next woodcut, No. 50, shows a wheel-made vessel of fine yellow clay, 4 mm. thick, with red painting. The vessel is broken on one side, and had apparently two handles, of which only one, seen in the picture, remains. Between a broad horizontal stripe round the border and a narrow one round the foot, one sees two horizontal bands, of which the upper one is formed by a thick waved line,

No. 50.—Vessel. Size 2 : 3. Depth not stated.    No. 51.—Vessel. Size 1 : 3. Depth 1 m

the lower one by seven parallel horizontal lines. The handle is painted; the inside is painted in light red.

Further, I show in the annexed woodcut, No. 51, a wheel-made vessel with one handle, of reddish clay, 3 mm. thick, with red painting. The rim, the handle as well as the whole lower part, are red. Round the body we see the horizontal yellow stripe of the clay-solution in which the vessel was dipped before being painted. Almost in the middle of the body is a breast-shaped projection, which probably was repeated on the opposite side, which is broken. The inner side is varnished red, only at the bottom there is a circle of a lighter colour.

I would also mention another wheel-made vessel, with

one handle, found at the same depth.   It is of fine yellow
clay, 3 mm.-thick, and has a reddish-brown painting on a
pale ground.   Under the border there is a broad dark
stripe, followed by a zigzag line; and below, round the
body, is a band composed of one strong and six fine lines.
The foot is also painted; inside the rim is painted red, and
the bottom is decorated with two concentric rings.

In the annexed woodcut, No. 52, is a wheel-made
broken vase, from the same depth, with only one handle,
but which most probably had two.   It is of delicate workmanship, and of dull-reddish clay, 3 mm. thick, with black
painting on light-red ground.   On the rim is a row of
dots; on the handle five spots.   On both sides between

No. 52.—Vessel with rosette.   Size 1 : 3.          No. 53.—Vessel with rosette.   Size 1 : 3.
　　　　Depth 1 m.　　　　　　　　　　　　　　　　Depth 1 m.

the handles, is a rosette surrounded with dots; there is no
other painting.

No. 53 shows a wheel-made vase, found about the same
depth.   It is of very fine yellow clay, only 3 mm. thick,
very delicately made, and decorated with red painting.   On
the edge of the rim is a circle of dots, and a large spot is
on the handle; on the body, between the handles, there
is a small rosette; the foot is small.   This vase has a
remarkable similarity to the last mentioned (No. 52), but
it is still more delicately and carefully made, and is less
baked.   The size of the two vases is about the same.

Another fragment deserving notice is of the upper
portion of a deep wheel-made bowl, of fine reddish clay,
3 mm. thick; it was found at a depth of 1·50 m.   It is

represented on Plate XXVI., Fig. *a*. The painting is
black on yellow ground. We see a line round the rim,
and beneath it a large rosette composed of three concentric
circles, of which the outside one consists of dots. The two
inner circles are intersected by a cross, with a dot in each
right angle.

Two other fragments of pottery, with similar rosettes,
have been found at Tiryns, of which I show one in the
annexed woodcut No. 54. The fragment consists likewise
of fine reddish clay, 3 mm. thick, with black painting on
yellow ground. The rosette lies here within a spiral, and
the field is bordered below by a band of eight almost
horizontal parallel lines, and to the left by a band of two
upright lines, on the outside of which is affixed a row of

No. 54.—Vase fragment with rosette.   Size 1 : 3.   Depth not given.

little arches. A similar ornament is seen on a vessel found
in one of the prehistoric graves in Nauplia, which is
preserved in the Mycenæan Museum at Athens.

Rosettes are extremely frequent in ancient Oriental art,
both Egyptian and Assyrian, and we repeatedly meet them
on Trojan * and Mycenæan † pottery and gold-work.
The remarkable sculptured ceiling of the Thalamos discovered by me in the Minyan treasury at Orchomenos,‡ is
adorned with not less than 184 large rosettes. Rosettes

---

* Schliemann, *Ilios*, p. 341, No. 230 ; p. 488, No. 835 ; p. 489,
Nos. 842, 843, 847 ; p. 495, No. 873.
† Schliemann, *Mycenæ*, p. 216, No. 327 ; p. 227, No. 336 ; p. 229,
No. 337 ; p. 234, No. 344 ; Pl. XII. Nos. 56, 57 ; Pl. XIII. No. 67.
‡ Schliemann, *Orchomenos* (Leipzig, 1881), Pl. I.

also appear on the pottery from the graves of Ialysos, *
and likewise on the bas-reliefs of Thutmes III. (XVIII.
Dynasty), in which the Khetas (Hittites) bring to Pharaoh
vases decorated with rosettes.

Professor Sayce thinks the rosette ornament originated
in Babylon, and was thence introduced into the manufac-
tures of the Phœnicians, who brought it to the West.†

The annexed woodcut, No. 55, is a representation of
a globular hand-made jug, with convex bottom; it is made
of fine yellow clay, and was found at a depth of 1·50 m.
The neck and handle are broken off. The painting is

No. 55.—Jug.  Size about 1 : 2.  Depth 1·50 m.

brown, partly dark and partly light; round the neck is
a horizontal border, from which depend on each side
two perpendicular chains of bow-shaped ornaments. The
decoration is completed by two rosettes, one on each
side.

No. 56 is a picture of a small wheel-made vase of light-
red clay, found at the same depth. Instead of the usual
handle, there is here only a small straight projection, of
which half at least must be wanting. The vase is painted
red on a yellow ground, as far as the middle; below
there are brown horizontal lines.

---

* A. H. Sayce, in *The Contemporary Review*, December, 1878.
† *Ibid.*

The terra-cotta vessel, whose form is the most common of all, both in Tiryns and Mycenæ, is exhibited in the annexed woodcut, No. 57.    It is a spherical jug of yellow

No. 56.—Vessel.   Size about 2 : 3   Depth 1·50 m.

clay, with a small flat foot.    Above there is a handle, with a rest in the middle for the convenience of the fingers, and greater solidity.    A little below this support is the spout.

No. 57.—Vessel with tube-shap d spout.   Size 1 : 3.   Found close to the surface.

The painting is in yellow and red-brown colours.    Above, around the support, are four figures in the form of lambdas ; on the rest itself concentric circles.    On the

body of the vessel, from top to bottom, there are horizontal lines of different colour and width, worked on the
potter's wheel.

There must have been a time when this very same
form of vase was excessively liked and universally used in all
the settlements of the great Asiatic race in the Greek world,
for in Mycenæ and Tiryns we find thousands of fragments
of it, as well as very many fairly complete specimens.   In
the few graves opened at Spata there were five specimens
found, one in those of Nauplia and one in the beehive
tomb of Menidi.   All these are exhibited in the Mycenæan
Museum.   The National Museum at Athens also possesses eight specimens of this form of vase found in
Attika ; the exact place where they were discovered is not
stated.   The Acropolis Museum of Athens contains five
complete specimens, and fragments of six others, found in
the lowest *débris* strata of the Acropolis.   The Director
of the Arsenal of Salamis, Captain Andreas Miaoules,
possesses in his collection one discovered in a grave at
Salamis.   The small collection of prehistoric pottery from
Thera, in the French School at Athens, contains one
specimen.*   At Knossos in Crete, five examples were
found.†

The same form of vase is common in Cyprus,‡ and in
Egypt, and the Museum of the Louvre contains six speci-
mens, four from the former and two from the latter place.§
The British Museum possesses no less than fifty-one speci-
mens of exactly the same form of vase ; five came from
Athens, three from Egypt, and forty-three from the graves

---

* Albert Dumont et Jules Chaplain, *Les Céramiques de la Grèce
propre*, pp. 38, 65.

† *Ibid.* p. 65.                                        ‡ *Ibid.* p. 44.

§ Sophus Müller, *Ursprung und Entwickelung der europäischen
Bronzecultur* (1882) ; German translation by Miss J. Mestorf, p. 333 ;
Rosellini, *I monumenti dell' Egitto e della Nubia*, II., Pl. 56, No. 99 ;
Leemanns, *Aegyptische Monumente*, II., Pl. 66, No. 415.

of Ialysos in Rhodes, which in a remote antiquity has for hundreds of years been inhabited by Phœnicians.

I would also mention that I found in Tiryns the upper part of a similar vessel, which had three holes in each handle for suspension.

On Plate XXVII., Fig. *b*, I give a drawing of a small *hand-made* saucer, of which six specimens were found by me in the palace of Tiryns ; they are made of fine yellow clay, not much larger than a spoon, and some of them bored through the edge. On most of these the decoration consists of two bands of four lines each, which cross each other at right angles and are coloured red-brown, or black ; on the smaller specimens there is only one painted line. A small saucer, with two little handles, was also found ; it is painted inside with white colour, on which two inter- secting red lines are drawn.

### 9. Various Objects of Terra-Cotta.

One of the most remarkable objects of terra-cotta found in Tiryns is that represented on Plate XXIV., Figs *d* and *e*. It was found at a depth of 1·50 m., and is part of a large bathing-tub. It is 0 70 m. long, and the rim is 55–60 mm. thick. The thickness of the clay lower down is but 15 mm. It consists of coarse red clay, with many small pebbles, on account of which the polish is defective. On the side is a large handle. The whole vessel is curved like our present bathing-tubs. The painting is in white colour on the reddish ground of the clay. Straight over the broad face of the rim there are stripes. Inside, following the rim, are three broad horizontal lines ; below this are large spirals. On the outside beneath the wide projecting rim, there are only two stripes visible. The handle is decorated with eight vertical stripes.

Of jars proper (πίθοι) of the Trojan form (cf. *Ilios*, page 378, No. 344) only fragments were found, one of them

had numerous vertical perforations in the rim; two other
fragments were pieced together with cramps of lead. We
found also many single lead cramps which may have been
used in the same way.

There were also found in one room of the palace, standing near each other, two jars of cylindrical shape of very
coarse dark-brown clay, about 30 mm. thick, unpolished
outside and inside; the diameter of one is 0·66 m., of the
other 0·54 m. Both were broken at the top, and in their

No. 58.—Torch-holder.    Size 7 : 24.

present condition only 0·60 m. high, from which we
suppose them to have been 1 m. high originally.

An exactly similar vessel was found in another chamber.
Vessels of cylindrical form, but somewhat smaller and better
worked, were also found under the ruins of the first and
most ancient town of Troy, but are wholly wanting among
the hundreds of *Pithoi* of the usual shape found in the
second, third, fourth, and fifth towns of Troy.

No. 58 is a remarkable object of dark-red clay, which
can be nothing else but a torch-holder. The height of it

is 225 mm., the diameter of the tube 48 mm.   On the middle of the tube, which expands above, is affixed a kind of saucer, the edges of which are now broken away.

Three similar torch-holders of clay and fragments of others, found in the lowest *débris* of the Acropolis at Athens, are preserved in the Acropolis Museum.   Professor C. T. Newton, of the British Museum, calls my attention to Plate XLIX., No. 6, in Mionnet, *Recueil des Planches*, where a very similar torch-holder is represented on a coin of Amphipolis.   From this it appears that similar torch-holders were still used in classical times, and yet, so far as I know, the three in the Acropolis at Athens and the one in Tiryns are the only specimens ever yet found.

The three woodcuts, Nos. 59, 60, 61, show a remarkable

No. 59.                    No. 60.                    No. 61.

Vase-lid, with perforated handle.   Depth unknown.

vase-lid, as seen from three sides.   It is formed of brown, well-polished, but unpainted clay; and has on the top a hori-zontally perforated excrescence, which appears to indicate that the cover belonged to a vase having on both sides a vertically-pierced projection.   As I have shown in *Ilios*, page 357, No. 252, the vases of this kind could be sus-pended, or carried and closed tight by means of a string drawn through the side holes and the hole in the lid.   On the lower surface of the lid, No. 61, we see a cross and fifteen points engraved.

On Plate XXVII., Fig. *c*, I show a small hand-made, pipe-shaped vessel of reddish clay, 4 mm. thick, with red decorations; it was found at a depth of 1·50 m.   It is orna-mented with a linear decoration on the body, and with little bows on the back.   The handle was broken, and has been restored in the drawing. The use of this strange vessel is a riddle to us; it cannot have been a lamp, and besides, I have never found among prehistoric ruins any trace of lamps; moreover, as I have shown,* lamps of all kinds were quite unknown even to Homer.

Two exactly similar vessels were found in the excavations in the Acropolis of Athens, and may be seen in the Acropolis Museum. There are two others in a private collection in Athens which came from Mycenæ; † a third, said to come from Cyprus, is in the Museum at Trieste. The Museum of the Louvre contains six vessels of precisely

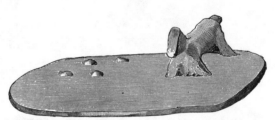

No. 62.—Dish with balls shaped like dumplings. Actual size. Depth 1 m.

No. 63.—Stand with a dog. Actual size. Depth 1·50 m.

the same form in the Cypriote, and four in the Etruscan collection.

A large fragment of a vessel was found at a depth of 1 m. It is of grey clay, 3–4 mm. thick, which before baking was dipped in a solution of green clay, and retains, therefore, a green colour. Only the outside rim and the inside are painted black.

In the above woodcut, No. 62, I show an object, from a depth of 1 m. of light-yellow clay, in the form of a dish with dumplings. It is 32 mm. across. No. 63 is an oval stand of reddish clay from a depth of 1·50 m. To the left a figure is broken away, of which the traces are still visible; to the right is a roughly made dog, on the

---

* Schliemann, *Ilios*, pp 620, 621 ; Schliemann, *Troja*, pp. 145, 146.

† Albert Dumont et Jules Chaplain, *Les Céramiques de la Grèce propre*, pp. 57, 58, Nos. 34, 35.

back of which we see four points.    Round the rim of the
stand is a black stripe.

No. 64.—Stopper of terra-cotta.  Size
about 1 : 2.  Depth 1 m.

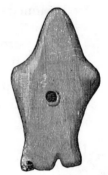

No. 65.—Object of clay.  Actual size.
Depth unknown.

The engraving, No. 64, shows a cone-shaped stopper of
coarse red clay.    It is 85 mm. long, and has excrescences

No. 66.—Object in clay.  Actual size.
Depth unknown.

No. 67.—Ear of clay.  Size 1:2.
Depth uncertain.

on both sides.    As far as I know, no similar object has been
found elsewhere.

At No. 65 I represent a horizontally-perforated object

of reddish clay, of which the use is unknown. It is quadrangular, with somewhat projecting corners. No. 66 is
a flat circular object of fine yellow clay, with a small perforated handle. Its length is 60 mm., its width 44 mm.
Use also unknown.

No. 67 represents an object of very coarse yellow clay
in the form of an ear. It is not polished, and, as the
breakage on the right side would seem to show, was fastened
to something and broken off. Below, it is pierced by a
hole, and in many places we see traces of rough painting.
The depth at which it was found is uncertain. Professor
Mahaffy remarks to me, that this object looks like an
*ex voto* fastened to the wall of a temple.

No. 68.—Object of clay in form of a foot.   Size 1 : 3.   Depth 2 m.

In the annexed woodcut, No. 68, I show a very curious
well-polished object, found 2 mm. deep, of slightly-baked
black clay. It is in the form of a foot, on which the
straps or strings used for securing the sandal seem to be
indicated by notching. It is 17 cm. long by 78 mm. broad
at the widest part, and 25–31 mm. thick. It is in a curved
form, and its front end is provided with a cylindrical stay,
which projects obliquely and seems to be intended for
fixing it. At the broadest end the rough surface shows
that it was broken off, and we are led to the conclusion
that we have before us the foot of a primitive statue of clay.

In the following woodcut, No. 69, I show an object of
well-baked red clay. Its length is 135 mm., its thickness

25 mm., the breadth is 35 mm. above, and below 70 mm. At the top is a large perforation, and lower down eight small ones.  Use unknown.

There were also found sixteen objects of coarse-brown clay, very little, or not at all, baked, of which one is given in the woodcut No. 70.  Its length is 80 mm., its width, above and below, 72 mm.  Towards the centre it is narrowed. Similar objects of unbaked or slightly baked clay are very common in Mycenæ, and are frequently found in Troy, both of stone and clay.  Apparently they were used as weights for looms.  It can hardly be that they were ever

No. 69.—Object of clay with nine pene-  
trations.  Size 1 : 3.  Depth 1 m.

No 70.—Object of clay.  Size about 1 : 2.  
Depth 1 m.

intended for weights to fishing-nets, as the unbaked clay would dissolve in water.  There also occur cylinders of unpolished, slightly-baked, brown clay, like that shown in the woodcut No. 71.  They are 10 cm. high, 6½ cm. across, and have two perforations running lengthwise. Most likely they were also used as loom weights.  Similar cylinders with perforations were likewise found in Mycenæ, but I believe not elsewhere.

There were also found numerous discs, with a hole in the centre, of slightly baked, very coarse yellow clay, of which I show a specimen in the engraving No. 72.  The outside is not polished.  They are on an average 62 mm.

thick and about 140 mm. wide, the breadth of the hole is 25 mm. They have been found in Mycenæ and Orchomenos of the same size. In Troy, however, all discs of this size, or near it, are of stone; the discs of clay, with a hole in the centre, are there but very small. The use of large discs of almost unbaked clay is a great problem to us, for they could not well have been used as quoits for throwing, on account of their fragility.

There were also found some small unornamented per- forated whorls of brown clay and conical shape, as well as

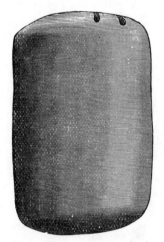

No. 71.—Cylinder with two perforations.
Size 1 : 2.   Depth 1 m.

No. 72.—Disc of clay.   Size about 1 : 3.
Depth about 1 m.

others of exactly the form of the stone whorl shown on Plate XXI., Fig. *g*. Of terra-cotta whorls of similar form, but usually with notched ornaments, I have collected in Troy more than 22,000 specimens.* In Mycenæ likewise were found about fifty unornamented clay-whorls. I also found in the ruins of the palace several perforated cones of black-varnished terra-cotta; their height and diameter were about 62 mm.; further, a couple of very large perforated

---

* See references under "Whorl," in Index to *Ilios*, and under "Spinning Whorl," in Index to *Troja*.

cones of brown, sun-dried clay, 320 mm. high and broad, which were a little broken, but seem to have weighed at least 25 kilogrammes when they were entire.

I bring before the reader in the woodcut, No. 73, a wheel-shaped ring with toothed edge, made of yellow clay covered with black varnish. It has an outer diameter of 38 mm. and an inner one of 23 mm. Several perfectly similar specimens were found, but none of the same form occurred in Mycenæ or elsewhere.

The annexed woodcut, No. 74, represents an object in the form of a disc of brown clay, on which traces of painting in red varnish can be seen. The diameter is 45 mm. The

No. 73.—Wheel-shape clay ring. Actual size. Depth not given.

No. 74.—Wheel-shaped clay disc. Actual size. Depth not given.

edge is jagged all round, and near it is a perforation. A large number of these were found. I am not, however, aware that discs of this kind occurred elsewhere.

The picture on Plate XXIII., Fig. *c*, represents an object of reddish clay, found at the depth of 1½ m.; it has the form of a three-legged chair, with double-back, of which the upper part at the right side is broken off. The painting is red. The outside of the back and feet is ornamented with broad stripes, the inside with concentric semicircles and waved lines. The upper side of the seat is painted in monochrome. The height of the chair is 67 mm., the width 62 mm. Similar miniature chairs of terra-cotta also occur in Mycenæ, and may be seen in the Mycenæan Museum at Athens.

No. 75 represents an animal of peculiar appearance, made of slightly-baked, brown, ill-polished clay, which, as

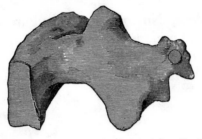

No. 75.—Handle of clay in form of an animal. Actual size. Depth not stated.

the broken parts of the back quarters seem to indicate, may have served as a handle to some other object. Of the character of that object, however, we can form no idea,

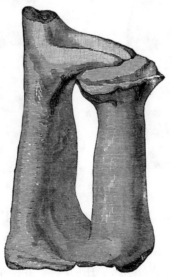

No. 76.—Bread-making figure. Size 7 : 8. Depth about 0˙60 m.

for the outward bent bow-shape of the back parts of the animal is unlike any vase-form known to us. If the animal was used as a handle, the humps on its back may have been intended as rests for the fingers. The head resembles that of a sheep. The eyes are made separately, and stuck on while the clay was still moist.

## 10. Idols of Baked Clay.

The woodcut, No. 76, shows a figure of yellow, unpainted clay, 70 mm. high, found at a depth of 60 cm. It stands in front of a cylindrical pillar, with a dish, in which it makes bread. The head of the figure is missing.

No. 77.—Idol. Actual size. Depth about 1 m.   No. 78.—Idol. Actual size. Depth 1·50 m.

In the following woodcut, No. 77, I exhibit an extremely rude and unpainted idol of coarse yellow clay, from a depth of about 1 m. The lower part, as well as the hands, are broken off; the eyes and mouth are very largely marked; on the left side and back are remains of braids of hair. The height of the figure is 90 mm.

Another very rough idol, 78 mm. high, is shown in No. 78. It is also unpainted, and of light-yellow clay. The face is simply pressed out between the fingers, and there are no indications of eyes, mouth, or breasts. Of the right arm a part remains, the left is broken off.

A similar unpainted figure of light-yellow clay, is shown in No. 79. It is 78 mm. high, and evidently a female idol. The eyes and breasts are marked; the mouth wanting; part of the arms is preserved. The depth of the find is stated to be 2 m.

Another equally rude, unpainted idol is seen in the woodcut No. 80. The face and the ears are likewise

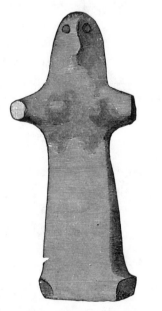 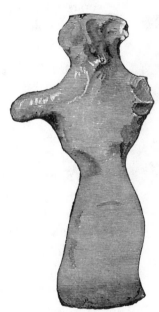

No. 79.—Idol. Actual size. Depth 2 mm.          No. 80.—Idol. Actual size. Depth 1·50 m.

squeezed out between the fingers; the mouth is not shown; the right arm remains; the left is broken away. The narrowing of the body beneath the breast seems to show that the primitive artist intended to represent a female idol. Depth stated, 1·50 m.

These five idols, Nos. 76-80, are extremely rude; so much so, that in the first efforts of the primitive man to represent the human figure, hardly anything more imperfect could be the result. The fact, however, that they were found in the chambers of the royal palace at Tiryns, proves beyond any doubt that they were still in common use at the time when the residence was destroyed.

As, however, the rudeness of their execution is in strong contrast with the artistic skill which is conspicuous in the pottery and its decoration, as well as in the wall-paintings of the palace, we are forced to conclude, that the ancient Tirynthians adhered with religious zeal to the primitive representation of their divinities, which had become conse-

No. 81.—Idol.
Actual size.
Depth 1 m.

crated by the precedent of ages. But, was this peculiar to Tiryns?—By no means. In the lowest layers of *débris* in the Acropolis of Athens, eighty-nine unpainted idols of terra-cotta were found, which are quite similar to the Tirynthian idols Nos. 77–79, and, if possible, exceed them in rudeness of execution. These may be seen in the Acropolis Museum.

Similar and equally rude terra-cotta idols were found during the excavations of the Archæological Society at the base of the Temple of Demeter in Eleusis. Strange to say, however, my excavations at Mycenæ, Orchomenos, and Troy produced no idol of even approaching rudeness, and no museum has anything similar to show.

On Plate XXV., Fig. *k*, I exhibit a perfectly flat idol, painted plain black, 11 cm. high, the execution of which already shows more artistic skill. On the head is a *polos*, beneath which, on the neck, projects a twist of hair. The eyes are large; no mouth is given; the arms are broken off. Depth of find, 1·50 m.

No. 81 represents a rude, unpainted female idol, 60 mm. high, whose face is formed in the same way as the previous ones. The eyes and breasts are formed by little lumps attached. No mouth is given. The right

arm is broken off; of the left remains a stump.   Depth,
1 m.

I mention, further, a rude idol, 48 mm. high, of yellow
clay.   The lower part is broken off, also the right arm; of
the left a stump remains.   The eyes, which are formed of
little lumps of clay stuck on, are, from want of skill in the
artist, placed below the nose.   The mouth is not marked.

No. 82.—Idol.  Actual size.  Depth 1·50 m.          No. 83.—Idol.  Actual size.  Depth 0·50-0·60 m.

The lower part of the body up to the arms is painted
black.

Further, I give in No. 82 the figure of a rude idol
of reddish clay, 80 mm. high, with a *polos* on the head.
The large eyes are indicated by lumps stuck on.   No
mouth is marked.   Of both arms only stumps remain.
The lower part of the body is red, the upper painted with
glossy-white.   Depth stated, 1·50 m.

The British Museum contains three idols of terra-cotta
from Ialysos and four from Cyprus, which approach nearly

in form and fabric to this and the preceding (Nos. 81, 82).

In the next woodcut, No. 83, I give a drawing of a better-made idol, of finer reddish clay, with a turban-like head-dress, which was attached after the idol was formed. This was also the case with the eyes and the neck orna-ment. No mouth is given. The left arm is stretched out wide; the right is broken off. The upper part of the body shows traces of painting. Depth of find, 50–60 cm. The ornament suspended from the neck is the Homeric *hormos;* for, as Helbig * very truly remarks: " The *hormos* † was not a band clasping the throat, but it was made to fall from the neck over the breast, and to display on the bust. This is abundantly shown in two passages in the Homeric Hymns. In one ‡ is described how the Horæ hang golden hormoi on " the soft neck and silver-white bosom of Aphrodite." In the other § it is said that the goddess of love wears beautiful golden hormoi on her neck, and " on her soft bosom, as if shone upon by the moon."

" And such neckbands hanging down on the bust are

---

* W. Helbig, *Das Homerische Epos aus den Denkmälern erläutert,* p 182.

† *Iliad,* XVIII. 401 ; *Od.* XV. 460, XVIII. 295; *Hymn. Hom.* I. (*in Apoll. Del.*) 103, IV. (*in Vener.*) 88, VI. 11.

‡ *Hymn. Hom.* VI. 10 :

δειρῇ δ' ἀμφ' ἀπαλῇ καὶ στήθεσιν ἀργυρέοισιν
ὅρμοισι χρυσέοισιν ἐκόσμεον, οἷσί περ αὐταί
Ὧραι κοσμείσθην χρυσάμπυκες·

§ *Hymn. Hom.* IV. 88 :

ὅρμοι δ' ἀμφ' ἀπαλῇ δειρῇ περικαλλέες ἦσαν,
καλοί, χρύσειοι, παμποίκιλοι, ὡς δὲ σελήνη
στήθεσιν ἀμφ' ἀπαλοῖσι ἐλάμπετο, θαῦμα ἰδέσθαι.

To this corresponds the considerable length of the hormos, which Iris promises Eileithvia in *Hymn. Hom.* I. 103,

μέγαν ὅρμον,
χρύσεον ἠλέκτροισιν ἐερμένον, ἐννεάπηχυν·

seen in Oriental,* old Greek,† and Etruscan monuments,‡
and corresponding examples have been found in Etruscan
graves, the contents of which offer points of connection
with Homeric art." §

The following woodcut, No. 84, shows the upper part
of an unpainted idol of yellow clay, 62 mm. high. The
eyes, the *polos*, and the plait of hair on the left temple are

No. 84.—Idol. Actual size. Depth
0·50-0·60m.

No. 85.—Idol with child on the arm.
Actual size. Depth 1·50 m.

made separately and stuck on. The mouth is not given.
The right arm is missing; of the left a stump remains.
Depth of find, 50–60 cm.

Further, I show in the next woodcut, No. 85, the

---

* E. g. On a Chaldean idol of Istar : Heuzey, *Les figurines du
Louvre*, Pl. II. ; Perrot et Chipiez, *Histoire de l' Art*, II. p. 82, Fig. 16.
On figures of the Cyprian Astarte : Cesnola-Stern, *Cypern*, Pl. 50, 3,
p. 235, Pl. 45 ; Gerhard, *Gesammelte Akademische Abhandlungen*,
Pl. XLVII.

† Thus on an archaic female figure from Kameiros : Salzmann,
*Nécropole de Camiros*, Pl. 15.

‡ Micali, *Mon. inéd.* Pl. XXVI. 3.

§ So *e.g.* Grifi. *Mon. di Cere*, Pl. III. 2, 3 ; *Mus. Gregor.*, I.,
Pl. LXVII. 3–5, Pl. LXXVII 1 ; *Mon. dell' Instit.*, VI. Pl. XLVI. b ;
*Mus. Gregor.* I., Pl. LXXIX. 5 ; Pl. LXXXI. 1, 2.

picture of the upper part of a rude unpainted idol of yellow
clay, 42 mm. high, which carries a child on the arm.  Of
the eyes, the right remains; of the left, we see only the
little hole in which the lump representing the eye was
fastened.  The mouth is half-moon shaped.  The child
and the ornament on the neck were made separately and
stuck on when the clay was still moist.  Depth 1·50 m.

The following woodcut, No. 86, shows the upper part
of an unpainted idol of brown clay.  The height of it is
80 mm., the width of the arms, 135 mm.  Both arms

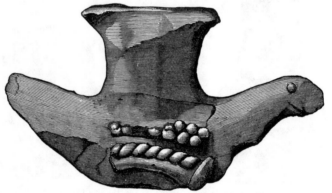

No. 86.—Upper part of an idol.  Somewhat more than 1 : 2 size.  Depth 0·50-0·60 cm.

remain, but from the right the hand is broken off.  The
head is a shapeless lump, with no indication of eyes, nose, or
mouth.  The breast is adorned with six bands of attached
clay mouldings, in which we may suppose we see fruits
and ears of corn.  Depth, 50–60 cm.

The next picture, No. 87, shows an idol 110 mm. high,
of reddish clay, represented as sitting on a seat.  The left
arm remains, the right is broken off.  The long head-
dress, which hangs down low behind, is very characterisic.
Its front is decorated with a disc; it has been made
separately and fastened on when the clay was still moist.  In
the same way the eyes, the circles on each side of the neck,
which probably represent earrings, the necklace (ὅρμος),
with a large circle in the middle, as well as the two bands

across the breast, which terminate on each side in a disc,
are separately made and attached when the figure was still
unbaked and moist. No mouth is given. A portion of the
lower part of the body and the feet of the seat are broken
off. This seat had only two feet, and was completed by the
fore part of the figure. Depth stated, 1·50 m.

The following woodcut, No. 88, also represents a sitting
idol, 90 mm. high. It is of red clay, unpainted, and very

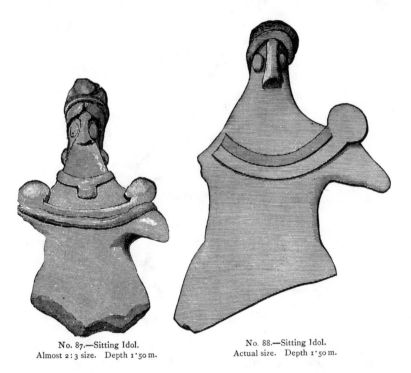

No. 87.—Sitting Idol.
Almost 2 : 3 size. Depth 1·50 m.

No. 88.—Sitting Idol.
Actual size. Depth 1·50 m.

like the preceding one, only differing in this, that here the
neck ornament, the feet of the chair, as well as the lower
part of the body, are missing. The left arm is preserved,
the right hand as well as the disc on the right shoulder
are broken off. Depth stated, 1·50 m.

In the next woodcut, No. 89, I exhibit a third sitting
idol; it is of reddish clay, 90 mm. high, and very like the
two last, except for the head-dress, which in this seems

to represent a crown. The lower part of the body and one foot are wanting. The depth of the find is not stated.

As analogous to these three idols (Nos. 87, 88, and 89), I mention two very similar sitting idols, found in the lowest layers of *débris* on the Acropolis of Athens, which are placed in the Acropolis Museum.

Besides these, the National Museum at Athens contains, under Nos. 1501–1531, thirty sitting idols, said to

No. 89.—Sitting Idol.   Actual size.   Depth not given.

be from the tombs at Tegea, which are, however, in most cases less primitive, and apparently all belong to a later period.

In the following woodcut, No. 90, I show the lower part of a sitting idol, 110 mm. high; the seat had four feet, of which two remain. Depth given, 60–70 cm.

The next woodcut, No. 91, shows a sitting idol of brown clay, whose feet are extended on the seat. Head, arms, and the four feet of the seat are broken away. Of the neck-band (ὅρμος) the central round ornament remains. The

length of the idol is 50 mm., the width 55 mm.; the
depth stated is 50–60 cm.

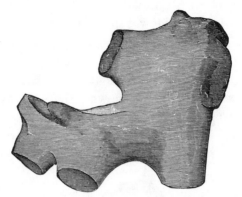

No. 90.—Lower part of a sitting Idol.
Size 1:2.   Depth 0·60–0·70 m.

No. 91.—Sitting Idol.
Actual size.   Depth 0·50–0·60 m.

I show further in the next woodcut, No. 92, a part,
50 mm. high, of an unpainted idol of yellow clay.

Only one eye remains; of the other only the little
hollow remains, in which the lump which represented the
eye was placed.   No mouth is marked; the head-covering

No. 92.—Upper part of an Idol.
Size about 7:8.   Depth not stated.

No. 93.—Head of an Idol with Phrygian cap.
Size 7 : 8.   Depth not stated.

is identical with that of the idols Nos. 82, 84, and 88.
Depth not stated.

In the following woodcut, No. 93, I give the head, 35 mm.
high, of an idol with a Phrygian cap.   This cap is represented as fastened by means of a strap or cloth round the

neck, which is marked by the projecting band. Depth is not stated.

The following woodcut, No. 94, exhibits the upper part of an unpainted idol of yellow clay, 40 mm. high, of which the lower part is broken away. The arms remain. The long plaits of hair are separately made and fixed to the figure while it was still moist. The face is simply formed by pressure between the fingers; the eyes, nose, and mouth are shown; the eyes by two lumps attached. Depth of find, o·15 m.

The next woodcut, No. 95, represents the head, 35 mm. high, of an unpainted idol, which shows considerable

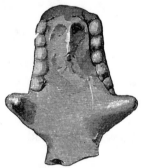

No. 94.—Upper part of an Idol.
Actual size. Depth o·15 m.

No. 95.—Upper part of an Idol.
Actual size. Depth not given.

artistic skill. It is, in fact, very remarkable that this naturalistic head should be found among numbers of the rudest idols. Forehead, eyes, nose, mouth and chin are all symmetrically represented, and the features may be called handsome. The ears are decorated with earrings in the form of two concentric circles. The plaits of hair are represented, both resting on the brow and falling on each side of the head, and are shown hanging down behind by notching. The depth of the find is not noted.

An idol, 132 mm. high, of red clay, is further shown on Plate XXV., Fig. c. The head, the arms, and the projecting feet, are broken away. Over the shoulders lie two projecting bands of clay, which, as Mr. James

Fergusson thinks, represent an ægis; they were, however, separately made and affixed while the clay was still moist. The lower band is ornamented with six vertical notches, and the panels so produced are decorated each with two, three, or four projecting points. These latter have been separately finished in the shape of little globules, while the clay was still soft, and were then stuck into little cavities fitted for them. In the same way the projecting points on the upper band were made. The figure is painted with a network of crossing red lines, which appear to show the colour of the dress. The depth is stated as 0·50 m. A similar idol found in a tomb at Tegea is to be seen in the National Museum at Athens.

I show, further, on Plate XXV., Figs. *h* and *i*, two idols, respectively 45 and 39 mm. high, of yellow clay, which are ornamented with a *polos*, and hold their hands upon their breasts. The painting is red and brownish-red. Round the rim of the *polos* is a line. to which is attached from below a band of little arches.

Round the upper part of the head is a horizontal line, from which fine strokes hang down at right angles and seem to indicate a veil. The nose and eyes are painted, and also the arms. The hair is indicated behind by four parallel horizontal strokes. The lower part of the body is ornamented in front and behind with two vertical parallel lines; it grows gradually wider, and is hollow. The depth is 2 m. Painted idols of the same, or very similar form, often appear in Tiryns, and are very numerous in Mycenæ.*

The Louvre Museum also contains a specimen of Assyrian origin which is very similar.

I would further draw attention to the female idol shown on Plate XXV., Fig. *a*, *b*, which is 120 mm. high, and of reddish clay. The painting is red. The face is squeezed

---

* Schliemann, *Mycenæ*, Pl. A, Fig. *c*; Pl. C, Fig. *l*; Pl. XVIII. Nos. 99–101.

out to a pointed form; the crown of the head is painted,
but there is no *polos*.  The hair is represented as hanging
at length down the back.  Between two horizontal bands, of
which one is round the neck, the other below the belly, the
middle of the body resembles a disc, in the shape of the full
moon, on which two round projections mark the breasts.
The lower part of the body is like that of the preceding
idol; it is decorated with straight, but the disc on both
sides with waving, lines.  The depth is given as 1·50 m.

A similar female idol, only 55 m. high, is shown in the

next woodcut, No. 96.  The eyes and the very
plump nose are separately formed, and were
attached while the clay was still moist.  The
lower part of the body is flat and not hollow,
like the preceding idols.  This figure was
painted simply with black colour, of which
we see traces on the head and nose.

Many specimens and fragments of similar
idols, with a disc-shaped middle and hollow
foot (Plate XXV., Fig. *a*, *b*), were found in
Tiryns.

No. 96.—Idol.
Size 7 : 8.
Depth not stated.

In Mycenæ they were also very numerous,
but nearly always in fragments.*  The National
Museum at Athens contains an idol of this
form, said to come from Bœotia.

A female idol of another form is shown on Plate XXV.,
Fig. *d*.  It is of black clay, painted black, and 122 mm.
high.  From the chest projects on either side an excrescence in the shape of a horn, so that, taken together,
the two excrescences represent the form of the horned
moon.  The head is decked with a high *polos*, the face
squeezed flat.  The lower part of the body widens gradually
towards the foot and is hollow.  The upper rim of the
*polos* is encircled by a band bordered by a row of little

---

Schliemann, *Mycenæ*, p. 73, No. 112 ; Pl. C, Fig. *m*

arches. Over the brow is another simple encircling line, meant, no doubt, to mark the limit of the *polos*. The nose has a branch-like decoration. The eyes are of extraordinary size. Two upward sloping lines on the neck seem to mark the end of the face. The middle part of the body is ornamented in front and behind with fine, the lower part with broad, vertical lines. The depth is not stated.

Idols of this form are very usual in Tiryns, and appear in a fragmentary condition at Mycenæ in countless numbers.*

Exactly similar idols found in the prehistoric tombs of Nauplia may be seen in the Mycenæan Museum at Athens. The Acropolis Museum contains two of the same form found in the most ancient layers of *débris* on the Acropolis. The National Museum at Athens also has two idols of this kind said to come from Bœotia. That the Phœnicians had idols of the same form, appears from the fact, that one was found in a tomb at Ialysos, which town, as already mentioned, was in very ancient days inhabited during many centuries by the Phœnicians. This idol is preserved in the British Museum, which also contains a similar one from Greece, but from what locality is not stated. I show on Plate XXV., Fig. *g*, another small idol of this kind from Tiryns. It is 60 mm. high, of red clay, and painted with horizontal red stripes. Otherwise the figure exactly resembles the form of the preceding idol. Depth of find not stated.

The head shown on Plate XXV., Fig. *e*, is exactly like that of the idol last described.

On Plate XXV., Fig. *f*, I show a somewhat different head of a similar idol. It is of light-yellow clay, and wears a *polos* which is very wide above. The painting is brown.

---

* Schliemann, *Mycenæ*, p. 12, Nos. 8, 10; p. 72, No. 111; Pl. A, Fig. *d*; Pl. B, Figs. *e* and *f*.

To the rim of the *polos* is attached a row of depending
arches.   The forehead is decorated with a band,from which
on each side six fine lines, which probably indicate the
veil, descend at right angles like a comb.   In contrast with
those of the former figures, the eyes of this idol are
extremely small.

I also found here again great masses of fragments of
idols in the form of small terra-cotta cows, and a considerable number of perfect ones, of which two are represented
on Plate XXIV., Fig. *a, b.*   In my excavations at Tiryns,
in the year 1876, I had found eleven such idols,* also in
Mycenæ many hundreds of more or less broken specimens,
as well as fifty-six golden cows'-heads, one of silver with
gold horns, and several cows'-heads engraved on gems.†
Most of the cow idols of terra-cotta have on a light-
yellow ground a painting of bright red, or brown; black
painting is also not uncommon.

Exactly similar cows of terra-cotta were also found in
the prehistoric graves of Nauplia by Professor Castorches,
and may be seen in the Mycenæan Museum at Athens.
Three similar cows, which were discovered in the lowest
layers of *débris* on the Acropolis, are preserved in the
Acropolis Museum ; and the British Museum contains
two similar cows of the same size and exactly the same
painting, which were discovered in the prehistoric graves at
Ialysos.

I have already shown in my earlier works ‡ that, just
as the hundreds of female idols and vases with female
figures and owls' heads, which I found in Troy, could

---

* Schliemann, *Mycenæ*, pp. 10, 11, Nos. 2–7, and Pl. A, Fig. *a, b.*
† *Ibid.* p. 74, Nos. 114–119; Pl. A, Fig. *d*; Pl. B, Fig. *e* and *f*;
Pl. C, Fig. *k*, and pp. 216, 217, Nos. 327, 328 ; p. 218, Nos. 329, 330 ;
p. 309, No. 471 ; p. 360, No. 531 ; p. 362, No. 541.
‡ Schliemann, *Mycenæ,* pp. 19–22 ; *Ilios*, pp. 281–290.  I recommend
the discussions in these passages, and especially the explanation of the
epithets γλαυκῶπις and βοῶπις to the particular attention of the reader.

only represent one goddess, and that Pallas Athene, the tutelary deity of Troy, the more so as Homer constantly names her γλαυκῶπις (literally " owl-faced "), and never bestows this epithet on any other goddess or on any mortal woman, so the countless numbers of idols in form of terra-cotta cows found in Tiryns and Mycenæ, as well as cows'-heads of gold, women with cow's-horn-like, crescent-shaped projections from the breast, or with the upper part of the body shaped like the disc of the full moon, and also the idols in Mycenæ, with cows' heads,† can only represent Hera, the tutelar divinity of Tiryns and Mycenæ, especially as Homer constantly gives this goddess the epithet βοῶπις, which originally can have had no other meaning than " cow-faced."

I have further shown that Tiryns and Mycenæ were in the immediate neighbourhood of the famous Heraion, and that in my opinion even the name of Mycenæ seems to have arisen from the bellowing (μυκᾶσθαι, with Homer always μυκᾶν) of the cow. This theory of mine was at once accepted by the learned Prime Minister of England, W. E. Gladstone,‡ as well as by the late François Lenormant,§ the latter one of the greatest authorities in the field of ancient Oriental literature, and I believe that the learned are now all well disposed towards the acceptance of this theory.

## 11. OBJECTS OF METAL.

Of gold there was found but one small object, which I represent on Plate XXI., Figs. *c, d, e.* It resembles the pedestals in the relief over the Lions' Gate at Mycenæ, on

---

* Schliemann, *Mycenæ*, Pl. D, Figs. *n, o, p.*

† Cf. W. E. Gladstone's Preface to Schliemann's *Mycenæ*, pp. vi–viii.

‡ François Lenormant, in the *Gazette des Beaux-Arts*, Feb. 1, 1879, p. 108.

which both the pillar and the fore-feet of the two lions rest. Of bronze there were also but few interesting objects found. In the accompanying woodcut, No. 97, is seen a bronze figure,* 92 mm. high, which represents an upright beardless warrior in the act of fighting. The head is covered with

a helmet having a very high cone-shaped top. The rest of the body is naked. Nose and eyes are fairly well preserved, the lower part of the face is injured, the ears are disproportionately large. The lance, held in the lifted right hand, as well as the shield fastened to the left, are missing. Beneath the feet are two vertical supports, which give us exactly the depth of the double funnel through which the molten metal was run into the mould. These reminiscences of the two funnels, which the primitive artist could not remove, not yet having files, as well as the general unskilfulness which is conspicuous in the whole figure, point to a high antiquity. I wish to draw attention to the remarkable similarity of this statuette to a Phœnician bronze figure from Tortosa in Spain, and which is preserved in the Louvre Museum.†

No. 97.—Helmeted warrior of bronze. Actual size. Depth 3 m.

Woodcut No. 98, shows a bronze chisel, which appears in the same form at Mycenæ,‡ and has the strongest likeness to the Trojan battle-axes.§ It is 90 mm. long, and the blade is 30 mm. broad. In

---

* This figure was found by me in my excavations in 1876, and is here reproduced from my *Mycenæ*, p. 14, No. 12.

† Georges Perrot et Charles Chipiez, *Histoire de l'Art*, III., pp. 404, 405, Fig. 277.

‡ Schliemann, *Mycenæ*, p. 306, No. 463.

§ Schliemann, *Ilios*, p. 476, Nos. 806–810; p. 485, No. 828; *Troja*, p. 166, Nos. 80, 81.

the handle is an engraved line, 20 mm. long.  There were two specimens of this tool discovered at a depth stated as from 1–1·20 m.  There are seven similar bronze chisels in the Museum at Copenhagen.*

In No. 99 I give a drawing of a bronze tool in the form of a bar, 135 mm. long and 6 mm. thick, with one

No. 98.—Bronze chisel.
Size 2:3.   Depth 1–1·20 m.

No. 99.—Tool of unknown use.
Size 2:3.   Depth 1–1·20 m.

end flattened like a chisel.  Similar tools were found at Mycenæ † as well as at Troy.‡   Depth stated, 1–1·20 m.

The woodcut, No. 100, gives a picture of a two-edged bronze battle-axe, 205 mm. long, 45 mm. wide, with a long oval hole in the centre.  Depth of find 1–1·50 mm. Two similar double-edged axes of bronze were found in

---

* Sophus Müller, *Ursprung und erste Entwickelung der europäischen Bronzecultur*, German translation by Miss J. Mestorf, 1882, p. 348.
† Such a tool from Mycenæ, is in the Mycenæan Museum at Athens.
‡ Schliemann, *Ilios*, p. 482, Nos. 816, 817.

my excavations at Mycenæ.* On the gold ornaments
in the royal tombs at Mycenæ I also found double-axes
of this form commonly represented, as *e.g.*, between the
horns of fifty-six cows'-heads.† We find, moreover, a
similar double-edged axe on a gold signet-ring of archaic
Babylonian style,‡ and another on a remarkable gem of
agate.§ A similar two-edged axe of copper was found in
Hungary.‖ This type of axe was characteristic of Asia
Minor; and Zeus Labrandeus in Caria derived his name
from *Labranda*, which in Carian meant a double-edged axe,
on which account it also occurs as a symbol on Carian
coins and on all coins of Tenedos. The double battle-axe

No. 100.—Double-edged battle-axe of bronze.  Size 1 : 2.  Depth 1—1·50m.

made of bronze is common in Assyria and Babylonia, and
two similar ones, but of copper, were found, one in the
lake-dwellings at Lüscherz,¶ and one on the lower Danube
respectively.** A similar double-bladed axe, also of pure
copper, was found by Dr. Victor Gross in the lake-dwell-

---

* Schliemann, *Mycenæ*, p. 111, No. 173.
† *Ibid.* p. 218, Nos. 329, 330.
‡ *Ibid.* p. 354, No. 530.
§ *Ibid.* p. 362, No. 541.
‖ Joseph Hampel, *Catalogue de l'Exposition préhistorique des Musées de province*, p. 139, No. 147.
¶ Cf. *Sitzungsbericht der Berliner Gesellschaft für Anthropologie, Ethnologie*, &c., for Oct. 18, 1879, Pl. XVII. Nos. 2 *a* and 2 *b*.
** *Ibid.* Nos. 3 *a* and 3 *b*.

ings at Locras, in the Bienne Lake, in Switzerland.\* A bronze axe from Cyprus of the same kind, and of Phœnician origin, is preserved in the Bibliothèque nationale at Paris.† This same type of double-edged axe is also found in Assyria, Asia Minor, South Russia, Central Europe, Sardinia, and on later Greek monuments.‡ The Museum at Copenhagen contains thirteen such bronze double-axes.§

Sophus Müller says, ‖ "Of votive axes over twenty were found in Olympia, 2–7 cm. long, all double-axes, the blades of which are more or less curved. Only in some is the handle preserved, in most it is lost, and in some the eye, though partly cut, does not go right through. That some at least of these objects, reach back to the oldest times of Olympia, is plain from the fact, that the votive objects generally lay in the lowest *strata* of *débris*. One of the swords and an axe were found even under the Opisthodomos of the Heraion, with a number of extremely primitive votive animals. These axes cannot, however, be attributed, any more than the other objects of bronze here described, to the culture of a general bronze age in Europe. Their forms are distinctly Greek, and votive objects of this kind are not found in Europe beyond the boundary of ancient Greek influence. At Olbia similar objects have been found of lead (Ermitage at St. Peters-

---

\* Victor Gross, *Les dernières trouvailles dans les habitations lacustres du Lac de Bienne* (Porrentruy, 1879), Pl. I. No. 1.

† Georges Perrot et Charles Chipiez, *Histoire de l'Art*, III. 867, No. 634.

‡ Sophus Müller, *Ursprung und erste Entwickelung der europäischen Bronzecultur*, 1882, Germ. trans. by Miss J. Mestorf, p. 329 ; Rawlinson, *The Five Great Monarchies* (London, 1862), II. 65 ; Perrot et Delbet, *La Galatie et la Bithynie* (Paris, 1872), p. 338 ; La Marmora, *Voyage en Sardaigne* (Paris et Turin), Pl. 34, 3 ; Lindenschmit, *Alterthümer unserer heidnischen Vorzeit*, II. 3, 2, Fig. 1. We also see the double-axe on many coins from Italy and Greece.

§ Sophus Müller, *op. cit.* p. 348.

‖ *Ibid.* p. 344.

burg), and from Siebenbürgen we have votive axes of the
same kind as those mentioned, but with three blades."*

Under Nos. 101, 102 I exhibit a small flat bronze
saucer found in the palace, the use of which is an enigma.
It had two handles, of one of which the half only remains,
and on each side of the handle was a holder of the same
length.   Dr. Dörpfeld thinks that the object may have
been used as an ornament for some piece of furniture.   Of
the other bronze things found in the palace of Tiryns, I
mention two punches; one bracelet, of which the ends

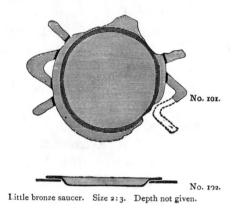

No. 101.

No. 102.

Little bronze saucer.   Size 2 : 3.   Depth not given.

run out in spirals; a brooch, with a globular head, stuck
through a lead bead; thirteen very common rings, and an
arrow-head of very primitive form without barbs, 55 mm.
long, which is extremely like the Trojan arrow-heads, but
somewhat longer.†

On the ramp leading to the gate on the east side of the
upper citadel (see Plans I.–III.), which was certainly roofed
and inhabited at a later date, were found, among many
bricks of Greek time, and many fragments of black and red-
glazed pottery dating from the 5th to the 2nd century B.C.,
a bronze lamp and an iron lance-head with a hole for the

---

* The find of Klein-Propstorf and Schelken in the Museum of
Hermannstadt.
† Cf. *Ilios*, p. 505, Nos. 931, 933, 942, 944, 946.

shaft ; but we need not further consider these objects, since they obviously belong to a comparatively modern date.

The above-described tools from Tiryns have not yet been analysed. The bronze objects from Mycenæ, analysed by the famous chemist, Dr. John Percy of London, gave the following result :—

FRAGMENT OF A SWORD ; ANALYSIS.

|  | I. | II. | Average. |
|---|---|---|---|
| Copper. . . . . | 86·41 | 86·31 | 86·36 |
| Tin . . . . . | 13·05 | 13·07 | 13·06 |
| Lead . . . . . | .. | 0·11 | 0·11 |
| Iron . . . . . | 0·17 | .. | 0·17 |
| Nickel . . . . . | 0·15 | .. | 0·15 |
| Cobalt . . . . . | Traces | .. | Traces |
|  |  |  | 99·85 |

FRAGMENT OF A VASE-HANDLE ; ANALYSIS.

Copper . . . . 89·69
Tin . . . . . 10·08

99·77

We may therefore suppose that the Tirynthian bronzes were similarly compounded.

Besides the iron lance-head of later date found on the ramp, there was not found during the excavations at Tiryns the slightest trace of iron. Of silver there was only found a simple signet-ring with a star engraved on it; yet, considering the numerous objects of this metal found in the royal tombs at Mycenæ, we cannot doubt that the inhabitants of the palace of Tiryns had silver in common use. Lead we found in many places, and this metal, among others, was used by the Tirynthians in repairing large

earthen vessels.   There were found numerous fragments
of large vases and jars bound together with clamps of lead,
as well as occasional lead clamps, which must have served
the same purpose.   We found, also, many large melted
lumps of lead, as well as one large piece in the form of half
a pig, and several fragments of sheet-lead.

## 12.  Objects of Stone.

Of the objects of stone, I mention, first, a small basin
of hard limestone, only 70 mm. long which I present to
the reader in the following woodcut, No. 103.   It has two
solid disc-shaped handles and a convex bottom.

As already mentioned (p. 80), a large number of

No. 103.—Basin of hard limestone.   Actual size.   Depth about 1 m.

almost globular corn-bruisers of granite, quartz, porphyry,
or diorite, were found in the ruins of the palace, as well as
several very rudely-formed hammers, without a hole, of
silicious rock or granite, and a pair of oval saddle-querns
of trachyte of the kind already described (p. 80). Of axes of
diorite, one solitary example was found in the palace; it
exactly resembles both those found by me in Mycenæ,*
and a specimen found in the neolithic necropolis of Tangermünde on the Elbe ;† its length is 54 mm., its width
38 mm. at the edge, and 25 mm. at the thick end.   Its
greatest thickness, which is about in the middle ·of its
length, is 10 mm.   The two surfaces, therefore, arch towards

---

* Schliemann, *Mycenæ*, p. 76, No. 126.

† *Zeitschrift für Ethnologie, Organ der Berliner Gesellschaft für Anthropologie, Ethnologie und Urgeschichte*, 1884, Heft III. p. 117, Fig. 2.

the centre; the sides are straight; the polish is good. In the lowest strata of *débris* on the Acropolis at Athens there were found four beautifully polished axes of diorite, which may be seen in the Acropolis Museum.

As in Troy and Mycenæ, so in Tiryns, stone implements were in use at the same time as tools of bronze. I wish to mention on this occasion, that, according to Professor Heinrich Brugsch, battle-axes with stone hammers were among the spoil which Thutmes III. brought back from the highly-civilized states of Western Asia, together with weapons and armour of bronze, and gold and silver works of art.*

A fine specimen of a slate whetstone was found; it is 342 mm. long, 61 mm. broad, and 30 mm. thick, narrowing somewhat to the end. Also a good specimen of fine clay-slate, which is 84 mm. long, 58 mm. broad, and 20 mm. thick.

If the primitive pottery described in the foregoing pages should not suffice to convince us that the palace of Tiryns was destroyed in prehistoric times, we must yield to the additional evidence afforded by the countless knives and arrow-heads of obsidian; for, as already remarked (cf. p. 78) these must, at the time of the destruction of the building, have been still in common use by its inhabitants. Of such knives, good average specimens are represented in the woodcuts Nos. 104–107, of the arrow-heads in those at Nos. 108–111. Knives of obsidian similar to those represented in Nos. 104–107, are also exceedingly common in Mycenæ.† On the other hand, the Mycenæan arrow-heads of obsidian have two barbs, and the three specimens ‡ found in the upper strata of *débris*, as well as the thirty-five § from the fourth royal tomb, are made

---

* Heinrich Brugsch, *Geschichte Aegyptens*, p. 344.
† Schliemann, *Mycenæ*, p. 76, No. 126.
‡ Schliemann, *Mycenæ*, p. 26, No. 176.
§ *Ibid.* p. 272, No. 435.

with great care, and are of the same type. In fact, the
Mycenæan arrow-heads are master-pieces when compared
to the only kind found in Tiryns—extremely rude and
primitive arrow-heads without barbs (cf. Nos. 108–111).

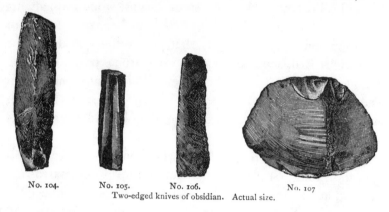

No. 104.        No. 105.        No. 106.                No. 107
Two-edged knives of obsidian.    Actual size.

That the knives and arrow-heads were made on the spot
appears to be proved satisfactorily as well by the obsidian
splinters as by the nuclei of obsidian from which they were
cut, and which we found in large quantities, especially in
the middle fortress

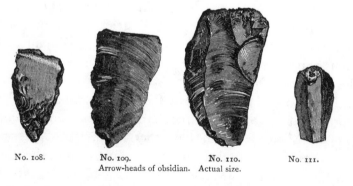

No. 108.        No. 109.            No. 110.        No. 111.
Arrow-heads of obsidian.    Actual size.

I further mention a flat implement of green stone,
20 cm. long, 2 cm. broad, the use of which is unknown, as
well as an egg of alabaster, which resembles the egg of arago-
nite * found in Troy, and which may have been an offering.

---

* Schliemann, *Ilios*, p. 430, No. 556.

We found many spinning-whorls of blue stone, also some of steatite (*lapis ollaris*); almost all are cone-shaped, are perforated vertically, and resemble exactly the 350 stone whorls found in Mycenæ.* There were, however, some stone whorls in the shape of a blunt cone, and among them a very remarkable one of violet-blue colour, which I show on Plate XXI., Fig. *g*. The surface is ornamented with two encircling engraved zones, of which the lower one is filled with a band of zigzags between two horizontal lines ; the upper one with bands of three slanting lines, which converge in the shape of triangles, between two slanting crosses, the arms of which are terminated by circles.

The same form of whorl appears in the prehistoric tombs in Nauplia, Spata, and Ialysos on Rhodes, as well as in Knossos, and in great numbers in the *débris* from the lowest strata in the Acropolis of Athens. The 157 whorls of *lapis ollaris* found there, with ninety of blue stone, are in the Acropolis Museum.

We also found numerous specimens of small discs of steatite, with an average diameter of 20 mm., which have on one side in the middle a projecting tube, 5–10 mm. high ; on the other side they are hollowed round the per-forated central point ; on account of their lightness and smallness they cannot possibly have been used as spinning-whorls. The projecting tube which occurs in all, and which must have occasioned the primitive artist no small trouble, must have had some special use, and I think these objects may have served as decorations on the doors into which they were secured by the tubes, and that in the hollow on the other side some small ornament of bronze or cobalt glass may have been placed.

In my excavations at Mycenæ, I found these objects in very great numbers, and for their form I refer to the draw-ing in my *Mycenæ*, p. 76, No. 126, to the right and left in

---

* Schliemann, *Mycenæ*, p. 18, No. 15.

the upper row. Exactly similar objects have been found in the graves at Nauplia and Spata * as well as in the excavations in the Acropolis at Athens, where twelve exactly similar specimens of steatite, and fifty-five somewhat more cone-shaped ones of the same stone, have been collected and placed in the Acropolis Museum. The National Museum at Athens has two specimens from Attica. The British Museum also contains numbers of similar objects found in the tombs of Ialysos. Of other stone objects, I can only further mention a pair of weights of beautifully polished hematite.

### 13. OBJECTS OF IVORY, WOOD, AND GLASS.

Of ivory there was only one broken comb, of common bone a bodkin, and an instrument 78 mm. long and in the broadest part 28 mm. wide, which has the form of a lance-head, and may have been used as an arrow-head. All the wood discovered was one piece of charred pine. I further mention a pearl of cobalt glass and some small objects of glass-paste. Exactly similar blue-glass beads appear among the finds of northern Europe, and many may be seen in the Museum at Copenhagen.† Precisely similar objects are found in Egypt.

--------

* Schliemann, *Mycenæ*, p. XLVI.

† Sophus Müller, *Ursprung und erste Entwickelung der europäischen Bronzecultur*, p. 340.

# CHAPTER V.

## The Buildings of Tiryns.

### By Dr. Wilhelm Dörpfeld.

### A.—The Citadel and its Wall.

Tiryns was built on an isolated limestone rock, which originally formed an island in the Argolic Gulf, but apparently was already surrounded in prehistoric times by land. The rock forms a ridge running from north to south, 300 m. long, and nearly 100 m. wide; its highest point S. rises about 22 m. above sea-level, and 18 m. over the present surface of the surrounding plain. As the rock is some metres lower on the northern than on the southern side, the *lower* citadel was built on the north, and the *upper* on the south part. Both divisions are of almost equal size, and both have an elliptical form. Separated from the upper citadel is a small section, somewhat lower in position, which divides the upper from the lower fortress, and which we shall call the *middle* citadel.

In the highest part of the citadel, which was surrounded by a double wall, lay the dwelling of the ruler, the royal palace. The middle fortress, which was in direct communication with the palace by means of a narrow staircase, contained apparently lodgings for the servants; in the lower citadel were probably situated the store-rooms, stalls for horses, and the rooms of retainers.

The two first portions were completely excavated by Dr. Schliemann in the summer of 1884, and have presented us with astonishing results.

# PLAN.

## THE FORTRESS
OF
# TIRYNS.

FROM THE EXCAVATIONS OF
DR. H. SCHLIEMANN IN 1884.

MADE AND DRAWN BY DR. W. DÖRPFELD.

CORNFIELD

[1 : 1000]

100 Meter

PLATE I.

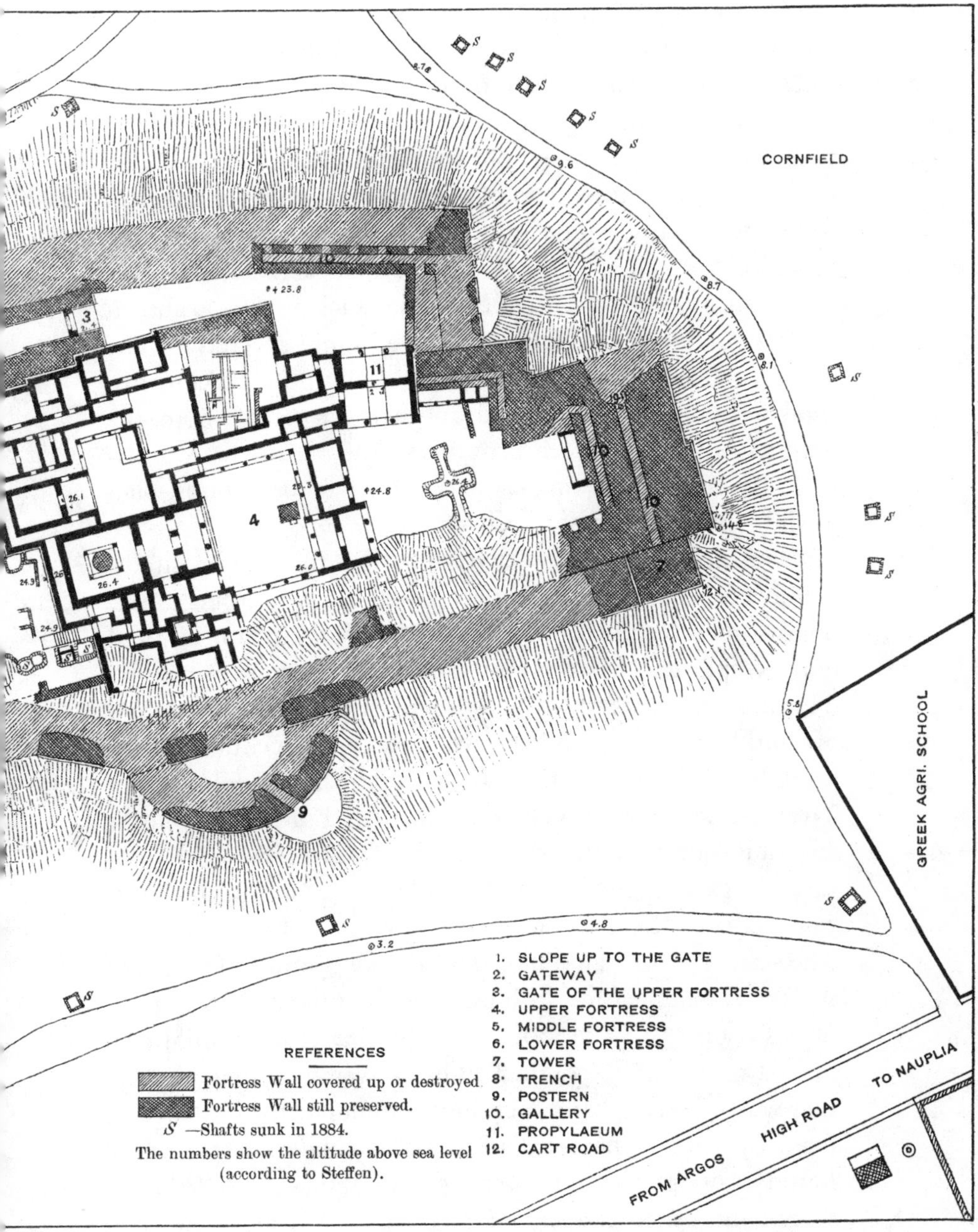

CORNFIELD

GREEK AGRI. SCHOOL

REFERENCES

Fortress Wall covered up or destroyed
Fortress Wall still preserved.
*S* —Shafts sunk in 1884.
The numbers show the altitude above sea level
(according to Steffen).

1. SLOPE UP TO THE GATE
2. GATEWAY
3. GATE OF THE UPPER FORTRESS
4. UPPER FORTRESS
5. MIDDLE FORTRESS
6. LOWER FORTRESS
7. TOWER
8. TRENCH
9. POSTERN
10. GALLERY
11. PROPYLAEUM
12. CART ROAD

FROM ARGOS    HIGH ROAD    TO NAUPLIA

In the upper citadel almost the entire palace, with its gateways, courts, great rooms and chambers, can be distinctly recognized. Most of the walls are still standing, ½ to 1 m. in height, numerous bases of pillars are still in their place, and in the doorways still lie the huge stone door-sills. The middle citadel yielded only the remains of foundation walls. The buildings were here of worse construction than in the palace of the upper citadel, and were therefore more frequently rebuilt in ancient times, and at the destruction of the fortress suffered more severely. The lower citadel is not yet excavated; though, by sinking two trenches, one lengthwise and another across, down to the natural rock, it has been proved that here also the foundations of various buildings still exist; what the ground-plan of these buildings was, is still unknown.

The massive *walls* which surround the whole citadel are formed of great irregular blocks of limestone. The huge stones are piled upon each other without mortar, and only keep their position by means of their great weight. The interstices are filled with small stones. This method of building is known as Cyclopean, on account of the legend which relates that King Proitos, the founder of Tiryns, caused the Cyclopes, skilled in building, to come and build for him the massive walls. Thus we learn that these huge walls excited the wonder even of the ancients, who believed them to be the work of no ordinary builders. The statement of Pausanias, that a yoke of mules could not stir the smallest stone in Tiryns, is, however, an exaggeration, for many of the stones of the citadel walls might be moved by a single workman. On an average the blocks are, however, of very great dimensions; stones of from 2 to 3 m. long, by 1 m. in height and 1 m. in thickness, are to be found among them in very great numbers. Probably there is no other citadel in Greece with walls built of such great blocks and in this rude manner. At Mycenæ, for instance, the average dimensions of the stones are distinctly less.  In fact, in respect of size and grandeur, these walls of Tiryns are unrivalled, and well deserved to be compared by Pausanias with the Pyramids of Egypt.

In the absence of a strong cement, we owe the comparatively good condition of the walls to the size of the individual stones; for had these been smaller, the walls would either have fallen down of themselves during the lapse of ages, or else the stones would have been carried off by the inhabitants of neighbouring towns and villages—to supply material for their dwelling-houses.

The walls stand at this day, almost as Pausanias saw them 600 years after the destruction of the citadel by the Argives, though more than 2300 years have passed since this destruction.

As the excavations were confined almost entirely to the inside of the fortress, very little new material for the reconstruction of the ground-plan or section of the walls has been obtained.  Only at isolated points has the plan of Hauptmann Steffen, drawn before the commencement of the excavations, been completed.*

Until further excavations take place, and the entire encircling wall is exposed, the object and meaning of the various walls, with their towers and gates, cannot be completely recognized and explained.

The course of the wall is shown in Plate I., which, according to the older plans, presents the whole fortress, together with its immediate neighbourhood, on the scale of 1 : 1000.  Those portions of the wall which are still visible, I have indicated by cross hatchings.  Where, on the other hand, the hatchings are single, there is no longer any trace of the walls; they are either destroyed, or concealed by heaps of ruins or earth.

Round the *lower citadel* the wall is simple, being of the same thickness above and below, without any set-off.  The

---

* *Karten von Mykenæ*, by Hauptmann Steffen, Pl. II.

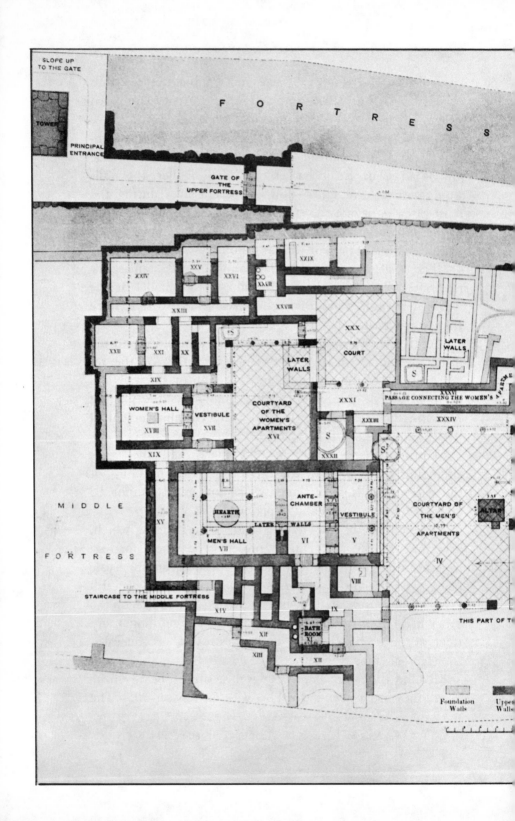

SLOPE UP
TO THE GATE

TOWER

PRINCIPAL
ENTRANCE

F  O  R  T  R  E  S  S

GATE OF
THE
UPPER FORTRESS

XXIX

XXIV

XXV

XXVI

XXVII

XXIII

XXVIII

XXX

COURT

LATER
WALLS

XXII

XXI

XX

LATER
WALLS

XIX

COURTYARD
OF THE
WOMEN'S
APARTMENTS
XVI

XXXI

LATER
WALLS

S

WOMEN'S HALL

XVIII

VESTIBULE

XVII

XXXIII

XXXVI
PASSAGE CONNECTING THE WOMEN'S APARTMENTS

XXXIV

XIX

S

XXXII

S

MIDDLE

HEARTH

ANTE-
CHAMBER

COURTYARD OF

THE MEN'S

APARTMENTS

ALTAR

XV

FORTRESS

LATER   WALLS

VESTIBULE

MEN'S HALL
VII

VI

V

IV

VIII

STAIRCASE TO THE MIDDLE FORTRESS

X

IX

XIV

THIS PART OF TH

BATH
ROOM
XI

XII

XIII

XII

Foundation
Walls

Upper
Walls

PLATE II.

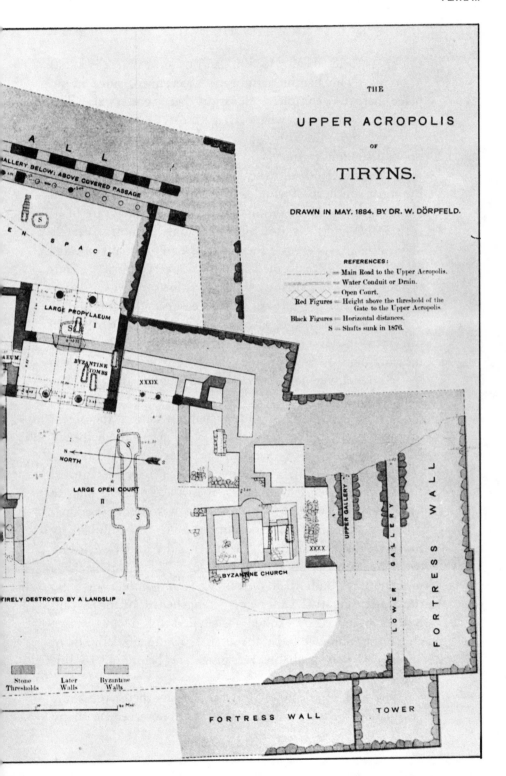

THE

# UPPER ACROPOLIS

OF

# TIRYNS.

DRAWN IN MAY, 1884, BY DR. W. DÖRPFELD.

REFERENCES:

----- = Main Road to the Upper Acropolis.
≈≈≈≈ = Water Conduit or Drain.
◇◇◇ = Open Court.
Red Figures = Height above the threshold of the Gate to the Upper Acropolis
Black Figures = Horizontal distances.
S = Shafts sunk in 1876.

WALL

GALLERY BELOW: ABOVE COVERED PASSAGE

OPEN SPACE

S

LARGE PROPYLAEUM
S
I

-AEUM-

BYZANTINE TOMBS

XXXIX

N ← NORTH
S

S

LARGE OPEN COURT
II

S

XXXX

UPPER GALLERY

LOWER GALLERY

FORTRESS WALL

BYZANTINE CHURCH

ENTIRELY DESTROYED BY A LANDSLIP

Stone Thresholds   Later Walls   Byzantine Walls

FORTRESS WALL          TOWER

thickness varies from 7 to 8 m., and in most places is about
7·60 m. The height cannot be ascertained, since in no
place has the complete elevation been preserved. The
height of the wall, where it is most perfect, is about
7·50 m., and this point lies about 3 m. above the ancient
floor of the lower citadel.

In the inner side of the eastern wall are left several niches,
the most southern of which can still be accurately measured
(3·20 m. wide by 3·70 m. deep). The others are filled
with *débris*, and their dimensions can only be approximately
determined. Apparently these niches had originally pointed
arches, which were formed merely by overlapping the ends
of the successive courses of masonry, for somewhat further
south, near the great tower on the east side of the middle
fortress, exists a niche, also given in the plan, which still
preserves its ogival vault; and although its horizontal
measurement is smaller than that of the niches in the
lower citadel, yet doubtless the method of roofing was the
same in all.

It is impossible to say with certainty what was the object
of these niches. Possibly they served as store-chambers.
More probably, as it seems to me, they were intended to
economize material in building the wall. On the top of
the wall, for defensive purposes, the widest possible plateau
was desirable, while lower down the wall might be considerably slighter. Both conditions were best fulfilled by
forming these niches on the inner side, and by closing
them beneath the upper wall-plateau. Many nations have
in later times built their fortress walls in a similar way; on
the inner side the walls were strengthened by projecting
buttresses, united by vaulted arches, and thus a wide surface
above was obtained. In the niches of the citadel-walls of
Tiryns we may probably recognize the beginning of this
construction.

The wall of the lower fortress has another remarkable
peculiarity. On its outer side may be observed, in many

places, a vertical joint extending the whole height of the wall. He who visits Tiryns for the first time and observes one of these joints, usually believes that in this place another wall was built on to the angle of a more ancient wall, and that this indicates a later extension of the fortress. When, however, he follows the course of the wall, and observes other joints of the same kind, this explanation will be found unsatisfactory. That the wall of the lower citadel should have been built at such varying periods as would correspond with all these complete joints, is most unlikely; it was certainly built, in its whole extent, at one time.

We must therefore seek for another explanation. As the vertical joints occur always either at a salient or at a re-entering angle, it might be supposed that the builders could not well produce with rough stones corners with an angle so obtuse as nearly to approach a straight line, and they therefore preferred to juxtaposit two corner-nocks.

But another explanation is perhaps more probable. Between two of those vertical joints on the east side of the lower citadel I measured a distance of 11·30 m. This measure corresponds exactly with the inner breadth of the great tower beside the main entrance to the citadel, and there being a complete vertical joint between this tower and the adjoining masonry, I am led to believe that the portion of wall between the two vertical joints must also have been a tower. If so, the probable origin of the joints is that the towers were first of all built at suitable places on the rock, and then they were joined by walls. This explanation, which has much in its favour, did not occur to me till after my departure from Tiryns, and I was therefore unable to test its application to all the other upright joints.

The lower citadel is separated from the *middle citadel* by a wall, the direction of which we can determine by many remains yet visible; but both height and width are as yet unknown to us, because the excavations stopped at this point. It was doubtless a retaining wall, as it supports

the higher middle fort, and has an outer front only on the
north side.   At its eastern extremity there appears to have
been a gate, which connected the lower fort with the main
entrance to the upper citadel which lies further south (see
Plans I. and II.).

The surrounding wall of the *Upper Citadel* is not constructed as simply as that of the lower fort.   The upper
plateau was too far above the foot of the rock to permit
of a vertical wall being built with rough stones without
mortar from the foot of the rock up to its level.   Such a
wall would have been thrown down by the thrust of the
earth settling behind it.   In order to build a high wall of
this kind, without exact horizontal joints or mortar, it is
necessary either to escarp the outside (that is to say, make
it slope at an acute angle), or to make the outside retreat
in successive steps.   The former method is particularly
suited to small stones, and was employed in the Acropolis
wall of ancient Ilion; the latter we find at the upper fort
in Tiryns.   Here a vertical lower wall is first built on the
rock, and over it there is a vertical upper wall, starting
about 6·50 m. behind the former.

On Plate III. I have given a section of the eastern wall
of the upper citadel on the scale of 1 : 250.   I have marked
the preserved parts with cross-hatchings, the restored with
single hatchings.   The section is made east of the larger
Propylæum (No. I. on Plan II.), because the wall is here
best preserved, and also partly cleared of the *débris*.

The whole thickness of the wall is 10·90 m., of which
4·45 m. belong to the upper and 6·45 m. to the lower wall.
The total height, from the way round the citadel to the
floor of the upper wall surface, is about 16 m., of which
nearly 5 m. belong to the upper wall.   The remainder
(11 m.), which gives the height of the plateau of the lower
wall above the plain, includes the height of the rising cliff
and that of the lower wall.   How much each of them is,
we cannot tell at the east side of the upper fort, because

there this lower wall is still covered with great blocks of stone and *débris*. We cannot therefore tell how much of the height is natural. The height given in the plan (6 m.) is a conjecture formed upon another part of the fort, where the wall is exposed.

While the lower wall, so far as we know, is a solid mass of stones, we find galleries introduced into the upper wall, which have often been examined and described. Their position and construction may be clearly seen in the section. Two parallel walls, the outer 1·15 m., the inner 1·65 m. thick, enclose a passage of 1·65 m. wide. To a height of about 1·75 m. both walls are perpendicular, with several courses of stones; but above this the stones gradually overlap, and so form a roof shaped like a pointed arch. For this purpose stones, which, when lying horizontally, have a side sloping inwards obliquely, are generally selected. Hence the inclination is made gradually, and not in steps. The result is that from within, the roofs of these galleries look like real vaults of pointed arches, whereas they are really not vaults at all. Some stones, indeed, because they do not lie horizontally, may exercise an inward thrust, and in some places the uppermost stone may really act as the key-stone of an arch; but these galleries cannot be regarded as real arches, because, generally speaking, there is no lateral thrust.

From this covered passage, the floor of which, made of beaten clay, is on a level with the plateau of the lower wall, a series of doors open on the lower wall. These are 1·50 m. to 1·70 m. wide, and about 2·75 high to their vertex. Their distance from centre to centre is on the average 4·75 m. On Plate III. (right corner below) there is a longitudinal section of a part of these galleries given, with a view of these doors, and below it a ground-plan of this part. The adjoining sketch, No. 112, gives also a section of the upper wall with an inner view in perspective. In both it will be seen that the doorways are

roofed by the converging of the upper stones in the form
of a pointed arch. Generally only two large blocks are
used for the purpose, which either lean against each other
at the upper edges directly, or against a third stone set
between them from above.

The object of these passages has long been disputed;
they were supposed to be storing-places for food and arms

No. 112.—Gallery in the Eastern Wall.

of the garrison, or stalls for horses or cattle.* Steffen was
the first to give a correct explanation in the text to his
maps of Mycenæ: they are covered passages inside the
upper wall, from which the defenders could step out upon
the lower wall, and resist the assailants. Small steps or

---

* E. Curtius, *Peloponnesos, II.* 387. Göttling (*Arch. Zeitung,* 1845,
p. 17, *sq.*) even thought he recognized in these galleries the chambers
of the daughters of Proitos, mentioned by Pausanias, II 25, 8.

ramps probably led down to the galleries from the upper citadel, but hitherto none of these have been discovered. Possibly of the two galleries situated in the south wall the upper one may be such a passage leading down to the lower gallery. For purposes of defence the lower wall must have had on its top either a breastwork or a covered passage; there are now no remains of either, for the upper portion of the wall is everywhere destroyed. In the cross section on Plate III. I have therefore conjecturally drawn a simple breastwork.

It must, on the other hand, be considered peculiarly fortunate that in one place important remains of the summit of the upper wall still exist, by which means we are better instructed regarding the shape of the upper than of the lower wall. The remains exposed by excavations consist of four bases of columns, which were found at the inner edge of the east wall opposite the greater Propylæum *in situ.* The bases consist each of a great stone, on the top of which a circle is raised by cutting. The diameter of the circles averages 0·55 m. The first, second, and fourth of these pillar-bases lie almost exactly on the same level, whilst the third, a larger square block, is about 0·28 m. higher. There can be no doubt that we have here the remains of a colonnade, which formed an upper covered passage round the wall. Of the construction of this colonnade we know very little, but from that of a later Greek wall, well known to us, we may form an approximate idea of it.

From the well-known inscription describing the resto-ration of the Athenian walls (Corpus Inscriptionum Atti-carum, II. 167) we know that on these walls, built of clay-bricks, a covered gallery was constructed. It consisted on the inner side of a row of separate piers; on the outside there was a continuous brick wall, with window-like open-ings, furnished with movable wooden shutters; it was roofed with strong beams of wood, clay, and baked tiles.

The passage on the citadel-walls of Tiryns was pro-

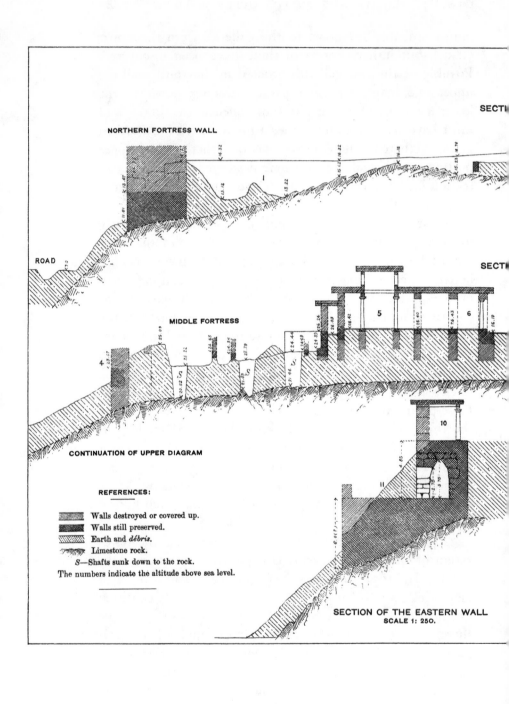

SECTI

NORTHERN FORTRESS WALL

ROAD

SECT

MIDDLE FORTRESS

4

5        6

10

11

CONTINUATION OF UPPER DIAGRAM

REFERENCES:

Walls destroyed or covered up.
Walls still preserved.
Earth and *débris*.
Limestone rock.
S—Shafts sunk down to the rock.
The numbers indicate the altitude above sea level.

SECTION OF THE EASTERN WALL
SCALE 1: 250.

PLATE III.

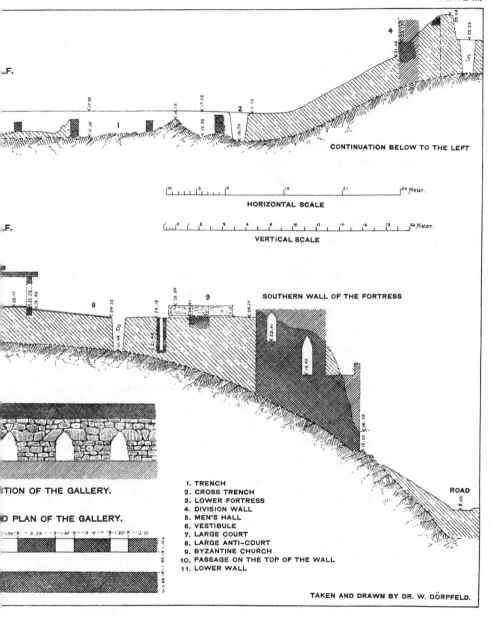

_.F.

CONTINUATION BELOW TO THE LEFT

HORIZONTAL SCALE

VERTICAL SCALE

_.F.

SOUTHERN WALL OF THE FORTRESS

TION OF THE GALLERY.

PLAN OF THE GALLERY.

ROAD

1. TRENCH
2. CROSS TRENCH
3. LOWER FORTRESS
4. DIVISION WALL
5. MEN'S HALL
6. VESTIBULE
7. LARGE COURT
8. LARGE ANTI–COURT
9. BYZANTINE CHURCH
10. PASSAGE ON THE TOP OF THE WALL
11. LOWER WALL

TAKEN AND DRAWN BY DR. W. DÖRPFELD.

bably arranged in a similar way.  On the inner side of the
wall, 4·45 m. wide, on bases of stone stood uprights of
wood at distances of about 2·15 m. ; on the outside we
must suppose a dead brick wall, which formed the back
wall of the passage, and was furnished with window-like
openings for defence.  That this wall was indeed built of
clay-bricks appears from the great quantity of half-baked
brick-*débris*, which is found on the upper wall, and the
set-off of the lower wall.  Over this hall-like passage there
must have been a simple roof of wood and clay.

The back wall of the passage in any case rose flush
with the outside of the great (hardly 5 m. high) upper wall,
and added an additional elevation.  As all evidence of the
height of this colonnade is wanting, that which is marked
in Plate III. is conjectural.

Thus the eastern wall of the upper fortress of Tiryns
affords us a very interesting and comparatively perfect representation of an ancient Greek fortress-wall.  The technical necessity of building the wall in two offsets was very
cleverly adapted to the purposes of fortification, affording
a double line of defence.

The enemy must first attack the outer wall, and if, after
a long fight, he carried this, he then found in the upper
wall a second line of defence, which, on the closing of the
steps which led down to the lower wall, was at least as
difficult to overcome as the first.

Whether the west and south walls of the upper citadel
were constructed exactly in the same way as the east wall
cannot with certainty be decided until the whole citadel-
wall is excavated.  Remains of similar galleries in the
south wall make such uniformity highly probable.

At the south end of the west wall are considerable remains of a great tower, which show us that the lower wall
did not surround the upper citadel in an unbroken line,
but that in several places on the lower wall towers were
raised, which hindered the free passage along it.  If therefore

the enemy had ever gained an entrance in one place on
the lower wall, the whole line of defence was not in his
hands yet, but he found himself in a comparatively narrow
space, from three sides exposed to the missiles of the defenders, who not only from the upper wall, but also from
the towers on each side, could discharge upon him stones
and darts.

In former descriptions of Tiryns one frequently finds
the statement that the citadel had two *chief entrances*, one
on the south-east corner, and one in the middle of the east
side. This, however, is incorrect, for the excavations show
that at the south-east corner there cannot have been any
entrance, and that therefore there was but one great
entrance to the citadel. How the south-east corner terminated is uncertain, for the wall there is not yet quite
exposed. But the position of the ground already shows
clearly, that at most a small side-door existed here, such as
occurs in several places in the citadel.

The only great gate lay about in the middle of the east
wall, that is, on the side of the citadel facing landwards,
and not towards the sea. A ramp, built of large blocks,
led from the north along the east wall up to the citadel. It
is still fairly well preserved, and might be restored at small
cost. Its width is 4·70 m.; the length cannot be fixed,
as the lower part is hidden by the ruins of the citadel-wall,
and on this account also we cannot measure the gradient
of the ascent. At the upper end of the ramp one comes
upon a passage, also 4·70 m. wide, in the wall, but the
lower part of this passage is reduced to a width of about
2·50 m. by blocks built up at its sides.

Here we confidently expected to find some remains of
a gate-portal; but our researches were without result, for
neither a stone threshold nor any doorposts have been
found.

On the north side of the entrance rises a tower which
is still, at the present day, more than 7 m. high, built of

gigantic blocks.   Its area forms a rectangle 7·50 m. broad
and 10·30 m. long.   The tower commanded the entrance
completely, for it lies, in accordance with the ancient law of
fortification, on the right and unshielded side of the assailants.   Whether we should supply a second tower on the
south side of the entrance cannot be decided from the
remains, but it might reasonably be concluded from the
position of the ramp in relation to the adjoining lower
wall on the south.   It would have been easy to reach the
lower wall from the upper end of the ramp, which is about
the same height, if it had not been shut off from the ramp
by a tower.

Having passed through the entrance, one reaches a
passage running from north to south, and shut in by high
walls on both sides.   On the N., or right hand, it leads
first to the middle fort, and then further down to the lower
citadel.   Going to the left, one soon comes to a great gate,
on passing through which a gradual ascent leads up to
the palace in the upper citadel.   Of this gate and way to
the upper citadel we shall learn more when we come to the
description of the palace.

The road on the right-hand which leads to the lower
citadel is not yet quite excavated, and therefore we know
not whether particular gates shut off the middle and lower
citadels. Huge boulders of stone, fallen from the side walls,
at present block the way.   We removed many of them
with great difficulty, but were unable to finish the work
before the conclusion of the excavations, which was rendered
necessary by the commencement of the summer heat.

Besides this chief entrance, the citadel had several
posterns or sally-ports, which apparently partly served for
purposes of defence.   Posterns of this kind are still to be
seen at the northern end and at the south-west corner of
the lower citadel; their disposition and construction can
only be ascertained by further excavation.

The small postern in the great semicircular building,

attached to the west side of the upper citadel, is of peculiar interest. We had just begun to clear this, when the intense heat put an end to our work. The purpose of this great screen is therefore not yet ascertained. Hauptmann Steffen conjectures that it was an assembling place, where the warriors gathered for a sortie, and that it was connected by steps with the upper fort. These steps and walled passages are very probably still preserved, and it would be a task likely to repay the trouble to continue the excavations at this point, and to bring to light that postern and its connection with the upper citadel.

In closing this description of the citadel wall and its gates, I cannot repress the earnest wish, that tne whole of these walls might be cleared as soon as possible, as completely as the inside of the upper fort has been by Dr. Schliemann. Then only will it be possible thoroughly to understand these interesting walls with their towers, galleries, gates, and posterns, and to answer with certainty the questions which still remain unanswered.

### B.—The Palace in the Upper Citadel.

In order the better to understand the description of the building of the various rooms, we shall first take a general survey of the Palace, its gateways, courts and chambers.

If we ascend the great ramp on the east side to the chief entrance, and, having passed the tower, turn to the south, we find ourselves in a high-walled approach, and in a few steps reach a great folding gate, which in dimensions and construction corresponds closely with the Lions' Gate of Mycenæ. If we pass through, we are led by an ascending way between the eastern citadel-wall and the terrace wall of the upper citadel to a large court, on the E. side of which we observe a portico, the covered passage on the citadel wall. On the west side of the court, opposite to the portico, lies a stately gateway. The folding-door is furnished with

a roomy outer and inner vestibule, both of which have
the well-known form of the temple *in antis,* that is, two
columns between two *parastades* or *antæ.* We cross this
Propylæum and come upon a large outer court, in which
we find again two small porticoes, and some chambers.
But the buildings of this outer court are much injured,
because here during the Middle Ages a small Byzantine
church was built, the foundations of which still remain.

At the north-west corner of this outer court lies a second
Propylæum, somewhat smaller than the first, but likewise
consisting of an inner and outer hall, adorned with pillars.
Through the double doors of this gateway we enter the
chief court of the palace, the court of the men's apartments.
On its four sides there are porticoes; on the south side,
beside the inner hall of the Propylæum, a narrow two-
pillared Stoa; on the north side, the spacious vestibule of
the megaron; and on each of the other two sides, a three-
pillared portico.

The floor of the court is composed of a strong concrete
of small pebbles and lime, and even now produces a very
fine effect. In the middle of the south side, immediately
beside the north-east pilaster of the Propylæum, stands
a great altar built of quarried stones. It was apparently
dedicated to Zeus, like the altar in the Palace of Odysseus.

The Megaron, the hall of the men, lies with its vestibule and antechamber on the north side, directly in the
axis of the court. We first come to the vestibule already
mentioned, which is formed of two columns and two *parastades* or *antæ.* Three folding-doors, side by side, lead into
the antechamber, and from thence by a large door we come
to the chief hall. Four pillars supported the roof of this
huge room, which is almost 10 m. wide by 12 m. long; a
large circle in the middle of the hall probably indicates the
situation of the hearth. The antechamber has in its west
wall a small side door, giving access to various corridors
and chambers. Of the last, one in particular is interest-

ing—the bath-room, of which the floor is composed of
one gigantic block of stone.

Near the great court of the men's dwelling, the palace
contains a second smaller court, with porticoes and
chambers, in which we may without hesitation recognize
the women's dwelling. This is only to be reached from
the men's dwelling by roundabout passages and narrow
corridors. As the Megaron of the men is connected
with the great court, so the Megaron of the women, with
an open vestibule, lies to the north side of this smaller
court. No separate anteroom like that in the men's
dwelling is found here, but from the vestibule one passes
directly through a wide single doorway to the women's
hall. A square place in the floor also shows where the
hearth was, in the middle of the chamber.

The women's room is surrounded on three sides by
corridors, leading to further chambers; one appears to
have had steps to the upper storey, or to the roof. In the
outermost north-east corner of the palace lies a separate
corridor, from which four chambers of various sizes are
accessible. Finally, on the east side of the court of the
men's dwelling many foundations of walls have been uncovered; but, on account of their ruinous condition, it is
impossible to give any comprehensible ground-plan of the
rooms in this quarter.

The picture which rises before us, as we thus wander
round the citadel, of the palace and its arrangements, is still
in some points misty; but, taken all in all, is surprisingly
complete. The dwelling-house of a ruler in the Heroic
age was until now only known to us by the descriptions of
Homer. Nothing remained of the palaces of Menelaus,
of Odysseus, or the other heroes; the few crooked walls at
Ithaka, which in histories of architecture usually pass for
the Palace of Odysseus, had in truth no claim to the
name

The nearest resemblance or approach to an ancient

royal palace was the dwelling of the ancient ruler of Troy, dug out two years ago among the buildings in the second stratum at Hissarlik; but these buildings were so destroyed, that no clue to the connection of the various rooms could be found.    How clearly, on the other hand, rises before us from these discoveries at Tiryns the image of the home of the prehistoric king!   We see the mighty walls, with their towers and gates, and enter into the palace by the pillar-decked Propylæa.   We recognize the men's court, with its great altar, surrounded by porticoes; we see, further, the stately Megaron, with its anteroom and vestibule; we even enter the bath-room; and finally pass on to the women's dwelling, with its separate court and numerous chambers.   This is a picture which floats before the mind of every reader of Homer—for example, in the description of the return of Odysseus and the massacre of the suitors — a picture which many a *savant* has endeavoured to reconstruct after the data given by Homer.

All attempts hitherto made at representing the "lordly house" of Homer have been to some extent unsatisfactory, because Homer never describes the palaces of his heroes minutely, but only gives us occasional and accidental allusions.   There always remained questions to which all the acuteness in the world on the part of Homeric scholars could give no answer in the words of the poet.   Many of these riddles are now solved by the palace at Tiryns. No doubt it must differ in some details from the palaces of Odysseus, Alkinous, and Menelaus, but in general it certainly gives us a true picture of a Homeric dwelling.

Having now taken a general survey of the palace of Tiryns, let us examine the details of the building.


## 1. The Gate of the Upper Citadel.

Between the eastern citadel-wall and the terrace of the upper citadel, about 15 m. south of the main entrance, the

way leading up into the higher citadel is barred by a gate.
This corresponds in arrangement and measurement very
closely with the celebrated Lions' Gate at Mycenæ. On
an enormous threshold, 1·45 m. broad and more than 3 m.
long, there stand two immense doorposts of breccia, 1·40 m.
broad, 0·95 m. deep, and 3·20 m. high; one of them still
in its place, the other, the eastern one, with its upper
half broken off. These uprights are not mere squared
blocks, but in the outer side a special door-rebate or door-
case is wrought (cf. the ground-plan on Plan II.) against
which the great doors rested. The width of the gate within
this door-rebate is 2·86 m., a measure recurring precisely
in the same part of the Lions' Gate at Mycenæ, and therefore probably some definite amount of ancient feet or
cubits (6 cubits are 9 feet). On the inner side the gate
is 3·16 m. in width. As its height is also 3·20 m., the
folding-door formed an exact square. In the threshold,
immediately behind each stanchion of the door-case, there
is preserved a round hole 0·15 m. in diameter, in which
the pivot of the gate turned. There were, no doubt, two
corresponding holes in the lintel. The latter is gone, but
most probably consisted, as at the Lions' Gate at Mycenæ,
of a large lintel, over which a relieving aperture of triangular shape was arranged. Nothing was discovered of
any relief which might have filled such an aperture. But
the arrangement for shutting the gate can still be clearly
seen. In each of the two uprights, 1·55 m. above the
threshold, and therefore exactly at mid height, there is a
cylindrical hole 0·17 m. in diameter, meant to receive a
large wooden bolt. This bolting beam was round, and,
when the gate was to be opened, could be pushed back
through the eastern doorpost into the wall of the fort;
when the gate was shut, the great bolt was drawn out of
the wall, and run across into the western post, where the
hole was only 0·41 m. deep.

The broad wall on the west side of the gateway, which

strengthens considerably the great eastern supporting wall of the palace, is clearly built for the defence of gate and gateway; for, as the rooms of the palace reach right up to the eastern edge of the terrace, there was on this latter no room for defenders. Hence an additional wall had been added along the terrace, from the top of which the gate could be easily defended. Another object was likewise attained by this wall; the gateway was narrowed, and therefore rendered more easily defensible.

## 2. The Great Propylæum of the Upper Citadel.

When we pass through the gate, and go up to the higher citadel, there lies before us a great outside court, on the west of which was a stately gate-building. The actual gate-wall, which held a folding-door, had vestibules before and behind it (east and west). Both these halls are built like temples *in antis*—that is, their respective fronts consist of two pillars between two pilasters. Simple as this plan of the gate is, its importance for the history of Greek architecture is great, for we see in it the form of later Greek gates almost complete. The idea of supplying the actual gate-wall with halls before and behind was substantially maintained throughout all ages in Greece, from this gate building of the heroic age to the rich Propylæa of the Acropolis of Athens.

The gate building is fairly well preserved. The great door-sill of stone lies in its place; the ancient floor is preserved in the whole building; the walls still rise up to 0·50 m. above the ground. Of three *antæ* (pilasters), the lowest large stone is still preserved; and of the four columns, the bases are all *in situ*. There cannot therefore be the smallest doubt about the ground-plan.

The ante-chamber, 5·50 m. deep and 11·25 m. broad, is surrounded on three sides with walls of limestone-rubble and clay, 1·05 m. to 1·18 m. thick. The north wall

varies in thickness, as it must correct the variation in direction between the gateway and the rooms adjoining on the
north side. A stone of the northern *anta* still lies above
the floor in its place, while of the southern *anta* only the
foundations remain. This stone is limestone, and is fitted
above with round dowel-holes to fasten in the wooden *antæ*.
The bases of the two pillars are formed of large blocks of
limestone with irregular edges, on the upper surface of
which is worked a circle of 0·75 m. diameter, and about
4 cm. high. We shall show, further on, that the pillars
themselves and the upper parts of the *antæ* were of wood.

The great door-sill is formed of a limestone block with
irregular edges, almost 4 m. long and 2 m. broad. In
order to fix it firmly on the foundation, it is supported
only at both ends; in the middle the foundation does
not reach its lower surface. The whole upper surface of
this door-sill is polished, and along its centre a band of
1·08 m. in width, corresponding to the width of the wall,
is brought up in relief about 3 cm. high. This band formed
the visible door-sill, against which the wooden folding-
doors were closed. The lower and irregular part of the
door-sill was covered with the composite of the floor, and
therefore, not visible. In the part of the threshold, which
projects from the line of the wall, the grooves were made
in which the pivots of the huge folding-doors turned.
They are round holes, 0·21 m. in diameter and 0·04 m. in
depth; in form, the section of a sphere. From centre to
centre they are 3·12 m. apart, from which it appears that
the clear width of the actual gates was about as great as
that of the gate above described (2·86 m.). The two
folding-doors were made of great beams of wood, as the
size of the pivot holes (0·21 m.) clearly shows. In the
description of the doors (below, § 6) it will appear that
the wooden posts did not work directly in the grooves,
but were shod with bronze. It was therefore bronze, and
not wood, which turned in the stone groove. The ruin

affords no evidence as to the arrangements for shutting
this gate.

The back vestibule, into which you pass by the folding
doors, was planned like the anteroom, but was somewhat
deeper (6·73–6·85 m. as compared with 5·50 m.). Its
front is formed of two pillars between two *antæ*. Of the
former, only their irregular bases are left, which show in
the upper surface the circle raised on the one 2, on the
other 3 cm. In both the spaces between *antæ* and pillars
there are now low walls, starting from the *antæ*, and not
reaching quite to the pillars. They end also in *antæ*-blocks
of their own. I thought that these walls were later, and
that the two pillars had been got rid of when they were
built, for the northern pillar base was found about half
covered by a later concrete floor. But there is this objection,
that the greater corner-*antæ* are not carefully worked on
their inner side, and were therefore never meant to be visible.
Two explanations are possible. Either the front of the
posterior hall consisted originally of two pillars between
two *antæ*; later on, the pillars were removed and the side
walls built, in order to have only one broad entrance.
Or else the two low walls were erected together with the
pillars, but were only 1–2 m. high; then the pillars must
have been removed later. In the plan, I have adopted
the former hypothesis, and have accordingly noted the
little walls as later work.

The whole floor was covered with a concrete of pebbles
and lime, which is still well preserved in most places. In
some can be seen later repairs done with a material almost
exclusively lime, and therefore less durable than the older
concrete. The holes about 2 m. long, seen in some parts
of this floor are Byzantine tombs, to be discussed when
describing the Byzantine Church.

In the central passage through the gate, indicated in
the plan by two lines, the concrete has sunk about 0·30 m.
as compared with the floor of the two 'side aisles,' so that

the threshold, which maintains its original level, is to that extent raised above the floor of the 'nave.' The cause of this lies in the variety of foundation. The side aisles rest in their whole breadth on huge foundation walls, while the nave or central passage has no foundation. The earth piled up under the floor of the latter subsided considerably even in olden times, as did the whole court west of the Propylæum. Hence the concrete of the central passage has sunk, while that of the sides, supported by walls, has maintained its original position.

But why were the sides supported by great foundations 7½ m. thick? It is obvious to compare the Athenian *Propylæa*; in those too the central passage, in contrast to the sides, is not on a foundation, no doubt because it must be passable for horses and carriages. Perhaps for the same reason the central passage at Tiryns was not supported by a foundation wall. Yet in this case it remains inexplicable how carriages could get over the high threshold, after the central way had already sunk considerably; it is also remarkable, that on this great threshold no sign of wheel tracks has been found. My architect friend, Herr Siebold, who during his long visit at Tiryns was kind enough to talk over all these problems with me, has proposed another theory for the supporting of the side aisles, which has much to be said for it, and which therefore I shall not omit. He thinks that the strong walls with a passage between them of about 2·75 m. wide are the remains of an older gate, whose floor lay much deeper, and was enclosed with thick walls. To support this hypothesis there are various grounds. First, there are in many parts of the palace, at a deeper level, undoubted traces of older buildings; secondly, the open court east of the Propylæum is made of *remblai* of red, or burnt-brick *débris*, which also points to an older destroyed settlement; thirdly, it could thus be explained how the foundation under the middle of the great threshold does not reach up to it, but lies considerably deeper.

In the north wall of the back vestibule a side door has been discovered, which leads to some rooms (XXXVIII.), and by means of a long corridor to the women's apartments. In this long passage the lime-floor is almost everywhere well-preserved, so that even now you can pass up easily between the walls, about 1 m. high, to the higher court of the women's residence.

Of the upper structure of the gateway we can form only a conjecture, as we know nothing, or next to nothing, about its height and artistic details. The principal (east) front had four supports, two pillars between two *antæ*; the latter were 1·35 m. broad, the lower diameter of the pillars may be assumed at 0·65 m., to judge from the bases. The central intercolumnar space was wider than the rest; the width in the clear from pillar to pillar was 3·45 m., while that of the others was about 3·15 m. But this difference was merely caused by the varying strength of the supports, for from axis to axis the three distances were exactly the same, 4·10 m. We know nothing of the form of the pillars, and can only surmise that their capitals were not unlike those of the great beehive tomb at Mycenæ, and the Lions' Gate there.

Over the four supports there must have been an epistyle, to receive the ends of the great roof-beams, for, considering the width in the clear of the gate (11·25 m.), the latter could not possibly have been set parallel to the front, but must have been at right angles with it. The ends of the beams were perhaps visible over the epistyle, and ornamented after the manner of triglyphs; otherwise they may have been round, like the beam-ends shown on tomb façades and the Lions' relief at Mycenæ. Over these great beams we must imagine boards, which, as a protecting entablature, reached out far beyond the edge of the roof. They were probably covered with rushes and a thick layer of clay, which formed a horizontal roof. In order to secure a better escape for rain water, the clay-coating was doubtless much thicker in the centre than at the sides. Thus the surface of the roof obtained the form of a very flat cupola, as we see it on the temple of Thetis in the well-known vase of Ergotimos and Klitias in Florence, generally known as the *François-Vase*. The appearance of the back hall probably corresponded to the front hall as now described.

As regards the Homeric word for the *Propylæum*, there can be no hesitation in identifying it with the πρόθυρον (or πρόθυρα). The palace of Odysseus had, according to Homer, apparently only *one* πρόθυρον (vestibule), the gate of the court; when the palace was larger, and had an exterior court as well, this latter must have had its own πρόθυρον.

### 3. THE GREAT FRONT COURT.

### (No. II. on Plate II.)

Having passed through the Propylæum, we come to a large court of irregular shape, surrounded with colonnades and some rooms. At its east side, immediately south of the Propylæum, there is a small colonnade (XXXIX. on the Plan). It was designed like a temple *in antis;* of its two pillars the stone bases, 0·47 m. in diameter, are still *in situ ;* they are of limestone and have the form of frustum of a cone, or a Doric capital turned upside down. Of the southern *anta* too, a great limestone block is still in posi- tion ; it has on its upper surface no dowel-holes, as is the case with other *antæ*. The northern *anta* is gone. The distance from axis to axis of the pillars is 2·06 m.; the depth of the colonnade about 2·40 m. The narrow space, 1·20 m. broad, behind the back wall was excavated pretty deeply, but we could not determine its object, or whether it had been at all accessible.

A second colonnade of the same form appears to have existed south of the Byzantine Church ; but this is not certain, as not even the pillar bases were preserved. By the building of this Byzantine Church, not only this colonnade, but all the other buildings on the south side of the court were much injured. Foundations only are left, and even these are so much destroyed, that the connection of the various walls is hardly to be made out.

The west side of the court is even worse. Here, at some time or other, the great citadel-wall gave way; the terrace of the fort thus lost its support, and slipped away with all its buildings and foundations. Hence every trace of ancient buildings is gone on the west side of the citadel. The great western citadel-wall is probably still preserved here in its lowest courses, but it will require considerable excavations to determine accurately its direction and construction.

The north side of the court is, fortunately, better preserved. The great Propylæum is joined on the west side by a small corridor, which was closed by doors, and formed a direct secondary connection between the main court and the preceding court. The floor of this corridor is still preserved, and consists of lime-concrete. As the difference of level of the two courts exceeds 1 m., the way leads up with a steep gradient to the Men's Court. Westward follow two chambers, first, a larger one 6·22 m. wide, and then one of 3·09 m.; both are 4·29 m. deep. There is no trace of the position of the doors, but as remains of the concrete floor of both rooms are preserved, it could be ascertained that the floors were only a few centimetres higher than the outer court, but about 0·67 m. lower than the court of the men's apartments, and so these chambers were intended to be entered from the former, and not the latter. The doors must therefore have been at that point of the south wall where there is now no masonry left. As to the use of the two rooms, nothing can be safely determined; we can only surmise that they may have served to lodge the door-keepers.

## 4. THE GATE INTO THE MEN'S COURT.

### (Πρόθυρον τῆς αὐλῆς.)

Westward of the rooms just described lies a gate building (No. III. on Plan III.), which connects the outer with the main court. Its plan agrees substantially with that of the great Propylæum, except that all the measurements are somewhat smaller. Here too the wall of the gate, which had folding-doors, was furnished with a front and back vestibule, both of which probably opened with two pillars between two *antæ*. I say *probably*, because we found the southern vestibule so destroyed, that its form was no longer discernible. For by the fall of the western citadel-wall this gateway was also greatly injured; its whole west wall is gone, and of the southern there are only scanty foundations left. The back vestibule, on the contrary, is still well-preserved; on its north side there still stand two pillar bases and two *antæ*-blocks, of which the western only is somewhat displaced. In the east wall we still see a large stone-sill belonging to a side door, which led into the south portico of the court; in the gate wall itself there yet lies the great door-sill of breccia with two pivot-holes for the double folding-doors; the lime concrete floor of the back vestibule is almost completely preserved.

As no trace of a pillar was found in the front vestibule, it might be considered doubtful whether the building was really a Propylæum. One might suppose that the room looking north was only the vestibule of a room adjoining it to the south. But this idea can be easily refuted. First, it would indeed be curious if a chamber furnished with a vestibule were itself no deeper than this appendage. Again, the well-preserved pivot-holes for the doors are found to be inside the north room, thus proving it to be the *inner* part of the structure, and that the room to the south was indeed the vestibule or entrance. Lastly, the way leading from the

great Propylæum rises considerably towards the west, and
only attains the level of the men's court south of our building.   This is therefore the point where the lie of the ground
forces us to place the connection of the two courts, even if
no trace of this lesser Propylæum remained.

Hence it is certain that the building under consideration
is a gateway, whose destroyed vestibule we can reconstruct
from the well-preserved back-hall, and in accordance with
the plan of the great Propylæum, as an open hall with
two pillars between two *antæ*.

The existing foundations of the gate are all of limestone rubble ; portions of the wall above ground are only
preserved at the east wall, and are of the same material, with
clay-mortar.   The foundation of the middle wall is widened
southward, after the manner of steps, probably because here
the *remblai* of the building ground required a broad foundation.   A real flight of stairs is not to be thought of here.
The great door-sill in the central wall is made of a single
block of breccia, 3·50 m. long, towards the south cut away
smoothly flush with the wall line, towards the north uneven,
and advancing beyond the wall.   In this advancing portion
the pivot-holes are set, each 0·19 m. in diameter.   Their
distance from centre to centre is 2·85 m. ; the width of the
door was therefore by some centimetres smaller than that
of the door in the great Propylæum.   The lesser door-sill
in the east wall of the back-hall is of limestone, and has
apparently no pivot-hole.   It is remarkably long in relation
to the possible width of the side door, and must therefore
have reached far southwards into the wall.

The two *antæ*-piers of the back hall are of breccia, and
show above holes bored for wooden dowels, which served
to fasten the wooden *parastades*.   Their front face is 1·30 m.
broad.   Between them lie the two pillar bases of limestone,
0·70 m. in diameter, so that the diameter of the wooden
pillar would be about 0·60 m.

The axes of the pillars are 3·67 m. apart, those of

pillars and *antæ* only 2·92 m.; hence the central inter-columniation was considerably. the wider (3·07 m. instead of 1·97 m.). This considerable difference, far exceeding that observed in the great Propylæum, appears to be due to the desire of giving the central passage the maximum width possible, in spite of the narrow dimensions of the whole Propylæum.

The Homeric word for our gate is πρόθυρον, or πρόθυρα. The court-gate of the palace of Odysseus must have been situated, at least in Homer's mind, just as it is in Tiryns, for he describes Athene standing on the threshold of the gate, and looking at the suitors, who in the court before the entrance to the men's apartments amused themselves with games.*

## 5. THE COURT OF THE MEN'S APARTMENTS.

### (ἡ αὐλή.)

Through the *Prothyron* we enter a great court, sur-rounded with colonnades. This is the men's court, the centre of the whole palace. The ground-plan is approxi-mately a rectangle, 15 75 m. deep by 20·25 m. broad, not counting the depth of the colonnades. The whole floor is still covered with thick lime concrete, injured only here and there. In the great shaft at the north-eastern corner of the court, which Dr. Schliemann sunk in 1876, the various strata of this concrete floor are plainly discernible. Lowermost on the *remblai*, there is a thick stratum (40–70 mm.) of stones and lime, a sort of *Beton*, intended as a secure basis for the actual concrete; then

---

* *Od.* I. 103–7 :

Στῆ δ' Ἰθάκης ἐνὶ δήμῳ ἐπὶ προθύροις Ὀδυσῆος.
Οὐδοῦ ἐπ' αὐλείου· παλάμῃ δ' ἔχε χάλκεον ἔγχυς,
εἰδομένη ξείνῳ, Ταφίων ἡγήτορι Μέντῃ·
εὗρε δ' ἄρα μνηστῆρας ἀγήνορας· οἱ μὲν ἔπειτα
πεσσοῖσι προπάροιθε θυράων θυμὸν ἔτερπον,

follows a second layer about 25 mm. thick, consisting of pebbles and a very solid reddish lime. Uppermost lies a layer of about 18 mm. thick, made of lime and small pebbles, and affording a most durable concrete. In some places, especially in the east colonnade, repairs had already been made in ancient times, and with an inferior mortar, consisting almost exclusively of lime.

The escape of rain-water is very carefully provided for, for the surface of the concrete is not a horizontal plane, but so levelled that the water runs off to a single point on the south side. There we find a vertical shaft, built of rubble, and covered with a stone flag. Through a hole in this covering stone the water fell down the shaft, and so reached a walled horizontal canal, which probably led it to some reservoir. No trace of this reservoir, which must have been some metres below the floor of the palace, has yet been found; but its existence may with some confidence be assumed, since the inhabitants of the citadel would hardly have left the water gathered by the roofs and floors to be wasted. E. Curtius (*Peloponnesos*, II. 388) indeed mentions a cistern, as lying near the south wall. We have found no trace of it.

The *south side* of the court was occupied by two colonnades, of which the western has already been mentioned as the back-hall of the gateway. The other (No. XXXV.) consists likewise of two pillars between two *antæ*, and immediately adjoins the gateway. The site of the pillars is only indicated by two irregular stones, which show on their upper surface no raised circle, as is the case with the pillar-bases before-mentioned. Hence the axal-distance of the pillars could only be determined approximately at 3·90 m. By means of a side-door, the colonnade stands in direct connection with the back-hall of the gateway, so that both really form but a single continuous *stoa;* but the back hall is considerably deeper than the colonnade (3·60 m. and 1·60 m. respectively).

On the *west side* of the court lie three pillar-bases, and a quadrangular pilaster; they are the pillars which Dr. Schliemann found in 1876, and which have been measured and described by many travellers. The quadrangular pilaster is an irregular block of limestone, on whose upper side a square of 1·05 m. is worked; it probably formed the east end of a wall coming from the west; but of this latter no trace has been found. The pillar-bases consist likewise of irregularly-edged limestone blocks, on the upper surface of which there is a circle raised a few centimetres, of 0·59 m. diameter. The distance of their axes is 3·20 m. To the north the pillars are flanked by no *parastas* or *anta*, as we should expect, but the epistyle over the pillars continued on the cross wall.

Unfortunately we cannot say whether this row of pillars belonged to a narrow *stoa* or a deep room, because no trace, even of foundations, of the back wall has been found. But the former was probably the case, as we may assume that a portico was arranged on the west side as on the other sides of the court. Between the south *anta* of this portico and the north-western corner of the gateway a narrow corridor seems to have led to rooms lying westward, but now destroyed. Digging deep in the neighbourhood of the western colonnade, we found about 1 m. under the floor of the court remains of older concrete, which proves that even in this part of the palace there were new buildings added in very ancient times.

On *the east* of the court lies a colonnade consisting of three pillars between two *antæ* (No. XXXIV.). Its southern *anta* of breccia belongs also to the south colonnade of the court. The three pillar-bases are not as well worked as those on the west side of the court, and are merely irregular stones, somewhat smoothed on the top; it is only from their equal distances that we could infer that they carried pillars. The north *anta* consists of two blocks of sandstone set on end, and resting on a stone base. Their

vertical joint, the close fitting of which reminds one of
the later masonry of the Greeks, is very remarkable.  On
the top of this *anta* there are square holes for the reception
of wooden dowels.  Neither height nor diameter of the
pillars can be determined; their axal distance can be fixed
at 3·90 m.  The depth of the colonnade without the pillars
is nearly 1·90 m.

The above-mentioned connecting corridor (No.
XXXVII.) which joins the court with the great front
court, forms precisely the southern prolongation of the east
colonnade.  At the north end a door leads into the little
room, No. XXXIII., which is separated from the colonnade
No. XXXI. by a very thin wall.  Unfortunately we do
not know whether this wall was carried up, or was merely a
sort of threshold.  If this latter was the case, then there
was here a connection between the men's and the women's
dwelling; but the existence of such a passage is very
questionable.

In the middle of the south side of the court, beside the
north *anta* of the lesser Propylæum, we found, in digging, a
quadrangular block of masonry, made of flat-shaped quarry
stones and clay.  It was 3·25 m. long by 2·68 m. broad;
on its west side, but not exactly in the middle, a small
square block of masonry is annexed.  We could have no
doubt as to the meaning of this structure; it was a great
*altar*, lying exactly in the central axis of the court opposite
the *megaron*.  Its size was sufficient to burn a whole victim
at once.  Perhaps the addition on the west side was the
place for the sacrificing priest to stand.  What the altar
once looked like, we could not tell; it is probable that the
rough rubble masonry was not meant to be visible, but the
surface was covered with a coating of lime or some other
material; of this, however, no trace remains.  The height
of the altar is also indeterminable; what remains rises only
0·35 m. above the floor of the court.

Such an altar Homer often describes in the inner court;

here the house-master, as priest, used to offer victims; Nestor, for instance, relates that he came with Odysseus to Peleus, and found him sacrificing.* "But the aged Peleus burned on the grass of the court the fat thighs of an ox to the thunder-loving Zeus, and poured from a golden goblet sparkling wine on the blazing sacrifice. You were busied with the meat of the ox, while we were standing in the vestibule."

In the palace of Odysseus also stood an altar of Zeus, for during the murder of the suitors Phemius the singer, who was in the megaron, deliberates whether he will run to the altar of Zeus, and sit there as a suppliant.† "He stood with the clear-toned harp in his hand, hard by the postern gate; and he meditated two ways in his mind, whether he should slip forth from the hall and sit down at the well-built altar of the great Hercæan Zeus, whereon Laertes and Odysseus had burnt many thighs of oxen."

Besides the altar, there is also a *Tholos* mentioned in the court of Odysseus' palace, on the shape and intention of which Homeric scholars are widely at variance. In the court at Tiryns there has been no circular building found, so that the question so far cannot be settled. By some scholars the *Thalamos* (bed-chamber) of Telemachus is also placed in the midst of the court, but this rests on what seems to me a false interpretation of the phrase περισκέπτῳ

---

\* *Il.* XI. 772-7:

　　. . . . . . . Γέρων δ' ἱππηλάτα Πηλεύς
πίονα μηρί' ἔκαιε βοὸς Διὶ τερπικεραύνῳ
αὐλῆς ἐν χόρτῳ· ἔχε δὲ χρύσειον ἄλεισον,
σπένδων αἴθοπα οἶνον ἐπ' αἰθομένοις ἱεροῖσιν.
Σφῶϊ μὲν ἀμφὶ βοὸς ἕπετον κρέα, νῶϊ δ' ἔπειτα
στῆμεν ἐνὶ προθύροισι

† *Od.* XXII. 332-6:

Ἔστη δ' ἐν χείρεσσιν ἔχων φόρμιγγα λίγειαν
ἄγχι παρ' ὀρσοθύρην. δίχα δὲ φρεσὶ μερμήριζεν,
ἢ ἐκδὺς μεγάροιο Διὸς μεγάλου ποτὶ βωμόν
Ερκείου ἵζοιτο τετυγμένον, ἔνθ' ἄρα πολλά
Λαέρτης 'Οδυσεύς τε βοῶν ἐπὶ μηρί' ἔκηαν.

ἐνὶ χώρῳ.  I think those are right, who place this chamber
close to the outer wall of the palace, so that Telemachus
could have a wide prospect into the country.  There
may have been several such Thalamoi at Tiryns, especially
on the west side of the court; inside the court nothing of
the kind has been found, and it contains no building but
the altar in its open space.

In describing a Greek dwelling-house, Vitruvius says *
that the Greek court (peristylion) had colonnades on three
sides, west, south, and east, and on the north side lay the
Prostas, a vestibule, to which the large rooms adjoined.
This is the very arrangement of the court at Tiryns.  On
the south side lies the back hall of the πρόθυρον and a little
αἴθουσα αὐλῆς, east and west larger αἴθουσαι; at the north
side, between two advancing antæ, the megaron is placed
with a vestibule (αἴθουσα δώματος).  This agreement is
striking, and is an important proof that the plan of the
late historical Greek dwelling-house was developed from
the Homeric dwelling-house.

Finally we note the two epithets which Homer gives
to the colonnades of the court, ξεστός and ἐρίδουπος.
The former probably refers to the polished plastering, which
covered the back wall of the colonnade, and to the polished
pillars of wood, which were probably covered with metal,
the latter to the loud echo which the colonnades of the
court produced.

## 6. THE MEN'S APARTMENT.

### (τὸ μέγαρον.)

At the north side of the court lies the largest room of the
palace, the *megaron* for the men, with an antechamber and

---

* Vitruv. *De Arch.* VI., 7.   Id peristylion in tribus partibus habet
porticus; in ea parte, quæ spectat ad meridiem, duas antas inter se spatio
amplo distantes . . . Hic locus apud nonnullos προστάς, apud alios
παραστάς nominatur. In his locis introrsus constituuntur œci magni . . .

a vestibule. The present condition of these three rooms
may be seen on the ground-plan of the palace (Plan II.),
in which the existing foundations are given in light colour,

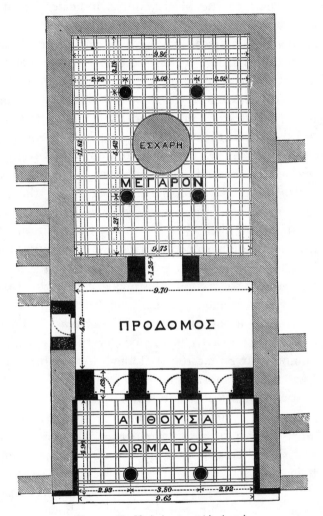

No. 113.—The Men's Apartment (τὸ μέγαρον).

the still-standing walls in a darker one. The next figure,
No. 113, gives a restored plan, to which we shall refer in the
following description. The light colour here indicates
masonry, and the dark, wooden structure. The little

squares denote the designs of the concrete floor produced
by scratched lines.

The megaron, with its entrance chambers, is the *most
important* part of the palace, and is indicated as such in
various ways. In the first place it occupies the highest part
of the citadel, as may easily be seen by the altitudes marked
in red on the Plan II. From the gate of the upper citadel
to the first Propylæum you ascend 3·33 m.; from there to
the second Propylæum, 1·07 m.; and the floor of the
megaron lies still 0·64 m. higher. Secondly, the vestibule
of the megaron is the only building of which the front is
furnished like a Greek temple with steps in its full width;
for two neatly worked stone steps lead from the court
up to the vestibule. Thirdly, the megaron is the largest
covered room in all the palace, and has therefore thicker
walls than any of the rest. Fourthly, the position of the
megaron in relation to the court shows the importance of
this building. The north side of the court is planned in
accordance with the axis of the megaron; to the front of
the vestibule are joined at either side walls 3 m. long, with
cross walls, which end in front with *parastades*. The altar
is likewise set up exactly in the axis of the megaron. All
these points prove that the building on the north side of
the court was the most important part of the palace, the
men's apartment, with its anterooms.

Let us now examine the details of the structure. The
*vestibule* is built as a ναὸς ἐν παραστάσι, its front consists of
two pillars between two *antæ* (pilasters). In the adjoining
sketch in perspective (Fig. 114) the western *parastas* and
one of the pillar bases are given; in front are seen the two
steps, which raise the floor of the vestibule above that of the
court. The upper step consists of slabs of red limestone
of various length, joined with great accuracy. The height
of this step is 0·08 m., and is therefore very small, the tread
measures 0·39 m. The lower step is built of sandstone slabs,
in height and width corresponding with the measurement

of the upper step, but the length of the single slabs is greater. As may be seen from the sketch and the plans, the upper step only lies *between* the two *antæ*, while the

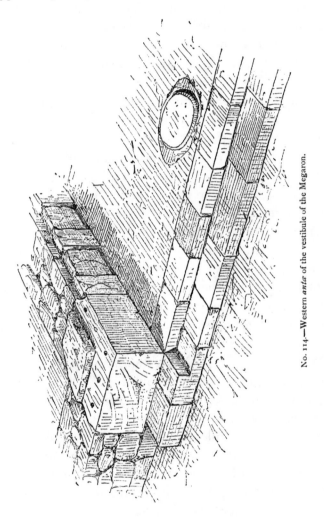

No. 114.—Western *antæ* of the vestibule of the Megaron.

lower reaches to their outer corners ; immediately in front of the *antæ* the lower step has double the height.

The two pillar bases are large irregular limestone blocks, with a circle, 0·76 m. in diameter, worked on the top. Their axal width is 3·80 m. Each of the *parastades* or

*antæ* consists of a large block of breccia, only worked on
two sides.   The other sides, being hidden in the masonry,
could be left rough.   The treatment of these *antæ* we shall
discuss in speaking of the materials used in the building.
The two surfaces which show, are on the average 1·43 m.
broad and 0·61 m. high.   On the upper side, and parallel
to the outer surface, a band 0·30 m. broad is smoothed
and furnished with five round dowel-holes; the rest was left
rough and is some centimetres higher (cf. Fig. 114).   There
was therefore no second stone laid over the first, for, to
secure it, the upper surface must have been at least approximately levelled.   We must rather conclude, from the form
of the surface, that the upper part of the *antæ* consisted of
wooden posts, fitted to the lower block by wooden dowels.
These posts must have been about 0·30 m. thick.   From
the number of the mortice-holes, we may infer that each
*anta* consisted of five vertical posts, but we must not
forget that possibly a horizontal beam may have been laid
immediately over the stone *anta*, the same beam which,
as longitudinal beam, went through the whole wall.   The
wood of the *antæ* was probably coated with metal, for we
know that such metal-coating took a prominent place in
the Homeric palaces.   No certain remains of such metal-
coating have, however, been found in Tiryns.

If we examine carefully the ground-plan of the vestibule, the remarkable relation of the pillar-bases to the *antæ*
strikes us.   For while they lie strictly in a line with the
inner surface of the *antæ*, they retire about 0·56 m. from
the outer line of the building.   Why was this? and of what
kind are we to imagine an architrave if one was resting on
the pillars?   Three possible explanations occur to me.   If
the architrave was about as thick as the diameter of the
bases, and lay exactly over the middle of the pillars, the
*antæ* advanced about 0·56 m. in front of the architrave
and reached probably up to the projecting *corona* (γεῖσον).
If, however, the architrave was of the breadth of the *antæ*

(1·42 m.), and agreed with them both back and front, then
we cannot understand why the pillars were not set under
the middle of it, the more so as it must have consisted of
several longitudinally-set beams, and therefore in the first
place required support in the middle.   In the third place,
we might suppose that the architrave lay as first described,
but that the front surface of the *antæ* was so much tapered
upwards, that at the top it matched the architrave.   If this
tapering of the *anta* were less considerable, this last hypothesis would be the most admissible, because in later Greek
edifices the upward tapering of the *parastades* was conspicuous.   But in our vestibule the tapering would have been
so considerable, that we cannot implicitly decide for the
third theory, and the first theory, which brings the *parastas*
in advance of the architrave, and up to the *corona* (γεῖσον)
deserves attention (see the *François-Vase* for bracket-
capitals).

Concerning the proportions of the *façade* we know
nothing, as all the altitudes throughout the buildings of
the citadel are completely lost.   We can only make a possible picture of the outside of the vestibule, which would
agree in the main with the view of the great Propylæum, as
we have described it (see p. 198).   On two low steps there
rose two pillars and two corner *antæ*.   The diameter of the
former is less than 0·75 m., the *antæ* are at least twice
as thick.   The four supports, counting from axis to axis,
are almost equidistant; but as the *antæ* are considerably
thicker than the pillars, the intercolumniations at the
sides must be less than in the centre.   The precise form
of the entablature is unknown to us; we only know that
the roof-beams did not lie parallel over the vestibule, but
at right angles to the front; that they must therefore have
been set on the epistyle and not on the side walls.   Perhaps
the beam-ends were visible over the architrave, and used for
a triglyph-frieze arrangement.

Inside the vestibule we have still to speak of the two

short side walls, which show one remarkable feature. Immediately behind the pilasters, the wall, which is built of rubble and clay, becomes about o·40 m. thinner, clearly because some coating of different material was here applied. Now on the south wall there still remain portions of a splendid alabaster-frieze, which we shall describe at length in its place. They occupy exactly the whole space from the *antæ* to the cross wall. But it will be clearly shown that the frieze cannot have stood here originally, but at some other place. We must therefore assume some other material for the wall-coating of the vestibule; I conjecture it to have been wood. As the back wall of the vestibule has been proved to have consisted entirely of wood, and as the pillars and *antæ*, with the exception of the bases and socles, were also of that material, the short side walls would have been the only plastered surfaces of the vestibule, if they had not also been cased with wood. Whether this wood was covered with bronze or some other metal, cannot be decided, but is probable.

The floor of the vestibule was covered with a concrete almost entirely of lime, which is mostly preserved; under the upper layer, about 15 mm. thick, lies another of inferior mortar. The upper edge of the concrete lies on an exact level with the top step, while the two pillar bases are raised about 2 cm. above the floor. In the north-west corner one can still see that it was divided into squares and narrow rectangles of scratched-in lines; in the restored plan (Fig. 113) the design is reproduced. The length of the vestibule contains thirteen, the depth about six of these squares. The latter measure could not be accurately determined, because close to the steps the lines are now gone. Each line in the plan was really formed by bands of three parallel strokes, as is shown in Fig. 116. for the floor of the megaron.

Three large folding-doors connect the vestibule with the *anteroom* (see woodcut No. 113, and Plan II., No. VI.)

They occupy almost the whole partition wall, leaving room
only for four narrow doorposts. The three huge door-
sills are still in their place—breccia blocks 1·50–60 m.
broad by about 2·30 m. long. On the short sides they
are irregular in edge, but at the long sides they are cut
smooth, not like the limestone thresholds, which are mostly
unfinished all round. Each door-sill has two pivot-holes,
about 90 mm. diameter and 25 mm. deep, and 1·72 m.
apart. These are not, as in the door-sills formerly described,
outside the course of the wall, but are set in the sill itself,
about 0·35 m. from its outer edge. Hence it follows, the
three doors must each have had a separate door-case about
0·30 m. thick, into which the doors fitted when shut.
When opened, they remained flat against the pilasters, or
fitted into the door-case so as not to narrow the entrance.
In the restored plan (woodcut No. 113) this is indicated
by dotted curves. Considering the narrow separation of
the doors, this arrangement *was necessary*, as, according to
the usual arrangement, the opened wings must have collided
in the interior of the *prodomos*. Of the posts between the
doors, Homer's σταθμοί, we shall speak again in our general
treatment of the doors; we need only here observe that
they were all four certainly of wood. Hence nothing of
them could be extant except the foundations.

The anteroom itself, which we enter through the three
great doors, is of about the same dimensions as the vestibule.
It is about 4·72 m. deep by 9·70 m. broad, thus in about
the ratio of 1 : 2. On the floor are the remains of concrete
made of lime and pebbles; there are no lines scratched
on it visible. The door in the west wall, leading to the
bath-room and other apartments on the west side of the
*megaron*, has still its great sill of breccia, with only one
pivot-hole left; it was therefore a single door, as the restored
ground-plan (Fig. 113) shows. Huge beams of wood, provided on the front side with a separate door-case, enclosed
the door on both sides. With the exception of some

×

0.680

FRIEZE·INLAID·WITH·BLUE·GLASS·RESTO

·FRIEZE·IN·ITS·ACTUAL·STATE·1: 50.

·SCULPTURED·ORNAMENT·1: 5.

DRAWN BY W. DÖRPFELD.

PLATE IV.

·PLAN·OF·THE·FRIEZE·1: 5.

GLASS·PASTE·FROM·MENIDI.

ZE·FROM·MYCENAE.

charcoal, nothing of these posts is left; but their existence is proved by the state of the adjoining wall, which is
thoroughly burnt through, and reduced to a solid mass.

When we discovered the small door, we expected to
find a similar one in the east wall of the anteroom, which
would have established a direct connection between the
men's apartment and the court of the women's habitation;
but this was not so. There was no door in the east wall,
for the masonry of the whole wall still remains unbroken.

A large door, about 2 m. broad, in the midst of the north
wall, leads us to the *Men's Hall.* The great breccia door-
sill, 3 m. long by 1·25 m. broad, is still in its old place.
On the left of the door, as the ground-plan (Plate II.)
shows, there still stand endwise two stone slabs terminating
the masonry. The doorposts were of wood, and were
destroyed with the citadel. In Fig. 113 I have denoted
them by a dark colour. Strange to say, in the door-sill we
were unable to find any pivot-hole. We must assume, therefore, that the doorway was only closed by drawing a curtain.

The *megaron* is a large room, 11·81 m. long by
9·75 m. to 9·86 m. broad,* thus having a ground surface
of 115·75 square metres. It exceeds in size the *cellas* of
many Greek temples, *e.g.* that of the Theseion at Athens is
only 75·5 square metres. So great a space could hardly
be spanned by a free roof, and therefore four inner pillars
were set, on which lay strong supports to carry the roof
beams. Of these pillars the round stone bases remain.
They are 0·78 m. in diameter and a little wider below.
On their surface is an inner circle about 0·66 m. in diameter, within which the stone is well preserved, while the

---

* The measurements at opposite sides of this hall do not agree,
as there were small variations in the building, and in the subsiding of
the walls. It must also be observed, that rude rubble walls admit of no
accurate measurements. I have therefore in most cases given average
measures. I note the fact here, on account of the large amount of the
variation.

surrounding edge was eaten by fire, and partly chipped away. This condition of the bases shows us that they were of wood, and smaller in diameter than the bases.

On the arrangement of the wooden epistyle we can say nothing, as we have no safe data to go upon. Either there were only two great beams from the south wall resting each on two pillars and reaching to the north wall, thus dividing the hall into three naves ; or the same arrangement ran east and west ; or both of these were used ; or else there was only a square of architraves lying on the four pillars, which did not reach the walls. Without deciding for any one of these, the last arrangement may fairly be rejected, as requiring four diagonal beams and a great many dragon-pieces (hammer-beams), a construction certainly avoided in ancient times.

Closely related to the roof-problem is that of *lighting*. We cannot decide the one without the other, and must therefore here say a word about the lighting of the megaron. There can be no doubt that the scanty light which the door admitted cannot have sufficed to light the megaron. For in front of this door lay not only the deep vestibule, but also the equally deep anteroom. Direct sunlight could therefore never be obtained from the south door, and the little indirect light was hardly sufficient to illumine the great chamber. There must have been some other supply of light. It may indeed be argued that Homer calls the megaron σκιόεις, and so implies its twilight. But σκιόεις only refers to the shady part of the men's apartments, in contrast to the sunny halls and courts.

How then was light obtained? not by windows, or apertures in the side walls, for the chamber was surrounded by others. At the south-east corner alone it adjoins the court of the women's apartments, but just there an opening of attainable height would hardly have been made. But it is very conceivable that the corridors and rooms surrounding the megaron were lower, and so over their roofs there could be apertures in the exterior walls of the megaron. In the case of horizontal roofs, which we must assume for Tiryns, this arrangement is peculiarly suitable ; with sloping roofs it presents many difficulties. The spaces between the beams of the roof were obviously suited for windows, and I do not doubt that such was the case in many rooms at Tiryns. But in the megaron we can imagine yet a different kind of windows.

The arrangement of the four inside pillars and of the great hearth in their centre appears to me to point to there having been some aperture in the middle of the hall. It might be assumed that the whole square between the pillars was open; but so large an aperture, even in the southern climate of Tiryns, would have made the hall temporarily uninhabitable in winter. It would answer much better to cover the square included by the pillars, after the manner of a basilica, with a higher roof; in the vertical walls of the upper structure (clere-story) smaller or larger apertures could be introduced, through which not only light would enter into the megaron, but also the smoke from the hearth would find an easy escape. I have therefore thus restored the megaron in the longitudinal section in Plate III. The vertical measurements of this reconstruction are, however, as I particularly mention, hypothetical, and are therefore not in any wise to be depended on.*

This basilica form of raising part of a building above the rest offers so many advantages, that it has been used from the oldest times for obtaining light and air in the

---

* Mr. James Fergusson observes to me: "The question whether Greek interiors were lighted by vertical triglyphal openings, or by horizontal skylights, is the principal subject discussed in my work on the *Parthenon* published in 1883. Either mode is no doubt applicable to this megaron ; but the dimensions of the various parts required for the Basilican arrangement suggested in the text, present to my mind such difficulties of construction, that on the whole I would prefer the theory that it was lighted by vertical openings in the upper parts of its side-walls."

case of closely adjoining buildings.    It is proved by monumental evidences that the pillared halls of the Egyptian
temples were often lit with this basilica upper-lighting
(clerestory windows); and it is well known that the
basilica was a form adopted in many Roman private and
public buildings.    Although Greek buildings with clerestory windows are not preserved, their existence cannot
be doubtful.*    There must certainly have been from the
earliest to the latest times many buildings in Greece which
had a basilical cross-section, and were therefore lighted
from a lateral clerestory.

In my opinion the megaron of Tiryns belongs to
these; its central part was probably raised above the roof
of the hall, and contained window-apertures in the vertical
walls under the eaves.    We have still to enquire whether
the whole central nave was so raised, or only the part
enclosed by the four pillars.    I think the form of the
ground-plan gives us the means of answering this question.
For if the whole central nave had been so raised, then two
strong beams must have rested as epistyles upon the pillars
from the front to the back wall.    Then the two pillars
intended for the support of each epistyle would probably
have been so set, that the three resulting intercolumniations
should have been about equal.    But this is not the case;
the distance between each pair of pillars is much greater
than their respective distance from the walls.    Hence it
seems to me to follow, that the higher roof lay only over
the part enclosed by the four pillars.

If we assume this kind of lighting, it follows that the
roof was constructed by laying two or four great girders

---

* Konrad Lange is about to treat fully the important question of the
origin and spread of the basilica in his forthcoming work : *Haus und
Halle, Studien zur Geschichte des Wohnhauses und der Basilika.*    Even
before he saw the ground-plan of the megaron of Tiryns, he thought it
probable that the megaron of the Homeric dwelling-house was lighted
like a basilica.

upon the pillars, which supported directly the beams of the
lower roof.  The beams covering the central structure lay
somewhat higher.  Over the beams of both portions were
cross-beams, covered probably with a layer of reeds or
straw, over which was laid a very thick layer of clay.*
Such a clay roof is very heavy, and requires powerful
beams, but leaves very little to be desired as regards solidity,
provided the clay when washed away by rain is supplied
with a new layer.

As regards the names which Homer gives for the
various parts of the roof, Buchholz (*Homerische Realien*,
p. 109), and those whom he has followed, seem to me to
have hit the truth.  I, therefore, simply repeat his words.
He first cites the passage in the *Odyssey* referring to the
roof:

"O, father, surely a great marvel is this that I behold with mine
eyes; meseems that the walls of the hall and the fair spaces between
the pillars, and the fir-tree beams, and the lofty columns, are bright as
it were with burning fire." †

and he continues—

"The very way in which here the τοῖχοι, μεσόδμαι,
δοκοί, and κίονες are brought together, seems to point to
their being the members of some system or plan.  But if
we enquire into the precise meaning of these architectural
terms, there can be no doubt about the τοῖχοι and κίονες—
the walls of the *Andronitis*, and the pillars or pilasters
which supported the beams of the roof.  More difficult

---

* In just the same way all the village houses in the Troad, and
all over Asia Minor, are roofed to the present day.  Besides, Mr.
Theodore Bent found many houses so covered in the more remote
Cyclades.  Cf. his recent book, *The Cyclades* (London, 1885).
† *Od.* XIX. 36–9.

’Ω πάτερ, ἦ μέγα θαῦμα τόδ’ ὀφθαλμοῖσιν ὁρῶμαι·
ἔμπης μοι τοῖχοι μεγάρων καλαί τε μεσόδμαι,
εἰλάτιναί τε δοκοὶ καὶ κίονες ὑψόσ’ ἔχοντες,
φαίνοντ’ ὀφθαλμοῖς, ὡσεὶ πυρὸς αἰθομένοιο.

is it to explain the μεσόδμαι and their relation to the δοκοί. Galen * gives of the μεσόδμη the following definition : τὸ μέγα ξύλον ἀπὸ τοῦ ἑτέρου τοίχου πρὸς τὸν ἕτερον διῆκον. Hence it was a beam, reaching from wall to wall, and with this again the notice in the *Etymologicum Magnum* (581, 5) that μεσόδμη is derived by syncope from μεσο-δόμη, is in perfect agreement, as the word, formed from μέσος and δέμω, means something inserted between two things, and combining them. Hence nothing prevents us from taking μεσόδμαι to be cross-beams between the τοῖχοι of the μέγαρον, and producing a junction between them. This agrees with the view of Rumpf, who translates μεσόδμη by *transversaria trabs.*† If we further enquire in what relation the μεσόδμαι stand to the δοκοί, I think the Schol. on *Od.* XIX. 37 can here lead us in the right track, who gives a gloss τὰ μεταξὺ δοκῶν on μεσόδμαι, which were accordingly the transverse beams between the longitudinal δοκοί.

" All the μεσόδμαι and δοκοί together form the whole frame on which the roof (ὀροφή) lies, which Homer designates as μέλαθρον, so that old commentators have identified μέλαθρον with the ceiling. So the Schol. on *Od.* XXII. 239 : μέλαθρον, τὴν ὀροφήν, and in *Etym. M.*, μέγαρον δέ ἐστιν ὁ οἶκος· μέλαθρον δὲ ἡ ὀροφή, ἀπὸ τοῦ μελαίνεσθαι ὑπὸ τοῦ καπνοῦ, ὡς Ὅμηρος, χ. 239.‡ The other rooms, as well as the Andronitis, are also supplied with a μέλαθρον, like the former Thalamos of Hephæstus,§ and of Jocaste.‖

---

* Cf. his 4th *Memoir on Hippocrates*, περὶ ἄρθρων, ed. Kühn, vol. xviii. pars I. p. 738.

† Rumpf, *De æd. Hom.*, pars II. p. 30 : Μεσόδμη illa fuisse transversaria trabs cuivis videbitur.

‡ *Adn. ad. Et. M. ed.* Kulenhamp, p. 960, where Block cites the above gloss from the Cod. Havn. Cf. Rumpf, *De æd. Hom.*, pars II. p. 34.

§ *Od.* VIII. 279 : πολλὰ δὲ καὶ καθύπερθε μελαθρόφιν ἐξεκέχυντο.

‖ *Od.* XI. 277 : ἡ δ' ἔβη εἰς Ἀΐδαο πυλάρταο κρατεροῖο, | ἀψαμένη βρόχον αἰπὺν ἀφ' ὑψηλοῖο μελάθρου.

In a wider sense the μέλαθρον is put for the whole roof (στέγη), as is said of the preying eagle, which Penelope sees in her dream, flying up after killing the geese, and lighting ἐπὶ προὔχοντι μελάθρῳ,* by which we must understand the outermost end of the roof, starting like a cornice from the wall."

I must add to these words, that the relation of the μεσόδμαι to the δοκοί is perhaps not quite rightly conceived ; to me the μεσόδμαι seem rather to be the main beams, the δοκοί the roof-beams.

In the exact centre of the hall, and therefore within the square enclosed by the four pillars, there is found in the floor a circle of about 3·30 m. diameter, within which there is no concrete. It is surrounded by an upright rim of plaster, which makes it probable that the core of the circle which rose over the ground was made of clay, or clay-bricks covered with mortar. Of this core nothing is preserved. There can be little doubt that this circle indicates the position of the *hearth* in the centre of the megaron. The hearth was in all antiquity the centre of the house, about which the family assembled, at which food was prepared, and where the guest received the place of honour. Hence it is frequently indicated by poets and philosophers as the navel or centre of the house.† In the oldest times it was not only symbolically but actually the centre of the house, and especially of the megaron. It was only in later days, in the great palaces of the Romans, that it was removed from the chief rooms, and established in a small by-room.

Homer generally calls the hearth ἐσχάρη ; it is only in the oath, " so may Zeus, first of the gods, attest it, and the hospitable table, and the hearth of the blameless Odysseus

---

* *Od.* XIX. 544 : ἂψ δ' ἐλθὼν κατ' ἄρ' ἕζετ' (ὁ αἰετὸς) ἐπὶ προὔχοντι μελάθρῳ.

† Winckler, *Die Wohnhäuser der Hellenen*, p. 120, *sqq.*

to which I come," * that the word ἱστίη is used. Homer
does not indeed tell us precisely in what part of the megaron
the hearth used to stand, but from his description of the
house of Alkinoos we can infer that it was placed as at
Tiryns ; for Nausicaa advises Odysseus to go as suppliant
to her mother Arete and embrace her knees. She describes
the way to the palace, and then says of her mother, " She is
seated at the hearth in the light of the fire, plying the
wondrous fair spindle with purple wool; leaning against
the pillar." † This description agrees very well with the
arrangement of the megaron of Tiryns, for the four pillars
stand at such a distance from the round hearth, that those
sitting at it must often have leant against them. Most
probably the ground-plan of the megaron at Tiryns was a
typical one, occurring in an identical manner in many
heroic palaces. The arrangement is indeed both simple
and practical ; the hearth, being in the middle of the hall,
could be approached from all sides to obtain warmth in the
winter. The four pillars surrounding the hearth are so far
apart, as to allow a convenient passage between them and
the hearth, and even room to sit there. The smoke, too,
did not fill the room, but found a convenient outlet
through the openings of the central dome.

In a later wall, built within the megaron, we found two
sandstone blocks, curved on the outer side, and thus belonging to a circular building. We thought at first that
they belonged to the hearth, but found that the radius of
their curvature was less than that of the hearth. They can,

---

* *Od.* XIV. 158-9;

> ἴστω νῦν Ζεὺς πρῶτα θεῶν, ξενίη τε τράπεζα,
> ἱστίη τ' Ὀδυσῆος ἀμύμονος, ἣν ἀφικάνω·

† *Od.* VI. 305-7 :

> . . . ἡ δ' ἧσται ἐπ' ἐσχάρῃ ἐν πυρὸς αὐγῇ
> ἠλάκατα στρωφῶσ' ἁλιπόρφυρα, θαῦμα ἰδέσθαι,
> κίονι κεκλιμένη· δμωαὶ δέ οἱ εἴατ' ὄπισθεν.

therefore, only belong to it if we assume that the hearth was built up in retreating steps.

It is hardly an accidental coincidence, that in the middle of the largest hall in the Pergamos of the Homeric Troy (second town at Hissarlik) a large circle is to be seen in the concrete of the floor. We have hitherto been uncertain as to the intention of the great hall at Hissarlik, and its central circle. Now that we know the plan of Tiryns, there can be no doubt that at Troy too the spacious hall, with its vestibule (the large so-called Temple A), was the megaron, and the circle in its centre marked the place of the hearth. A special ante-room does not exist at Troy, but then both vestibule and hall have larger dimensions than those at Tiryns. Even the diameter of the Trojan hearth, which can only approximately be fixed at 4 m., exceeds that of the hearth at Tiryns by about 0·75 m.

In the adjoining figure, 115, by way of comparison, the central part of the Acropolis of Troy is given. Of the three separate buildings the largest contained the main hall with a vestibule. The second smaller one adjoining possessed, besides megaron and vestibule, a large back-room. The relations of these two buildings—whether the greater was the men's, and the lesser the women's dwellings, or whether the second was a smaller men's house—we cannot determine. As in Tiryns, so there lies in Troy, opposite the megaron, a small gateway, the door of which is furnished with a large stone door-sill.* This is wrought just like the thresholds of Tiryns. This agreement in ground-plan and details of construction between the citadels of Tiryns and Troy is of course of great importance, and gives us additional evidence to solve the Trojan problem.

Round about the hearth in Tiryns the whole floor of the megaron was covered with excellent concrete, which

---

* In the plan of the Acropolis in Schliemann's *Troja*, by a mistake of the lithographer, this door is filled up by a continuous wall.

still occupies a great part of the hall. It consists of two successive layers, which are not, as might be supposed, of different periods, but of which the lower, and less solid, is merely the substratum for the more carefully smoothed upper layer. In the polished surface are deeply scratched lines, the pattern of which may be seen in the adjoining

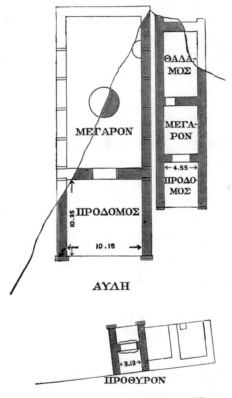

No. 115.—The central part of the Pergamos of Troy.

figure, 116, and in the restored ground-plan (Fig. 113). It is identical with that of the vestibule, but the squares are somewhat smaller. In the northern part of the hall there are still distinct traces of red colour on the larger central squares of the concrete. On the small strips separating these are faint traces of blue. Hence the floor was originally of a bright simple carpet-pattern.

I may here mention a small basin, which was found in the megaron before the middle of the east wall (cf. Plan II.). It is formed of a row of slabs, rising only a few centimetres over the floor, and enclosing an oblong rectangle. The fact, that several of these slabs had on their hidden face a spiral ornament in relief, shows that the basin is not contemporaneous with the building of the megaron, but later. The object of this basin, or whatever it was, is unknown.

The outer walls which surround the hall are all preserved

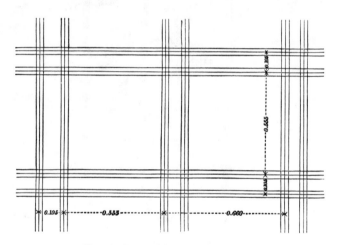

No. 116.—Pattern of the floor in the Megaron.

to a height of o·40 m., except at the north-west corner; they are built of limestone with clay-mortar. The single stones are on the average o·65 m. long by o·35 m. high, and larger than the rubble used in the other walls of the palace. The wall, so far as it now exists, has only one course of stones. There is, indeed, some higher masonry on the east wall, but this belongs to a later complete alteration of the megaron. Above the lowest course there appear to have been on both faces of the wall wooden longitudinal beams, such as we find them also in the Trojan buildings. Over these beams the surrounding walls were probably of clay-bricks, as the inside of the megaron was almost filled up with half-burnt *débris* of bricks. These bricks are discussed in the section on the building materials (pp. 256–273). The wall was covered on both sides with a coating 1–8 cm. thick of clay, over which was a good lime plaster; remains of both are found on the west wall, showing clear traces of fire. The clay-plaster has in places been reduced to red terra-cotta.

Almost all authorities on the Homeric house assume a door in the back wall of the megaron, leading directly to the women's apartments. They support this by a number of passages (*Od.* I. 333; XVI. 415; XVIII. 209; XXI. 64, 236), in which they suppose it to be implied. But in the first four of these passages, the doorposts of the great door into the megaron are intended, and in the last the poet only speaks of the well-folding doors of the women's apartment, without in the least implying that it opened into the men's hall. We may even infer from the fact, that here Odysseus orders the door of the women's hall to be shut, not to keep the suitors from escaping, but to keep the women undisturbed within, that this door did not open on the men's hall, in which the suitors were afterwards shut in. In the megaron of Tiryns there is no such direct connection, and it may even safely be asserted that such never existed. Whoever wished to pass from the men's to the women's hall could only do so by going around long corridors and passing several doors.* In the Odyssey the account of the massacre of the suitors mentions another door into the megaron, about which Homeric scholars differ widely in opinion; it is the ὀρσοθύρη, mentioned *Od.* XXII. 126,

---

* Professor J. P. Mahaffy observes: "This is strongly corroborated by a passage in *Od.* VI. 50, where Nausicaa is represented as proceeding διὰ δώμαθ', *through the buildings*, not through a door to find her parents. She finds her mother sitting at the hearth, but meets her father face to face (ξύμβλητο), as he was *coming out of the main door* of the μέγαρον, on his way to a council. Hence she came in by no side door."

132, and 333. The last passage has already been mentioned. The other two are contained in the following:—

> Ὀρσοθύρη δέ τις ἔσκεν ἐϋδμήτῳ ἐνὶ τοίχῳ,
> ἀκρότατον δὲ παρ' οὐδὸν ἐϋσταθέος μεγάροιο
> ἦν ὁδὸς ἐς λαύρην, σανίδες δ' ἔχον εὖ ἀραρυῖαι·
> τὴν δ' Ὀδυσεὺς φράζεσθαι ἀνώγει δῖον ὑφορβόν
> ἑσταότ' ἄγχ' αὐτῆς· μία δ' οἴη γίγνετ' ἐφορμή·
> τοῖς δ' Ἀγέλεως μετέειπεν, ἔπος πάντεσσι πιφαύσκων,
> Ὦ φίλοι, οὐκ ἂν δή τις ἀν' ὀρσοθύρην ἀναβαίη
> καὶ εἴποι λαοῖσι, βοὴ δ' ὤκιστα γένοιτο; *

" Now there was a certain postern in the well-built wall : and near
the furthest threshold of the well-reared palace was a way to a narrow
passage, but well-fitted doors enclosed it ; this Odysseus bade the godly
swineherd to guard, standing near it, for it was the only approach. But
Agelaos addressed them, and declared the word to all : ' Friends, will
not some one go up to the postern, and tell the people, and an alarm
would be raised straightway ? ' "

Even the ancients differed about the meaning of ὀρσοθύρη and λαύρη, and among recent commentators there
are hardly two (independent) who are agreed about them.
Unfortunately the discoveries at Tiryns cannot altogether
decide this problem. There are indeed small corridors,
which may be identical with the λαύρη, but no ὀρσοθύρη has
been discovered. No doubt this may have been a peculiarity of the palace at Ithaca, and need not therefore have
occurred at Tiryns. But even supposing it had existed at
Tiryns, it could hardly have been preserved, as it clearly
follows from Homer's words that it was situated not on the
floor, but in the upper portion of the wall or in the ceiling.
These parts of the megaron are irrevocably destroyed.
Under these circumstances it is useless to waste time on the
ὀρσοθύρη, for it is not the object of this book to add new
hypotheses to those already existing on the subject. The
case is the same with the ῥῶγες μεγάροιο of Od. XXII. 143 ;
some think them small passages, others a stair leading to
the upper storey. We pass by this controversy, as the
excavations afforded us no materials to explain it.

---

* Od. XXII. 126–34.

Lastly, I must mention the reconstruction of the megaron carried out in later days. The changes made may be seen in Plan II., where I have denoted the later walls by yellow colour. The new plan was a narrow rectangle containing a square vestibule and a hall about 15 m. long by 6 m. broad. The west longitudinal wall was completely rebuilt. No special foundation was laid, but the old concrete was used as such. The eastern longitudinal wall was built on the remains of the older and thicker walls. The date of this reconstruction cannot be determined, but was certainly not till after the complete destruction of the older megaron. The doorposts and pillars cannot have been standing when the new walls were built. The fact too that these latter contain no marks of fire, is another proof of their later construction. It is not impossible that here, on the summit of the hill, there was a Greek temple built in later times, and that the remaining walls were its foundations. Possibly, also, the pieces of Doric architecture, which we shall discuss presently, belonged to this building. In some places we had to break away small pieces of the wall, to uncover what they had hidden of the old structure: originally the wall was as shown in Plan II.

## 7. The Bath-room and other Apartments West of the Megaron.

The north-west corner of the palace is occupied by a number of small rooms and corridors, whose connection and use it is scarcely possible to determine ; the walls are in part too much damaged, in part wholly destroyed. We now proceed to discuss the rooms in detail.

Next to the great court comes Room VIII. ; its southern half is so destroyed that we can no longer tell whether the door lay west or south. The northern part is better preserved ; the rubble masonry still stands 0·50 m. high, and the concrete floor is still in its place. On two

sides this room is bounded by a corridor (IX.) which leads
from the west colonnade of the court to the anteroom.
At both ends it could be closed by doors provided with
stone sills. A third door leads to a little antechamber, and
then into the BATH-ROOM (XI.). The position of this was
most convenient, for if a stranger was to be brought there,

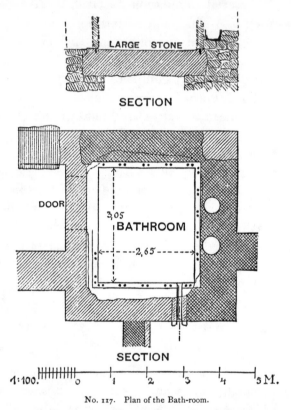

No. 117.  Plan of the Bath-room.

before entering the megaron, he could reach it at once
from the west colonnade of the court through corridor IX.
When washed and anointed, he went through the same
corridor to the anteroom, and thence into the megaron.

The bath-room is certainly one of the most interesting
discoveries at Tiryns, for who could have imagined that
we should ever find one of the rooms in which the Homeric

heroes actually bathed and anointed themselves? The adjoining figure, No. 117, gives a ground-plan and cross-section of the chamber. The walls surrounding the room are cross-hatched; where only foundations are preserved, there are merely simple hatchings.

The whole floor is occupied by one gigantic block of limestone, over 3 m. broad, nearly 4 m. long, and averaging 0·70 m. in thickness. It contains therefore about 8½ cubic metres, and it weighs more than 20,000 kilogrammes. Its edges are not worked, if we except a smoothed edge at the southern side; the under side is quite rough, the upper surface carefully levelled and polished. There was no solid foundation built to support this enormous block, but it was laid on walls supporting its four sides, with a cavity under its central part. The upper surface is the most important part; the well-polished surface forms a rectangle of 2·65 m. broad by 3·05 m. long, surrounded by a border raised about 3 mm. and 0·12 m. to 0·13 m. broad. The projecting parts of the block are or were covered up by the masonry of the walls. In the border along the wall are bored a large number of holes, about 3 cm. in diameter, marked in the above ground-plan by dots. They are not made at random, but alternate regularly between 0·11 and 0·12 m., and 0·50 and 0·52 m. in distance, the latter measure being slightly diminished at the corners. The intention of these holes was clearly to receive round wooden dowels, which served to fasten the wainscot to the floor. The present condition of the still standing fragments of the wall shows clearly that this wainscot consisted of *wooden* panels, for the stones of the wall are burnt partly into lime, the clay-mortar into red terra-cotta. The panels were about 0·12 m. thick, and, as may be safely inferred from the arrangement of the dowel-holes, they were 0·61 to 0·64 m. wide. They stood upright in a row, and were dowelled together below at both corners; hence the vertical joints occurred

regularly between the closer pair of dowel-holes. On
the shorter sides of the room there were four such panels,
on the longer, five; at the corners there were set up
special posts.

Had this wainscot left its traces on all the four walls,
we might have assumed the building to have been a great
reservoir for water. But the dowel-holes are wanting for
the most part of the south wall; there remain only four
at its eastern end. Hence this southern wall had only one
panel, the rest of it no coating. As the small antechamber
lies exactly outside this uncased part, there must have been
a door, which, with its lateral jambs, occupied the space of
four panels. Hence the room cannot have been a reservoir.
But what was it? Another feature in the stone floor tells
us. At its north-east corner a square gutter is cut out
which carries off all the water from the floor, and takes it
eastward; where the large stone ends, a stone pipe is applied,
which reaches through the eastern wall. From the existence
of this pipe, along with the other arrangements of the room,
I think it certain that we have here found the bath-room,
which must have existed in every Homeric palace.

In the room there must have stood a *tub*, to be filled
with water for the bather. By a fortunate accident we
found a fragment of such a bathing-tub, which teaches us
that it was made of thick terra-cotta; that its form agreed
pretty nearly with that of our bathing-tubs; that it was
furnished with a thick upper rim and with strong handles
on the sides, and that it was painted within with spiral
ornament. Such then were the ἀσάμινθοι εὔξεστοι, the
well-polished bathing-tubs, often mentioned by Homer.

The using of this tub required a stone floor, for had
the latter consisted merely of lime concrete, the water
would soon have destroyed it. No doubt it was from
unpleasant experiences that the architect felt himself compelled to construct his floor in so expensive a way, of one
huge stone. For after the bath the water need only be

PLATE V.

WALL PAINTING IN THE PALACE OF TIRYNS.

emptied on the floor, to escape through the gutter and pipe without damage to the floor.   No doubt also, the masonry of the walls of quarry-stones and clay would soon have been injured and destroyed by the water, had it not been wainscoted with thick panels, which, like the sides of a ship, were no doubt well joined and made water-tight.

The bath-room contains another peculiar arrangement of which the object is uncertain.   As the ground-plan and section show, there are in the north wall two round re-ceptacles, coated on the inner side with well-smoothed lime-plaster 25 mm. thick.   Their diameter is above 0·44 to 0·48 m. and diminishes somewhat below.   How high they reached we cannot say; they are now only 0·20 m., their bottom being 0·25 m. higher than the great stone floor.   We presume they were intended to hold water, or rather oil, which was largely used by the ancients after bathing.   If the lime-coating of the receptacles seems insufficient to retain the oil, we may assume large earthen jars built into the wall.   Our visitors at Tiryns made many other conjectures as to the use of these receptacles, but none of them seemed to me satisfactory.

The lighting of the bath-room was obtained either by carrying up its walls higher than the adjoining walls, and making apertures in the clerestory, or the adjoining room, No. X., was not roofed, and so the bath in this direction would have an ordinary window.

Room X. has a floor made of stone slabs, which has a considerable slope, and lies 0·50–0 75 m. under the level of the bath-room.   The channel coming from the bath-room opens into the southern part of it; the water gushing out was led through box-shaped pipes of terra-cotta into a larger drain of masonry, which led it beneath the ground out to the south-east.   I conclude that this latter is identical with the canal which Dr. Schliemann already discovered, in 1876, in the room XXXII., east of the megaron.

The  shape  of  the  earthenware  pipe  is  given  in  the

adjoining cut, No. 118; it consists of pieces 0·68 m. in
length, open on the upper side, and having a rectangular
cross-section. Their junction is contrived by making them
considerably narrower at one end, so that they could
be simply fitted one into the other. The clay of which
they are made is very coarse, and very insufficiently
baked. Similar earthenware pipes have been lately discovered in the famous aqueduct of Eupalinos at Samos.*
The single pieces have almost exactly the same proportions as those at Tiryns; but there is a marked difference
in the method of joining them. There the width in the
clear of each pipe remains constant, but nevertheless the
single pieces could be easily fitted, the thickness of the clay
of both pipes having been reduced to one-half where the

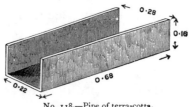

No. 118.—Pipe of terra-cotta.

pipes join. This is a much more advanced construction
than that of the pipe at Tiryns, which is, therefore, older
than the conduit of Eupalinos, which dates from the
6th century B.C.

Room X., which contains this drain-pipe, is also of the
greatest importance, because here were found the largest
and best fragments of pottery, and the best remains of the
painted wall-plaster. This room must have been used in
ancient times as a lumber-room for broken vessels and all
kinds of *débris*, for the many objects here found were
mixed with perfectly black earth, such as is not found
anywhere else in the palace.

---

* Cf. E. Fabricius in the *Mitth. des deutschen archäol. Instituts in
Athen*, 1884, p. 185.

On the west side, by the bath-room, lies a long corridor (XII. on Plan II.), which is comparatively well preserved. It retains almost all its concrete floor, and the lime-plaster of the walls is still there in many places. In the south-west part there are still traces of colouring on the floor. Geometrical ornaments were painted in red on the yellow or white concrete. In one field is a zigzag pattern of straight lines, in another wavy red lines. Although these traces of an ornamental painting of the floor are very scanty, we may use them as important evidence of the rich style of decoration of the whole palace. For if the floor of an unimportant side-corridor was so adorned, we may be sure the floor of the greater rooms must have been similarly, if not more richly worked.

In corridor XII. there are also remaining three stone sills for single doors, one leading to the bath-room, the others to rooms adjoining the west wall of the citadel, and now almost entirely gone. In the remaining corner of one of them (XIII.) there is still a fragment of lime-concrete floor coloured red. A fourth door led to corridor XIV. It never possessed a stone door-sill, but rather one of wood, as the charred remains of this material here clearly show. We shall meet such wooden door-sills at several other doors.

The object of the walls which lie between corridor XIV. and Room X. is not clear. Although they are preserved above the floor-level of the corridor, they show no openings for doors.

But the rooms contained by them may possibly, for some reason unknown to us, have had their floors on a higher level, so that doors may have existed in the higher parts of the walls now destroyed. It is also possible that here there were stairs leading to the upper storey or the roof. But no certain traces of such steps have been found. It is also to be observed that these walls, as well as those lying to the north-west of them, have a direction somewhat different from those of the megaron and the bath. This variation was probably caused by the orientation of the adjoining west wall of the citadel.

From corridor XIV. you can pass down to the middle citadel by a comparatively well-preserved flight of steps; nine steps and a large landing-step of stone are still discernible. It is remarkable here, as in the two steps leading to the αἴθουσα δώματος, that the height of the step is so small in relation to its depth, on the average 0·10 m. to 0·44 m. In later Greek times steps were not so comfortably built, and even nowadays such proportions are very rare. The steps consist of stone slabs of various length, very regularly worked, and joined without any cement.

## 8. THE COURT OF THE WOMEN'S APARTMENTS.
### (XVI. on Plan II.)

In the north-west part of the palace lies a small court, with colonnades and adjoining rooms, which has no direct connection with the main court; it is the court of the women's dwelling. You must pass many doors and corridors to reach this inner part of the palace. There appear to have been three ways of reaching it. First, from the back-hall of the great Propylæum, through the long passage XXXVI., to the colonnade XXXI.; and from this, through the outer court XXX., to the east colonnade of the women's court. Secondly, you could go from the great court or from the megaron, past the bath-room, into corridor XII., and then through passages XIV., XV., and XIX., to reach the vestibule of the women's apartments. A third way probably went from the east colonnade of the great court, through Room XXXIII., into the colonnade XXXI., and then along the first way into the court of the women's apartments. All these three approaches are stopped in several places by doors, and the women's apartment was therefore quite separated from the great hall and men's court.

The commentators on Homer have disputed much whether the heroic palace had a separate women's court, like that described by Vitruvius in later Greek houses. The latest inquirer * concludes his discussion of this question thus: " Everywhere in Homer an αὐλή is mentioned, never αὐλαί, so that the view of those who assert that there were two, may be regarded as finally disposed of." This sentence is directly refuted by the palace at Tiryns. There may indeed have been palaces in Homer's time which had only one αὐλή; but we now know for certain that some there were which contained two. Whoever concludes from Homer's always mentioning *the* court of the royal palaces, that in addition to this main court (the court κατ᾽ ἐξοχήν), there was no second, forgets that Homer never gives us a formal description of a palace, but only mentions such parts of them as are necessary or desirable to explain the scenes taking place there. In the Homeric palace the court of the men's apartments is the αὐλή; the women's court is subordinate, and so happens never to be mentioned by the poet.

The women's court at Tiryns is a rectangle of 18·45 m. long by 9·20 m. broad. In the plan I have marked both courts with cross-lines, so that they might at once be recognized as such. The floor is of sand and coarse pebbles, in some spots (especially at the north side) there are under this some traces of lime-concrete. In front of the vestibule leading to the women's hall there are found, several centimetres under this floor, traces of an older, carefully-smoothed concrete floor, which have a steep decline to the north, and go down under the door-sill of the vestibule. They point to ancient rebuilding on this site.

As the great court was well arranged for carrying off

---

* E. Buchholz. *die Homerischen Realien*, II. p. 93.

the rain-water, so the women's court also possesses a good
system of drainage.    There is a vertical shaft of rubble
masonry at the lowest point of it, covered with a slab 0·50
to 0·55 m. in size.    Through a hole in the middle of this
slab the water of the court passed into the shaft, and so
reached a horizontal drain of rubble masonry which carried
it away.    The upper edge of the covering-slab lies 0·29 m.
deeper than the floor of the women's hall, and 0·53 m.
deeper than that of the men's.    Closer information about
the proportions of level of the court and its surrounding
halls can be obtained from the figures on Plan II.

On the east side of the court lay a colonnade with a
front of two columns between two quadrangular pilasters.
Both column bases of limestone are still in their place, and
have a diameter of 0·41 to 0·45 m.    The pilaster at the
north corner is a sandstone block, 0·76 m. broad, 0·85 m.
long, and 0·53 m. high, on whose upper surface ten square
dowel-holes are visible.    One of these holes was found full
of charcoal, and so proved that these holes contained
wooden dowels, which fastened the upper part of the
pilaster, which was of wood, firmly to the stone basis.    The
unusually large number of the dowel-holes is owing to the
pilasters being made of several parallel pieces of wood.    The
south pilaster of the colonnade is considerably longer than
the northern, because it forms the side wall of a small antechamber which lies before the main entrance to the women's
apartment.    This door, whose limestone sill is still in its
place, was single, and led directly, not to the court, but
into the east colonnade, so that one could pass from all
rooms of the women's apartment, even in rain, to the
entrance, under shelter.    The east colonnade is immediately
joined on the north side by another smaller portico which
has only one pillar between two pilasters.    The round limestone pillar-base is 0·62 m. in diameter, and shows clear
traces of burning.    In its centre is a circle of 0·30 m. in
diameter, which is not so affected, while the outer edge is

much damaged by fire. We infer from this, that the diameter of the burnt wooden pillar was only a little above o·30 m. Clear traces on the concrete floor and the plaster of the back wall show that there were benches here for sitting, presumably of wood ; their breadth is, on the average, o·45 m.

In speaking of the court, we have lastly to consider the reconstruction undertaken at its south-east corner. There a room was built in, which was entered from the east colonnade. Although its walls are of the same rubble masonry as the walls of the palace, and its floor is covered with a well-smoothed lime-concrete, yet this room must be a later addition, because it disfigures the court, and shuts up part of the east colonnade. But it must also have been built before the destruction of the citadel, for its walls show evident traces of the great fire which destroyed the whole palace. We cannot tell whether, before the building of this room, there was in the south-east corner of this court a second door for direct communication between the court and outer court, or, as indicated in the plan in dotted lines, the south wall of the court reached without interruption to the east colonnade. The probabilities are in favour of the latter plan

## 9. THE WOMEN'S HALL AND ITS VESTIBULE.

As the men's apartment with its anterooms lies on the north side of the great court, so the megaron on the north side of the lesser court is arranged as the women's apartment. The similarity of these halls in proportions is obvious on the plan of the palace. The women's apartment with its vestibule is a reduced copy of the great megaron ; but almost all its dimensions are considerably smaller, and the anteroom between the vestibule and the men's hall is not here repeated.

The vestibule forms a rectangle of 5·05 by 5·59 m., and

therefore nearly a square. In the middle of its north wall
is the main door leading to the hall. The two side walls
have each a side door, and end in *parastades*. The south
side, looking into the court, is quite open. The separation
of the two *parastades* is so small (5·59 m.), that the architrave over them required no support. The two still-existing
*antæ* blocks are 1·03 to 1·06 m. broad, 0·58 m. high,
and at most only 1·23 m. long; they are made of hard
limestone. Only the visible surfaces are well worked, those
hidden by the masonry have remained more or less rough.
On the upper side are round dowel-holes, of which every
two are, curiously enough, so close together as to form
one oblong hole. The front line of the *antæ* is connected
by a stone sill, which separates the floor of the vestibule
from that of the court. Such a threshold seems to have
surrounded the whole court, for in front of the east colonnade it can still be made out in all its length.

The floor of the vestibule now consists of a lime concrete, 5–15 mm. thick, which in many places crosses the
door-sill. But this is not the original floor, for underneath
are found remains of an older concrete beautifully smoothed,
which agrees perfectly with the older concrete discovered in
the court.

The existence of the two side-doors, which led from
the vestibule into a corridor surrounding the megaron, is
proved by the two great door-sills of limestone, which still
show the pivot-holes for single doors. One of these doors,
the ground-plan of which is seen in No. 121, we shall
discuss in treating of the doors generally. The same is
to be said of the main door in the middle of the back-
wall, which connects the vestibule and women's hall. The
ground-plan is given in Fig. 119.

The *megaron of the women*, a rectangle, 5·64 by
7·60 m., is considerably smaller than that of the men, but
is still to our notions a large room ; a considerable number
of people could find comfortable room in it. Both side

walls still stand 0·50 m. high in their southern half, the front
wall is also fairly preserved ; of the back wall only the foundations remain.   All these walls are of rubble, with clay-mortar,
they were covered with clay-plastering, and over it with
lime-plastering.   In the south-east corner this coating is still
well preserved; even the early painting is here still visible.
These scanty remains of wall-painting are very valuable
to us, because all the other fragments of painted plaster
found in the other rooms have fallen from the walls.   The
women's hall is therefore the only place in the palace where
we can study this decoration *in situ*.   In the section on
wall-painting we shall return to it.   The floor of the hall is
still almost completely covered with the old lime concrete,
consisting of two layers, each 18 mm. thick.   The upper
one shows in some places scratched-in lines and red colour.

In the middle of the room was a square place where
there was no concrete—its breadth 1·24 m., its length not
accurately determinable.   The analogy of the men's hall
leads us to regard this as the place of the *hearth*, which
could hardly have been dispensed with in this room.   The
smoke of the fire must have escaped through the door, or
high lateral windows in the walls.   The latter is the more
probable conclusion, the more so as such high windows
were the most obvious way of lighting the room.   But it
must be admitted, on the other view, that the door, if left
quite open, would give light enough for the room.   But as
keeping the door open at all times and seasons was not
convenient, it can hardly have sufficed to let the light in
and the smoke out.   Sufficient window-apertures could be
easily managed, if the roof of the corridor running round
the hall was lower than that of the hall; it would then
only be necessary to leave the interstices between some of
the roof-beams (what were later the *metopæ*) open, to obtain
light enough and excellent ventilation.   I regard the existence of this method of lighting the women's megaron as
highly probable, if not actually proved.

In the south-west corner of the megaron we discovered
an imperfect rectangle built into it, which I have noted in
Plan II. in yellow. It does not belong to the original
building, but has been added later. Yet it was there before
the destruction of the citadel, as it shows strong traces of
the great fire. For the clay bricks of which it consists are,
together with the mortar, turned into regular baked bricks.
Near the wooden door-posts, where the heat was greatest,
the bricks are even melted on the surface, and now covered
with a thick glaze. As to the intention of this building
I cannot even offer a conjecture.

On three sides the megaron and its vestibule are surrounded by the corridor XIX., which is 1·39 to 1·48 m.
broad. Its main object seems to have been to establish
such a connection between the men's apartments and the
chambers at the north-east corner of the palace, as to avoid
passing through the women's rooms. At its south-western
end it was stopped by a wall, which is now indeed destroyed,
but of the existence of which there are clear traces. At its
south-eastern end there is a stone door-sill, which proves the
existence of a single door connecting the passage with the
north hall of the women's court. The corner pilaster still
standing at the eastern side of this door is of sandstone, and
provided with square dowel-holes.

### 10. The Thalamoi in the North-east corner of the Palace.

In Odysseus palace there were, according to Homer, in
the farthest recess of the building (ἐν μυχῷ δόμου) a series
of rooms, among which are expressly named the husband
and wife's bedroom, the armoury, and the treasury. The
last is called (*Od.* XXI. 8, 9) the θάλαμος ἔσχατος, and therefore the furthest from the entrance gate. In Tiryns also we
find in the north-east corner, furthest removed from the
great court and its *prothyron*, a number of chambers, which,

from their position and form, we may clearly identify with those just described in Odysseus' palace. There is first the Thalamos XXII., a square of about 5 m.; it had a broad folding-door, whose great limestone sill is still *in situ*. The anteroom XXI. separated it from the corridor XIX. From the anteroom you reached a closed passage (XXIII.) upon which three other thalamoi opened. The largest is XXIV., occupying exactly the north-east corner of the whole palace; was accessible from the corridor through a single door, whose sill we found. Beside it lies the small thalamos XXV., provided with a very small anteroom, and therefore capable of double closing; the sills of both doors are still *in situ*. The third thalamos (XXVI.) was directly accessible from the corridor; its doors appear to have had not a stone, but a wooden, sill. There are in addition two small rooms together (XX.) in the north-east corner of the palace, which from their dimensions (on the average each is only 1·50 m. wide) cannot have been dwelling-rooms. I think I can recognize in them the place of the stairs leading to the roof or upper storey, and will describe them more fully in treating of the ὑπερῷον.

We have, accordingly, in the μυχός of our palace, besides corridors, four thalamoi and two anterooms. If we desire to compare them individually with those of Odysseus' house, XXII. would correspond best to the bedroom of the royal pair, and the doubly closed room XXV. to the treasure-room; the other two may have served for keeping arms and other valuables. But as these details cannot be certain, I have not mentioned them on the Plan II.

As regards the construction of these thalamoi and their internal arrangements, we can say even less than in the other parts of the palace, because these rooms, lying at the edge of the upper citadel, were naturally most damaged. The outer walls, which form also the boundary wall of the upper citadel, are nowhere preserved higher than the floor of the thalamoi, and therefore we can neither tell how thick

the outer walls were in their upper part, nor can we give
the accurate dimensions of these chambers. The measures
of breadth of the out-walls given in the Plan II. only indicate those of the foundations, that is, of the terrace wall of
the upper citadel. Of the partition walls of the thalamoi,
on the contrary, several still stand about 1 m. high, and
their plastering is here and there extant. Both walls and
coating, as well as the remains of concrete floor found in
some of the rooms, are made in the same manner as those
already described in other parts of the palace.

When we found in the wall between the corridor XXIII.
and the eastern portico of the women's court the two stone
pilasters noted in the plan, we surmised that there was a
door between these pilasters. Whether such a connection
was originally planned, is difficult to decide ; this much is
certain, that it did not exist when the citadel was destroyed,
for the wall between these pilasters happens to be particularly well preserved, and is still covered on its eastern face
with the old coating of plaster.

## 11. The Outer Court XXX. with its Adjoining Rooms.

South-east of the women's court lies an open space, which
we may best designate as the outer court of the women's
apartments. That it was not covered, is proved, both by its
measurements, and by the portico along its western side.
Neither traces of a concrete floor, nor of a water-escape
have been found in it. The front of the *stoa* on the western
side was formed by two pillars between two *antæ*. Both
pillar-bases and the bases of both *parastades* are still *in situ*.
The northern intercolumniation was closed by a later wall
built of clay-bricks. Into this *stoa* the long corridor opens
which comes from the south between the Propylæum and
the women's habitation, and which was ended at its entrance
to the portico by a door with a wooden sill. The three

little rooms to the west of the portico were most probably accessible from here, but it can only be proved in the case of Room XXXII., in the eastern wall of which a door is to be seen. There are indeed clear traces of a door connecting the two other rooms, but the rest of their walls is too much destroyed to determine any other door-places with safety.

In Room XXXII. Dr. Schliemann sunk a shaft in 1876 (noted by S on Plan II.), in which the water-drain already mentioned was found. This canal is built of rubble masonry with clay-mortar, and covered with slabs of the same material. To save it from injury by the water, its lower surface is formed by a quadrangular pipe of terra-cotta, open above, like that which we found east of the bath-room. But its pieces are smaller than those there described, and the edges rounded as well within as at both ends. The strength of the clay of the pipe is below, 23 mm., at the upper edge, only 12 mm. The material is very impure clay, only slightly baked. The level of the actual water-course is about 1·75 m. under the floor of the chamber. It may safely be assumed that this canal is connected with the water-drain of the bath-room, the escape pipe in the women's court, and also with the vertical shaft in the great court, so that the palace possessed systematic draining arrangements.

Of the rooms east and north-east of the court, Nos. XXVII. and XXVIII. only are sufficiently preserved to enable us at least to recognize their doors. In the latter were found three curious clay-cylinders, at a place marked on Plan II. Their manufacture is very rude, with no smooth surface within or without. They have an average diameter of 0·50 m., and are about 1 m. high, but broken at the top. When found, they were filled with red burnt brick-*débris*. As to their use, I can offer no suggestion.

The three rooms connected with them to the south are so changed or destroyed, partly by the ruin of the citadel, partly by later restorations, that I could not recover their original ground-plan. They suffered particularly, because immediately east of them lies the way, 4 m. lower, which leads to the upper citadel, and into which most of the walls tumbled down.

The part of the citadel lying south of the outer court XXX. is even worse preserved; there we find a mere chaos of intersecting walls, from which it is impossible to guess any ground-plan. Some of these walls are so destroyed, that even their direction is lost. Even the various directions of the walls shown in the plan, prove that here we have buildings of widely different epochs. On Plan II. I have coloured all the thin walls, which show about the same system of orientation, yellow, to indicate them as later buildings. But they too cannot all be of the same date, for some cross others and some have foundations, while others have not. We do not know when these thin walls were built, but one thing we may assert; they are later than most of the other walls of the palace, all of which have thicker walls.

On a level with these later walls we discovered two water conduits, marked on Plan II. The western was built of stone slabs set on end, and covered with the same; the eastern is made of square terra-cotta pipes. The single members of this latter agree in form with those before described, which were found close to the bath-room and in the room XXXII.; but the measures of the profile are smaller. The box-shaped pieces are 0·69 m. long, the actual aperture 0·07–0·10 m. broad and 0·08 m. high. The thickness of the sides varies from 35 mm. below, to 15 mm. at the upper edge; the corners are rounded. Both watercourses fall towards the south, and appear to have led the rain-water into some reservoir lying in that direction.

In some places under the thin walls, as shown in Plan II., there are remains of older foundations of greater strength, which, strangely enough, have almost the same direction as the great Propylæum. We conclude from these founda-

tion-walls that the eastern part of the palace had once quite
a different arrangement; but the scantiness of the extant
remains will not admit of a reconstruction. What rooms
there were here earlier and later, whether work-rooms for
female servants or their bedrooms, we cannot decide.

The east supporting wall of the palace-terrace seems
to have been here exceptionally thick, but is destroyed so
completely as to allow no safe measurements. At its south
end only, where the ascending way to the upper citadel
widens into a larger space, the wall is comparatively well
preserved. It is here as much as 5·30 m. thick, probably
because there was here a tower to defend the approach to
the citadel. How far this tower reached north is, however,
not to be determined.

Finally, we may mention briefly the rooms immediately
north of the great Propylæum, lying, two of them west, and
three east of the long corridor leading to the women's apartments. Of the two former the northern is accessible from
the great court, while the other is connected by a door with
the short corridor between the great Propylæum and the
men's court.

The opening in the east wall of this room is no door,
but a gap made by the digging of a shaft by Dr. Schliemann
in 1876. The three rooms lying east are so connected by
doors, that the first two must be passed through to reach
the third. This latter has now, indeed, by an opening in
the western wall, a direct connection with the corridor
XXXVI., but this hole was also made by Dr. Schliemann
in 1876. In the north-east corner of Room XXXVIII.
there is a great rude clay cylinder, such as we have already
found in Room XXVII. As to the use of these rooms,
it seems likely that one or more were meant for door-
keepers, but there can be no certainty about it.

## 12. The Roof and the Upper Storey.

### (τὸ ὑπερῷον.)

We have frequently alluded, in describing the great Propylæum and the Megaron, to the fact that they had horizontal roofs. We must assume this kind of roof for the whole palace, as will be shown presently in discussing the roof-question. Flat roofs, on which people can walk about and can sleep, are still common in the East, and that they were also usual in antiquity is proved by many passages in classical authors and in the Bible.* As the Greeks and Orientals now often sleep in the open air on roofs or balconies, so people, no doubt, did in early days. Thus Homer, in the 'Odyssey,'† tells how Elpenor, when intoxicated, goes up on the roof of Kirke's house, and there falls asleep; awakened suddenly by the noise of his companions, he forgets where he is, and by a false step is killed. To sleep on the open roof was of course only possible in fine weather, so that probably from the earliest days there were rooms on the roof partially closed, to protect from wind and rain, while admitting the cool night-air. If the building-ground was limited, and the room required by the family considerable, there were no doubt many such rooms in the upper storey. But in general the ancient house, as appears from its ground-plan, was one-storeyed; if an upper storey existed, it was appropriated to the sleeping-apartments.

We found no trace in Tiryns of an upper storey itself, as the walls are nowhere preserved more than 1 m. in height, but there are traces of stairs which must have led to the roof, which consequently thus formed the upper storey. The Room XX., lying between the women's apartment and the thalamoi, is divided by a cross-wall into two

---

* Cf. Winckler, *die Wohnhäuser der Hellenen*, p. 56.
† *Od.* X. 552–60, and XI. 60–5.

narrrow compartments each about 1·50 m. broad; in the
northern of them the concrete floor is still well preserved,
and moreover slopes considerably upward from west to east.
I presume that the proper stairs began at the east end of
the southern compartment; that here it rose from east to
west, then passed into the northern compartment, and there,
going west to east, reached the roof. In this way the form
and position of these two rooms can be very well explained.
The slight rising of the floor in the north compartment
may have been caused by the intention, that the steps might
also be reached from the corridor XXIII. as well. In
speaking of the rooms south of the megaron, it was said
(p. 235) that possibly there was here also a stair to the
roof, but the extant traces of it are less clear than in the
case of the stair in the women's apartment. Still it is quite
conceivable that there were two stairs.

Whether they led to the roof, or whether upon it there
were also rooms (ὑπερῷον), we cannot decide. The existing
walls of the ground-floor are in any case strong enough to
sustain the walls of upper rooms.

We now close our description of the plan of the palace.
It is very circumstantial, perhaps too much so for some
readers. But I had my reasons for making the description
of the individual rooms, and especially of the important
halls and courts, very full. The remains of Tiryns, after
the recent excavations, must be regarded of the first importance in the history of Greek architecture. Not merely
the architect and the archæologist, but every cultivated
man must regard and study the plan of Tiryns with
peculiar interest. From this alone I was bound to give as
accurate a description as possible, in order to make the
understanding of it easier and clearer. But there is a
further reason. Those parts of the palace which are built
of imperfect materials—e.g. the floors of lime and the walls
of rubble and clay—are doomed to certain destruction. The

Greek Government, indeed, intends to cover a large part of
the palace with a roof, and in other ways to protect the walls
and floors from destruction; but such measures can only
delay, they cannot prevent, their destruction.  It was therefore imperatively required to explain fully and accurately
the present state of the ruins, so that it might hereafter be
certain what still remained of the palace of Tiryns when it
was excavated, and what was already destroyed.*

## C.—The Architectural Remains of an older Settlement.

In describing the palace, we have repeatedly spoken of
remains of walls and floors, which, when the fort was destroyed, were already covered by other buildings, and must
therefore have been older than the palace as shown in Plan II.
We must not attribute all these remains to an older
settlement, but must distinguish between such as belonged

---

* " I trust Plan II. and its full description may suffice to persuade
Herr Hauptmann Bötticher of the Prussian artillery, the discoverer of
the ancient cremation ovens, that Tiryns was not a 'fire-necropolis of
terraced construction,' but an inhabited palace.  I shall surely not be
expected to add a word of refutation to so original a hypothesis.  But
I cannot resist the temptation of quoting a few sentences from the
latest 'epoch-making' essay of the gallant officer, as characteristic of the
man and diverting to the reader.  He says (*Zeitschrift für Muscologie,
&c.*, 1884, pp. 189–91) : 'A year has passed since my fire-necropolis
illumines the nations.  The recognition of the necropolis of Hissarlik
and Tiryns is of vast application.  It is the beginning of a new epoch
(*sic!*) in archæology and extends its widening circles !  No wonder that
antiquated (!) and tottering systems strain themselves against it.  They
must fall, for they are built up on error, on the confusion of tombs and
dwelling-sites, and can only explain the utensils of the dead, often
shabby and unusual, by want of civilization, as if they had always been
in parallel use among the living.  Let us build up the primitive history
of mankind on a thoroughly different foundation, fair and beautiful;
for such a brutal condition, as is sketched in some theories, has never
existed !' "
This may suffice for the reader.

to the great palace itself, and were only put out of use by alterations in its details, and such as really belong to a much earlier epoch. Most of the remains we have mentioned belong to the former kind. A careful examination of the ground-plan (Plate II.) will convince any one that it cannot have come into existence as an unity. As a whole, the palace may from the beginning have had the general character it now exhibits, but in the course of decades or centuries many changes of detail were certainly undertaken. We cannot here enter upon these successive changes of structure, as the number of original fragments of the palace is not enough to tell us what was the original plan and what the various changes. To obtain materials for writing an architectural history of the palace of Tiryns it were necessary to undertake deep excavations in many parts of the fort, and uncover completely various older pieces of masonry.

We, however, may briefly discuss the older remains of the second kind, in order to prove the important fact, that Tiryns was occupied before the building of the palace. The clearest traces of earlier settlement were found in the south-west corner of the middle citadel. In a shaft (S on Plan I.) sunk immediately west of the little connecting stair between the upper and middle citadels, there was found at the depth of 3·30 m. under the level of the lowest step a concrete floor, consisting of clay, and showing strong traces of fire. Digging further, we found also two walls of about 0·75 m. height, built of rubble with clay-mortar. They belong to a room, whose floor was made of that clay concrete. The *débris*, which filled and covered the room several metres deep, consisted chiefly of clay, wood-ashes, and fragments of brick burnt red. Among the latter are several broken and even whole burnt bricks. They are c·36–7 m. long, by 0·21 m. broad, and 0·12–3 m. high, and were of clay and straw. In the *débris* there was also found pottery almost exclusively monochrome, which is described in Chapter III.

There can be no doubt that we have here the remains
of a settlement older than the palace ; for in the first place,
all the objects of clay found here belong without exception
to an older epoch than those found in the palace ; secondly,
their age is proved by the great depth of the walls and
floors ; thirdly, it can clearly be seen on the spot that this
deep room was long covered up by *débris*, when the boundary wall and stairs of the upper citadel were built.  This
latter ground seems to me indeed decisive ; it can easily
be shown at the west part of the terrace wall of the upper
citadel, that to make a foundation for this wall a trench
was dug in the brick *débris*, and that, after laying the
foundation, the remaining empty space was filled with
clay and sand.  Hence the terrace wall cannot have been
built till the red-brick *débris* covered the older house, with
its clay floor, several metres high.

In the other shafts sunk, both in the middle fort and in
the palace, like incontestable traces of an older settlement
have not been found ; but they almost all disclosed some
faint traces of it.  Several of these shafts contain one or
two deeper floors of clay, others showed traces of older
walls ; in almost all were found wood-ashes and potsherds.
In several shafts there also turned up the *débris* of burnt
walls made of sun-dried bricks.  In the great cruciform
trench dug by Dr. Schliemann in 1876 in the south part
of the citadel, when it was being widened, 2 m. under the
floor of the palace were found pieces of lime-plaster with
traces of colour, which exactly correspond to the plaster
found in the palace.  It is indeed doubtful whether these
fragments of lime-plaster belong to the older settlement,
or whether they belong to the palace, and at the fall of the
west fort wall and of the buildings close to it, found their
way down so deep.  This I do not venture to decide.

The existence of an older settlement in Tiryns is therefore certain, but of its size and form we know hardly
anything.  We do not even know whether it was surrounded with a wall.  For I regard it as certain that the

present gigantic wall, which is still preserved, does not belong to the earlier settlement, but was built at the same time as the stately palace.

## D.—Building Material and Construction.

### 1. The Walls.

The principal building materials found in the walls of Tiryns are limestone, breccia, sandstone, clay, lime, and wood. Let us first consider the various kinds of building-stone.

*Limestone* has been used both in the rough shape from the quarry and in a hewn form ; the rough stones being employed for the fortress-walls, the foundations, and the rising walls of the houses ; the ashlars for thresholds, *antæ*-blocks, pillar-bases, steps, and for the floor of the bath-room. It was quarried from the rocks lying to the south and east of Tiryns, where there are still distinct traces of ancient quarrying. For rubble building the blocks broken from the rock were not further hewn, except, perhaps, roughly with a hammer. The larger blocks were used for the outer wall of the citadel, the smaller for the walls of the buildings inside. But whenever they were to be employed as ashlars for *antæ*-blocks, steps, &c., the surfaces were regularly cut with saws, hammers, and other instruments.

*Breccia*, a conglomerate of pebbles, is used as free-stone for door-sills and *antæ*-blocks ; the gigantic doorposts of the gate of the upper fort are also of this material. In proportion to limestone, breccia was very little used ; for it is harder, and hence more troublesome to quarry. It is not certain where the blocks used at Tiryns came from ; possibly from Charvati, a village close to Mycenæ (about eight miles distant), since there are there large beds of breccia, which

have also furnished the material for the buildings of
Mycenæ. But there may be, for all I know, beds of
breccia in greater proximity to Tiryns, at the foot of the
eastern mountains.

*Sandstone* is used even less than breccia; only, indeed,
for some *antæ*-blocks and for the lower step of the
great megaron. Whence these blocks came, I could not
discover.

Among the walls built with these various sorts of stone
we have to distinguish two kinds, according as mortar was
used or not. The fortress walls and foundations of the
houses are built without it, whereas for the rising walls of
the buildings clay-mortar has always been used. In the
fortress walls mortar could be spared, because only huge
blocks were employed, which were kept in their place
by their great weight, and therefore required no cement.
Although smaller stones were used in the foundations of
the houses, no mortar was used, because the mass of
earth on either side prevented any giving way of the individual stones. But for the comparatively light house-walls,
mortar, and indeed exclusively clay-mortar, was necessarily
employed. The masonry of these house-walls, consisting
of limestone rubble and clay-mortar, was just such as is
now common, not only in Greece, but also in many other
countries. All the interstices of the stones, which are for
the most part very irregular, are filled up with small pebbles
and with clay-mortar. This mortar consists of clay and
water mixed with straw or hay.

Burnt lime was known to the builders of Tiryns, for
they have made the wall-plaster of pure lime, and that of
the floors of lime and gravel, but they did not use it as
binding material for quarry-stone work. This agrees
exactly with the long-established fact, that the Greeks
from the earliest times made plaster and concrete floors
of lime, but that the use of lime as binding material for
quarry-stone or brick walls became usual with them only

very late.* Only in aqueducts do the Greeks in early
times seem to have used lime-mortar.

Walls of rubble and clay would not have resisted the
direct effects of the weather had they not been covered on
the outer surface with a good plaster, for rain would soon
have washed out the clay from the joints of the wall, and
so in a short time produced the fall of the walls. Such a
wall-coating consists, in Tiryns, first of a layer of clay of
very various thickness, because it levels all the unevennesses
of the masonry, and then of a plaster of lime 1–2 cm. thick,
smoothed on the surface, and painted.

Besides this protecting plaster, another means is used
to strengthen the walls. Beams were built longitudinally
into the outer surface, which greatly contributed to the
solidity of the walls. This sort of building is still much
used in the East, and was often used in antiquity, as we
know from allusions in classical authors.† The lowest

---

* Nissen (*Pomp. Studien*, p. 45), cites two instances, where in comparatively early days lime-mortar was said to have been used in Greece ;
first in the foundations of the long walls of Athens, and secondly in the
Philippeion at Olympia. If this were really so, then the statement in the
text would be wrong, but both instances are exceedingly doubtful. The
former is taken from Plutarch's description of the long walls (Plut. *Cim.*
13), where he says : χάλικι πολλῇ καὶ λίθοις βαρέσι τῶν ἑλῶν πιεσθέντων.
The word χάλιξ, however, need not mean lime, but is more correctly
translated *gravel.* A foundation of pebbles and larger stones was in any
case better on a marshy site than one of stones and lime-mortar, for the
lime, unless it were hydraulic or water-lime, would not have hardened
in the marsh. That the Greeks frequently used gravel and pebbles in
the foundations of walls has been sufficiently proved by excavations.
The second alleged instance has been confuted by the excavations at
Olympia. From the notice of Pausanias, that the Philippeion was built
of baked bricks, Nissen concludes that lime-mortar must have also been
used in it. But it has been shown that the cella-wall of the Philippeion
was of ashlar-masonry in poros-stone. The notice of Pausanias is
therefore false, and perhaps refers only to the roof, which indeed was
made of baked tiles. Hence the Philippeion can no longer be considered
as a brick-building, and still less as a building with lime-mortar.

† Cf. Winckler, *Die Wohnhäuser der Hellenen.* p. 77, *sqq.* Such
quarrystone-walls with longitudinally placed beams have also been found

longitudinal beam in those walls of Tiryns, which are so
constructed, lies 0·45–0·60 m. over the floor.   The wood
itself is gone; but in several places one can distinctly trace
the empty space in the walls which it once filled.   In the
south-east corner of Room XVIII. there was even charcoal found in such a hollow space.

Before such a beam could be built in longitudinally,
there must first be a horizontal bed made for it with thin
slabs of stone, which are still to be found in several walls.
Generally the masonry immediately over the empty space
is much burnt—another proof that these longitudinal holes
have once been filled with wooden beams.   Whether cross-
beams were used in addition to the long beams we could
not ascertain.

Whilst the lower part of all the house-walls was constructed of rubble masonry, in the upper part *clay-bricks*
appear, besides the former material.   There must have been
a very extensive use of bricks in Tiryns, for almost all the
rooms of the palace were filled with half-burnt bricks and
red brick-*débris*.   Unfortunately, however, but in a few
places of the palace brick masonry is preserved, for at
highest the walls are now only 1 m. over the ground, whilst
for the most part the brick-work only commenced at that
height.   In two places alone (in the Women's Hall XVIII.
and in the Court XXX.) the brick-work walls started from
the ground, and therefore are still in good preservation.
During the destruction of the citadel both these walls were
so thoroughly burned, that the sun-dried bricks became
fire-baked.   In the first place named, those bricks which
were in immediate contact with a large wooden doorpost
were even completely vitrified.

When one observes the partially well-baked bricks, the

---

at Thera (Bursian, *Geogr. von Griechenland*, II. 523).   In Troy, too,
there is preserved in a quarrystone-wall a round longitudinal bed for a
wooden beam.

PLATE VI.

IVORY ORNAMENT FROM MENIDI

GOLD ORNAMENT FROM MYCENAE

WALL PAINTING IN THE PALACE OF TIRYNS.

first idea is that they are really baked bricks, burnt before they were used. But the circumstance, that the mortar between the bricks is baked in the same manner as they are, satisfactorily proves that the baking only took place after the building of the wall. The burnt mortar, however, is not only to be seen in the brick-walls still *in situ*, but also among the loose bricks found inside the rooms, which are frequently baked into lumps together with the mortar. For the burning of the bricks there are but two conceivable solutions. Either the walls having been built of raw clay-bricks were then purposely baked, or the baking resulted from the fire used by the conquerors for the destruction of the citadel. With the brick walls of Troy, I was led from peculiar technical indices to infer at first the possibility of the former solution, but later I convinced myself on the spot of the incorrectness of this judgment. The Trojan citadel and house-walls were unbaked clay-brick walls until the destruction of the city, and the holes in them were intended for the reception of cross and longitudinal beams.

As in Troy, so in Tiryns, the baked bricks were originally sun-dried clay-bricks, which during the destruction of the citadel first became baked bricks. That during the excavations almost none but baked-brick masonry was found can be plainly accounted for by the fact, firstly, that in the course of ages the unbaked portions of the wall crumbled away; and secondly, that during the excavations the few remaining raw bricks can only be observed and saved by the greatest possible attention. Many may wonder why the strong clay-brick walls found in Troy should have been so completely and regularly burnt in the conflagration at the destruction of the city as was in fact the case. This appearance is, however, easily explained by the material of the bricks. The clay of which bricks and mortar are alike composed had been mixed with a quantity of straw, which furnished fuel to the flames, and when consumed, the hollows left gave free access for the heat to penetrate the bricks and walls. The beams built-in also, if they had not decayed before the destruction of the fortress, would everywhere abundantly feed the fire.

On account of the importance of sun-dried brick building in antiquity, and more especially in the most ancient period, it may be permitted in connection with the notices of Vitruvius,* and on grounds of the discovery of ancient brick walls, to give some more accurate account of the sun-dried brick and its uses.

As material for the sun-dried brick, Vitruvius names as most suitable chalk (*terra cretosa*), or an argilliferous sand (*sabulo masculus*); but practically all kinds of earth have been used. Especially in building the fortress they were not very critical, and usually employed the earth thrown out in digging the trench round the fortress for the manufacture of bricks, even should this not be very suitable for the purpose. The clay to be used should further be as pure as possible; but this requirement has also frequently been disregarded. For example, the bricks of Troy contain countless shells, large and small, and in Troy as well as Tiryns I have frequently found potsherds and large pebbles in the bricks.

In order to strengthen the bricks and at the same time to facilitate drying, cut straw was mixed with the clay, and its presence can still be distinctly recognised even in the burnt bricks. The clay was kneaded with water, mixed with straw, and then the mass was shaped. The drying took place either in the open air, or, still better, under a sheltering roof, and lasted a long time. If the bricks were to be

---

* The two most important passages are Vitruv. II. 3, and II. 8, 8–18. Cf. also Blümner, *Technologie bei Griechen und Römern*, p. 8, *sqq.*, and Nissen, *Pompeianische Studien*, p. 22, *sqq.*

perfectly dry, they had to remain two full years, for only after the lapse of this time did the inside of the brick lose all its moisture.   In Utica, indeed, as Vitruvius informs us, the clay-bricks were not used till they were five years made, and until their age was attested by an official certificate.* For the manufacture of bricks the most suitable seasons were spring and autumn, for in summer they were so quickly and completely dried outside by the great heat, that the moisture contained inside could hardly escape; and if such bricks are used, they soon split, and the masonry is not lasting.

The forms of the bricks were very various.   According to Vitruvius, there were three kinds: (1) The Lydian brick, 1½ ft. long and 1 ft. broad (0·44 m.–0·30 m.), which was specially used in Italy; (2) the Pentadoron, which was 5 palms (0·37 m.) square, and was particularly used in the public buildings of the Greeks; (3) the Tetradoron, of 4 palms (0·30 m.) square, which was used in Greek private houses.

At the time of Vitruvius probably only these kinds were in common use.   But of the bricks whose origin was centuries earlier, those of Troy, Hanaï-Tepeh, Tiryns, Mycenæ, and Eleusis, for the most part, show other sizes.† For more convenient survey I place the principal sizes of the bricks

---

* See Vitruvius, II. 3.

† Herr Hauptmann Bötticher maintains in the *Zeitschrift für Museo-logie*, 1884, p. 190, that it is "absolutely impossible" to build a wall of dry clay-bricks and moist clay-mortar; that clay-bricks can only be used when they are moist, as otherwise they do not bind with the mortar. What Vitruvius writes of sun-dried brick-buildings in antiquity is evidently unknown to Herr Hauptmann Bötticher; neither, evidently, does he know that to the present day in the East many houses, nay whole cities, are built in exactly that manner, which he considers to be "absolutely impossible." If the "village-architect," whom Herr Hauptmann Bötticher cites as his authority, is still ignorant of this kind of building, I can recommend it to him for imitation, from my own experience, in the strongest manner.

of these different towns in a table together—the numbers
mean centimetres.

| | | Length. | Breadth. | Height. | |
|---|---|---|---|---|---|
| Troy . . . | 1. | 67–72 | 44–48 | 12–13 | } II. City. |
| | 2. | 66 | 30 | 12 | |
| | 3. | 69–71 | 19–20 | 11–12 | |
| | 4. | 30 | 30 | 7 | } III.–V. City. |
| | 5. | 42 | ? | 8 | |
| Hanaï-Tepeh * | 6. | 28 | 14 | 7 | |
| | 7. | 25–28 | 20–25 | 6–7 | |
| | 8. | 45–48 | 30–31 | 7 | |
| | 9. | 41 | 21 | 9 | |
| | 10. | 49 | 24 | 7 | |
| Tiryns . . | 11. | 47–48 | 36 | 10 | in the great Megaron. |
| | 12. | 36–37 | 21 | 12–13 | { in the primitive settle-ment. |
| | 13. | 52–53 | ? | 9 | in the Room XXX. |
| | 14. | 43 | 25–26 | 9 | in the Room XVIII. |
| Mycenæ . . | 15. | ? | 35 | 8–9 | |
| Eleusis . . | 16. | 44 | 44 | 9 | |

This list shows how extraordinarily various the sizes of
ancient bricks were. Among the bricks cited, evidently only
very few correspond in measurement with any of the kinds
mentioned by Vitruvius. This may in part arise from the
difference of the cubits which were used in the different
towns, for it makes no trifling difference in the size of a brick
whether we assume the Græco-Roman cubit of 0·44 m. or
the Samian cubit of 0·52 m. Thus, for instance, in the
first case, the Lydian brick of Vitruvius would measure
0·44 m. by 0·30 m.; but in the second, 0·52 m. by 0·35 m.
In order, therefore, to compare the sizes enumerated with
the notice of Vitruvius, we must know in the first place

---

* The bricks of Hanaï-Tepeh are described by Frank Calvert in
Schliemann's *Ilios*, p. 709. I have myself measured most of these
bricks.

what cubit was in use in Troy, in Mycenæ, in Tiryns, or
elsewhere. This preliminary inquiry as to the size of the
individual cubits cannot be here discussed completely. I
mention, however, for those who wish to compare in detail
the dimensions of the bricks mentioned with the statements
of Vitruvius, that, according to my computation, in Troy
a cubit of about 0·51 : 0·52 m., in Mycenæ and Tiryns
a cubit of 0·48 m., and in Eleusis the Attic cubit of 0·44
appear to have been in common use.

The first is the Samian cubit of Herodotus, of which a
specimen has been found lately on a measuring table at
Assos; the second is the so-called Olympian cubit, which
was used in the older buildings of Olympia, and by which
Herakles is said to have measured off the Stadion there.
These results are, however, only afforded by a proximate
computation, and are therefore by no means perfectly
assured. We hesitate, therefore, to compare the dimensions of the bricks found with the measurements of Vitruvius, and confine ourselves to the above table of the
various sizes of the bricks without regard to their absolute
measurements.

Of square bricks there are but few among them,
namely, No. 14, from the cities above the ruins of Troy,
and No. 16 from Eleusis. But as in building a wall with
square bricks of more than one brick in thickness it is impossible to effect a systematic bond without half bricks, we
must add to the number of square bricks those whose
length is double their width. Of such half bricks we find
several in the table, for instance, No. 2, from Troy, Nos. 6,
9, 10, from Hanaï-Tepeh, and perhaps, too, No. 13, from
Tiryns. All the other bricks mentioned are rectangular,
and therefore resemble the Lydian brick of Vitruvius, but
besides the proportion of 2 : 3, between the sides of the
latter, 3 : 4 and 3 : 5 also occur. With bricks of such
dimensions, even without half bricks, an exact bond
could be effected, in which neither on the surface of the

wall, nor within it, two joints come vertically one above the other.

The common brick of Tiryns appears to have been No. 11; several perfect specimens of this sort have been found in the great court as well as in the men's hall. The length of 0·47–0·48 m. corresponds probably to a cubit or six hands, whilst the width is 0·36 m. or 4½ hands. In the wall of the megaron, which is 1·33 m. thick, a good bond could best be made by two bricks in length and one brick in width to form the thickness of the wall. Each course then contained two bond-courses and one stretching-course, and these changed so, that in one course the stretchers were inside and in the following outside. But we cannot make an accurate statement of the bond adopted at Tiryns, the two well-preserved brick-walls being only half-brick thick. At Troy, on the other hand, we could determine, that with the bricks of the size No. 1 a wall had been built in such a manner, that the courses consist alternately of two bond-courses and one stretching-course. The bond of the two half-brick thick walls in Tiryns is a simple block-bond, which is not, however, quite regularly carried out, for mostly the side-joints do not hit exactly in the centre of the brick beneath.

That in Tiryns also longitudinal beams and cross-beams were used in the brick walls, may be concluded with reasonable certainty from the presence of such wood in the basement of some walls. The way in which these beams were used for the strengthening and securing of the brick walls, we can best learn from the ruins of Troy. In the two buildings A and B, of which the ground-plan is given Fig. 115, beams were built-in longitudinally both outside and inside, one over another; in the building A, in every fifth course. To connect these longitudinal beams there were cross-beams laid between them at intervals of 4 m., which had a height equal to three courses of bricks, and thus reached just from one long beam to the next above. The beams thus formed, in building A, a strong frame, which was filled with bricks and clay-mortar (cf. *Troja*, Figs. 20–22*).

The sun-dried brick-walls were undoubtedly coated with clay and lime-plastering in the same manner as was the case with the quarry-stone walls. Remains of this, however, have not been preserved.

## 2. THE PARASTADES (PILASTERS).

As all walls were formed of quarry-stones or clay-bricks, and so of perishable materials, their frontal sides must be strengthened by a facing of a more solid material, either free-stone or wood. Without such a provision all the exposed corners would in a short time have been injured or destroyed. And thus arose the well-known *parastades*, or *antæ*, which never fail in the later Greek stone-temples, but in them had no constructive but only an artistic intention to fulfil. The *parastades* were not applied to every wall-corner, but only where an end of wall was exposed in three directions, for instance, in the facing-walls of the vestibules and in the doorways.

Whilst in Troy the *parastades* consisted of juxtaposited posts of wood which rested on a common base-stone of inconsiderable height, in Tiryns their lower part was all of stone and only their upper part of wood. In the description of the various buildings composing the palace at Tiryns we have already learned something about these *parastades*. The base-stone is mostly 0·50–0·60 m. high, and is either of a single block, or made of several flat pieces set edgeways together. Altogether there are twenty-six such *antæ*-stones in the different parts of the palace *in situ*. They are partly of breccia, partly of sandstone, and partly of hard limestone. Especially interesting is the manner of

---

* In Figs. 20–22 the places in which the beams rested are erroneously represented as hollows.

preparation of the smooth surfaces of the breccia and limestone blocks. From the present appearance of the vertical
outer surfaces one can easily see that they were not worked
with a pick-hammer or chisel, but with a saw. In fact, on
the stone one can see numerous bow-shaped lines, which
arose from the backward and forward motion of the saw. At
Fig. 114 I have distinctly drawn these curves on the outer
surface of the *antæ*. This stone was cut from above, from
below on the left, and from below on the right, until it
was only attached by a small part in the middle to the
mass from which it was to be separated. Then this piece
was broken off, and in this way there remained on the
stone a visibly fractured surface showing the form of a
spherical triangle.

As all the traces of the saw visible on the stone are
concave, they cannot have been caused by the common
stone-saw, which is held at each end by a workman and
drawn backwards and forwards, for in that case the traces left
would be straight lines or convex curves; but the saw must
have had the form of a common knife, which a single
worker grasped by the handle, and with the point of which
he made the incision. The saw had certainly no teeth, for
only the very softest stone can be cut with the toothed-
saw. The hard limestone, and particularly the breccia of
Tiryns, belong, however, to the class of hard stones which
could only be cut through with a smooth saw and extremely
sharp sand (emery).

On several stones in Tiryns and on some in Mycenæ the
width of the incision made by the saw can be measured,
it is only 2 mm. When the stone was sawn some centimetres deep, the piece to be removed was struck off, as far
as the incision reached, and the sawing was begun anew. It
is of these separate incisions that the still visible curves
remain on the stones. This primitive method of sawing
had the effect of leaving the surface not quite even, but
often very warped. On this account, too, the *antæ* seem

to have been all covered with lime-plastering, although traces of this coating only remain on some of them.

The cutting of stone by means of the saw (λιθοπρίστης πρίων) was much used in antiquity. Many authors tell us of it, and in Egypt, Greece, Italy, and Germany undoubted traces of stone-sawing have been observed in ancient quarries and on the buildings.*

The buildings of Tiryns and Mycenæ afford a valuable addition to the known evidences. These two citadels are probably older examples of the use of the stone-saw in antiquity than any others in Italy or Greece.

Among the stones of Tiryns on which the traces of the saw may be most clearly recognized, I would mention the ántæ of the vestibule to the men's hall, those of the great Propylæum, and those of the vestibule to the women's hall. In Mycenæ there lies in the space between the ring of slabs encircling the tombs and the outer citadel-wall a block of breccia, upon which we can study the manner of sawing very completely; even the width of the sawn incision can still be measured on this stone.

Whilst the blocks of hard limestone and breccia which were used for antæ and door-sills have probably all been sawn on account of their great hardness, it may be that other instruments were employed for cutting the softer sandstone; yet I do not venture to speak with certainty on this point. The outer surface of the sandstone blocks is, in almost every case, too much injured by fire to allow observation on the method of their preparation.

The same difference which is seen in the manner of working the different sorts of stone, is to be observed again in the making of the dowel-holes in the upper surface of the antæ blocks. Thus while the two hard stones have round-bored holes, the sandstones have squared-cut hollows. In the soft sandstone it was possible with a sharp instru-

---

* Cf. Blümner, *Technologie bei Griechen und Römern*, II. pp. 216–222, and III. pp. 75–78, where all information about the saw is given.

ment to cut or sink a square hole without much difficulty.
But with the hard breccia or the fine-grained limestone this
was scarcely possible, for these stones it was, therefore,
necessary to use the auger.*

That this instrument was known to the ancients is
proved by the accounts of numerous authors, and by the
bore-holes found in buildings and on statues.† For boring
stone, the hand-bore was naturally not suited, but a drill
or revolving auger would be needed, which in antiquity was
usually set in motion by a bow-string twisted round it.
This kind of boring is very clearly described to us by
Homer in *Od.* IX. 382–386,‡ where Odysseus bores the
burning stick into the eye of the Cyclops.

> "They, seizing the bar of olive wood, sharp at the point, thrust it
> into his eye, while I from my place above moved it round; as when a
> man bores a ship's beam with an auger, while his fellows below, having
> bound it with a thong on each side, move it, and the auger runs round
> continually."

A similar drill-auger, twisted backwards and forwards by
means of a string, was certainly used in Tiryns. The lower
end of the auger had, however, a different shape from the
common bores of antiquity, which Blümner describes
*loc. cit.*, and which exactly resembled our modern ones.

The appearance of the Tirynthian bore-holes shows us
rather that they were made with a simple cylinder, hollow
inside, and that thus the auger had the form of a strong
reed. With even very rapid twisting one could not bore a
hole in a hard stone with such an auger, unless, as with the

---

* A very curious auger of bronze was discovered by Dr. Schliemann
in the second, the *burnt city* of Troy; see Schliemann, *Troja,* p. 99,
Fig. 34A. This appears to be the first auger ever found in prehistoric
remains.

† Cf. Blümner, *Technologie bei Griechen und Römern,* III. pp. 223–
226.

οἱ μὲν μοχλὸν ἑλόντες ἐλάϊνον. ὀξὺν ἐπ' ἄκρῳ,
ὀφθαλμῷ ἐνέρεισαν· ἐγὼ δ' ἐφύπερθεν ἀερθεὶς
δίνεον, ὡς ὅτε τις τρυπῷ δόρυ νήϊον ἀνὴρ
τρυπάνῳ, οἱ δέ τ' ἔνερθεν ὑποσσείουσιν ἱμάντι
ἁψάμενοι ἑκάτερθε, τὸ δὲ τρέχει ἐμμενὲς αἰεί.

saw, a sharp sand (emery) were strewed into the bore-hole. When the sand was moved about by the auger, it rubbed away small particles of the stone, and thus there was gradually formed a cylindrical hole, in the middle of which a thin cylinder of stone remained standing. When the hole reached the required depth, this cylinder was removed by some instrument, and the dowel-hole was complete. As might be expected, the central stone-cylinder was not always by this procedure completely removed at the lower end, but generally a portion of it remained at the bottom of the hole. These upright remains of the little cylinders can be still plainly seen in many dowel-holes, and it is from them we have obtained an insight into the method of boring.

The diameter of the holes varies from 28 to 45 mm., and the depth from 40 to 60 mm.*

Whilst in most of the *antæ*, the bore-holes stand alone, and at a great distance from each other, we find in the *antæ* of the vestibule to the women's hall always two holes immediately beside each other, so that both together form a single long dowel-hole which has somewhat this form ◯◯. Its breadth is 29, its length 55, and its depth 45 mm. What advantage these coupled-holes had over the simple dowel-holes is not clearly seen; it must have been that the tenon fixed in it, and consequently also the upper wooden-beam of the *anta* could not turn on its axis.

---

* The English archæologist Flinders Petrie has published, in his work, *The Pyramids and Temples of Gizeh* (p. 173), an investigation on the tools used by the ancient Egyptians n the working of the hard kinds of stone. He comes to the result that, as in Tiryns, the hard stones were worked with saws and cylindrical augers of metal, but he believes the edges and points of these tools to have been laid in with diamonds or other jewel stones. I take this notice from the *Centralblatt der preus sischen Bauverwaltung*, 1884, p. 24, and do not know whether such instruments have really been found in Egypt. I believe that, even without inlaid diamonds, very hard kinds of stone can be cut and bored with common emery.

The *parastades* of sandstone have quadrangular dowel-holes, which are partly square and partly oblong rectangular; the dimensions of such a dowel-hole are, for example, breadth 30, length 52, and depth 80 mm. The number of these dowel-holes varies in different *antæ*, in some there are only three, in some many more. The north-east corner pillar of the women's court has even as many as eight dowel-holes.

We have already shown in the description of the two *parastades* in the vestibule of the megaron that wooden beams stood over the stone basement. We concluded this particularly from the surface of the *anta*, which was quite unfit to receive another stone-block. This proof, however, is not forthcoming for all the other *parastades*, for most of them are perfectly smoothed on the top, and could have well supported a second square stone. We are able, however, to prove that these *antæ* also had only a base-stone, and that their upper part was also of wood.

In the palace there are in all twenty-six *antæ* blocks remaining *in situ*, and in every case these are the lower stone of the compound pilaster. In five places the base-stone is missing, and these all occur in the periphery of the palace; in the inside there is but one base-stone missing, that is to say, at the door of the men's hall. These numbers show, first of all, that the destruction of the palace was not effected by the carrying away of building materials by the destroyers for use elsewhere, but that they burnt the palace, and perhaps tore down the roofs, but left all the materials on the spot.

But if such is the case, we must consider it further impossible that a second square stone ever stood upon the preserved *antæ*-blocks, for surely on at least one we should expect to find such a square stone remaining. On the other hand, we must not conclude that the whole palace was levelled to the height of the lower *antæ*-blocks, for in many places the quarrystone-walls are preserved to a height of above 1 m., whilst the *antæ* are everywhere only about ½ m. high.

When we consider that almost all *antæ* blocks have dowel-holes above, and therefore must have borne some other material than rubble-masonry or clay-bricks, there can in my opinion remain no further doubt that the upper part of the *antæ* consisted of wood.

About the construction of these wooden *antæ* we cannot say much, as not a single one has been preserved. We can only conclude from the position of the dowel-holes, and the cutting of the upper surface of the stone-base, that the wooden lining of the wall-ends was 0·25–0·30 m. thick, and consisted of posts or boards of this strength. Such *antæ* were applied not only at the frontal side of the walls, but wherever a beam of the epistyle reached the wall. It is in the very same places exactly that the *antæ* stand in the stone temples of the Greeks, though they no longer fulfil any constructive purpose. But while in Tiryns the *antæ* were still intended to strengthen the ends of the walls, which were of less resisting material, and to sustain the heavy pressure of the architrave-beams on the wall; in later Greek buildings they merely suggest artistically these functions, which they no longer perform. We have accordingly here an important instance how the Greek artistic forms of the later stone-buildings were derived from the constructive members of older buildings.

### 3. The Pillars.

The pillar plays a prominent part in the palace at Tiryns; thirty-one pillar-bases being still extant in the upper fort, besides several others, whose bases are missing, which can with certainty be restored to their places. For a single palace this number is considerable, especially if we consider that hitherto the Homeric house has been credited with but very few columns.

As to the form or decoration of these pillars we know
almost nothing, as only their stone bases have been preserved; both shafts and capitals are gone. Among the
bases now discovered there are two kinds; first, large calcareous blocks with irregular edges, on the smoothed
surface of which is raised a circle about 3 cm. high;
and secondly, irregular foundation blocks, which are only
smoothed on the surface. The former kind is both
more usual and older; the second, which only occurs at
the east and south porticoes of the great men's court,
is due to the later reconstruction of the palace.

The appearance of the first kind is given in Fig. 114,
where the western base-stone of the vestibule of the megaron
is given. The block, which is quite rough on its sides and
lower surface, always lies so deep in the ground that the
rough parts are not seen, as the lime concrete of the floor
exactly covers the deeper lying portion of its upper surface.
The central circle stands up 1–2 cm. above the concrete
floor. As the diameter of the pillar was a little less than
that of this circle, it afforded a visible basis for the pillar,
just as Egyptian pillars are generally provided with a simple
base much greater in breadth.*

All the pillars and capitals were of wood, as can be easily
proved. First, not a single stone drum has been found,
whilst of twenty-six *antæ* the lower block of stone is preserved; it is, accordingly, inconceivable that all traces of
the drums would have disappeared unless they had been
of wood. They must have been of some material which
could be destroyed with the fortress. It is proved,
secondly, by the diameter of the bases, which is far smaller
than that of the *parastades*, that the pillars cannot have
been of stone. Thirdly, all the *antæ* consisted, as we have
seen, of wooden posts; but to wooden *antæ* naturally
would belong wooden epistyles and wooden pillars, for had

---

* Cf. Perrot et Chipiez, *Geschichte der Kunst*, p. 103.

the latter been of stone, why not the *antæ* also?  Fourthly, we can adduce as evidence the present condition of some of the pillar-bases.  For several of them are severely burnt round about with fire, while their centres show only slight traces of being burnt.  This peculiarity is to my mind only to be explained by assuming the shaft of the pillar to have been of wood.  If the pillar was set on fire, the centre of the base could hardly be injured, whereas the outer edge was subject to all the damage of the flames.

These reasons are so convincing, that no one would dream of the existence of stone pillars had not an old Doric capital of sandstone been found on the upper citadel, which will be more closely described in the section on the architectural members found in the ruins (cf. Fig. 122).

But this capital did not lie in one of the rooms of the palace, but was built into a rude later wall, which ran in a bow shape above the great court.  Above the altar we have left *in situ* some blocks of this wall, which only consisted of a single course of stones; the rest we have taken away.  When this wall was built, the palace was already hidden under the ground, and hence the capital may very well have been dragged up here in the Middle Ages from some other part of the citadel.  It is further to be noticed, that two fragments of a Doric gable-*sima* (γεῖσον) of the very same sandstone were found at the eastern declivity of the upper citadel close to the gate, where also several clay tiles, some fragments of Hellenic pottery and iron objects were found.  Hence it seems certain that in early Hellenic days a building in the Doric style was erected close to the main ascent to the fort, to which the stone capital, the *sima* (γεῖσον), and the tiles belonged.  I have already (p.t229) offered the conjecture, that the later walls discovered in the megaron of the palace are the foundations of a Doric temple.  If this be so, the palace must have been destroyed very early, for the capital, and the antefix, which probably belongs

to the same building, seem to be older than the fifth
century B.C.

But neither the capital nor the rest of these members
can possibly belong to the old palace, for had its pillars
and cornices consisted of sandstone, and the roofs of tiles,
then in the *débris* filling the courts and rooms there must
have come to light at least a single fragment of sandstone
or of clay tiles. This was not so, and is therefore conclusive.

If the pillars of the palace were of wood, then first we
can explain why their basis was raised above the floor. The
wooden pillar must not reach the floor, or it would be
affected and soon destroyed by damp. The wooden pillars
of the palace were probably of single stems, for had they
been constructed of several uprights fastened together, then
the single posts would surely have been fastened into the
bases by dowels, as has been done in the case of the *antæ*.
For a single thick tree no dowel was required.

As regards the capitals, we can only conjecture that they
were of the form seen at the Lions' Gate of Mycenæ, and
at the entrance of the so-called Treasury * of Atreus. The
exact correspondence of these two, the only capitals still
extant from the days of the building of Tiryns and
Mycenæ, gives great probability to this conjecture.

## 4. The Roof and Roofing.

In describing the details of the palace we have often
already touched the question of the roofing. To answer
this we must first of all determine the roofing material employed, as it is of vital importance for the form of the roof,

---

* In the newest work on the subject, *die Architektonik der Hellenen*,
by Dr. R. Adamy (p. 84), the capital from the Treasury of Atreus is still
represented as a pillar-base, though it has long since been proved to be
a capital.

PLATE VII.

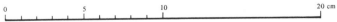

WALL PAINTING IN THE PALACE OF TIRYNS.

and also of the roofing, whether baked tiles, or rushes, or clay, or some other material was used for the thatching.

As repeatedly mentioned, not a single tile of baked clay was found anywhere in the palace; it is therefore impossible that the roofs can have been covered with clay-tiles. Between the main entrance to the citadel and the gate of the upper fort, some good Hellenic tiles and an archaic *antefix* were indeed discovered, and near the Byzantine Church at the south end of the fort, various Byzantine roof-tiles have been found, but neither can be assumed as used on the roof of the palace. It must have been thatched with a material which was either burnt up when the palace was burnt, or at least has left no visible trace. It seems to me that accordingly only two substances can come into question, rushes and clay.

The tent of Achilles was covered with rushes, as we read in the *Iliad*, XXIV. 450-1.

> ἀτὰρ καθύπερθεν ἔρεψαν
> λαχνήεντ᾽ ὄροφον λειμώνοθεν ἀμήσαντες.

"But they thatched it from above, having gathered a rough roofing from the meadow."

Rush-thatching, according to Herodotus (V. 101), was in use at Sardis, when the town was taken by the Ionians (καλάμου εἶχον τὰς ὀροφάς). If these rushes were frequently used in olden times, yet it can be easily shown that the roofs of the palace of Tiryns were not so covered. A rush-thatch, like one of straw, requires a steep roof, that the water may not penetrate, but run down the individual straws. Such a roof may be well suited for an isolated house; but to thatch a great system of buildings like the palace of Tiryns in such a way is simply impossible, for if the whole building were to be provided with one single ridged roof, the height at its centre would be far too high; but if you make several, then there must be gutters between each of them, which could never be made water-tight with rushes.

There remains the covering with clay. Every clay roof must be nearly horizontal, if the first heavy shower is not to wash down the whole covering. We have above indicated how such a roof is to be conceived. Over the great epistyles and girders came the rafters proper, either separated or close together, like the round timber on the façade of the beehive tombs, or in the lions' relief at Mycenæ. In the former case, the intervals were bridged with cross-pieces or boards of wood; in the latter, rushes were sufficient to afford a close bed for the clay. As lime was well known to the builders of Tiryns, it might be supposed that they covered the roof with lime-plaster instead of clay. But in the first place, a lime concrete is not better for a roof than a coat of clay, because it easily cracks, and is then no longer impervious. In the second place, had the roof been so covered, we must have found remains of this lime-coating in the palace. This not being the case, we must assume that the whole roof, as is still commonly the case in the East, was covered with a thick layer of clay.*

While with raised roofs there was often in the interior of the houses a separate horizontal covering, in horizontal roofs these two are always identical. In most rooms of Tiryns the ceiling therefore consisted either of a number of juxtaposited roof-beams, or a smaller number of beams joined by cross-timbers. In the larger rooms, especially in the men's hall, there were added strong girders or sleepers, to diminish the span of the roof-beams. All the woodwork of this ceiling was doubtless carefully polished, so far as

---

* " All over Asia Minor the horizontal wooden roofs of the village-houses are covered with a layer of rushes or sea-weed. Thereon is put a thick layer of clay, which is consolidated by a powerful stone cylinder, or in most cases by a smooth drum of an ancient marble column. I have myself built at Hissarlik a dwelling- and a kitchen-house with such a roof, and can testify to the fact, that if it is once yearly slightly repaired, it is perfectly solid and rain-proof. In the Troad this is the only kind of roof used in the villages ; indeed, I have never seen there any other kind of roof."—HENRY SCHLIEMANN.

it was visible, as Homer often calls the woodwork of his palaces *shining*. Still in the course of years the fire of the hearth and torches blackened the ceiling, which he therefore calls *sooty* (αἰθαλόεις).*

### 5. THE FLOOR.

Homer describes the floor in the palace of Odysseus as simply beaten-in clay, in which Telemachus planted the axes in the contest with the bow.† This is the sort of floor in the megaron, and in several other rooms of the Pergamos of Troy. At the destruction of the town it was covered, in consequence of the intense heat, with a sort of glaze, but was originally nothing but a layer of clay stamped or beaten smooth. A similar floor we also find in the oldest settlement on the hill of Tiryns, the remains of which we have described above (p. 251).

The palace of Tiryns, however, shows right through another kind of floor, namely a concrete made of lime and small pebbles, or altogether of lime. In describing the various rooms, we have already noticed the still remaining portions of these floors, and mention therefore only briefly the various kinds now. In some rooms there is only a single layer of mortar immediately on the substratum of earth and clay; in others this layer is doubled, and in this way that below is a thick, less firm layer of mortar as a bed for the upper tough concrete. Pebbles are added to the mortar wherever it was peculiarly exposed to the weather, *e.g.* in the great men's court and the great Propylæum. In the latter the pebbles so predominate, that we may describe the floor as a mosaic of pebbles.

In the rooms these pebbles are generally absent, and

---

* The tools for working wood in Homeric times are described by Helbig in his recent work, *das Homerische Epos*, p. 76. The Homeric names for the parts of the roof or ceiling we have already cited above.

† *Od.* IV. 627; XVII. 169; and XXI. 120.

accordingly they have a smoother floor; but instead, the mortar in several of them is made into a carpet-pattern of scratched-in lines. Such may still be recognised in the men's hall, its vestibule, and the women's hall. Remains of red and blue colour found in several rooms show that the floor was also painted. In one place (corridor XII.) we could still perceive the colouring of the floor with red geometrical ornaments (circular and waving lines). Floors of wood or of stone slabs, such as are now almost universal, were not known in the palace of Tiryns, for the floor of the bath-room, consisting of one great block (p. 230), cannot be counted among the stone-slab floors.

## 6. THE DOORS.

The excavations have added greatly to our knowledge of the door-arrangements in the Homeric palace. More or less distinct traces of forty doors are preserved. Among them seven are certainly double-winged or folding, some were apparently closed only with a curtain; the rest were single. The folding-doors were in the gate of the upper citadel, the two Propylæa, the vestibule of the men's hall, and in Thalamos XXII., which was probably the bed-chamber of the prince. Homer calls the door θύρα or θύρετρον; the plural, θύραι or θύρετρα, seems frequently to mean folding-doors, not several doors.

As to the material of the door-sill or threshold, Homer distinguishes between stone, oaken, ashen, and bronze thresholds.* Accordingly we find in Tiryns stone and wooden door-sills: twenty-two well-preserved stone speci-mens lie still *in situ ;* the wooden are gone, but remains of charcoal testify to their place. It might be suspected that this charcoal comes from the doors, so that here too three

---

* λάϊνος, δρύϊνος, μέλινος, and χάλκεος οὐδός, *Od.* VIII. 80 ; XVII. 339; XXI. 43 ; and *Il.* VIII. 15.

were originally stone sills.  In some cases this is possible, but in most one can easily convince oneself that they can never have had a stone sill.  Of the twenty-two extant door-sills, only six are of breccia, the rest of close-grained limestone.  The kind of wood in the other sills is not known, nor whether perhaps some of them were covered with bronze plates.

To explain the arrangement and construction of the doors, I choose two specimens, which are particularly well preserved.  Let us first examine the door of the women's apartment, the plan of which is given in Figure 119. The present condition is as follows : in the middle of the wall separating the apartment from its vestibule lies a great door-sill of limestone with irregular edges on all sides; its extreme dimensions are 2 m.–1·25 m.  The upper face is all smoothed, but not in one plane, for in the middle is a strip 0·90 m. broad, about 2 cm. higher than the irregular edge of the stone.  The deeper part was covered by the concrete of the floor, and was not visible, while the higher strip was so, and formed the real door-sill, raised very little above the floor of the rooms. At the ends of the threshold there adjoin it on both sides three irregular stones, the smooth surface of which is on a level with it.  Next to these come great sandstone blocks, regularly cut, the form of which can be seen in the ground-plan.  Each of these piers is made up of two blocks of different sizes, and is 0·78 m. broad, 1·20 m. deep, and 0·60 m. high.  At the side facing the aperture of the door there are two grooves worked, each 0·15–0·16 m. broad, and 0·03–4 m. deep, forming a rebate of 0·08 m. from the outer edge.  On the upper side, both towards the vestibule and towards the women's hall, there is a strip sunk 0·02–0·04 m. deep and 0·28–0·32 m. wide, which probably held the lowest longitudinal beam of the adjoining rubble-masonry wall.

If the door-sill were not there, any one would suppose

that the two sandstone piers were the *antæ* of the door, and so that the latter had a width of 2·90 m. in the clear.

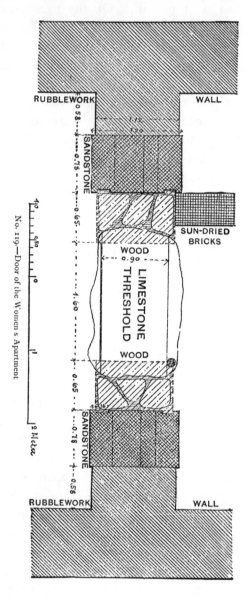

No. 119—Door of the Women's Apartment.

At most, it might have been inferred from the rebates in the sandstone piers that there was some thin coating, and

so have subtracted a few centimetres from the width of
the door. The door-sill proves for certain that such an
inference is false; the door had only a width of 1·60 m.,
and was enclosed by stout wooden pilasters, about 0·65 m.
broad and 1·04 m. deep. The facts from which we infer
this are as follows: of course the irregular ends of the
threshold, and the rude foundation stones adjoining, were
not visible; moreover, the door-sill must have carried the
door-posts on both ends, because the most important object
of every sill is to afford a safe and uniform support for them.
Further, it can be distinctly seen, from the different degrees
of wearing on the surface of the threshold, that the passable
aperture of the door was only 1·60 m. wide. With this
agrees, that just where the surviving traces of the eastern
door-post end, the groove for the door pivot occurs.
Lastly, the existence of a wall of sun-dried bricks, which
from the north side meets the western door-post, shows that
the door-aperture cannot have reached to the sandstone
pier. All these reasons confirm the width of the door
as only 1·60 m., and on either side huge posts.

Of what material were these door-posts? The very
existence of the rebates in the sandstone piers proves that
they must have been of wood, for to join one stone to
another such cutting is useless. The condition of the
sandstone piers and of the sun-dried brick wall also points
to wooden pilasters, for they have both been much affected
by fire, the sun-dried bricks near them have been even
completely glazed. But quite decisive is the circumstance,
that not only here, but at *at all the doors of the palace* the
side-posts are gone, and must therefore have been destroyed
with the palace. Indeed, the walls preserved are completely
burnt near the doors, and in many doorways we found
remains of charcoal.

I have insisted with much detail on the former existence
of wooden door-posts, because this question is of vast importance for all ancient architecture. The Greeks, and

especially the Dorians, associated them so intimately with the very idea of a door, that even in the marble structures of the fifth century, *e.g.* the Parthenon and its Propylæa, they made the door-jambs of wood, though such a construction in marble buildings is to us inconceivable. The fancy for wooden door-posts is only to be accounted for by the late and exceptional occurrence of regular ashlar-masonry in Greece, and that in older times all, in later times most, buildings were made of poorer material, of quarry-stone with clay-mortar and of sun-dried bricks.

As regards our Tirynthian door-posts, we have still to inquire whether they were made of one thick tree, or of planks with the inside hollow. While the absence of dowel-holes in the door-sill speaks for the former view, for the latter the two rebates suggest a construction with boards of about 0·16 m. thick. I prefer the former, because I think that for a hollow post made of several juxtaposited planks the base would have consisted of a single block. But I do not therefore think that the post was all of one stem, but rather of two at least (each 0·57 to 0·65 m.).

In Fig. 119 I have given the cross-section of the door-post a perfectly rectangular shape, but probably it was *fascia*-like profiled like the stone doorcase in the so-called Treasury of Atreus. So also is it explained why the door-post immediately beside the sandstone block has a depth of 1·04 m., while the breadth of the door-sill is only 0·90 m. The diminution of the post in thickness was therefore 0·07 m. on each side.

But if the doorposts were of wood, then what were the sandstone blocks beside them intended for? If they lay flush with the rubble-masonry of the wall, it might be assumed that they were intended to finish off the irregular rubble-work of the wall; but as they stand out 4 cm. like *antæ* from the wall, they must really have been pilasters, which enclosed the door on both sides. They were therefore like the two semi-columns at the Treasury of Atreus, which also enclosed a door framed with a double band (*fascia*). Similar *antæ* occur in Tiryns elsewhere only in the great door of the men's hall, and probably also in the Propylæum of the court; all the other doors had only a wooden framing.

Concerning the upper part of the doorway the ruins of Tiryns give us no information; if we wish therefore to imagine a picture of it, we must refer to the doors of the beehive tombs at Mycenæ, Orchomenos, Menidi, &c. They all agree in this, that the side jambs with the same, or at least similar profile, also form the upper door-frame, or lintel. This is how we must restore the doors at Tiryns.

The presence of *only one* pivot-hole in the sill of the

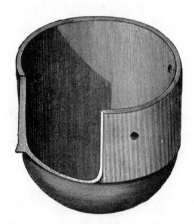

No. 120.—Bronze sheath for the pivot of a door.

door into the women's apartment shows, that in spite of its width (1·60 m.), the door was single. Of the appearance of this door we know nothing. But by a lucky chance we are well informed about the arrangement of its turning-joints. For in excavating the door we found the great bronze pivot, represented in Fig. 120, still in its socket. From its position we could tell that the door was half-open when it caught fire and was burnt. The pivot was a hollow cylinder of 118 mm. diameter inside, and closed below like a ball. It therefore formed a sheath for the strong wooden turning-pivot of the door, to which it was secured with three

nails.  The square cut in the cylinder is to receive the lower
frame of the door, which was morticed into the side beam
used as the turning-post.  The lower frame, to judge from
the dimensions of the cut in the cylinder to receive it, was
75 cm. broad and 95 mm. thick.  When the door opened,
the bronze pivot turned in the socket drilled into the stone
door sill.  How the corresponding pivot at the top of the
door was managed we cannot tell.

Besides this door, we give in Fig. 121 as a second
specimen a simpler door—one of the side doors in the
vestibule of the women's hall.  Here, too, distinct traces
were found of the great wooden posts, which framed in the
door.  The walls of quarry-stones and clay-bricks joined

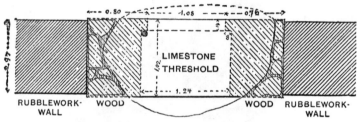

No. 121.—Side-door in the vestibule of Women's Hall.

these posts; there were no additional *parastades*, as in the
door before described.  The door-sill of limestone was
worked just like that of the door into the women's hall;
its limit inside the vestibule I was obliged to indicate by
dotted lines, as it was covered by the concrete floor, and
therefore not visible.  The material difference between the
two doors is the way in which the door-wing is applied.
While in the door to the women's hall the wing from
without strikes against the door-posts, the post was here
provided with a special rebate, against which the wing lay
when the door was shut.  When open, the wing lay against
the inner side of the door jamb.

Of the doors of the palace, the stone sills of which are
extant, the majority show this latter construction.  Only a

few, such as the doors of both Propylæa, opened like that
of the women's hall, but differ from it in being double.

As regards the doors with wooden sills, they were probably similarly constructed to those with stone sills.   But
the pivot was probably not provided with a bronze shoe,
the wood turning immediately in the wooden socket.   So
it was, at all events according to Homer, with the door
leading to the armoury of Odysseus, for ' as a bull roars that
is pasturing in a flowery meadow, so mightily roared the
beautiful doors stricken with the key ' (*Od.* XXI. 48, 49).
Whoever has heard the noise of the primitive Oriental
carts, where the wooden axle turns in its wooden bed, will
well understand Homer's simile.

Our knowledge of the locking-arrangements on the
doors of the Homeric palaces has not been increased by
the excavations.   I therefore avoid any discussion of either
bolts and keys, and merely refer to Winckler and Proto-
dikos,* who have brought together the existing materials.

In conclusion, I mention the principal names, which
Homer has given to the various members of the door.
That he calls the door-sill οὐδός, and knows four different
kinds of it, has already been said.   He often calls it ξεστός
(*Od.* XVIII. 33, and XXII. 72), which suits the smooth
sills at Tiryns very well.   For the door-post he frequently
uses the word σταθμός (*e.g.*, *Od.* VI. 19; XVII. 96;
XXII. 120); in the palace of Odysseus they were in part of
cypress-wood, κυπαρίσσινος (*Od.* XVII. 340); and in that
of Alkinoos, covered with silver (ἀργύρεος, *Od.* VII. 89).
The lintel is ὑπερθύριον (*Od.* VII. 90).   The door-wings
consisted of planks (σανίδες), " polished," " well joined,"
and " closely fitted " (εὔξεσται, κολληταί and πυκινῶς
ἀραρυῖαι, *Od.* XXI. 137; II. 344).   The door-posts are
themselves called by these epithets (*Od.* XXIII. 194).

---

* *Die Wohnhäuser der Hellenen*, p. 42; and *De Ædibus Homericis*,
p. 64, *sq.*

## E.—ISOLATED FRAGMENTS OF ARCHITECTURE.

In this section we shall speak of those separate pieces of architecture found in the upper citadel, of which the place in the palace, or in the building to which they belong, is unknown. These are a great frieze of alabaster inlaid with glass paste, a sculptured spiral ornament, a Doric capital, and an archaic *antefix*.

### 1  THE KYANOS FRIEZE.

In the vestibule of the men's hall we found at the western wall a large frieze composed of several alabaster slabs, which occupied the whole space between the *anta* and the southern wall of the vestibule. On Plate IV. at the left centre is given a sketch of the frieze as it appeared when found. On the left is the *anta* of the vestibule, to which seven slabs join on to the right; four of them are less in breadth than height, and resemble Doric triglyphs; the three others are square, and look very like metopes. In the small plan under the restoration on Plate IV. we can see that the narrow slabs overlap their square neighbour slabs, just as in many Doric buildings the triglyphs overlap the edge of the metopes. All the slabs are much injured, especially those to the left, on which no trace of ornaments is now left. As the small sketch shows, the lower part of those to the right are best preserved. Here it is still distinctly to be seen that the frieze was decorated with sculptured ornaments, and adorned with inlaid blue-glass paste. From the remains here preserved the reconstruction on Plate IV. is attempted. As unfortunately there remained in no slab the finishing at the top, the reconstruction must remain incomplete in that part. So also some parts of the frieze were left blank, because the ornament applied to it could no longer be determined.

The reconstruction shows to the left a half-triglyph (as we may call the narrow slabs, for brevity's sake); next, a metope; then another triglyph; and to the right again, part of a metope. The sculptured ornaments are given by shading, the inserted pieces of blue glass by blue colour. The triglyph shows in its lower edge a row of rectangular pieces of glass, each 19 mm. broad and 24 mm. high; over it is a continuous strip of glass, 9 mm. broad. The upper part is divided by four vertical rows of little pieces of glass (10–13 mm.) into three fields, of which the two outer ones are adorned with rosettes. The centre field, as the plan shows, is rounded off in profile, and seems to have had no ornament. The form of the rosettes could not be accurately determined, as the extremities of the leaves were broken off. The middle of each rosette is occupied by a round piece of glass of 26 mm. in diameter. How many rosettes there were in each field is uncertain, as we do not know how high the triglyph was, and whether there was not at its upper edge a band which corresponded to the lower strip.

The metopes are even more richly adorned than the triglyphs. Two semi-ellipses, which touch in the middle, occupy the whole field. The whole of each is treated as a great rosette with nineteen double leaves. How the centre was designed we do not know. The rosette is surrounded by a broad band, which consists of a band of spirals encompassed by two bands of inlaid pieces of glass. The pieces of glass of the inner row are rectangles, of 9 by 16 mm., the outer, 9 by 18 mm. The eyes of the spirals are also formed of round pieces of glass-paste, inlaid.

All kinds of ornaments which are conspicuous in the frieze are already known to us from other finds belonging to the same epoch at Mycenæ, Menidi, Orchomenos, &c. The rosette is indeed the favourite ornament of this period, and the spiral strip framed with two rows of little rectangles meets us in the very same form in the semi-columns and

in the capitals of the Treasury of Atreus. But besides
the separate ornaments, the whole composition of the
frieze does not appear here for the first time; for among
the finds at Mycenæ there are two different stone friezes,
which show the same series of metopes with two semicircles,
and triglyphal vertical stripes, and in the beehive tomb at
Menidi little pieces of glass-paste with the same composition have been found. I have given one of the friezes of
Mycenæ, and the glass-paste of Menidi on Plate IV. for
comparison. The Mycenæan friezes are smaller than our
alabaster frieze, and therefore not so richly ornamented;
above all, they want what makes our discovery so important, the inlaid pieces of blue glass.

The object of glass from Menidi is much smaller in
scale, and therefore much more reduced in its ornament.
But it is of great value, because it teaches us that we have
hitherto misunderstood the composition of the frieze. It
is not the two semicircles standing together and touching
in a so-called metope, which belong together, but the two
semicircles which stand one at each side of a triglyph form
the group. They represent the parts of an elongated ellipse,
joined in the middle by a band. We may best conceive
such ellipse as a richly formed clasp (agrafe); the whole
frieze is then a chain of agrafes linked together. If in our
alabaster frieze the analysis of the separate parts does not
agree with this theoretical division of the ornament, it is
owing merely to technical difficulties. In the first place,
the single blocks would have been too large, if we only had
a joint at the junction of such two ellipses, and in this case
also a great part of the slab's thickness must be cut away
over the semicircles. The composition chosen by the
archaic artist was no doubt the most advantageous, and
technically the soundest, even though its joints do not
agree with the divisions of the ornament. Our indication
of the slabs as triglyphs and metopes is therefore not quite
accurate; there are indeed sundry external resemblances

between this frieze and the triglyph of a Doric edifice, but the form of the ornament does not allow us to regard the frieze of Tiryns as a proto-Doric triglyph.

But this circumstance gives to our frieze a peculiar interest, that Homer mentions such a frieze adorned with blue glass in the Palace of Alkinoos. In describing the palace he says, *Od.* VII. 86-7 :

$$\text{Χάλκεοι μὲν γὰρ τοῖχοι ἐρηρέδατ' ἔνθα καὶ ἔνθα,}$$
$$\text{Ἐς μυχὸν ἐξ οὐδοῦ · περὶ δὲ θριγκὸς κυάνοιο ·}$$

viz., " bronze walls ran this way and that from the threshold to the inmost chamber, and round them was a frieze of *Kyanos.*" It is due to R. Lepsius * to have first proved clearly that κύανος was not blue steel, as was universally believed, but either the natural *lapis lazuli,* and the real ultramarine colour, or the artificial blue Egyptian glass. Prof. Helbig has fully accepted and further developed this in his recent book.† The reader will welcome the extract which I here append in Helbig's words.

" Kyanos is generally explained as blue steel, an assumption warmly defended still very recently by Evans.‡ But there is this objection, that the word always has another signification in later Greek. For it means first the stone, called sapphire (σάπφειρος, *lapis lazuli*) ; and next the blue ultramarine colour, which is obtained by pulverising this stone ; and, thirdly, the minerals used for imitating this stone or the true ultramarine. The classical passage is in Theophrastus (*on Stones,* § 55). This author distinguishes between the natural (αὐτοφυής) and artificial (σκευαστός) kyanos. That by the first *lapis lazuli* is intended, appears from another passage (§ 39), when the gold-dust distinctive of the *lapis lazuli* is cited as the

---

* *Die Metalle in den Ägyptischen Inschriften,* Abhandlungen der Berliner Akademie, 1871.

† *Das Homerische Epos,* p. 79, *sq.*

‡ *The Age of Bronze* (London, 1881), p. 14.

peculiarity of the natural kyanos. After distinguishing
the natural and artificial kyanos, Theophrastus continues:
'There are three kinds of kyanos, the Egyptian, Scythian.
and Cyprian. The best for the darker colours is the
Egyptian, for the lighter the Scythian. The Egyptian is
artificially prepared. And those who write about the
kings tell which king first, to imitate natural kyanos,
prepared the melted kyanos (κύανος χυτός), and allege that,
amongst others, from Phœnicia came a tribute of kyanos,
partly natural and partly burnt (τοῦ μὲν ἀπύρου, τοῦ δὲ
πεπυρωμένου).'

"By the interpretation of the Egyptian inscriptions and
wall-paintings, and by chemical analyses applied to Egyptian
works of art, Lepsius succeeded in identifying all the kinds
mentioned by the Greek writer. The different materials,
which the Greeks call κύανος, are indicated in Egyptian
inscriptions by the word χesbet. Lapis lazuli and the
ultramarine colour gained from it are called χesbet-ma,
e.g. genuine χesbet, sometimes " good χesbet from Babylon,"
or " good χesbet from Tefrer (Teflel)." The main source of
lapis lazuli is Tartary, particularly the present Badakhshan.
From here the precious stone came through Parthia and
Media to Babylon, and to the coasts of the Mediterranean.
Tefrer, or Teflel, was probably not the mine, but, like
Babylon, one of the marts, through which the stone came
on its way to Egypt. As the present Badakhshan, where
most of the lapis lazuli is found, is reckoned by post-
Herodotean writers to Scythia, there can be little doubt
that Theophrastus means by Scythian kyanos this very
material and the colour obtained from it.

"The inscriptions distinguish from the genuine χesbet
the artificial χesbet-irī-t, which corresponds to Theophrastus'
κύανος σκευαστός. This was a glass-paste coloured blue
with copper ore, sometimes with cobalt, which imitated
lapis lazuli. The Egyptians moulded or carved out of it
little figures, amulets, e.g. scarabæi, and ornaments, such

PLATE VIII.

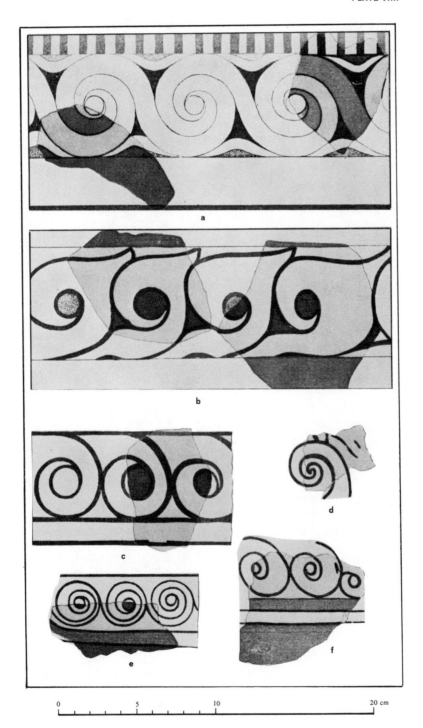

a

b

c

d

e

f

0    5    10    20 cm

**WALL PAINTING IN THE PALACE OF TIRYNS.**

as necklaces and breast-jewellery. Besides, this glass was pounded, and the blue powder used as a substitute for the genuine ultramarine, a proceeding known even to the old Memphitic dynasties. Finally, smaller or larger objects of clay or stone were covered like faïence with blue or greenish χesbet paste, and denoted as made of χesbet.

"In near relation to our investigation stands the practice of coating parts of walls with tiles enamelled in this way. That this custom reached back to the days of the Old Empire is proved by the great pyramid of Sakkárah, where the entrance of a chamber is framed with several courses of blue glazed tiles.*

"Theophrastus' unfired kyanos (ἄπυρος) was clearly the pigment which was mixed with the glass, the azurite, or mountain-blue. This material occurs in crystals, or in more earthy form near copper-beds, and a blue colouring powder can be made of it, which, however, under the action of the air easily loses its tone,—a difficulty which the Egyptians sought to meet by combining the azurite with glass fluor, and using this, when powdered, as a pigment. As we know that the main source of copper in the south-eastern part of the Mediterranean is Cyprus, and the Phœnicians had for a long time complete control of this island, all probability speaks for the ἄπυρος kyanos, which the Phœnicians (according to Theophrastus) brought to the Pharaohs, being the azurite found in the mines there.

"We have now to determine which kind of kyanos is to be assumed in the megaron of Alkinoos. As lapis lazuli is only found in small pieces, it is not to be assumed that long bands on the walls, as the frieze, could be encrusted with this precious material. Still less can we suppose painting with ultramarine or a colour imitating it, for the poet could not possibly speak of such a frieze as consisting

---

* Perrot et Chipiez, *Hist. of ancient Egyptian Art*, Vol. II. pp. 369, 399 (Eng. ed.).

of kyanos. There only remains blue-glass fluor or smalt. The Mycenæan and kindred discoveries* show that various objects of this material were already used by the Greeks in the pre-Homeric epoch. Such are also square, oblong, or circular little plates of bluish or greenish smalt, the decoration of which shows several of the ornaments characteristic of the period. As the great majority of these plates have holes or sockets, and the ornamented specimens are generally repeated in many examples in the same tomb,† we may assume with certainty that these little plates, set in rows on some under-surface, formed some sort of frieze-pattern. Of course it is doubtful whether such friezes were applicable to the walls of a tomb. The small size of the plates points rather to wooden sarcophagi or chests. But even in the latter case these friezes are of importance to us, for it was no great stride to transfer them from a piece of furniture to a wall. It was specially suggested, when the early Ionians, as might easily happen, had heard of the practice common in Egypt, Chaldæa, and Assyria, of coating parts of the walls with blue marked tiles. Hence I think it reasonable to conjecture, that the poet conceived the upper band of the wall in the megaron of Alkinoos as coated with blue glass-paste or smalt."

Helbig's conjecture has been brilliantly confirmed by the discovery of our frieze, and there can be no doubt that, in mentioning his θριγκὸς κυάνοιο, Homer had in view a frieze, which—like that in Tiryns—was inlaid with blue glass-paste.

---

* In one of the deep graves were found blue-glass cylinders (Schliemann, *Mycenæ*, pp. 157-8), and in two other objects of bluish smalt, p. 241, Nos. 350, 351 ; p. 242, No. 352.

† Such a specimen was found at Mycenæ, not in a deep grave, but in the *débris* (Schliemann, *Mycenæ*, pp. 109, 110 ; cf. the moulds, pp. 107, 109). From Menidi we may cite *Das Kuppelgrob von Menidi*, Pl. III. 12, 13 ; IV. 3, 12, 13, 15, 17, 19 ; V. 32, 43, 45. From Spata, *Bulletin de Corresp. hellén.*, II. (1878) pp. 192-204. From Ialysos, Dumont et Chaplain, *Céram ques, &c.*, I. p. 61, Fig. 36.

Regarding the chemical composition of the material used for the frieze, Professor Virchow writes: " The stone consists of sulphate of lime (gypsum), but in a form which reaches here and there the transparent blue of alabaster. The glass-paste consists of a calcium-glass, which is coloured with copper ; it contains no admixture of cobalt."

We have still an important question before us : What place did the alabaster frieze occupy at Tiryns ? We found it at the western wall of the vestibule of the men's hall ; it stood on the ground, and occupied the whole surface from the *anta* to the back wall of the hall.   But this cannot have been its original place, as can be proved by sure evidence. (1) In the north-western corner of the vestibule the floor is still pretty well preserved ; its western limit, clearly to be recognised, was in a *straight line*.   But the lower border of the frieze forms a broken line, seeing that the metopes are about 4 cm. thinner than the triglyphs ; the gap so caused between the foot of the metopes and the edge of the floor is filled with earth.   Hence it was certain that when the frieze was set up, the floor was already made.   (2) The alabaster slabs are from 0·15 to 0·20 m. thick, while the shrinking of the wall, where the frieze stands, is nearly 0·30 m. Hence the slabs could not occupy the whole space, and so the interstice between them and the wall is filled with *débris*. But this is no construction suitable for so splendid a frieze. The thinning of the wall by about 0·30 m. probably served, as was explained (p. 214), to admit a panelling of thick boards.   At the eastern wall of the vestibule we found the room thus saved filled up half its height with a layer of rubble ; nothing of an alabaster frieze was there to be seen. (3) The triglyphs have on their under-surface a pretty smooth border, 0·10 m. broad, and then a dowel of 0·07 m. width, rising 0·02 m.   This tenon-shaped addition has no meaning where the frieze now stands ; it rather points to the frieze being originally pretty high in position, and that the tenon was meant to obviate the falling of the

slabs. These are the grounds which have persuaded us that
the frieze was only transferred to the western wall of the
vestibule in later times, and that it was once placed elsewhere.
We cannot determine where this place can have been.


## 2. SCULPTURED SPIRAL BAND.

On Plate IV. to the left below, a sculptured ornament
is represented of which several pieces were found in the
men's hall. It is a corner-piece ; the ornament terminates
to the left and continues on the adjoining surface. The
material is a light-green very hard stone, and the pieces
are therefore in most cases very well preserved. Most of
them can be put together. They formed a continuous
moulding, o·12 m. high, which was sunk in the wall about
o·28 m. deep. On the upper and lower surfaces are bore-
holes, 26 mm. in diameter and 15–25 mm. deep ; they
evidently contained wooden pegs, by means of which the
moulding was fastened.

The ornament represents a spiral band, such as has
been already observed in Mycenæ, and also occurs in the
wall-paintings of Tiryns (Plate VIII., Fig. *a*). The
corners between the separate spirals are filled with flowers.
Although the spirals are not drawn with perfect regularity,
yet the execution is so excellent and the profile of the
moulding so fine, that the artist who made the spirals
must have possessed tools quite perfect. The position of
this find unfortunately gives us no certainty as to the place
which this moulding originally occupied. We found the
separate pieces in the small hollow which is in the middle
of the east wall of the men's hall. In a later reconstruction
of the palace, when a part was already destroyed, they were
used as common building stones in such a manner that the
ornament was not visible.

## 3. DORIC CAPITAL.

In a later wall which ran across the great court about ½ m. above the concrete-floor, there was found an old

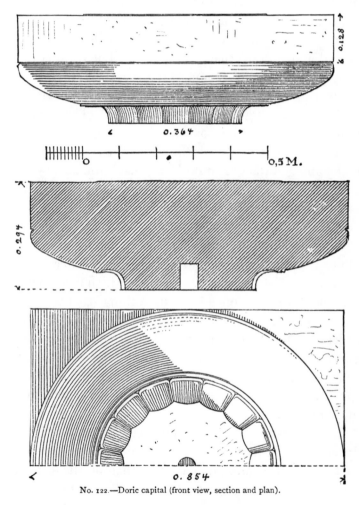

No. 122.—Doric capital (front view, section and plan).

Doric capital, of which the plan, front view, and section are given in No. 122.    The material is a porous sandstone of light colour, which did not very well bear the weather, and was therefore covered with fine lime-plaster 1–2 mm. thick.    Although the capital is only partly preserved, and is broken in many pieces, yet fortunately all the important measures could be taken. The only parts no longer distinguishable were the upper termination of the flutings and the form of the annulets. The capital belongs probably to the oldest Doric capitals in existence; in any case, it is older than the fifth century B.C.*

It has sixteen shallow flutings, which evidently terminated above as overhanging leaves. The *echinus* is very strongly curved, and is connected with the shaft by two narrow rings below. The *abacus* is comparatively high, even somewhat higher than the *echinus*. The projection of the capital must be considered as very marked, for the upper diameter is to the width of the *abacus* as 3 : 7. The lower joining surface is smooth, and has a round dowel-hole 44 mm. in diameter and 70 mm. deep. The upper surface has a quadrangular *scamillum* and an irregular hole, which latter may have been made later.

To which building this capital belonged is unfortunately unknown to us. Conjectures have been offered above (p. 229) on this subject. Of the shaft which belonged to it, and which assuredly once existed, nothing has been found.

On the other hand, between the gate to the upper citadel and the chief entrance two fragments of *cymatium* have been dug up, which most probably belonged to a gable *geison*. They are formed of the same material as the capital, and may therefore be supposed to belong to the same building.

I would here recall the fact, that in the Acropolis of Mycenæ also, remains of an old Doric building were found, which were of similar material to that of the capital of Tiryns. In Mycenæ, besides the capital, triglyphs, metopes and an architrave have been preserved.

---

* Mr. James Fergusson holds this capital to be of about 600 B.C., and observes to me : " There are some in Sicily probably older, but not much."—See *Serra di Falco*, plates of Artemis at Ortygia and elsewhere. See also *Parthenon*, page 71.

## 4. ARCHAIC ANTEFIX.

In the doorway to the north of the gate to the upper citadel, together with a number of Greek roof-tiles, an

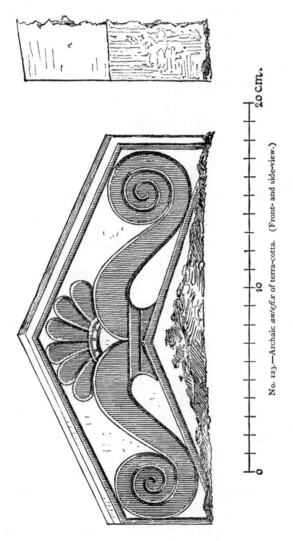

No. 123.—Archaic *antefix* of terra-cotta. (Front- and side-view.)

*antefix* of baked clay was found, of which the front and the side views are shown (No. 123)    It forms the end of a common gable-shaped coping-tile, about 0·21 m. wide.

The material of the *antefix* is a light-yellow clay, with many small red stones. Its whole outside was covered with a layer of well-cleaned yellowish clay, on which the hatched ornament in the drawing is executed in red-brown colour. The pattern has not been drawn, but it is impressed in low relief, as was often done on *antefixes*.

This *antefix* particularly deserves notice, because it accurately preserves the profile of the coping-tile, and does not, as is commonly the case, project considerably beyond it; the consequence is that the *palmetto*, which crowns the two spirals, is relatively extremely small; hence its very archaic appearance. Apparently the *antefix* belonged to the same building as the Doric capital. An *antefix* of similar form, which also had a remarkably small *palmetto*, was recently found in the excavations at Eleusis.

## F.—The Wall-paintings.

Among the finds of Tiryns the numerous remains of wall-paintings take one of the chief places. As up to the present time almost nothing was known of early Greek painting, the smallest remains would have been of great interest; and the numerous pieces of plaster found in the palace of Tiryns, which show not only a great number of different ornaments but also representations of figures, are the more deserving of universal attention.

All the walls of the palace had first a plastering of clay, and over this a plastering of lime. In spite of the great destruction which the palace has undergone in the course of ages, this can be proved with certainty, because there still exist in nearly all rooms at least small remnants of wall-plastering. The wall-painting has, of course, everywhere disappeared, for owing to the inconsiderable thickness of the layer of earth which covered the ruins, the rain-water could easily reach the plastering and destroy the colours. The only chamber in which we still found remains of

PLATE IX.

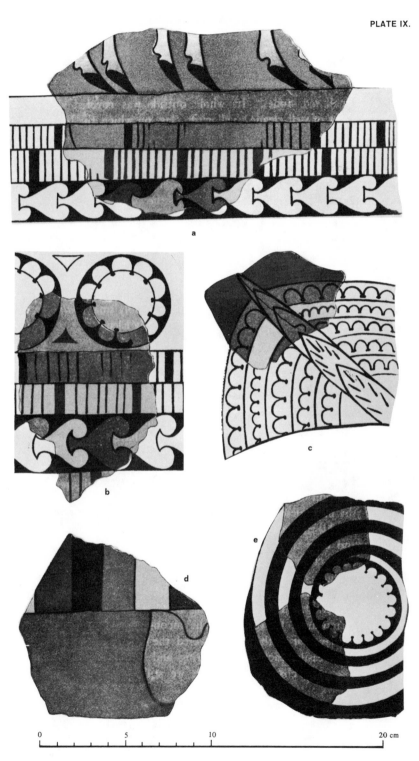

0       5       10       20 cm

WALL PAINTING IN THE PALACE OF TIRYNS.

painting on the plastering is the women's hall.  In its south-
east corner we distinguish, still fairly well, the shape of the
ornaments, but the colours are not so clear.  But many
fragments of plastering with well-preserved colours were
found in the *débris* of the various rooms, most of them
in the room which borders the bath-room on the north-
east side.

All these fragments had fallen from the walls, and were
preserved by the covering *débris* from the influence of the
weather.  Those fragments were best preserved of which
the painted surface lay downwards.  Altogether several
baskets were filled with fragments of such plastering.  The
most valuable pieces have been brought to Athens, but the
larger number are in the Museum fitted up at Tiryns.

A selection of the best-preserved pieces is given on
Plates V.–XIII.  The original fragments of the ornamental painting are represented with their colours; the
restored parts are rendered in black tone.  The colours are
not in every case a facsimile, but from the colours of the
best-preserved pieces I have decided on that of the more
injured.  On Plates V.–XI. all objects are represented half
the actual size.  In order, however, to give some idea of
the real condition of the paintings in their natural size, on
Plate XII. a fragment is shown in exact facsimile.  Plate
XIII. contains a bull in facsimile colours, but somewhat
diminished in size.

It appears to me that in all these paintings only five
different colours occur—namely white, black, blue, red, and
yellow.  Only simple pure colour has been used, no mixed
colour occurs; even green colour is altogether excluded.*
At the same time we frequently see among the pieces
found, blue or red colour of quite different shades; but

---

* According to Perrot and Chipiez (*Aegypten*, 5, 743, German
edition), the six colours, white, black, red, yellow, blue, and green, occur
in the Egyptian wall-paintings.

these deviations are due not to a different mixing of the colours, but to the different degree of preservation of each piece. One can best see this by comparing two fragments found at different places, but which originally formed one piece, for they frequently show greatly differing tones of colour, though they were undoubtedly originally painted with the same colour.

The greater or less moisture of the *débris* in which the separate fragments lay for ages imbedded, or even a different composition of these *débris* has altered the colours in a different manner.

The painting was executed *al fresco*, as may be seen in many fragments. For instance, while the white parts which show the ground-tone of the lime remain for the most part perfectly white, in painted parts we can often clearly observe how the pencil has entered into the lime and has made the surface rough. Especially in pieces painted blue I have been struck by these pencil-strokes.

Let us now consider, on Plates V.–XIII., the decorative and figure painting.

Plate V. shows an ornament composed of four fragments, in which at the first glance we recognise the pattern of the ceiling of Orchomenos, a corner of which I represent here in No. 124. We see a frieze composed of two rows of spirals, which is bordered above by plain stripes, below by stripes and a band of rosettes. The large spirals are drawn with black lines on a white ground; their centres are red. The spaces between each group of three spirals are filled with large flowers, which have the same two-leaved cup and the same long stalk as the flowers in Orchomenos.

The upper border consists of a yellow band with red strokes, and a blue band with black strokes. These narrow bands, which are apparently imitations of the rows of gay-coloured pieces of glass in the alabaster frieze, recur in very many paintings, as, for instance, in the bull, Plate XIII., and in the ornament still *in situ* in the women's hall. Also in the ceiling at Orchomenos, and in the pillars of the treasure-house of Atreus we see them in plastic form.

The lower edge is formed by a row of single rosettes, which are again enclosed on each side by such double bands as are described above. The rosettes, which are more simple than those of the ceiling at Orchomenos, show us by a very instructive example that the wall-paintings of Tiryns were all executed, not by the *stencil*-board (Schablone), but by free-hand. No rosette exactly resembles another; most of

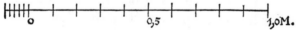

No. 124.—The sculptured ceiling of Orchomenos.

them are slanting and irregular, and we see plainly that the whole painting was made off-hand and carelessly.

Plate VI. shows below (Fig. *e*) a large and peculiar object. Its importance first became clear to me after I left Tiryns, and when it was therefore no longer possible for me to search among the mass of plaster fragments for the pieces which belonged to it. The curious figure is a part of a large-winged creature, of which the neck and the joint of one wing remains.

The most easily distinguished part is the neck-ornament, which is formed of a row of strung-beads, long in shape and

blue and red in colour; and of three rows of drop-shaped
beads of the same colours. The face-like ornament connected with it appears to be a clasp or agrafe, with which
the wing-arm is fastened to the body. The arm itself is
covered with several spirals, which gradually diminish in
size towards the end. At the last spiral we can see the
beginning of feathers. The wing, which was immediately
connected with the arm, is represented on Plate VII.

Further than this we have, so far, found nothing of this
winged creature, but the existing pieces are sufficient to
show that the creature represented must have had a similar
shape to several small gold winged-figures found in Mycenæ.
One of these is placed for comparison on Plate VI., Fig. *a*
(cf. Schliemann's *Mycenæ*, No. 277). On this figure also
we observe the neck-ornament, and we seem to recognise
the clasp and the spirals of the winged arm.

On Plate VI., Fig. *c*, there is also represented another
fragment, on which are traces of a drawing of another
similar winged creature. The neck-ornament is here formed
of small pendent flowers, alternating with small beads. The
wing was here to the right of the clasp. Only a corner of
the spirals and the beginning of the feathers are preserved.
For the sake of comparison, I have adjoined (Plate VI.,
Fig. *b*) a drawing of an ivory ornament from Menidi, which
evidently represents a perfectly similar clasp.

Further, I have drawn to the right above (Plate VI.,
Fig. *d*) a fragment of a wing, which is particularly interesting from the fact, that the feathers are arranged to
right and left of a central line. The fragment must therefore have belonged to some figure of which the two wings
met below.

Plate VII. shows some fragments of a wing half the
actual size. Fragments of this kind are found in large
numbers among the plaster remains, a proof that winged
creatures frequently appeared in the wall-paintings of the
palace. Besides the wing-joint, we see small feathers, painted

with red colour on a yellow ground; these are joined by
four rows of larger feathers, and by rotation a yellow, a
blue, a yellow and a white row; the separating strokes
of each feather are drawn in black, the middle-lines in
red.    The rayed long lines which divide the various
feather groups are not only painted, but cut deep into
the plaster.

With how little care the wall-painting was here and
there executed is seen in the example of these wings.    Not
only have the individual feathers quite different forms, and
are in part very irregularly drawn; but, besides this, the
inaccurate painting of the differently coloured feathers is
very characteristic.    The points of the large yellow feathers
are often blue, and those of the blue often yellow.    This
inaccuracy arose thus: the painters first drew a band of
blue and then a band of yellow of the same width, and
then marked off on these the various feathers with black
and red lines, without caring that the points of the feathers
often stretched over into the neighbouring colour.

On Plate VIII. I have placed six different spirals
together, all in half the actual size.    Fig. *a* shows a spiral
combined from two fragments which exactly corresponds
with the sculptured ornament (Plate IV.) described on
pp. 284–292.    Each spiral is composed of a blue and a
yellow band, unfolding on a white circle.    The spiral Fig. *b*
is simpler and more irregularly drawn.    One might even
doubt whether it should be described as a spiral, since it has
but one winding.    It agrees with the plastic spiral-band on
the metopes of the kyanos-frieze.    Fig. *c* looks like the preceding example; the spiral is drawn with a broad black line
on a white ground, the eye is red.    Fig. *d* shows the fragment
of a red spiral painted on a white ground.    The meaning of
the adjoining yellow spot is unknown.    Fig. *e* is a black
spiral drawn on yellow ground; by its irregular form we
judge that it was drawn rapidly with a free hand.    The
fragment shown under Fig. *f* contains red spirals on a

yellow ground, which apparently diminish in size towards the right.

Plate IX. gives five different fragments. Fig. *a* shows six bulls'-feet walking towards the right on a blue background. Below these come the gay-coloured stripes with cross-lines, described above (Plate V.). Below are leaves of various colours on a black ground in a row, and in the following order: yellow, red, white, blue, yellow. Similar leaves of glass-paste are among the finds of Mycenæ.

Fragment *b* contains in its upper part rosettes like those drawn on Plate V.; in its lower part leaves, which are very like those before named. In Fig. *c* I have drawn a part of a flower of the same pattern as on Plate V., because on this piece the little leaves or anthers between the calyx and the stalk are painted differently. The connected semi-circles make the flower still more like those in the ceiling of Orchomenos (see No. 124). The representation in Fig. *d* is not quite comprehensible. Fig. *e*, put together from two fragments, shows a very large spiral, black on white ground.

On Plate X. I have placed together various different patterns. Fig. *a* shows spirals of very small proportions, with black drawing on yellow ground. The fragments Figs. *b* and *c* belong to some figurative representation. We recognise in it starfishes, with arms red and blue in colour, painted on a black ground, on which the white points have been superadded in glossy white. Figs. *d* to *l* suggest no remark; indeed some among them (Figs. *f* and *l*) are inexplicable.

Plate XI. contains three variations of one *motif*, which was largely applied in later Greek art, and is even yet frequently used among us in tapestry patterns. In Fig. *a* the pattern is in red on a yellow ground. What is intended by the comb-like object which occurs in the separate fields of the pattern is not clear to me. The fragments Figs. *b* and *c* give the same pattern in black and red colours; the first is broader in its proportions, the latter considerably smaller. A similar pattern occurs on vases (cf. Plate XXVII., Fig. *a*).

Plate XII. gives a piece of the winged creature shown on Plate VI., namely the clasp of the wing; it is a fac-simile, and shows the actual size of the original. The colours are exactly those *now* visible on the fragment, and therefore they have not their original brightness, which, however, returns in the original when the plaster is mois-tened.

On Plate XIII. the largest preserved fragment of the wall-plastering is shown somewhat diminished in size; it represents figures, and therefore commands special interest. Dr. E. Fabricius, who gave particular attention to this fragment, has kindly furnished me with the following remarks upon it:—

"On a frieze-like band, which is limited above by a painted ornament, there is represented running wildly towards the left a *mighty bull*. He has his head lifted up, and his long curved horns reach up into the border; the mouth is closed. The wildness of the animal has been chiefly expressed by the artist by means of its large round eye. The breast is very high; the short, thick forelegs are advanced as if for a leap; the hind legs are stretched far backwards; the long tail is raised high, and swung forwards. The genitals are indicated. Above the back of the beast we see *a man* in a very peculiar position, also in profile to the left. He kneels with the right knee on the back of the bull, so that the knee only and the tip of the toe touch the back. He has stretched the other leg far back, and so high that the heel almost touches the upper edge of the frieze. In this unnatural position the figure is supported by the grasp of the right hand on the horn of the bull; the left hand is beneath the breast. The colours used in the painting are the following:—The ground round the figures is *blue*, and this blue is painted up to the outline of the bull, which has been first painted-in in *white*, and of which the contour is quite clear from the blue, although the blue is thicker. The nose of the bull is drawn with fine blue lines.

"Thus, while the bull has at first hand been *grounded* white, the artist has painted the man's figure in *glossy white on the blue ground.* In spots where the glossy white has been chipped off, the blue ground appears again. Following the outline of the bull, there are painted all over large semicircular spots in *red;* smaller red spots in groups of three or four are executed on the white ground between the larger ones. Drawn with somewhat thicker paint, and therefore showing darker, there are painted on the large spots waved lines, which give life to the whole. There are other parts brought out with *red*—the feet above the hoofs, the shoulder-blades by a fine line, the upper half of the tail and the genitals. The eye of the bull is put in with *black,* and here and there the contours are strengthened by a black line—for instance, on the extended leg of the man, and on the tail of the bull. Just below the body of the bull there was drawn a black line, as if it were to indicate the shadow, but it is now almost washed away, in consequence of which the genitals appear at present as if they were separated from the body.

"The muscles and genitals of the man's figure are brought out with black and *yellow* lines, and the extended left leg is covered with black cross-bands; yellow bands may be observed also on the hoofs of the bull. The ornamented border on the upper edge of the picture, reckoned from above downwards, consists of a blue, a yellow, and a white band; in the yellow band there are vertical red lines.

"DIMENSIONS.—The thickness of the fragment measures between 0·02 and 0·04 m.: length, 0·47 m.; height, 0·29 m. Height of the ornamental border above, 0·031–0·032 m. For the sizes of the separate parts I refer to the drawing.

PLATE X.

**WALL PAINTING IN THE PALACE OF TIRYNS.**

" PRESERVATION.—Below and on both sides are distinctly seen broken edges.  The whole was found in seven pieces.  A piece is wanting just from the middle of the bull, which is determined by the following four points: the onset of the back of the bull, the middle of the back, the middle of the body, and the onset of the fore legs with the right knee of the man; the hind legs of the bull are also wanting, which were originally stretched far behind.  The piece on which the head of the bull is preserved is much obliterated.

" In the figure of the man, the glossy white is chipped off the extended right arm, the upper part of the thigh of the left leg, also off the head, the shoulders, and breast; but the outline can still be distinctly traced.  Further, the blue underground is in many places almost washed out, and in consequence parts of an original grounding of the bull have come to light: we see that the artist had at first painted the bull somewhat longer, that he had twice grounded the tail differently before he gave it its present position, and the fore feet were also originally drawn somewhat higher.  The parts of the first grounding were, as we plainly see from what remains, completely covered with the blue ground colour.

" THE DRAWING is peculiarly free and skilful: the forms of the bodies are, as in the early archaic vase-paintings, too slender ; the head of the bull (height without horns, o·o58 ; horns, o·o75 m.) is too short in proportion to the height of the breast (about o·ioo m.) and to the back.

" As both the TECHNIQUE of the painting and the preparation of the colours, as well as the style of ornamentation on the upper border, are quite the same as the other wall-paintings of Tiryns, where especially the yellow band with vertical red stripes often appears, the idea is precluded that this piece with the bull might belong to a different epoch from the other fragments.

" As regards the *explanation* or *meaning* of the representation, we might suppose that the man on the back of the bull should be regarded as a performer of feats of bull-riding or a bull-tamer, who shows his skill by leaping on the back of the beast in wild career, just as in the well-known passage in the *Iliad* (XV. 679), the horse-tamer leaps from the back of one of the four galloping horses which he has yoked together, on to the back of another."

All these paintings, as well those of artificial design as those with figures, were certainly applied to the walls of the rooms, for the roof consisted of wood and was not plastered, while the concrete floor, wherever it was at all coloured, had a much simpler design.   But we may ask what the arrangement of the paintings on the wall was, whether they covered the whole wall, or were applied only above or below as friezes or *dados*.   We should be quite in the dark as to the answer, had there not been preserved a large piece of the wall-plastering with its painting *in situ* in the S.E. corner of the women's apartment.   We there see that a *dado* about 0·60 m. high is separated by a band of several colours from the upper part of the wall, and painted with ornaments.   The separating band is like that given on Plate V., and consists of a yellow band with red cross-strokes, and a blue band with black strokes.   This *dado* resulted from the construction of the wall, which often consisted of materials differing below and above.   If, for example, the wall was made of sun-dried bricks it was necessary, to save it from damp, to have a *dado* of stone. So we find in the palace of Tiryns the very same painted wall *dado* which we find in most of the Pompeian houses. Above the *dado* the surface of the wall had at Tiryns partly a single uniform colour (numerous pieces of plaster painted simply blue or red were found), partly it was certainly covered with ornaments and figure subjects.

As Homer never, either in Iliad or Odyssey, distinctly mentions plastered walls, Helbig infers that wall-painting was at that time not yet known in Greece.   He says (*das Homerische Epos*, p. 76) " Thus we must imagine the walls [of the Homeric palace], even if built of stone, as panelled within with wood, for plaster-coating was, as has already been remarked, unknown."   But as we now know that wall-plaster occurs both at Mycenæ and Tiryns, this statement of Helbig's is incorrect.   Though Homer makes no direct mention of plaster, we may perhaps infer from the epithets ξεστός, which he gives to porticoes, and παμφανόεις, which he gives to walls (ἐνώπια), that he alludes to the smooth, painted plaster-coating of the walls.

## G.—Later Remains on the Citadel.

We cannot determine accurately when the stately palace with its crowds of pillars and its wall-paintings perished. All the architectural finds we made on the citadel are older than the 5th cent. B.C., and so far confirm the ordinary tradition, that Tiryns was destroyed not later than 468 B.C. and never again rebuilt.   But among them there are found some (the Doric capital, the *geison*, and the *antefix*) which did not belong to the palace, but to a building erected after the destruction of the palace (cf. p. 229).   If this be so, then the palace must have been destroyed long before the year 468.   Nor do the architectural designs of the palace refute this view, so far as we know them ; for the sculptured frieze of Kyanos, the wall-paintings, and the construction of the *antæ* and pillars not only may, but must, be older than the Doric architectural remains just alluded to.   While therefore it is very probable that the account of the destruction of the Argives in 468 refers to a second destruction of the Acropolis, and of the Doric temple thereon, yet it is not impossible that the palace was destroyed along with it in the 5th cent. B.C.

After this last destruction the fort seems to have remained uninhabited, for of later Hellenic or Roman buildings there

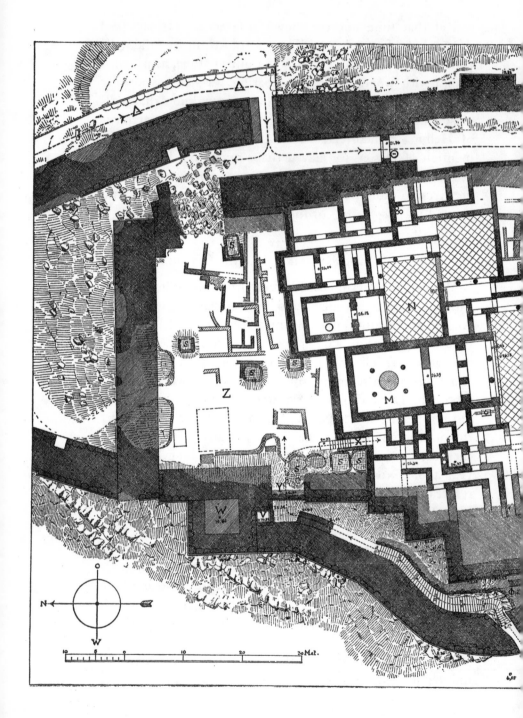

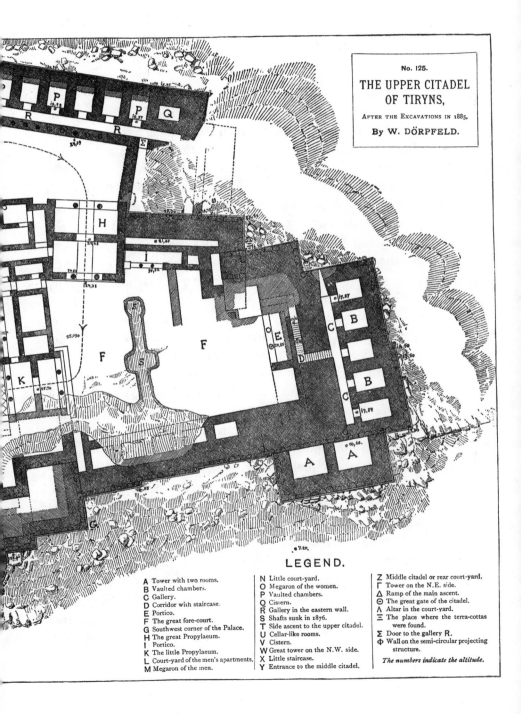

No. 125.

# THE UPPER CITADEL OF TIRYNS,

AFTER THE EXCAVATIONS IN 1885,

## By W. DÖRPFELD.

## LEGEND.

A Tower with two rooms.
B Vaulted chambers.
C Gallery.
D Corridor with staircase.
E Portico.
F The great fore-court.
G Southwest corner of the Palace.
H The great Propylaeum.
I Portico.
K The little Propylaeum.
L Court-yard of the men's apartments.
M Megaron of the men.

N Little court-yard.
O Megaron of the women.
P Vaulted chambers.
Q Cistern.
R Gallery in the eastern wall.
S Shafts sunk in 1876.
T Side ascent to the upper citadel.
U Cellar-like rooms.
V Cistern.
W Great tower on the N.W. side.
X Little staircase.
Y Entrance to the middle citadel.

Z Middle citadel or rear court-yard.
Γ Tower on the N.E. side.
Δ Ramp of the main ascent.
Θ The great gate of the citadel.
Λ Altar in the court-yard.
Ξ The place where the terra-cottas were found.
Σ Door to the gallery R.
Φ Wall on the semi-circular projecting structure.

*The numbers indicate the altitude.*

was not found a trace on the Acropolis. The fortress then was merely a large hill of *débris*, from which only the great walls stood up. This was the appearance of Tiryns when visited by Pausanias.

It was not till Byzantine days that active building again began there. At its south end, over the buildings of the great ante-court, a Christian church was erected, the foundations of which were found in our excavations. What remains of it can be seen on Plan III., where the extant remains are coloured red. The ground-plan of the church cannot indeed be accurately determined, on account of the complete destruction which it too has suffered; but the apse facing East and the three aisles can still be recognised. As the church was small in dimensions, so its ornamentation was very poor, for in addition to a marble slab, badly worked, only some rude stucco-cornices and remains of coloured plaster were found. As among these there were neither pillars nor Byzantine sculptures, all data for fixing the age of the building are wanting.

Both within and about the church we came upon a large number of tombs, all oriented to the East. Made as they were partly of stone slabs, partly of rubble-masonry and lime-mortar, partly of semicircular roof-tiles, they were almost all not laid deep enough to reach the old concrete floor. In a few places only, where the *débris* was shallow, they went below it, *e.g.* in the great Propylæum and in the gate of the men's court. On Plan III. I have indicated some of these tombs with red colour. In all about fifty were found, containing in every case besides bones a rude earthen vessel, but nothing to fix their date.

Both church and graveyard went also to ruin, and were covered by a layer of vegetable soil. Right over the church, at the south end of the fortress, there lay, when the excavations began, a threshing-floor made of stones, I suppose a work of the present century.

# CHAPTER VI.

## The Excavations of the Year 1885.

### By Dr. Wilhelm Dörpfeld.

In describing the citadel-wall (see pp. 177-189), we had concluded with the expression of a wish that the whole outer wall
of the stronghold might, as soon as possible, be brought to light
in the same way as had been done by Dr. Schliemann in regard
to the palace situated in the interior part of the castle. " Then
only will it be possible thoroughly to understand these interesting
walls with their towers, galleries, gates and posterns, and to give a
decided answer on those questions which at present, unfortunately,
must still remain open."

This wish has been fulfilled more quickly than could be hoped
for. Dr. Schliemann resolved upon taking the work upon himself, and entrusted to me the direction of the excavations. The
work was begun in the middle of April, and ended in the middle
of June, when the summer heat set in. During these two
months—not counting a few holidays and one rainy day—the
excavations were continued without interruption ; the number of
the workmen varying from thirty to forty. As in the year 1884,
Ilos, of Maguliana, again acted as overseer. To assist me in
superintending the excavations, and in making the drawings,
Dr. Schliemann, with kindly readiness, had engaged a second
architect, Mr. Georg Kawerau, of Berlin.

The Greek Government had sent the Phylax of Antiquities,
Mr. Georgios Chrysaphis, as its representative, to remain as long
as the excavations at Tiryns lasted. He superintended the
gathering-together and the storing of the finds with unsurpassed
care and great zeal.

Shortly before the excavations were concluded, and when
Dr. Schliemann had already gone to London, in order to receive
the " Gold Medal for Art and Science," which had been
awarded to him, Dr. Ernst Fabricius came for several days to

Tiryns, in order to examine the terra-cotta vases, bronzes, idols, and so forth, which had been discovered. The reader will see his report on these subjects in the following pages (see pp. 344–357). During the last days of the excavation, after Dr. Fabricius had left, we came, in an inverted wall-corner on the S.E. side, upon a great find of terra-cotta figures which Dr. Koepp has been good enough to describe (see pp. 358–367).

The task entrusted to us was twofold. First, the object was, to remove the great masses of *débris* which, last year, during the excavation of the upper citadel, had been thrown upon the slopes of the castle-hill ; and then to bring the enclosure wall of the upper citadel to light on every side. The earth had to be levelled on the fields all round the castle ; and the numerous small and large stones had to be heaped together on separate spots.

We began the digging on the southern side of the citadel by removing the mass of *débris* lying on the wall, and clearing the two galleries there, which were already known. Soon it was observed that the upper gallery, in accordance with what we had suspected before, contains a staircase leading to the lower gallery. But a further discovery was for us a most unexpected and surprising one. It was found that to the lower gallery were joined five vaulted rooms, each of which was connected with the gallery by a door.

When we passed over, in our clearance work, to the western side of the citadel, a large tower, projecting from the castle-wall, appeared on the S.W. corner. This tower contains two inner rooms, divided by a party-wall. The adjoining wall on the N. side is very much destroyed, and therefore could only be uncovered, in its lower layers, after many blocks of stone had been removed and great masses of earth carted away. The greatest obstacle was, the large semicircular projecting structure in the middle of the western wall. Its interior being wholly filled with colossal blocks of stone, that had fallen from the upper citadel, and the access to it being only possible through the little gate on the W. side, the clearance could only be effected with the greatest difficulty, and under constant danger of life for the workmen. Many of the colossal blocks of stone had first to be laboriously split so as to enable us to lift them with our strong levers, and to get them out. Several times, seeing the enormous difficulties, and doubting whether, after all, any noteworthy result would be obtained, we were on the point of desisting from its further prosecution. It was, therefore, to our great delight that suddenly, within the projecting structure, a well-preserved stone staircase came to view, of which we gradually uncovered sixty-five steps.

Further north, the western wall offered no special difficulties. After the *débris* and a few stone-blocks had been removed, the wall as well as the rock on which it is built, were disclosed.

After the whole western wall of the upper citadel had been brought to light, we turned to the eastern wall and began, at the S.E. corner, with the removal of the old and new masses of *débris* and the complete clearance of the great gallery which had already been known for a long time past. As was to be expected, this gallery too proved to be a corridor, which even now is connected, by six doors, with as many vaulted rooms. Although we could not fully finish the carting away of the masses of earth on this side, because the beginning of the great summer-heat put a stop to the continuance of the work, we were yet able to trace nearly the entire course of the eastern wall. Only very little remains to be done ; and that can easily be finished, when the lower citadel—which, last year, was investigated only by means of a small trench, but which in the present year has been left quite untouched—is to be fully excavated.

As, in these diggings, the *débris* to be carted away consisted principally of that which last year had been thrown from the upper citadel, and which, therefore, had already once been searched, we could not reckon upon many finds. Vases and other objects could only be found on approaching the older layers of *débris*. Nevertheless, the number of the finds has been a comparatively large one. Two places more especially—the surface of the semicircular projecting structure on the W. side, and an inverted corner on the S.E. side of the castle—yielded a particularly rich booty. In the last-mentioned place, we dug out very many terra-cotta figures and small vases of a later period ; in the former place, a large number of fragments of ancient vases (of geometrical and Mycenean style), and numerous fragments of painted wall plastering.

In general, the finds were made singly ; and moreover— as was natural, considering the kind of earth that had been excavated—very ancient vases were intermixed with later ones. For, the *débris* which covered the walls, had gathered there in the course of ages, and consequently could not but contain products of widely varying periods, embedded in the most different layers of earth. Under these circumstances, it would have been useless, nay, even misleading, if we had noted the depth below the surface, at which the several objects were found.

Passing over to the special description of the results of our excavations, I may mention that the best pieces found have been sent to Athens, in order to be exhibited there in the Mycenæ Museum, together with the objects discovered last year. The less important objects remain in Tiryns, where they are kept in the watchman's hut.


## A.—THE CITADEL WALL.

As a basis for the description of the castle wall, we adopt the subjoined plan No. 125 which, drawn up on the scale of 1 : 400, has been reduced, by photographic process, to about three-quarters. I have chosen the orientation in such a way that the magnetic north directly points to the left ; hence the east is at the top. For those who desire an exact statement as to the orientation, it may be observed that the axis of the Megaron deviates from the magnetic north line by about $6\frac{1}{2}°$. The plan does not embrace the whole castle, but only that part in which the new excavations took place—namely, the palace properly speaking, with its fore-court and outer court.

The lower citadel, which is represented on Plate I., I have not included in the new plan, because its picture has in no wise been changed by the new excavations, and because I thus gained the advantage of being able to take a larger scale for the upper citadel. Though a short explanation has been added to the plan, I think it necessary to add a few more remarks by way of illustration. The citadel wall, as far as it is preserved and is now visible, I have marked by cross-hatching, and moreover I have put its outer side in relief by a double line. Where this double line is wanting, we have not found the outer course of the wall. On the other hand, a simple hatching indicates those portions of the wall which have only been preserved in their foundation layers, or which are not visible now. As the present surface of the circuit wall, in many places internally, remains below the level of the palace floor, whilst externally it lies several meters above the more deeply situated rock, the exterior face of the wall in the Plan had to be patched in many places in a darker tone, but the interior face more lightly, although the inner edge is nearly everywhere preserved at greater height than

PLATE XI.

a

b                    c

0        5        10                    20 cm

WALL PAINTING IN THE PALACE OF TIRYNS.

the outer part. Furthermore, as, in the galleries, the imaginary section-plane has been assumed to be close above their floor, the columns situated above the eastern gallery ought not, properly speaking, to have been represented in the ground-plan. Yet, their presence on the Plan seemed to me absolutely necessary; and I have, therefore, drawn the four preserved bases of columns quite black, indicating the supplemented ones merely by circular lines, in the hatched wall surface.

Of the inner walls of the palace, those the foundations of which only have been preserved, are also marked by a simple hatching, whilst those which rise above the floor, are cross-hatched. The three open inner courts of the palace are marked by a square net, and thus they will be recognised at a glance. The inserted numerals indicate, in meters, the height of the point in question above the level of the sea.

The foundations of the Byzantine Church, which were discovered at the S. end of the citadel, and which are delineated on Plate II., I have left out on the new Plan, in order the better to give a full idea of the antique plan of the great fore-court.

A comparison of our new plan with the one drawn last year (Plate I.), and that of Captain Steffen (*Maps of Mycenae;* sheet II.) shows at once how successful this year's excavations have been. Hitherto, the few visible wall-corners had been connected by dotted lines, and thus an outline of the castle had been obtained which is now shown to have been by no means correct. Instead of the long, almost unbroken lines of the wall, we have found numerous projecting and inverted angles; and instead of the uniform wall profile, which we had thought was to be assumed for the whole upper citadel, very great variety in the depth and form of the wall has presented itself. Amongst the numerous sections of the circuit wall, there are scarcely two parts which have been built on the same scale and in like manner. This fact is the more remarkable because the wall of the lower citadel, in its whole extent, possesses the same profile and almost exactly the same thickness. We are forced to assume that this difference has arisen partly from the configuration of the castle rock, partly from the manner in which the paths of ascent have been formed, partly from the desire of establishing store-rooms and cisterns within the wall.

Before we turn to the description of the several sections of the wall, let us first try to obtain a general survey of the citadel, as represented.

The core of the upper citadel is formed by the palace

properly speaking, with separate dwellings for men and women. Even as, towards the south—therefore, on the right of our Plan —the somewhat deeper situated great fore-court adjoins, so in the north, also a few meters lower, that section adjoins, which we have called the middle citadel. These three parts possess in common a strong circuit wall, which, roughly speaking, forms an oblong rectangle stretching from north to south. The several sections are separated by thinner walls. The connection between the palace and the fore-court (F) is effected by the Gate K and two side-doors ; between the palace and the middle citadel (Z) by the staircase and the door X.

On the eastern longitudinal side of the great quadrangle lies the chief ascent to the castle. The carriage-road begins at the N.E. corner ; it gradually rises in a southerly direction to the level of the citadel, and ends at the fore-court F, with the great Gate structure H. On its outer side, this long road is protected by a strong embattled wall. A second ascent, which only served as a side ascent and was not passable for horses and carriages, is situated on the W. side. Here, the approach is from the opposite direction—that is, from south to north—by means of a flight of steps : first, the middle citadel is reached in this way ; whence the ascent to the higher palace may be made by the staircase Z. This ascent, too, is protected against hostile attack by a strong embattled wall which at its lower end terminates in a great semicircle.

Three sections adjoining each other, of which the central and highest one is occupied by the palace ; a great practicable carriage-way on the eastern side, which abuts upon the southern section ; and a side ascent formed as a staircase, which leads to the northern section : such are the general features the upper citadel of Tiryns presented to us after the excavations of the present year. This division of the upper citadel we shall follow in the subsequent description, when, first, we shall consider the out-wall of the palace proper ; then, that of the southern section—viz., of the great fore-court ; and further on, that of the northern section—or middle citadel. Finally, we shall discuss the two ascents, with their protecting walls.

## 1. The Out-Wall of the Palace.

In the fifth chapter we were only able to fix the limits of the palace on the north, east, and south, whilst the boundary wall on the western side was then still unknown. This gap is now, to some extent, filled up.  Though the walls on the W. part of the palace are mostly quite destroyed, the great out-wall itself nevertheless remains.  Externally, it consists of very large blocks of stone, whilst on the inner side smaller stones have also been used.  It is impossible to say what were the dimensions of the wall above the floor of the palace, and whether, on the W. side, a corridor lay along the wall in the same way as on the north side ; for, the wall has disappeared down to the depth of several meters below the upper floor.  In its lower preserved part—as may be seen from the Plan—it has a considerable thickness which, although not exactly measurable, amounts in some places to 12 m.  In its S.W. corner (see U in the Plan), the wall contains some cellar-like rooms, the bottom of which, composed of a concrete flooring, is in part still well preserved.  This floor lies 21·90 m. above the sea ; therefore about 4·50 m. below the floor of the palace.  The ceiling of these rooms was not made of stone, but undoubtedly of strong wooden beams ; for, in no part of the palace are the vestiges of the great fire which brought about the destruction of the castle, to be more clearly seen.  In the red *débris* with which the interior was filled, we even found still great pieces of burnt and unburnt wood.  The rooms were at all events accessible, from the upper chambers, by means of a wooden staircase, and probably were used as cellars for the storing of food, etc.  Their situation within the great out-walls may be seen from the profile in Fig. 130, where they are indicated by dotted lines and marked by the letter *e*.

A noteworthy fact is, that the western boundary wall of the palace is not in a straight line, but forms a whole series of in· verted and projecting angles, as is the case with the northern and eastern wall.  These many angles are by no means capriciously arranged, but correspond—as may be seen from the Plan—to the inner walls of the palace.  *The circuit wall and the palace are consequently in close connection ;* and in this we may recognise a further valuable proof of the thesis repeatedly mentioned before, that the construction of the palace and of the embattled walls took place simultaneously.  It cannot be denied, it is true, that in some cases also the configuration of the rock on which the wall was to be built, prescribed the erection of projecting structures.  But in Tiryns itself it can be clearly seen that in many places where the formation of the castle-rock by no means required it, inverted angles were nevertheless arranged on account of the interior division of the palace.

At the corner G, situated to the west of the gate-structure
K, the western circuit wall of the palace ends.  It bends here
into a right angle, and runs exactly in an eastern direction towards the gate structure.  Thus, the palace on its S. side also
was separated from the fore-court F by an embattled wall ; and
this wall had been constructed simultaneously with the western
wall of the palace, but a little earlier than the circuit-wall of
the fore-court.

## 2. THE OUT-WALL OF THE FORE-COURT F.

On the western side of the fore-court, before the most recent
excavations had been begun, only insignificant vestiges of the
circuit-wall were visible, and therefore it could only be indicated, on Plate I., by dotted lines, in a hypothetical form.  The
assumed shape of the wall has, however, proved to be an erroneous one ; for in reality the wall lies—as is shown by Plan 125
—several meters farther away to the east.  Its comparatively
slight thickness has been the cause of its nearly entire destruction.  Only in its southern part, where the great tower projects,
it still stands upright, several meters high.  In its northern part,
after prolonged excavations, we have only brought to light one
or two courses of stone on the outer side.  Here, the present
upper edge lies on an average 8–9 m. under the floor of the fore-
court.

The outer edge of the wall forms a broken line, which is
composed of several straight pieces, 10–12 m. in length.  A reason
for this slight deviation from the straight line is not visible ; it
cannot possibly have been caused by the configuration of the
rock.  Whilst the wall in the neighbourhood of the tower has a
breadth of 8·15 m., it is only half as thick (4·10 m.) further
north.  By way of compensation for this reduction, a second,
parallel wall, 1·65 m. in breadth, has been set up at a short
distance within.  This second wall is composed of smaller
stones, and seems to be connected with the outer wall by several
cross-walls.  At least, one of these cross-walls has been brought
to light.  The space between the outer and the inner wall is now
filled with earth, and in ancient times also does not seem to
have been a hollow space.  The idea suggests itself that the
inner wall, which in quite a similar manner recurs also in other
parts of the castle, formed the foundation for a colonnade
running along the inside of the castle wall.

At the S. end of the western wall, a mighty tower projects
from the line of the wall.   Its breadth is 8·30 m. ; its length
19·20 m.   It is built on a natural prominence of the castle rock ;
for, even now, the rock shows itself on the three unenclosed
faces of the tower.   Inside there are two rooms of equal size
(4·95 m. to 6·0 m.), separated from each other by a party wall,
1·70 m. in depth.   They were therefore completely isolated,
and could only be entered from above by means of wooden
stairs or ladders.   On the outside of the western wall of the
northern room there is a broadening of the wall, which, at a
first glance, might easily be taken for a stone staircase, leading
up from without.   But a closer investigation will soon convince
everyone that it was solely the shape of the rock on that spot,
which caused the broadening of the footing of the wall.

As scarcely any stones, but almost exclusively half-baked,
sun-dried bricks and red rubbish have been found in the interior
of the rooms, their ceilings cannot possibly have consisted of
stone, as was the case with the ceilings of the chambers B and P,
but must have been formed of strong wooden beams.   At the
destruction of the castle, the beams caught fire ; and by the
glowing heat thus created the upper parts of the tower, consisting of sun-dried bricks, were burnt red.   The remnants of the
burnt brick-walls afterwards filled the rooms.   It is not possible
to decide how many storeys the tower had.   As there is a difference of about 8 m. between the floor of the rooms (+ 16·60 m.)
and that of the fore-court (+ 24·50 m.), there were probably
two storeys even below the level of the floor of the fore-court.

It would be of great importance, in deciding the object of the
rooms, if we could find out whether light was imparted to them
by windows.   Unfortunately, a single layer only of their western
wall, which was 3·30 m. strong, has been preserved above the
floor ; and as the windows had at any rate to be placed in the
upper layers, the ruins do not offer us any data for answering
that question.   If the rooms were dark, they may have been
cisterns.   Otherwise we might regard them as prisons, or as a
provision cellar.   For cisterns two circumstances speak, which I
will mention though they do not afford a full proof.   First, the
out-walls of the two rooms are built with clay-mortar which can
be clearly recognised even now, on the inner side of the walls,
between the stones.   As the walls were consequently water-tight,
the two rooms may very well have served as cisterns.   This
conclusion is, however, not a certain one ; for, the last excava-

tions have proved that nearly *all the walls*, the outer citadel walls as well as the inner walls of the palace, *were built with clay-mortar.* If the portions of the castle-wall which were hitherto visible, do not show any mortar, but only small stones in the joints between the large blocks, it is the natural consequence of the rain which during thousands of years has struck the wall and washed out the mortar. The mining work of lizards and rats which live by hundreds in the walls, has also contributed to the removal of the clay from the joints. Almost throughout, wherever we have laid bare pieces of wall which for many centuries had been covered with *débris*, the mortar within the joints still showed itself well-preserved ; the light colour of the clay, or loam, forming a clear contrast to the dark vegetable earth and the red brick rubbish.

Secondly, it is to be noted that unquestionably there must have existed, in the castle, several reservoirs for storing the rain-water (comp. p. 204). If, therefore, we meet with two rooms which by their construction, their dimensions, and their elevation are very well fitted for being used as cisterns, we may no doubt assume them, with some degree of probability, to have been cisterns.

A transverse section through the tower is to be seen on Fig. 127, to the left, in *b* : the preserved portion of the wall is coloured dark ; the supplemented one lighter. The indicated division of the height by an intermediate ceiling is, in accordance with what we have above stated, simply a hypothesis.

A structure of the highest interest is the southern citadel wall of the fore-court, with its vaulted corridors and chambers. It had long been well known that the southern wall contained two galleries ; but it was not known what was the form of these vaulted passages ; both having partly fallen in, and being partly filled with *débris*. One of our first objects was, to decide this question. Great difficulties, however, lay in the way of an effective clearance. In many places, the ceiling had fallen ; and the large blocks of stone had been so firmly wedged together in the small space that they could only be removed with the greatest labour. Again, in several places, the preserved portion of the ceiling, and the side-wall which still stood upright, threatened to fall in during the clearance. As this, of course, had to be prevented by every means, we found ourselves compelled to shore-up the dangerous spots of the ceiling by means of strong iron bars, and to repair the decaying portions of the walls by cement masonry.  Only after this securing work had been effected, could the galleries be cleared without danger to the lives of the workmen engaged.   The result of these labours repaid us richly for all the trouble and the expenses.   Within the corridor D, which is still, in part, covered with its vault, nine steps of a stair-case leading down are preserved.   A little further to the west, the corridor bends, at a right angle, to the south, and shortly afterwards opens into the broader and higher corridor C. In the southern wall of the latter are five arched doors.   When we discovered these, we thought that, outside the doors, the

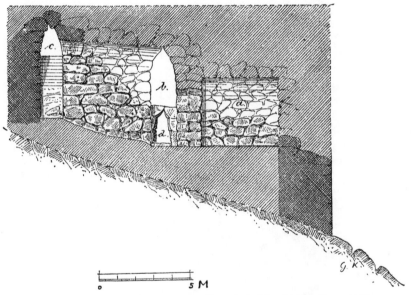

No. 126.—Transverse section of the southern wall.  *a*, vaulted chamber ; *b*, gallery ; *c*, gallery with staircase ; *d*, window of the gallery *b*.

plateau of the under-wall would extend itself.  But how great was our astonishment when, instead of the under-wall, we found five separate rooms, all of which were once vaulted with colossal blocks of stone in ogival form !

As soon as we had made this discovery, we also examined, with some workmen, the great, already known gallery (R) in the eastern wall, in order to see whether there, too, similar rooms did exist.  Soon it was found that the six doors existing there also led into six separate, vaulted chambers.  By this discovery, at one blow, everything we had said on p. 184, and

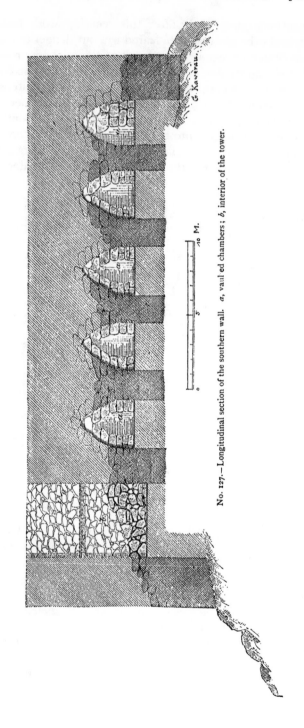

No. 127.—Longitudinal section of the southern wall.   *a*, vaul ed chambers ; *b*, interior of the tower.

following, in accordance with Captain Steffen's attempt at an explanation, was proved to be untenable. An isolated under-wall, with a passage along the top, such as we had imagined, has never existed in Tiryns at any place, but the whole under-wall was occupied by rooms; and only above the ogival ceiling of those chambers was the top wall-way situated, from which the castle could be defended.

In order to be able to inquire into the object of the casemate-like chambers and corridors, a short architectural description of them will be necessary. We take as a basis the ground-plan (Fig. 125), the transverse section through the southern wall (Fig. 126), and the longitudinal section through the same (Fig. 127). The transverse section (Fig. 126) shows, on the right, the middle one of the five rooms (*a*); it intersects, further to the left, the door of the same and the great gallery (*b*); and then follows the N.S. arm of the second corridor (*c*). In the background, to the right, the eastern wall of the middle room is to be seen; in the centre, at the east end of the passage (*b*), is the window (*d*), and to the left, the second arm of the corridor *c*, with the remaining steps of the staircase. The longitudinal section (Fig. 127) is taken through all the five vaulted chambers (*a*), and through the tower (*b*); one sees the wall with the five doors, behind which lies the gallery. The standing portions of the structure are in both profiles drawn dark; those which could be supplemented with certainty, in light colour.

Both arms of *the upper passage* (D in the ground-plan) are about 1·35 m. wide, and contained a great stone staircase, by which the corridor C could be reached from the fore-court. Of this staircase, nine steps, rudely made of unwrought limestone slabs, are still *in situ*. The rise of each step is 0·16 m.; its tread 0·37 m. Now, as the lowest remaining step still lies 3·20 m. above the floor of the corridor C, about 20 steps, which are destroyed now, must have existed below it. And, in fact, as many steps can be accounted for on the lower end of the passage; as indicated by the dotted lines in the ground-plan. Towards above, the staircase is short of about 18 steps, if we assume the height of the fore-court at that place to be about 25·0 m. It is no longer possible to decide how they were arranged, because we do not know at what place the staircase opens into the fore-court. When the Byzantine Church was built—the foundations of which I have left out in the new Plan, for the sake of affording a better synopsis—the upper part of the staircase D was also destroyed, together with the other antique structures in this region of the citadel. From the fact of a Byzantine grave and several Byzantine vases having been found under the lower, destroyed parts of the antique staircase, we conclude that the lower part of the staircase also was destroyed in Byzantine times.

The *corridor C,* which was likewise provided with an ogive-like stone ceiling, is in its eastern part 1·70 m., in its western only 1·50 m. wide. Its western end is closed against the some-what deeper situated Tower room A by a wall, 2·50 m. deep. At the eastern end, the closing wall is considerably stronger (4·60 m.), and contains, several centimeters above the floor, a *window* which contracts towards the outside, and consequently had the shape of a loop-hole. Seen from the inside, it is trian-gular; 1·30 m. broad, and 1·80 m. high. A measurement of its breadth at the outside of the wall is no longer feasible, because the front of the wall is destroyed at this spot; but from the sloping of the preserved portion of the window, we can compute an outer breadth of 0·10 m. to 0·20 m. Although, therefore, the window was outside so small that it could scarcely be distin-guished from a joint; and though it was impossible to enter through it: yet, on account of its inner broadening, it admitted light enough for the whole corridor. The profile of the latter may be seen from the transverse section (Fig. 126). Whilst its breadth, in the main, agrees with that of the eastern gallery (p. 184), its height is greater by a whole meter. Of the ceiling, which was formed of mighty overlapping blocks of limestone, only a few portions are preserved; the greater part has fallen in. The cause of this was, partly, the bad construction of the thick northern wall, the inner side of which consists of rather small quarry-stones and clay mortar, and is only lined outside with a layer of large stones.

All the five doors leading to the chambers are still preserved; though partly very much damaged. Their breadth measures 1·45 m. (at the easternmost door only 1·25 m.); their height, up to the crown of the arch, about 2·80 m. Each door is pro-vided with a great stone threshold. Contrivances for locking the doors we have not been able to detect.

Of the five rooms, the two western ones are 5·30 m., the three eastern ones 4·30 m. deep. Their breadth is 3·30 m.; only the eastern one is 3·05 m. broad. The greater depth of the two western chambers is certainly caused by the projection of the outer edge of the wall towards the south ; for the inverse supposition, that this projection has been formed with the intention of thus obtaining two larger chambers, appears to me improbable for many reasons.   The chambers—as may be seen from Fig. 127—were covered with blocks of stone in such a way that the intermediate walls converged, at a certain height, so far as eventually to join one another.   Portions of these heavy ogival stone-ceilings are yet preserved ; but the greater portion has fallen in, and their *débris* filled the chambers.   From four chambers we have cleared out the *débris ;* only in one (the second from the west) have we left them lying there.

As the ridges of the arches lay parallel to the intermediate walls, the trifling pressure which the ceilings possibly exercised on the intermediate walls, was mutually neutralized.   Only the outer walls of the first and fifth room had to bear the pressure, if any existed.   These are, therefore, constructed more broadly than the intermediate walls (2·75 m. against 1·90 m.).   The southern outer wall in all the five chambers is much destroyed, because the ceilings, in falling in, dragged these walls along with them.   Only of the lowest stone-layer, several ashlars are still preserved, so that their thickness at least (2·75 m.) could be measured.   Undoubtedly, these outer walls reached up to the ceilings of the chambers, so that the latter were quite closed.   On the other hand, it is impossible to decide whether these walls also contained windows for lighting the chambers.   As, however, the corridor C has a window, each room probably had a similar one.   These apertures must have been so small, that from the outside they were either not visible at all, or very slightly indeed.

Interesting and important as the whole system of these case-mate-like rooms is in itself, it obtains still greater importance by the fact, that *quite a similar system of construction has been found in several Phœnician colonies* on the northern coast of Africa—namely, in the Punic cities of Carthage, Thapsus, Hadrumetum, Utica, and Thysdrus.*   In Fig. 129 I have given, after Perrot

---

* Professor Rudolf Virchow directs my attention to the fact of his having been reminded by Prof. P. Ascherson : "that some written evidence has been preserved from antiquity as to the architecture of the wall of Punic Carthage and the object of the rooms contained in it.   *Appianos*, of Alexandria (*Hist. Romana*, I. ; ed. Bekker, 1842 ; p. 220, 1–8)—whose report is probably founded on the lost account of *Polybios*, who as we know, was an eye-witness of the capture and destruction of Carthage, having been among the suite of the younger Scipio—describes this colossal and peculiar structure in the following words : ' The upper part of each of the (triple) walls was

and Chipiez (*Histoire de l'Art*, III. p. 351) part of the ground-plan of the wall of Byrsa (the Acropolis of Carthage) ; and I added (Fig. 128), for the sake of comparison, a piece of the ground-plan of the eastern wall of Tiryns, drawn on the same scale. Although, in Byrsa, the chambers lie towards the inner part of the Castle, and are not of square, but circular formation, the great similarity in the whole arrangement is unmistakeable. The conformity even goes so far that the length and breadth of the chambers in Byrsa almost exactly recur in the two central rooms in the southern wall of Tiryns (3·30 m. in breadth to

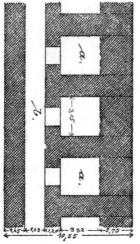

No. 128.—Ground-plan of the eastern wall of Tiryns. *a*, vaulted chambers; *b*, gallery.

No. 129.—Ground-plan of the wall of Byrsa; *a*, vaulted chambers; *b*, gallery.

4·20 m. in depth). Scarcely anybody will venture to declare this surprising similarity to be fortuitous. Surely, an underlying connection is here traceable. Either Phœnician builders raised the castle walls in North Africa as well as in the Argive plain ;

provided with a double roof; and in the hollow and covered room below there stood 300 elephants. Close by, there were magazines for their fodder. Above, there were stables for 4000 horses, as well as store-rooms for green vegetable provender and barley, together with quarters for 20 000 infantry and 4000 cavalry. So large a military force found shelter in the walls alone' :—διώροφον δ' ἦν ἕκαστον τείχους τὸ ὕψος καὶ ἐν αὐτῷ κοίλῳ τε ὄντι καὶ στεγανῷ κάτω μὲν ἐστάθμευον ἐλέφαντες τριακόσιοι καὶ θησαυροὶ παρέκειντο αὐτοῖς τῶν τροφῶν, ἱπποστάσια δ' ὑπὲρ αὐτοὺς ἦν τετρακισχιλίοις ἵπποις καὶ ταμιεῖα χιλοῦ τε καὶ κριθῆς, ἀνδράσι τε καταγωγαὶ πεζοῖς μεν ἐς δισμυρίους ἱππεῦσι δὲ ἐς τετρακισχιλίους· τοσήδε παρασκευὴ πολέμου διετέτακτο σταθμεύειν ἐν τοῖς τείχεσι μόνοις."

HENRY SCHLIEMANN.

or we see here an architectural arrangement which, invented in the oldest times by some nation, had gradually become typical and therefore was executed by several races in similar manner. Strabo, it is true, states that the Cyclopes, the builders of Tiryns, had come from Lycia. The ancients, consequently, knew nothing of Phœnician architects having built Tiryns. Nevertheless, I give preference to the former of the two possibilities mentioned. As long as a similar casemate-like construction has not been found in Lycia or in any other district of Asia Minor, which had not been visited by Phœnicians, the conformity between the structures of Tiryns and Byrsa must be looked upon as a proof that both were erected by Phœnician builders.

The style of the wall of Byrsa, it is true, appears to be a more advanced one—according to the statements of Beulé, the discoverer of that wall—than the style of the fortification-works of Tiryns. But, in the first place, this difference may partly have arisen from the diversity in the building material; the walls of Tiryns consisting of hard limestone, those of Byrsa of soft tufa. Secondly, assuming an interval of several centuries between the construction of the two strongholds, our hypothesis would again hold good.

Whilst formerly, when only the galleries in Tiryns were known, a great deal of controversy went on as to the purpose they had served, we think all differences of opinion as to the object of these underground rooms will now cease, since the chambers have been discovered. They can no longer be assumed to have served the purpose of fortification ; for even supposing that each room had a window that could serve as a loophole, yet, within the whole southern wall, only six combatants could have found standing-room for the defence. And for six defenders so great a construction would certainly not have been made. The chambers and corridors cannot have been anything but cellar-like *magazines*, in which all kinds of provisions and other things could be conveniently and safely stored.

Beulé (*Fouilles à Carthage*, p. 60) attributes a similar object also to the chambers in the wall of Byrsa. Perrot (*Hist. de l'Art*, III. p. 352) is of a different opinion. In accordance with the idea of other French scholars who preceded him (Daux, *Recherches sur les Origines des Emporia Phéniciens*, pp. 190–192 ; and Graux, *Note sur les Fortifications de Carthage*, p. 196), he takes the cellar-like rooms to have been water-cisterns. This hypothesis seems to me less probable. As regards Tiryns, at any rate, it is quite untenable. For, first of all, a water-reservoir has never been planned in such a shape as occurs in Tiryns and also in North Africa. For a cistern, either a single room is taken; or, if several reservoirs are wanted, they are at least so arranged that one of them can remain filled, when the other is emptied. Secondly, this hypothesis is utterly at variance with the existence of a window in the corridor of Tiryns, which is absolutely incompatible with a cistern. Thirdly, the doors with their stone thresholds, and the handsome staircase, seem scarcely suitable to a cistern. But the disposition of the ground-plan is excellently adapted to a store-room, seeing that the cellar-like rooms could be very well used for storing various things, whilst at the same time each room could be separately closed.

Above the chambers and the passages, the several walls were united in a single huge mass of masonry, which had the enormous breadth of 17·50 m. It cannot be said with any degree of certainty what it was that stood on the plateau of this broad wall: whether magazines or dwellings were erected there, or whether only a broad rampart way was laid out on it. A few wall-remnants perhaps point to the former conclusion. The inner side of the wall seems to have been joined by a portico (E); at least, several bases exist there, which apparently were destined for columns.

On the *eastern side of the great fore-court*, the castle-wall is still preserved a few meters high on the outer side; and here also it forms several far-projecting angles. In one of the inward angles (near $\Xi$ in Fig. 125), the many terra-cotta figures which Dr. Koepp describes on pp. 358–364, were found in a heap together. The wall here also consists of two parallel courses, the outer one of which is 4·20 m. broad, whilst the inner one, constructed of smaller stones, is only 1·0 m. broad. We have excavated the intermediate space behind the little portico J, about 3 m. deep down to the rock. It was filled with *débris* which probably has lain there since the construction of the wall. The northern part of the eastern wall is occupied by the great gate structure (H) which we have already described in Chap. V.

### 3. The Enclosure Wall of the Central Citadel (Z).

The central part of the castle, which, as distinguished from the great fore-court to the S. of the palace, may also be called the rear court-yard, lies, on an average, 2–3 m. lower than the

floor of the palace. Its *southern boundary wall* is the northern
enclosing wall of the palace, which has already been described,
and which contains the small stone staircase X. To the *east*,
the central citadel is bounded by a wall 6·80 m. broad, which
separates it from the main ascent. The northern portion of this
wall appears to have contained a gate. But in order to obtain
any certainty in this respect, the many blocks of stone lying
about there, would first have to be removed. The *northern limit*
of the rear court-yard is formed by the strong fortification wall
which separates the upper citadel from the lower one. A great
part of this wall, which on Plan 125 I have marked with a light
tint, is still covered with earth and shrubs, and can only be fully
brought to light together with the lower citadel. Possibly it
consists of two parallel wall-courses, separated from each other
by a narrow interstice. To the *west* we find, as a boundary wall
of the rear court-yard, in the northern half, a wall 5·55 m. broad,
with a mighty tower (W), of 11·60 m. breadth and 8·05 m.
depth, built out from it. The tower is unfortunately so much
destroyed that we have no means of deciding with certainty
whether it had a room in its interior, also—of which there are
some indications—corresponding to the tower A. Immediately
to the south of it, a small cistern (V) has been found, the sides
and bottom of which are even now partly covered with a coating
of loam : it is 2 m. to 2·20 m. broad and about 3 m. deep ; it lies
16·85 m. above the sea-level. The tower and the cistern form
the northern limit of the great stone staircase which we shall
describe in the following paragraph.

The south-western limit of the rear court-yard is formed by a
wall only 2 m. broad, but the base of which broadens by 3 m. on
the inside. Between this wall and the small cistern (V), the
boundary wall (Y) is still narrower and only very low. Here,
most likely, is the spot where the path formed by the great
staircase reached the central citadel.

## 4. THE SIDE ASCENT TO THE UPPER CITADEL.

Besides the chief carriage-way to the castle on the eastern
side, the recent excavations have brought to light, in the west, a
side ascent only serviceable for pedestrians. Its discovery has
already been shortly reported in discussing the course of the
excavations. Its situation and shape is to be seen from the
ground-plan (Fig. 125), from the transverse section (No. 130),

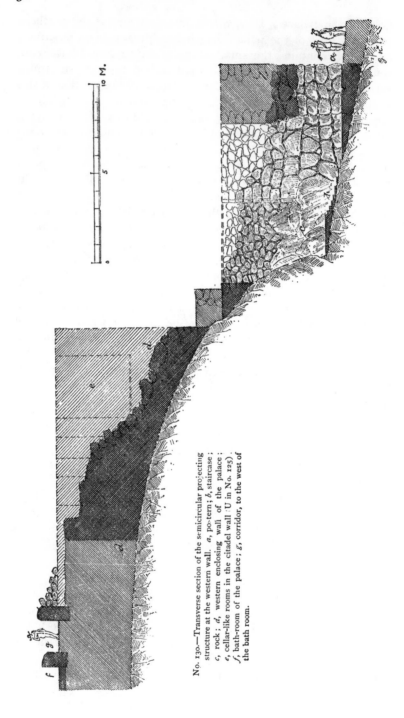

No. 130.—Transverse section of the semicircular projecting structure at the western wall. *a*, po-tern; *b*, staircase; *c*, rock; *d*, western enclosing wall of the palace; *e*, cellar-like rooms in the citadel wall (U in No. 125); *f*, bath-room of the palace; *g*, corridor, to the west of the bath room.

and from the perspective view (No. 131). The transverse section shows, to the right, the entrance gate (*a*) ; further, to the left, a section of the lowest steps of the staircase (*b*), with a view of the rocks (*c*) between which the staircase passes ; and it gives, quite to the left, a profile of the strong western wall of the palace (*d*), the preserved portion of which is hatched dark. Fig. 131, on the other hand, offers a glimpse of the staircase from the surface of the projecting semicircular structure : to the left is seen the outer

No. 131.—Perspective view from the crown of the semicircular projecting structure on the staircase of the lateral ascent. *a*, external citadel-wall ; *b*, rock ; *c*, lateral wall of the staircase ; *d*, enclosure wall of the palace.

embattled wall (*a*) ; in the centre, the staircase with the walls enclosing it ; to the right, above, the commencement of the great enclosure wall of the Palace (*d*).

One enters the side ascent near the little gate (T in the ground-plan) which occupies the centre of the semicircular structure. This gate was already known before ; only, it was not known whither it led. Outside it has a breadth of 2 m., which gradually decreases upwards, in the shape of a pointed arch. The passage of the wall which is 7·50 m. broad, is only vaulted for one-third of its length ; the remaining portion, as well as the whole remainder of the staircase, was uncovered. The breadth of the passage somewhat diminishes in the first third of its length ; afterwards, it gradually increases to 3·20 m. On entering the gate, the floor is at first found to be paved with large stones, and rises but very little. At a distance of 5·40 m. from the entrance, the *steps* commence. The two lowest ones are cut into the castle-rock ; all the others consist of limestone slabs, and are constructed like those in the passage D. The lowest part of the staircase lies E. and W., but it makes a bend at about the eighth step, and then takes a S.N. direction. The clear width, as far as the twentieth step, up to which the staircase is on both sides limited by the natural rock, is about 1·50 m. From there, it suddenly changes to 2·30 m. ; then gradually decreases to 1·75 m. ; again increases to 2·15 m., and at last, in its upper end (at the sixty-fifth step), amounts to 1·65 m. The rise of the step varies from 0·10 m. to 0·17 m., and amounts, in the mean, to 0·135 m. The lowest step lies 8·72 m., the topmost 17·50 m. above the sea. For the breadth of the tread of a step, 0·45 m. may be given as the average measurement.

Unfortunately, above the sixty-fifth step not a single step has been preserved *in situ*. The *further course of the staircase* might, therefore, be doubtful if, about 10 m. to the north of the last step, a wall had not come to light, in which a piece of the substructure of the staircase may, without much hesitation, be recognised. Its elevation is just sufficient to admit of the stair-case being carried on above it. In our Plan (Fig. 125) we, therefore, have drawn the dotted line, which is to mark the direction of the ascent, through the wall. This substructure is unfortunately only preserved for a length of 6½ m. Where it ends, every further vestige of the staircase ceases at the same time. We can consequently only make a surmise in trying to fix the end of the ascent. First of all, it is clear that the stair-case cannot have led further to the north, because there the small cistern V bars the way. Neither can it have had a north-eastern direction, because the wall east of the cistern is even now preserved to such a height that the staircase cannot have passed over it. The way must, therefore, certainly have made a bend to the east, and passed over the thin wall Y. The upper *edge* of the latter lies only 22·24 m. above the sea ; an altitude which the staircase could easily attain. I suspect that the wall Y is the remnant of a gate-structure through which the rear court-

yard of the palace could be entered. The little staircase X—
with which we are already acquainted from the excavations of
last year—afforded access to the interior of the palace itself.

At the place where the great staircase now ends—that is, at
the sixty-fifth step—a narrow path seems to have branched off to
the right, which, doubling back on the same level, formed an
approach to the semicircular projecting structure. This conjecture rests on the observation, that the eastern side-wall of the
staircase always remains at a distance of, at least, 2 m. from
the highly rising western revetment of the Palace, and that the
upper edge of the wall Φ—whose eastern arm perhaps forms a
buttress wall of the same path—lies exactly on a level with the
sixty-fifth step. The form of the surface of the semicircular
projecting structure is quite unknown. I only remark that the
highest point, in the best state of preservation at present, of the
projecting structure ($+ 17·46$ m.) still lies 9 m. below the floor
of the palace, and that therefore this projecting structure was
scarcely as high as the palace. Probably its height was not
much greater than we assumed in the profile (Fig. 130).

A further fact worthy of notice is, that in the inverted angle
of the wall Φ a very great number of the most ancient vases,
fragments of ancient painted wall-plaster, and other objects have
been found. The whole corner was filled with all kinds of
things as compactly as the chamber near the bath-room, described
on p. 234 ; and in ancient days this must have been a place
for depositing broken vases, fallen wall-plastering, and the like.

If, lastly, we ask ourselves why the builder of Tiryns has—in
addition to the main ascent to the upper citadel on the eastern
side—constructed this side ascent on the west, we cannot doubt
that they were chiefly reasons of fortification which induced him
to do so. But for the wants of daily life in times of peace also,
an ascent on the western side, turned towards the sea, must
have been very desirable. In any case, the builder has admirably
solved the task set before him. For, the staircase rose to the
rear court-yard of the palace on the shortest line by closely
hugging the rock and the castle wall. Moreover, a strong
embattled wall which followed exactly the same direction, protected it against all hostile attack. The situation and breadth
of this wall is shown in the ground-plan.

### 5. THE MAIN ASCENT TO THE CASTLE.

The reader is already acquainted with the main ascent on the
eastern side of the upper citadel, from the fifth chapter (p. 187 *seq.*)
What was said there, has been completely confirmed by the new
excavations.   This was the only way to the upper citadel available for carriages and horses.   In order to reach the considerable
height of 20 m. by an easy gradient the builder commenced the
ascending causeway as far as possible in the north, then carried
it on along the whole eastern side of the upper citadel, and made
it debouch in the fore-court lying at the southern end of the
citadel.   The first part of this road was a ramp buttressed by a
strong wall, which lay outside the castle, and had externally no
special embattled wall.   The upper part, however, was protected
by an outer wall.   The form of the latter, although not cleared
up in some particulars, is now known in its main features, as
shown on Plan No. 125.

The most important piece of this wall-course is that which
contains the stately *gallery* (R).   We have already mentioned
that this gallery, too, is joined on the outside by six chambers (P).   In their arrangement and construction, these rooms
fully harmonise with those in the southern wall ; only in regard
to their dimensions they somewhat differ from them.   Their
breadth, on an average, is 3·05 m. ; the width of their party-
walls, 1·70 m. ; whilst the corresponding dimensions in the
southern wall are 3·30 m., and 1·90 m.   The depth of the
chambers can unfortunately not be fixed, because in not a single
one has the slightest remnant of the outer boundary wall been
preserved.   We therefore, in our Plan, have marked the inner
part of the outer wall only with a light hatching.   But as we are
able to measure the depth of the chamber including the outer
wall (the measurement is 6·05 m.), and as we may assume that
it was, at least, about as broad as in the rooms of the southern
wall (2·75 m.), it results that the probable depth of the chambers
was $6·05 - 2·75 = 3·30$ m.

The reconstructed *profile* of the *eastern wall*, given on
Plate III., below, to the left, may now be supplemented as follows ;
namely, above the under-wall, a section is drawn through the
chamber similar to that shown by the cross-section through the
southern wall (No. 126).   We have abstained from indicating
this redintegration here and giving a new restored cross-section
of the eastern wall, because there are no data whatever for fixing

its upper limit, and because it cannot be the object of this book to offer fanciful reconstructions. The fact of a colonnade having been built on the wall, is certainly assured by the existence of the bases of the columns ; but it is completely unknown where the hinder wall of this hall lay, and whether, besides the colonnade, there were rooms on the top of the wall, and a separate wall-way with parapets.

In No. 132, we, however, give a picture of the *present condition* of the well-preserved eastern gallery (R.). It offers a view, from the south, into the gallery. At the right wall of the passage, six doors (*a*) are still to be recognised, which lead to the chambers. Through the first door, one looks into one of the latter, where a piece of the party-wall (*b*) is still recognisable between the first and the second chamber. The last door is situated directly at the hinder boundary-wall.

South of this magazine, the wall still contains a rectangular room (Q), which is accessible from no side, and therefore probably formed a *cistern*. This room only came to light on the last day of the excavations, and therefore could not be fully cleared out. Like the cistern V, it contained almost nothing but red brick *débris*.

As the floor of the chambers lies about 5·30 below the threshold of the great Propylæum, a *staircase* must, of old, have led to the magazine in the eastern wall. By analogy with the staircase existing in the southern wall we may assume that it led, from the door Σ, westward along the wall which has been uncovered, and that, perhaps, it ended within the small colonnade (J). Both magazines, the one in the eastern wall as well as the one in the southern wall, were consequently in direct connection with the great fore-court. It is true, we have not found any further trace of this staircase ; this part of the castle wall being in the worst state of destruction. A few wall-fragments which we had drawn, at this place, in Plan I. were found, during the recent diggings, to have been modern structures, probably erected by herdsmen ; for they had no foundations. Hence we had to be content, for the present, with indicating the wall by dotted lines. It will be necessary to dig yet deeper than we have done, in order, here also, to discover the remnants of the castle wall.

The great destruction of almost all the antique walls at this spot may, however, be explained by the circumstance of the magazine of the eastern wall having for centuries been used as a

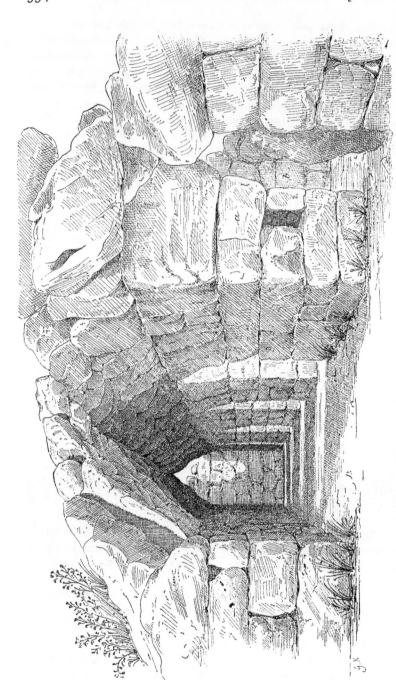

No. 132.—View into the gallery of the eastern wall.   *a*, doors to the chambers;   *b*, partition-walls of the chambers.

fold for sheep, and that, for this object, an ascent had to be formed from the south by pulling down the antique walls. The favour in which the cool underground room must always have been held by the herdsmen of Argolis, is shown by the fact of nearly all the sharp angles of the lower stone-layers in the interior of the gallery having been rubbed down by the sheep, and several stones being smoothly polished on their whole outer surface.

In Chapter V. (p. 187) we have already explained that, in antiquity, no main ascent can have existed at the S.E. corner of the castle. The new excavations have only confirmed these statements. If an ascent existed here, it can only have been a lateral ascent, by means of winding stairs taking several turns, owing to the great variations in the ground. But most probably, there was no ascent at all at the S.E. corner of the castle.

## B.—TECHNICAL REMARKS.

As building material for the strong castle walls and the thinner walls of the Palace, *limestone* was chiefly used, quarried in the two mountains in the neighbourhood of Tiryns. There are *two different kinds of this stone ;* one of which has a light grey, the other a reddish, colour in its inner parts   Whilst the former is very hard and extremely weather-proof, there are, among the red stones, many which in the course of ages have become very rotten, and are no longer able to bear a heavy strain. Probably, therefore, it was those red limestones which led to the falling-in of most of the stone ceilings and the destruction of many a wall. A single stone only had to be decomposed by the action of the air, in order to bring about the fall of all those lying above it, and subsequently of the whole upper portion of the wall. At several corners we, therefore, replaced the red limestones which had deteriorated, by cement.

In the old quarries of Tiryns, the blocks of stone were probably loosened by metal wedges or simple pickaxes ; the limestone rock being stratified in pretty regular layers, and very loosely. *Bored holes,* which are found in several blocks of the castle wall, prove however that the stones were partly obtained by other methods. Two such stones are shown in Nos. 133 and 134. In the one, the hole is in the centre of a face ; in the other, right in the corner. We suppose that the holes, as well as the mortices in the pilaster blocks, were made with *wimbles ;* then

filled with dry sticks of wood ; and that finally, by wetting the
wood, the stones were cleft.

In regard to the *manner* in which the great blocks of stone
were wrought, it may be seen from those pieces of wall, which

No. 133.—Stone with a bore-hole.          No. 134.—Stone with a bore-hole.

are but little decomposed, and which have only now been brought
to light, that the separate stones had, after all, been more dressed
than was hitherto supposed.   Almost all the stones, before being
used, had been wrought on one or several faces, with a pick-

No. 135.—Portion of the western citadel-wall.

hammer.   In this way, some of the stones have received a better
lower bed ; others a smooth facing.   Thus, the walls of Tiryns
must not be spoken of as being composed of unhewn, but of
roughly dressed stones.

PLATE XII.

**WALL PAINTING IN THE PALACE OF TIRYNS**

In treating of the Tower A (p. 318), we have already pointed to the important fact, that *all the walls of Tiryns are built with clay-mortar*, and that this mortar, wherever it is wanting now in the joints, has been removed by rain or other agencies. Only in a few foundations, do the stones seem to have been joined without mortar.

The *horizontal arrangement* of the blocks of stone has been effected in the outer walls more regularly than is usually assumed. In most places, the several layers of stone run in pretty exact horizontal lines. As a characteristic example of such a regular style of building, a fragment of the western wall (No. 135) may serve. On the other hand, a second picture (No. 136) shows a wall fragment in which the layers do not all run right through ; the bonding being an irregular one.

In regard to the *sawing* of the stones used for the interior of the Palace, we have observed at one of the thresholds (south of the bath-room) that the sawing was only done after the stone had already been put in its proper place. For, at this threshold, one of the incisions made by the saw has also touched the basement stone which lies next to it.

## C.—SUPPLEMENTS TO CHAPTER V.

### I. THE ALTAR IN THE COURT-YARD OF THE MEN'S APART-MENTS.

In discussing the Doric capital (pp. 293, 294) I mentioned a rudely constructed wall, of late date, which was built right across the great court-yard, and into which that capital had been inserted. As the wall did not even reach down to the floor of the court-yard, it must have been of not very remote, perhaps even modern, origin. We, therefore, did not hesitate to pull it down, only leaving a piece standing above the altar, so that later visitors to Tiryns should also be able to examine the shape and situation of the wall. This mural fragment, standing as it does on a broad layer of earth, was the cause of our having over-looked, last year, an important part of the altar.

During this year's excavations I by chance observed after a heavy rain that, in the centre of the altar, some round stones were lying under the later wall. I at once had the wall removed ; and to our surprise, a circular opening, 1·16–1·21 m. in diameter, and surrounded by a layer of sandstone, made its

appearance.  At first we thought that our altar must, after all, have been a cistern, or a well.  But when we had the central

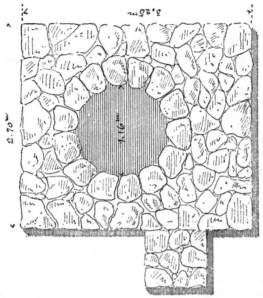

No. 137.—Ground-plan of the altar (sacrificial pit).

hole excavated, it was found that the circular masonry only reached to a depth of 0·90 m.  Further down, there were neither

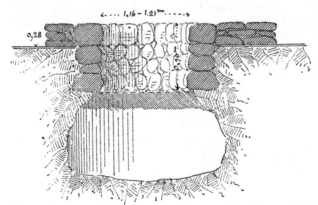

No. 138.—Transverse section of the sacrificial pit.

side-walls of masonry, nor any artificial floor.  As the hole, consequently, could by no means have been either a cistern or a

well, it must have been a *sacrificial pit*.  I cannot offer any
other explanation.

The present aspect of the structure is shown in Figs. 137
and 138.  The first gives the ground-plan, the latter a section.
The central ring of the ground-plan is formed of sandstone ;
the square surrounding it, of small slabs of limestone.    The
ring seems to be older than the square ; for, as may be seen
from the cross-section, the floor of the court-yard reaches below
the outer limestone masonry.

Leaving the conclusions to be drawn from this discovery to
more competent men, I will only mention that similar sacrificial
pits have been found in the Asklepion at Athens (Köhler,
*Mittheilungen des Athenischen Instituts ;* II. p. 233), and in
Samothrake (*Untersuchungen auf Samothrake ;* I. p. 20, and
II. p. 21).

## 2. The Gate of the Men's Court.

### (K, on Plan No. 125.)

In describing this gate structure (p. 201), we pointed out
that, in its southern vestibule, there was no longer any base of a
column *in situ*.   Since the winter rains have thoroughly cleansed
the walls, it is now seen that, after all, the eastern base of the
two columns does exist.   It is certainly very much damaged,
and therefore scarcely recognisable as a base ; nevertheless, its
identity does not seem to me doubtful.   Our reconstruction of
the Gate is fully confirmed by this find.   To the south of the
vestibule there were probably one or two steps ; in this way, the
foundation projecting to the south, in front of the columns, is
best explained.

## 3. The Megaron of the Men.

Dr. Philios, who during last winter, by order of the Greek
Government, covered the floors of the palace with earth to
the height of 10–20 cm., in order to preserve them, pointed
out to me that, in the interior of the Megaron, at the northern
rear-wall, twelve circles were visible in the floor.   He conjectured
that these circles may have been the standing-places for twelve
chairs.   In consequence of this communication I also examined
those circles.   Over the painted plaster-floor a coarse mortar

has been laid ; and in this mortar, circles are visible, which can clearly be traced as being produced by terra-cotta vases. At the rear-wall of the Megaron, a row of large jars (*pithoi*) seems to have stood. But it is not possible to decide whether this was already the case in the oldest times, when the Megaron was still a single great hall, or whether the *pithoi* were only set up after the Megaron had been entirely reconstructed (compare p. 229).

### 4. A Drain.

To the drains hitherto known, and described in Chapter V., a new one has to be added. In the small room to the west of the vestibule of the Megaron, there is one half of a great square slab of sandstone, in which is a round hole, 0·51 m. in diameter. Under the hole there is a low vertical shaft which opens below into a horizontal drain. I suppose that this drain is identical with the one proceeding from the bath-room, and I have therefore united both on Plan 125 by a dotted line.

### 5. The Roof-Tiles of Terra-cotta.

Whilst during the excavations of 1884, terra-cotta tiles were only found here and there, in the neighbourhood of the Byzantine Church, we have met with such tiles very often this year, in the rubbish lying outside the Castle. They were most numerous near the lateral ascent on the western side ; and they were, all of them, simple bent tiles, of bad make, such as are still used in Greece. They are probably from a later Greek building, erected at the place where the great stone staircase now ends. It need not be said that this fact in no way affects the statement repeatedly made in Chapter V., that within the Palace proper no tiles were found, and that therefore the Palace was most likely covered with horizontal earth-roofs.

### 6. Additional Wall-paintings.

We have already mentioned (p. 331), that close to the wall marked Φ in Plan 125, at the top of the semicircular projecting structure on the western side, numerous fragments of ancient vases and wall-plastering were found. Most of these stucco fragments show painted ornamentation, which corresponds

to the specimens discussed in Chapter V., and represented on
Plates V.—XII.  Thus there were, among these, fragments of
the spiral ornament (Plate V.) which also occurs in the *tholos*
(ceiled roof) of Orchomenos ; pieces of the great wings (Plate
VII.), which we attribute to a sphinx-like being ; lastly, also
some new pieces of the star-fish represented on Plate X. *b*.
Among the recently found ornaments, the two fragments Nos.
139 and 140 are especially noteworthy.  On a yellow ground
is represented a black-bordered white leaf which contains
black and red stalks and flowers, or leaflets.  The large
leaf grows from a black and white-edged blue border.  In the

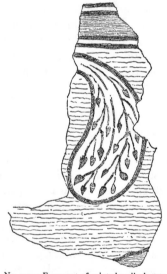

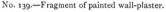

No. 139.—Fragment of painted wall-plaster.    No. 140.—Fragment of painted wall-plaster.

smaller fragment, two blue and black pencilled feathers join the
leaf.  The latter seem to belong to some large winged creature ;
for, a great many fragments of the same kind were found, which
however, unfortunately, do not fit into each other.

The fragment shown in Fig. 141 merits mention because it
has formed the lower end of a wall.  It contains many parallel,
party-coloured stripes, arranged in the following succession :
white ; blue ; white ; red ; blue with black strokes ; yellow with
red strokes ; and lastly, a black drawing on yellow ground.  What
the latter represents, cannot be made out.  The two last stripes
but one recur in similar manner in many of the wall-paintings

which we have represented; but nowhere are they executed so regularly as in this case.   That is to say: at certain fixed

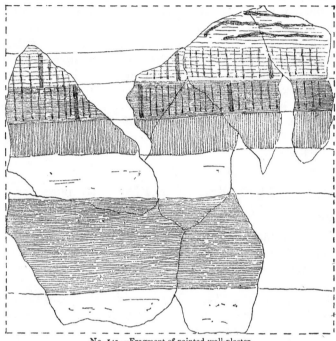

No. 141.—Fragment of painted wall-plaster.

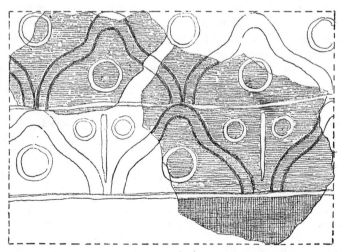

No. 142.—Fragment of painted wall-plaster.

intervals the little *thin* lines are replaced by broader ones ; the red and black broad lines alternating regularly.

In Fig. 142, lastly, a fragment is shown, which represents, in three different specimens, the ornament shown on Plate XI. It varies but very little from these in the form of the ornamentation (the little vertical cross-lines are wanting); but the distribution of colours is quite different. Whilst the lower broad stripe is a dark red, the ground of the ornament shows a bright-red colour ; the two strokes of the scale-like ornament are black, the little circles and lines within the scales white. Very noteworthy is the simultaneous occurrence of two different shades of the red colour ; a fact hitherto not yet observed among the other monumental paintings.

## D.—THE SEPARATE FINDS IN 1885.

### By DR. ERNST FABRICIUS.

The excavation of the Royal Palace of Tiryns, in the summer of 1884, had yielded an abundance of interesting separate finds, more especially as regards terra-cotta vases more or less completely preserved, on which Dr. Schliemann has treated in Chapters III. and IV. When the old fortress walls of the upper citadel were more completely brought to light in the summer of 1885, great masses of fragments of terra-cotta vases, together with not a few noteworthy objects made of other material, were again discovered. These new finds, although far less important than those of the first excavation campaign, still supplement and amplify the results already obtained, so that it seems desirable to offer a short survey of them.*

I. POTTERY.—The excavation works of the second year had simply for their object the clearance and bringing to light of the

---

* In making the notes required for the present report in the only two days that were at my disposal, it was unfortunately impossible to refer to the finds made last year ; much less—as ought to have been done—to institute a comparison with the new finds *in loco*. By order of the Greek Government, the insignificant objects found— especially the smaller vase fragments, filling eight or ten baskets—were sent to the Museum at Charvati (Mycenæ), whilst all the more valuable pieces—at present preserved in the Polytechnicum at Athens—were not yet rendered accessible. Again, as the report had to be written in Asia Minor, I could neither look into the detailed description of the finds of 1884, given by Dr. Schliemann, nor make use of any literary material. The references and arguments, drawn simply from memory or from casual notes, have therefore, of necessity, turned out very meagre. My friend, Dr. Koepp, at Athens, was kind enough to add some quotations.

fortifications.　It is, therefore, easy to understand that—whereas, during the uncovering of the Palace, a larger number of complete vessels, as well as of magnificent fragments fitting into each other, had been discovered—the new finds of vases consisted almost exclusively of small fragments accidentally scattered among the masses of *débris* under which the old walls had until lately been hidden.　The endeavour to find pieces belonging to each other was attended with success in but few cases.　On the other hand, as regards quantity, the recently-found material is comparatively little inferior to the vase-finds of last year.　Whole mounds of potsherds had been heaped up on the site of the excavation.　For days, some workmen were busy cleaning them, so far as was possible.

The sifting of these masses of larger and smaller potsherds, which had to be undertaken in order to make a selection of the serviceable fragments, at once gave occasion for purely statistical observation, which claims attention before we discuss individual objects found.

Setting aside a considerable number of very beautiful frag-ments of Byzantine vases,* at once recognisable by their shape and make, the whole material exhibited a very noteworthy uniformity.　Among a thousand fragments of earthenware which is usually designated as Mycenæan, scarcely a single fragment of a more recent kind occurs.　And these potsherds of later make decrease numerically in the same proportion as the time of their certain or probable origin recedes from the art-epoch of the "Mycenæan" vases.

A short survey of the fragments belonging to the later period of fictile art, will serve to prove the fact just mentioned— a fact of some importance for the history of Tiryns.

Let us begin with the pieces of the latest make.　Of fragments of red-figured Greek vases, scarcely anything has been found. A few small potsherds, on which only the black varnish was well preserved, are the solitary representatives of that *tech-nique* from the best days of Greek vase manufacture.　It is scarcely otherwise with the black-figured vases: here, too, a single fragment is to be noted, on which two horse-legs have

---

* These Byzantine vases, the insides of which are mostly covered with a yellow or green glaze and decorated with Byzantine ornaments and figures, but which are unglazed outside, were nearly all found in graves and in the neighbourhood of the Byzantine Church.　In the galleries also, they came to light here and there. (D.)

been preserved.   In the same way, potsherds of vases of Corinthian type are very rare.   A small but unmistakeable fragment,
showing the front of an animal's head (black and reddish-brown
on yellow ground, the drawing etched in), leaves however no
doubt as to its occurrence.

In greater number there appear, first, potsherds of a peculiar
species of little vases, whose system of decoration is characterised
by thin parallel lines, drawn by the potter's wheel in brilliant
red or yellowish-brown varnish on a finely polished shining
yellow ground.   The best preserved piece of this kind, that has
come to light in the excavations, is shown in the adjoining engraving, No. 143, at about half its real size.   It is the lower

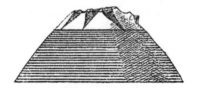

No. 143.—Vase-fragment with brown parallel lines.

portion of a small bottle with flat bottom, made very finely
and lightly of yellowish clay (breadth 0·065 ; preserved height
0·030 m.).   The painting is brown.   The neck and the handle
are broken off.   But the joint of the handle is preserved.   Of
the neck, round the fracture, the decoration of the lowest portion
(composed of six leaflets turned downwards) is still to be seen.
The body of the bottle is decorated with twenty-two parallel
lines, drawn with admirable regularity by means of the potter's
wheel.   A bottle of quite the same shape is known from Sicily,
where the only hitherto published specimens of this kind of vase
have as yet been found : it is represented in the *Annali dell'
Instituto* 1877, tavol. ag. C D 1.   The other Sicilian vessels shown
on that Plate, and which are as remarkable in shape as in their
decorative style, are also matched by a moderate number of
quite similar fragments found in Tiryns.   Besides Sicily, this
kind of vases occurs in Ægina and Eleusis, where I found
them, in company with Dr. Ferdinand Dümmler, who recognised
their conformity with those Sicilian fragments.

Most of the Tirynthian vase fragments, which are not of the
specially Mycenæan sort, belong to vessels of the geometrical
system of decoration : in particular, to that kind which is represented by the Dipylon vases.   A large number of fragments

which only came to light in the excavations of the second campaign, need not be discussed separately here, because these
fragments evidently belong to vessels the same as, or kindred to,
those of which Dr. Schliemann had already found fragments
in the first year of the excavations, and which he has described
and shown in the present work.

Of such vases also which, so to say, form the first step in
the decorative system of the Dipylon vases, and which indicate
the connection between the latter and the vases peculiar to
Mycenæ and Tiryns, the number of fragments has been increased
by a few specimens. Thus, for instance, a new large fragment
has been found of the vessel shown in Plate XVIII., on which
horses are represented, with fishes between their legs.

The same numerical proportion in which the potsherds
of the Ægineto-Sicilian kind, and of the Dipylon vases, stand
to the great mass of the vase fragments found, recurs among
the remnants of that very old, monochromatic pottery, of
which Dr. Schliemann has already treated, when discussing
in Chapter III., p. 70 *et seq.*, a number of such specimens
belonging to last year's finds.

We now turn to the remnants, so surprisingly predominant
in Tiryns, of that vase manufacture the products of which, from
their peculiar mode of decoration, have been called vases in the
"naturalistic" style, chiefly illustrated by the finds at Mycenæ,
Nauplia, Spata, Ialysos, and Knossos.

I. First, as regards shape, we again, among the finds of this
year, meet with a large number of the very peculiar, so-called
stirrup-can (see p. 138, No. 57). It is a nearly ball-shaped vessel,
with a stirrup-like handle, which in the centre of the top is provided with a support. Lower down, at the side of the central
support of the handle, there is the spout. This vessel occurs in
all the places above mentioned, and is thoroughly characteristic
of that whole epoch of vase manufacture. Among the potsherds
inspected by me I have counted fragments of at least *nineteen*
specimens. Whilst the differences of size are trifling (diameter
up to 0·15 m., breadth of the stirrups 0·07–0·08 m.), the painting (concentric circles in the centre of the stirrup-handle; also,
concentric circular arcs on the top of the support; also concentric circular arcs on the shoulder; and horizontal lines and
stripes on the body of the vessel) is sometimes red, sometimes
reddish-brown; or black.

In comparison with the results of last year, a whole series of

new finds has been made, consisting of fragments of large jars
which show the same shape of the handle and the spout as the
stirrup-jugs, but with a much slenderer form. The original
height of these jars must have been between 0·40 and 0·50 m.
The breadth of the stirrup-handle, of which alone I have
counted eleven different specimens, measures, on an average,
0·20 m. The clay of these vessels is generally but slightly
washed. The painting, consisting of lines lightly painted round
the handle and the spout, is restricted to horizontal stripes and
wave-lines on the body. A splendid specimen of such a stirrup-
jar is in the collection of the Archæological Society of Athens
(No. 1944). It is from Crete ; 0·40 m. high ; and shows, in red
colour on yellowish ground, a large marine creature (an octopus),
whose wave-like twisted tentacles surround the whole of the
vessel. Several specimens of the same shape and size, but only
decorated with large wave-lines, quite similar to those tentacles,
are known to me from Knossos, whence the specimen now at
Athens may also have come.

Just as the stirrup-jug is very frequent in the epoch of
vase-manufacture of which we are here treating, but afterwards
wholly disappears, so there is a second form of vessel, almost
exclusively to be met with at the places above mentioned.
It is a funnel-shaped goblet on a high, thin, cylindrically
formed stem, broadening into a wide foot, and with one or
two little ears on both sides near the upper rim (comp.
Schliemann's *Mycenæ*, p. 233, No. 343 ; p. 350, No. 528 ; and
above, p. 117, No. 27, Plate XXI. *f, et seq.*). In Tiryns, this
type occurs in two kinds, differing from each other in size and
painted ornamentation. The larger sort (height about 0·25 m.),
of which there were comparatively few specimens (ten or twelve,
all of them only recognisable by fragments) shows horizontal
stripes on the cylindrical part of the stem, and on the foot (which
is about 0·10 m. in diameter) mostly three or four concentric
rings in reddish-brown painting. On the upper rim of the goblet
there is either a thin line, or a row of dots, whilst the centre of
the vessel, between the ears, is decorated on both sides either by
a rosette of the forms shown here (No. 144), or by one of those
ornaments so characteristic of this whole epoch—the so-called
purple-fish, *murex* (Schliemann's *Mycenæ*, p. 138 ; *Tiryns*, Plate
XXII. *b*, p. 109, Nos. 24, 25).

II. The second, smaller sort of goblets occurs in Tiryns in
*hundreds* of specimens ; unfortunately all of them, without

exception, broken. Their height, on an average, is only one-half of the first sort, but varies much according to the more or less slender shape. The clay is, throughout, a light-yellow, and finely washed. Of painting, there is no trace.

In regard to the smaller fragments, it is in most cases scarcely possible to decide whether they belonged to goblets of the first

No. 144.—Rosettes of different form.

sort, or to a kind of deep bowl uncommonly frequent in Tiryns. These latter, a few specimens of which Dr. Schliemann has discussed on p. 135, Nos. 52, 53 *et seq.* (comp. Plate XXIV. *c*, p. 118) are of an average height of o·10 m. They are provided with two ears, placed about halfway; and the sides of the vessels are always made of very thin, well-washed clay, generally of a yellowish colour; and they show a twofold system of painting. That is to say: they have either rosettes between the ears, as is the case with some specimens shown by Dr. Schliemann in this work; or a horizontal border of delicate parallel lines, like a frieze, marks off, on the upper side, a neck-piece, which is divided by two vertical stripes on each side between the ears, into rectangular squares. The last-named stripes consist of vertical lines, between which are drawn waved or zigzag lines, met at the outside by smaller or larger semicircles.

2. The fragments of larger vases are, almost without exception, so small that the original shape of the vessels in question is no longer distinguishable. They are therefore only interesting on account of the *ornamentation* preserved on them.

When treating of the cups, we mentioned that ornament, so characteristic of the whole Mycenæan class of vases, which is composed of straight and curved lines and dots, and which has been explained as an imitation of the purple-fish (Plate XXII. *b*). In Tiryns this ornament also appears on fragments of large vessels with thick sides, the thickness of which is, of course, always proportionate to the size of the vessel. New to us, on the other hand, is an ornament which has great affinity with the purple-fish (I am only using this expression for shortness' sake), and which—together with the latter, though not quite so richly elaborate, but in that simpler form, of which the fragment on

Plate XXII. *a* shows a sample—occurs also on a cup from
Attica (No. 2078 of the collection of the Archæological Society
at Athens). This splendid ornament, two fragments of which
are shown in No. 145 *a* and *b*, was repeated at least twice, and
is carefully drawn in dark-brown, on a large vessel of reddish
clay, 6–7 mm. thick. Seven fragments—among them, two of
the upper rim of the vessel, under which the ornament is placed—
allow a nearly complete reconstruction of its original shape. We
gather therefrom that a support, formed of six vertical lines
which are joined outwardly by small semicircles, upholds a
horizontal ornament, reminding one of the shape of the Ionic
capital. Above this, there is an elaborate finish of concentric

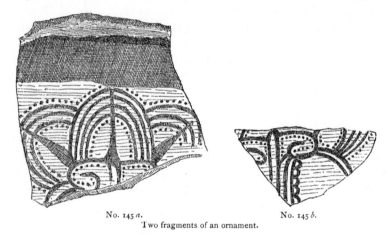

No. 145 *a*.                    No. 145 *b*.
Two fragments of an ornament.

arcs, three of which occur twice and four once (viz., in the
centre); combined with rows of dots, and strongly accentuated
middle lines.

The origin of this ornament, as before mentioned, has been
connected, on that Attic vessel, with the supposed purple-fish.
I, for my part, rather see in it an adaptation of types from
the vegetable world. As to the decoration of a second, also
very large, vessel with wide mouth, of which two middling-sized
fragments have been preserved, its origin might perhaps be
proved to be an animal type, albeit the patterns themselves
allow the supposition of a vegetable prototype. Those fragments (No. 146 *a* and *b*) have a thickness of 5 mm. The
clay is light-red, and very well polished on the surface The
painting is of a dark-brown colour. The fragments allow of a
row of stripes being recognised, which end in fan-like spread

spirals. In the spandrels between the border (relieved by a coloured stripe) and the spirals, one of those rosettes of concentric circles is observable, surrounded by a border of dots, which form, in similar or little-varied shape, the permanent orna-

No. 145 a.                       No. 146 b.
Two fragments of an ornament.

ment of so many bowls and cups in Tiryns. As to interpreting that fragment, there is at least a possibility of doing so by comparison with a large jar from Spata, preserved in the collection of

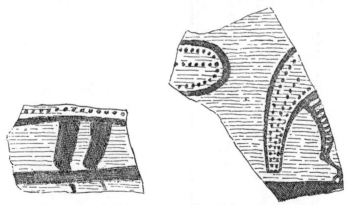

No. 147.—Legs of a bird.          No. 148.—Fragments of two birds.

the Archæological Society at Athens (shown in the *Bulletin de Correspondance Hellénique*, II., 1873, Plate XIX.). Between each of the three handles of this jar, a large marine creature is represented, somewhat similar to the octopus, which widely extends its four upper tentacles (the lower ones are not preserved), ending as spirals. Perhaps, therefore, those stripes ending as spirals, on

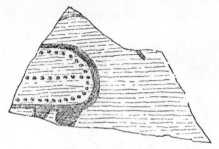

No. 149.—Body of a bird.

the potsherds of Tiryns, are also to be looked upon as tentacles of a marine creature.

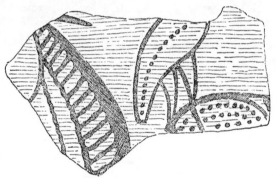

No. 150.—Fragments of various animals.

At the side of those fantastic transformations, for decorative purposes, of prototypes from the vegetable and animal world,

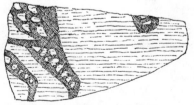

No. 151.—Fragment of a horse.

there appear however, in addition, on numerous fragments, figures chiefly of animals, in faithful imitation of nature.

PLATE XIII.

WALL PAINTING IN THE PALACE OF TIRYNS, REPRESENTING A MAN DANCING ON A BULL.

Unfortunately, among the recently-found vase fragments, there are scarcely any larger pieces which would permit of those figures being fully recognised. We see swans, turned to the right, the head bent downward, the body adorned with a series of dots;

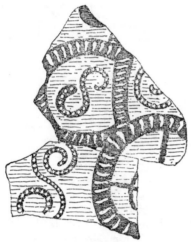

No. 152.—Fragment of a chariot.

as well as other aquatic birds and horses, whose bodies are covered as with scales (Nos. 147–151). Again, there are fragments of those richly-ornamented vessels on which warriors are

No. 153.—Vase-fragment with a horse-head and warrior.

No. 154.—Vase-fragment with horse-feet.

represented, each dressed in a skin the tail of which is visible between the legs of the warrior (Plate XIV. p. 103); portions of chariots (No. 152), and dogs running to the right (*ibidem*): all

executed in red and red-brown colour, and the whole adorned
with white dots and stripes.

Very noteworthy in style are two fragments which seem to
be a portion of one and the same large vase (yellowish clay, dark
red-brown painting ; the inside of the vessel was coloured all
over). The fragments are shown in Nos. 153 and 154. One of
them is a portion of the rim : it shows, below the stripe which
runs round the rim — to the right if I do not mistake—the

No. 155.—Vase-fragment with a warrior and a chariot.

head, arm, and shield of a warrior ; to the left, the head of a
horse (?) with the bridle. On the other fragment the fore-legs of
a horse galloping to the left are clearly distinguishable. Compare the vase from Mycenæ in Schliemann's *Mycenæ*, Plate X.,
No. 47.*

In the great mass of the other potsherds, only a few ornaments,
already known from other sources, can be distinguished. A short
notice will, therefore, suffice. First of all, there appear, in many
hundreds of specimens, the spirals in every shade of colour—
from red to yellow on the one hand, and black on the other.
(Comp. p. 110, *et seq.*) Most of those spirals served to ornament large bowls. They were, in part, not simply strung
together, but the outer ends of the twisted line were bent apparently into a loop. Next to the spirals, we may mention the
peculiar ornament of curved lines, which sometimes net-wise
covers a whole vessel—as may be seen in the splendid vessel
shown in Plate XXVII. *a*, which the excavations of last year have
brought to light. Among the wall-paintings also (on Plate XI.)
the same ornament occurs. On p. 124 *et seq.* Dr. Schliemann

---

* Later on, the most remarkable potsherd of the same style, shown in No. 155,
was still found. Two teams, placed one above the other, are represented so that the
hind-legs of one of the horses above (of a second, no trace is preserved) stand on the
extended left arm of the man who stands on the lower carriage, with couched lance.

has already pointed out the many analogies of this kind of decoration among the finds of Ialysos, Spata, Nauplia, and Knossos. The potsherds found in the two excavation campaigns show that the same ornament has likewise been used in Tiryns— as in those other places—merely as a simple stripe, and not in net-like continuation. Sometimes it appears in Tiryns as a simple curved line ; sometimes doubled or trebled. In the interspaces (spandrels) between the upper edge of the whole stripe and the individual leaves (for as such, I assume, the members of the ornament have to be regarded¹, as well as inside the leaves themselves, there are concentric circles, corner ornaments, and so forth. (Compare Plates XI. and XXII. c ; also, No. 141.)

A further noteworthy circumstance is, that on potsherds, especially on those of smaller vessels (there were fragments before me of at least thirteen vases), there is frequently to be seen the border ornament, consisting exclusively of a series of N strung together. The proof of the extensive use of this peculiar ornamentation is thus furnished. New to us, in Tiryns, however, is a fragment on which a stripe of ornamentally joined Ǝ has been preserved (dull black colour on yellow ground ; the vessel of red clay).

What were, without doubt, most frequently met with, were the potsherds with remnants of a painting, the system of which —an alternation of jambs and of ornaments merely used for filling in, distributed over a frieze-like stripe—may justly be called an architectonic one, on account of its likeness to the Doric triglyph frieze, as pointed out by Dr. Schliemann. A special discussion of those potsherds may be omitted here, as there is nothing essentially new among the finds of the second excavation campaign.


### 3. OTHER FINDS. TERRA-COTTA OBJECTS.

Again a large number of clay idols has come to light, which with the exception of a single new type, appearing in three specimens, repeat the forms known from Mycenæ and from the former excavations of Tiryns. Those new idols are small conical clay figures, only about 0·03 m. high, ending trilaterally above, and slightly bevelled on the upper surface (see No. 156). One of the three sides of the top is pierced. The whole was conse- quently intended to be hung up, and was perhaps worn as an amulet. Four or five horizontal lines are the only ornamentation of this most primitive work of art.  Numerous figures of animals also have again been found, which fully correspond to the specimen shown on Plate XXIV.

To a probably much later time belongs a roughly-made

No. 156.—Idol for suspension.          No. 157.—Two figures sitting on a couch, of terra-cotta.

terra-cotta group (No. 157).  It represents a man reposing on a couch ; to the left, at his feet, sits a woman, *en face*, with her garment thrown over the back of her head, exactly as on the relievos of late Greek art, which represent the so-called

No. 158.—Weight of terra-cotta with a number.

funeral meal.  The group is o·095 m. long ; o·085 m. high ; made of red clay, and open below.  The head of the man is half broken off.  Deserving of notice is, lastly, the clay weight (shown in Fig. 158) with a neatly engraved sign, resembling an Arabic 4 turned upside down.

BRONZES.—The number of bronzes found during this year's excavations is again very small.   Special mention is to be made of the upper part of the leg of a medium-sized tripod, 0·11 m. long, to which the plate (0·6 m. broad, 0·05 m. deep, but not thoroughly preserved) is still attached, with which the leg was joined to the kettle of the tripod.   The rivets which served for the junction of both the plate and the kettle also still exist. The tripod was of the same size and form as that of Mycenæ, the well-known prototype of the numerous tripods of Olympia, Delos, and Krete.   The Mycenæan tripod was found in the fourth tomb, and is shown in Schliemann's *Mycenæ* (No. 440).

Furthermore, a bronze ear-ring is to be mentioned, formed of a wire-ring (diameter : 38 mm.), adapted for opening and locking below, and on one half of which three little balls—at a distance of about twice their diameter—are represented ; each ball being composed of two hollow hemispheres.   Similar ear-pendants—complete sets, of gold, silver, and bronze—are in the collection of the Archæological Society at Athens.   Lastly, we mention a part of a heavy object—0·13 m. long, 0·06 m. broad—formed like a lance-point, and rounded off as if it were to be fixed to a pole.   Though of bronze, it might probably have served as a plough-share.

## E.—THE FIND OF TERRA-COTTA OBJECTS MADE AT THE SOUTH-EAST CORNER OF THE CASTLE.

During the last days of the excavations, a large quantity of figures and other terra-cotta objects were found in an inverted corner of the south-eastern castle-wall (near Ξ on Plan 125), immediately under the surface.   All the pieces lay close to the circuit-wall, but outside of it, and therefore must at some time have been thrown from the Castle.   We need not wonder, there-fore, that most of the objects found were broken.   If, never-theless, so many, still well-preserved, figures and vessels were brought to light, we have mainly to thank the Greek Phylax of Antiquities, Mr. G. Chrysaphis, who for several days, most indefatigably, and with great care, cautiously extracted these pieces from the earth with a knife.

As the objects seem almost all to have been votive offerings, they must have belonged to some sanctuary existing above in the castle.   Where was this sanctuary situated ?   With the exception of the altar in the great court-yard, there are no archi-

tectural remnants of any kind, which we could attribute to it
with certainty. But we can quite imagine that on the same
spot where the Christians afterwards built their church—that is,
at the southern end of the castle—there existed, in older times,
a temple or some other sanctuary. In building the church,
they perhaps collected the votive gifts found near the ancient
sanctuary, and threw them down from the castle wall.

As Dr. Fabricius had already left for Pergamon when the
terra-cottas were found, Dr. Friedrich Koepp was kind enough
to give the following description of them for this book :—

"The fact of idols of the most archaic style, together with
little images of deities of a rather late time, as well as little
vessels which cannot possibly have served for a practical object,
having been found here in large numbers, renders it probable
that we have before us a deposit of rejected votive gifts of an
over-stocked sanctuary—such as have also been discovered
elsewhere. Its tutelar Goddess appears to have been Demeter.
At least, her image is by far the most frequent among those to
which we can give a name at all.

"Nameless, no doubt, must remain the idol of a seated Goddess, which, if it is not of remotest antiquity as regards make,
certainly represents the oldest type. It is now pretty generally
believed that such archaic images were still imitated in later
times when art had already attained a far higher stage. The idol
in question, of which a whole series of specimens, more or less
broken, has been found here (Fig. 159, side-view No. 160 ; comp.
above, pp. 157, 158, Nos. 87–89), represents a sitting female as flat
as a board, with great protruding eyes, bow-like prominent nose,
and with no indication of the mouth. The head is adorned with
a coronal ; the breast with the breast-plate peculiar to many
archaic terra-cottas—the ends of which rise above the shoulders.
(Comp. Schliemann, p. 157 *et seq.*). On the occiput, the tuft
of hair seems to be indicated. The arms are quite misshapen—
not to say stunted—stretched forward and bent in volute shape ;
without hands. The tips of the feet are visible. Instead of a
chair, two legs, apparently growing out of the body of the idol,
support it in sitting posture. These legs, as may be imagined,
are nearly, if not quite, broken off. The height of the
figure is about 0·130 m. Some specimens still show a well-
preserved painting : a broad red stripe on the upper and lower
rim of the breast-plate ; a similar, though narrower, framing of
the diadem ; a red stripe round the neck, and another round the

hips; lastly, on the dress, three horizontal stripes, probably representing branches of a tree. Similar idols, from Tanagra, are in the collection of the Archæological Society ('Αρχαιολογικὴ Ἑταιρία). The same ornamentation is found on Trojan vessels

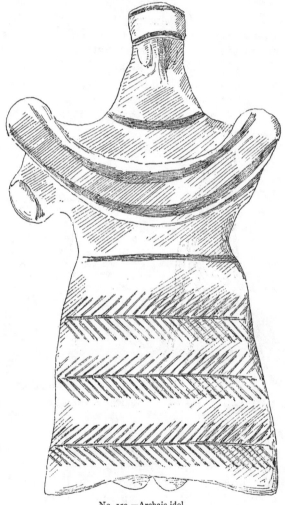

No. 159.—Archaic idol.

See *Ilios*, Nos. 257, 260 and 349 ("The Burnt City"); comp. Sayce, Appendix III.

"To the same type, but to a later development of art, belongs an idol which, it is true, still shows the same manner of sitting

and the same stunted arms, but which has human features, and
also otherwise finer forms. Under the diadem we see a crown
of ringlets; on both sides, long curls fall down to the shoulders.
There is some indication of the breast: the monotony of the
board-like garment is somewhat broken, on both sides, by
straight folds; the feet are placed on a stool. Height: about
0·120 m. (Fig. 161). Considering this more skilful formation
and the completely horizontal position of the shoulder-volutes,
one might imagine that the artist rather wished thereby to
indicate the back of the seat, if only there were any trace of

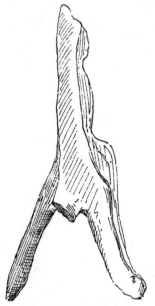

No. 160.—Archaic idol. Side view.　　　　No. 161.—Sitting idol of terra-cotta.

arms. Another figure of the same kind has no longer the
stunted arms, but appears to have the arms drawn stiffly close
to the body, with the hands on the lap.

"Further progress is indicated by a little sitting figure
(height: 0·085 m.), which, to compare small things with great,
might in some degree bring to mind the figures of the Sacred
Way near Miletos. On a high seat of small depth, sits a woman
in a stiff posture; the hands laid on the side-arm of the seat:
the feet are parallel. At the height of the neck, the corners of
the chair-back project on both sides. She wears a diadem and

has shoulder-curls.     On both sides of the dress a broad fold ; in
the centre, three small ones.

  " A similar little figure (height : 0·075 m.), but again formed
with greater artistic intelligence, shows us a woman with a bird
on her lap ; consequently, Aphrodite.

  " More numerous is the group of female figures standing
upright.  The most important among them are those representing
a woman holding a pig under her left arm.  The pig was sacred
to Demeter ; and similar representations of the Goddess have

No. 162.—Terra-cotta figure ; woman with a pig.     No. 163.—Terra-cotta figure ; woman with a pig.

also been found elsewhere among the terra-cottas.  A clay figure
from Eleusis has been published by F. Lenormant in the
*Archæologische Zeitung* (1865), Plate CXC.  Another has been
found by Newton in the district of Demeter of Halikarnassos
(*Discoveries*, p. xlvii. 4).    One is in the collection of the
'Αρχαιολογικὴ 'Εταιρία (No. 16, Martha ; No. 576, from Tegea,
published in *Nuove Memorie*, Plate VI. 6).   One, from Sardinia,
is published in *Annali d. I.*, LV., 1883 ; tav. d' agg. D.

  " The right arm is in most cases quite broken off, or partly so.
In one specimen it is preserved, but the attribute of the right

hand, a spherical object, is no longer recognisable.   In this specimen the figure stands on a rather high plinth.   (Height : 0·165 m.
Fig. 162).   Another (height : 0·170 m. Fig. 163) has no plinth.
but is open below ; and the front half of the feet is elaborated.
Both figures have long curls ; the latter a very slender neck, such
as occurs in other female figures standing upright.   A third
figure, the lower part of the body and the right arm of which are
broken off (height : from the girdle to the crown of the head,
0·062 m. Fig. 164) has a shorter neck, no curls, and the head thrust
forward.   The breasts are more strongly indicated.   The right
arm and the pig are very coarsely formed.   All the figures have
a rather youthful aspect for Demeter ; none of them is archaic ;
all are of hasty or crude workmanship.   To fix the period
of such products exactly is impossible ; but they can scarcely
be assumed to be older than the third century before our era.
Possibly, they are even of more recent date.   A similar kind
of female figure has in her left hand, instead of the pig, an
object which most probably is a deep bowl, such as two clay
figures from Halikarnassos also hold in their hands.   (Newton,
*Discoveries;* Plate XLVII., 3 and 6.)   This figure, too, stands
on a plinth hollow below.   The right lower arm is extended ; but
the open hand which is held sideways, and the fingers of which
are broken off, has probably not held an attribute.   (Fig. 165.)

"Another standing figure, of which the torso only is preserved, gives an archaic impression.   By its narrow and upright
parallel folds, which only show by a very slight curve that the
right leg is the one in motion, it reminds us of the archaic so-
called Hestia.   The action of the arms is no longer recognisable
(height : about 0·115 m. Fig. 166).   The head (height from the
chin to the crown : 0·030 m.) which is described as belonging to
the figure, reposes on a slender neck.   Wavy thick hair sur-
rounds the face ; long curls fall down to the shoulders.

"An archaic impression is also given by the lower part of the
legs of a woman standing on a high plinth, with parallel folds on
both sides and in the centre of the dress.

"Worthy of mention are perhaps also the head and shoulders
of a woman with a *polos* (height from the chin to the *polos*-point :
0·050 m., Fig. 167), of crude workmanship, massive, and flattened
behind ; and two feet, standing parallel on a plinth, the toes and
sandals of which are pretty carefully worked.   Of women with
the *polos* there are several other specimens, more or less mutilated
and insignificant.

"Among the several little heads there is nothing archaic.
Some betray an Oriental influence ; but they, too, seem to belong

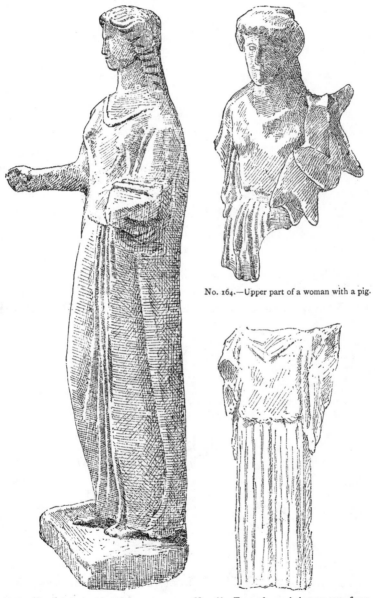

No. 164.—Upper part of a woman with a pig.

No. 165.—Standing woman of terra-cotta.      No. 166.—Torso of an archaic terra-cotta figure.

to a later time. A little head of very skilful workmanship, with abundant curls and a high crown of leaves has a round, softish form. The upright leaves of the diadem are separately placed

No. 167.—Head with polos of terra-cotta.

in moulded sockets ; two of them are broken out. The occiput is broken off or was not finished. (Height from the chin to the leaf-point : 0·045 m.). Another head of the same kind has a more

No. 168.—Female head with diadem.

Oriental appearance. (Height from the chin to the leaf-point : 0·042 m., Fig. 168). Below the diadem two rows of luxuriant curls. Long curls fall down to the shoulders in serpentine lines.

Specially characteristic are the thick lips, the protruding eyes, and the ribbon round the neck, in the centre of which there is a round boss.   A thicker boss is on the right shoulder ; a similar one has probably been broken off on the left.

"A like ribbon, with medallion, is on a more rudely-worked, larger head of the same kind, from which all the leaves are

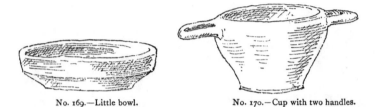

No. 169.—Little bowl.                    No. 170.—Cup with two handles.

broken out ; the diadem itself is injured.   (Height from the chin to the rim of the diadem : 0·045 m.)

" From a better period is a female half-length figure (*protome*), broken into three pieces, which, however, fit into each other. It is broken above the breast ; but, with this exception, nearly perfect.   The head is adorned with a high coronal (*stephane*) and a garland of leaves ; under it there are two rows of curls.

No. 171.—Tripos kettle.                  No. 172.—Little pan.

Long shoulder-curls of curious shape.   (Height from the chin to the upper rim of the coronal : 0·062 m.)

" Of archaic character, but rude workmanship, is the head of a bust (*protome*) with diadem, encircled by flat curls.   (Height from the chin to the point of the diadem : 0·050 m.)

" Amongst the smaller heads, one which reminds us of the most beautiful little heads from Tanagra, merits special mention.   The parting of the hair is very deeply graven ; the hair itself tolerably

worked ; in the nape of the neck there is the remnant of the
chignon.   The chin is full and round.   The type is related to
that of Aphrodite.   (Height :  o·030 m )    Another little head
strikes one as strange by its features being flattened, and by its
curiously broad arrangement of the hair.    (Height :  o·025 m.)

"The fore-part of a pig might perhaps have belonged to one
of the Demeter figures above described : but then, the latter must

No. 173.—Small dish.          No. 174.—Basket with openings in the body of terra-cotta.

have been rather large.    Possibly, also, the animal was a votive
offering for the Goddess.

"To a rather tall, standing female figure belongs a preserved
fore-arm, of good workmanship.

"The vessels are all so small that, owing to their shape, the
idea of their having been put to real use is, in most of them,
excluded.   On the other hand, they all agree in size.   They

No. 175.  Vessel with three openings in the body.        No. 176.—Vessel with two handles.

are shallow little bowls, with considerably convex bottoms
(Fig. 169 ; upper diameter : o·06 m.) ; two-handled cups (Fig. 170 ;
upper   diameter :  o·048 m.) ;   tripod kettles  (Fig. 171), etc.
Specially noteworthy are the handle of the little pan (Fig. 172 ;
diameter in the centre : o·058 m.), and the three double-ears of
the plate (Fig. 173) ; but more particularly, two little baskets with
openings in the body, and a dentated upper rim (Fig. 174), which

have a counterpart in a vessel in the collection of the Archæological Society.   In the latter case, however, the openings are
formed quite regularly in rectangles, whilst in the vessels from
Tiryns they are often awry and crushed.   A vessel in beaker

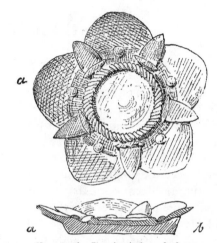

No. 177.—Little vase with two handles.          No. 178 *a, b.*—Flat plate in form of a flower.

(*skyphos*) snape also has two rectangular openings ; another
(Fig. 175) three.   Besides the two little vases (Figs. 176 and 177),
I lastly mention a curious flat plate in the form of a blossom, of
which Fig. 178 gives a plan and a cross-section (diameter from
one leaf-point to the other : 0·085 m.)."

# APPENDIX.

M. PANAGIOTIS STAMATAKIS, Director-General of Antiquities in Greece (whose untimely death, a few weeks ago, we sincerely deplore), was kind enough to let me have a couple of amber beads from the royal tombs at Mycenæ for investigation. I sent them to the well-known chemist M. Otto Helm, of Danzig, whose very accurate analyses I give in this Appendix. The most interesting result appears, that the amber comes from the Baltic, and that therefore, in those very remote times to which the royal tombs of Mycenæ belong (the second millennium B.C.), there was already traffic between Greece and the inhabitants of the Baltic coast. It will probably ever remain unsettled whether this traffic took place by land or by means of Phœnician ships. But in the former case we may easily conjecture that the traffic, as happened again later, especially in the Middle Ages, took its way through Russia and the Balkan peninsula. Or may the amber perhaps have been brought through Russia to Colchis, and thence by Phœnician ships to Greece? At all events, the only time that Homer mentions amber for sale, it is in Phœnician hands :

ἤλυθ' ἀνὴρ πολύϊδρις ἐμοῦ πρὸς δώματα πατρός,
χρύσεον ὅρμον ἔχων, μετὰ δ' ἠλέκτροισιν ἔερτο·
τὸν μὲν ἄρ' ἐν μεγάρῳ δμωαὶ καὶ πότνια μήτηρ
χερσίν τ' ἀμφαφόωντο, καὶ ὀφθαλμοῖσιν ὁρῶντο,
ὦνον ὑπισχόμεναι· ὁ δὲ τῇ κατένευσε σιωπῇ·
ἤτοι ὁ καννεύσας κοίλην ἐπὶ νῆα βεβήκει·

" For a wily man (a Phœnician from a ship) came to the palace of my father, bringing a collar of gold set with beads of amber. This, in the hall, the servant-women and my noble mother were handling and admiring, bargaining for it, and he nodded secretly to the woman, and then was gone to the hollow ship."

That the amber trade in later prehistoric times was in Phœnician hands is beyond doubt.

H. S.

## A.

Danzig, 20th Nov. 1884.

Dr. Schliemann at Athens has been so kind as to send me some fragments of amber beads, which he had himself found in the royal tombs of Mycenæ. I desired to analyse them chemically, in order to see if they were related to the amber found on the Baltic coast. My interest in this question was excited by the analyses made by me three years ago of amber articles from the Necropoleis of Upper and Central Italy, which belong to the oldest Iron Age and the so-called Etruscan Epoch.* I then showed that the amber articles I examined were made of Baltic amber, and not from that found to-day in Sicily and Upper Italy. The chief evidence of this I considered to be the high percentage in them of amber-acid ($4 \cdot 1$–$6 \cdot 3$ per cent.). I observed the same thing lately in the objects of amber from Hallstadt.

I regret to say the fragments now before me of amber beads from the royal tombs at Mycenæ afforded too scanty a material for a chemical investigation; they only weighed 2 grammes. I subjected the larger part of them for the quantitative determination of the amber-acid they contained, and obtained by dry distillation $1 \cdot 6$ per cent. pure amber-acid from them. There were besides $3 \cdot 2$ per cent. of mineral constituents, of silicious earth, calcareous earth, oxide of iron, carbonic acid, and sulphuric acid.

The particles of amber were extraordinarily disintegrated, and easily crumbled away by pressure between one's fingers. The large quantity of mineral substances has plainly found its way into the decaying amber in the course of thousands of years, as sound amber of any kind only contains $\frac{1}{10}$th of the proportion of the mineral substances found here. We may also assume that even the organic part of the amber has suffered loss and change by reason of this disintegration, and that the amount of amber acid was originally higher. Baltic amber yields by distillation 3 to 8 per cent. of amber-acid.

Most of the fragments from Mycenæ were of a dark hyacinthine red, especially in the fracture—the very colour which clear Baltic amber assumes after disintegration. One little piece was wax-coloured, and in this also not different from certain Baltic amber. The Mycenæan pieces also had, when burnt, the same

---

* Cf. *Schriften der Naturforschenden Gesellschaft zu Danzig*, 1862.

peculiar odour as Baltic amber. They differed from it really only in the smaller amount of amber-acid.

I cannot therefore now assert with absolute certainty that Baltic amber lies before us in these pieces; all I can say is that I know no fossil resin now found which so closely resembles the Mycenæan amber as the Baltic amber.

It is certainly not Sicilian or Apennine amber, for I examined both these fossil resins in various pieces, and found them all devoid of amber-acid. In the amber from the Lebanon, gathered and brought to me in some pieces by Professor Fraas, I also found no amber-acid. K. John was able to show small quantities of amber-acid in the brownish-yellow kind of this amber, but none in the red resin.

In the dark-red fossil resins of Galicia (Schrauffit), and some others found in Hungary and Austria, there were also found some traces of amber-acid, but these resins occur very rarely and sporadically; the same is true of the Roumanian amber, and of that found in the Bukowina. These latter contain as much amber-acid as the Baltic amber, but are easily distinguished by a competent judge from it by their colour, hardness, and disintegrated layer. Besides, as far as I know, we have no notice handed down to us that these resins, which occur so rarely in the earth, were already known to the ancient inhabitants of those countries.

On this evidence I may assert, that the objects of amber exhumed by Dr. Schliemann from the royal tombs at Mycenæ are very probably made of Baltic amber.

OTTO HELM.

---

## B.

Danzig, 17th Dec. 1884.

The doubtful result of the analysis of Mycenæan amber, made by me on the 20th November of this year, caused Dr. Schliemann to send me an additional piece of the amber from the royal tombs, which I examined on the 15th and 16th of this month.

The piece was better suited to my purpose than the former; it was the fragment of a large bead, weighed 4·1 grammes, and showed only a slight disintegration.

The colour, when the outer particles of earth were removed, was bright ruby-red, and quite transparent. The outer layers were easily scraped off witn a knife ; as this scraping went on, the amber was found harder and clearer. The ruby colour changed to that of hyacinth, then to bright orange-red ; finally there remained a core of the finest clear amber. This was almost as transparent as water. The beads of this kind must once have been of great value, for this colour is now, even in Baltic amber, very rare, and much prized. I know no other fossil resin which has it with the same degree of hardness. Even the disintegrated layer passing from bright wine-yellow to ruby red, is characteristic of Baltic amber. Equally characteristic was the smell ; when a particle was heated on a platina-sheet and brought to evaporation, the smell excited violent coughing, like the Baltic amber.

To complete my former report, I undertook to make with 2 grammes of the parts scraped off a quantitative determination of the amber-acid contained therein, and here describe the process often used by me. I pour the broken-up amber into a tubular glass-retort, connect it with an ample receiver, and then heat the retort in a sand bath. At first thick clouds of smoke are developed in the retort, which pass into the receiver, then the amber melts and gradually begins to boil ; the clouds of smoke are condensed to a turbid liquid and a brown oil. I continue the distillation as long as vapour passes into the receiver. Then I stop it, allow the apparatus to cool, and cut off the lower part of the retort with an appropriate instrument. The neck of the retort and the receiver I then rinse carefully with distilled hot water, boil the mixture of watery fluid and oil, and separate them with a paper-filter ; the latter I wash again with some distilled water. The filtered fluid I evaporate in a steam-bath till it is dry. Water and volatile acids thus volatilize, and the amber-acid remains in brilliant crystals. I purify the latter again by resolution, filtration, and re-crystallization ; then I weigh and identify them by their peculiar chemical reactions and physical form

In the case before us, and after I had found in my first investigation that a not inconsiderable quantity of earthy substances, especially of calcareous earth and oxide of iron, had got into the amber, I altered the process by mixing with the amber a quantity of sulphuric acid corresponding to both earths. I thus obtained the combination of these kindred earths with the sulphuric acid, so that the amber-acid could be separated by distillation.

The result answered my expectations. I obtained from the 2 grammes of Mycenæan amber 0·12 gramme amber-acid = 6 per cent. The redistilled brown oil was like that of the Baltic amber, and equally sulphureous. The elementary analysis of the amber gives varying results; the more advanced its disintegration, the more oxygen it contains. Here, where an unweathered core was before me, I undertook the analysis. It produced

> 78·60 per cent. carbon.
> 10·08   ,,    hydrogen.
> 10·98   ,,    oxygen.
> 0·34   ,,    sulphur.

An elementary analysis I made of Baltic amber in 1881 gave

> 78·63 per cent. carbon.
> 10·48   ,,    hydrogen.
> 10·47   ,,    oxygen.
> 0·42   ,,    sulphur.

The agreement is here, too, nearly attained. I have therefore no hesitation in declaring the amber beads found in the royal tombs of Mycenæ to be Baltic amber; there are no facts known to show that any product corresponding to the above results can be found elsewhere, *i.e.* anything chemically and physically resembling Baltic amber.

To obviate misunderstandings, I will add, that by *Baltic amber* I mean such as the type dug out of the Tertiary formation of the Prussian *Samland,* and on the coasts from the Russian Baltic provinces as far as Jutland and Holland; also in Southern Sweden. The limits of its spreading southward are not accurately determined; but it becomes rarer and rarer in that direction. It has been found in North Poland, in the Prussian provinces of Posen, Silesia, Brandenburg, Westphalia, and Saxony, in the kingdom of Saxony and in Oldenburg. The great mountain chains of Central Germany appear to have formed the limits of the old diffusion of the Baltic amber. I have analysed chemically a number of specimens found in these lands, and found them not materially different from that dug out in the *Samland.* I therefore call them all by the name "Baltic amber."

OTTO HELM.

# INDEX.

---

during 6th and 7th century B.C., corresponding to that from the Dipylon graves, 87 ; inscription regarding the restoration of its walls, 185.

*Atreus*, treasury of, 272, 280, 286.

*Attica*, the graves of Menidi, Spata, and Aliki in, 56, 84 ; Cape Kolias in, 84 ; the revolution following on the Doric invasion in, 87.

*Auger*, its use in boring dowel-holes, 266 ; found at Troy, *ibid.*

*Axes*, stone, 81 ; of diorite, one specimen at T., 172 ; four at Athens, 173 ; bronze, found at T., 167 sq. ; as symbols on Babylonian ring, on Carian coins, and coins of Tenedos, 168 ; Soph. Müller on, 169.

*Azurite*, 289.

## B.

*Baalbek*, 18, 28.

*Babylon*, χesbet from, 288.

*Badackshan*, 288.

*Baltic* amber, found at Mycenæ, 368–372

*Basilica*, principle of, in Greek buildings, 218 sq.

*Basin*, found in the megaron, but later in construction, 226 ; of unknown use, 226.

*Basis*, of pillars, found *in situ*, 185, 199, 238 ; affected by fire, 238-9 ; discussed, 270.

*Bath-room* at T., 229 sq. ; its place, 230 ; its floor of one gigantic stone, 231 ; its panelled walls, 231 ; draining of, 233, 341.

*Bathing-tub* of terra-cotta, 140.

*Beads* of blue glass, 82.

*Beams* of wood, longitudinal, in walls, 226, 255-6, 262 ; in ceilings, 317.

*Bellerophon*, myth of, 32.

*Benches* in women's court at T., 239.

*Bent, Mr. J. Th.*, cited, 25 ; his excavations at Antiparos, 56, 60. 65, 78, 114 ; on flat roofs in the Cyclades, 220.

*Berlin Anthropological Society*, quoted, 62-3, 78, 168.

*Bernburg*, Historical Society of, 63.

*Beton*, 203.

*Beulé*, on architecture at Byrsa, 325

*Bikellas, Dr. D.*, visits T., 10.

*Blocks*, stone, of the walls of T., 17.

*Blue glass*, Egyptian, 287, 289, 290.

*Blümner, H., Technologie bei Griechen u. Römern*, cited, 26, 258, 265-6.

*Bodkin* at T., 176.

*Bolting* of gates at T. described, 193.

Βοῶπις, meaning of, 46, 165.

*Bötticher, Herr Hauptmann*, his theory of a fire-necropolis, 250 ; on building with clay-bricks, 259.

*Bottle*, fragment, 346.

*Boulpiotes, M.*, Greek Minister of Education, his zeal to promote the excavations, 2, 3.

*Bovolone.* (*See* TOMBS.)

*Bow*, ornament on a vase, 128, 129, 137.

*Bowl*, cup, and kettle, 365.

*Bracelet*, bronze, found at T., 170.

*Branches*, like larch, on a large jar, (πίθος), 69.

*Breccia*, used for door-sills, &c., 193, 202 ; its use discussed, 253 ; in *antæ*, 264.

*Bricks*, sun-dried, of clay, 256 ; glazed with heat, 242, 256 ; of oldest settlement, 252 ; manufacture of, 256 sq. ; the burning of, discussed, 257 sq. ; Vitruvius on, 258 ; comparison with those at Troy, *ibid.*; forms and sizes of, 259-62 ; specially mentioned by Hesychios, 19.

*Brizio, E.*, cited, 61, 67.

*Brockhaus, Dr. E.*, visits T., 10.

*Bronze* objects found at T., 166 sq. ; at Olympia, with geometrical patterns, 88 ; warrior, 166 ; battle-axes, 167-9 ; various objects, 170 ; shoeing of door-pivots, 195 ; drawing of a bronze sheath for the pivot of a door, 281 ; tripod, ear-ring, 357.

—— analysis of Mycenæan, by Dr. J. Percy, 171.

—— coins discovered at T., 48.

*Buchholz*, his *Homerische Realien* cited, 220 ; refuted as regards women's αὐλή, 237.

PORTION OF A LARGE VASE REPRESENTING
TWO WARRIORS, A HORSE AND A DOG.

PLATE XV.

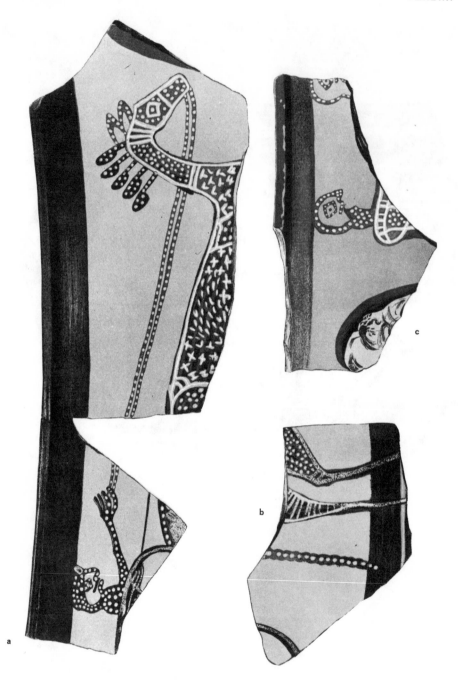

PORTION OF TWO LARGE VASES,
REPRESENTING A MAN IN A CHARIOT.
AND PART OF TWO OTHER MEN.

PLATE XVI.

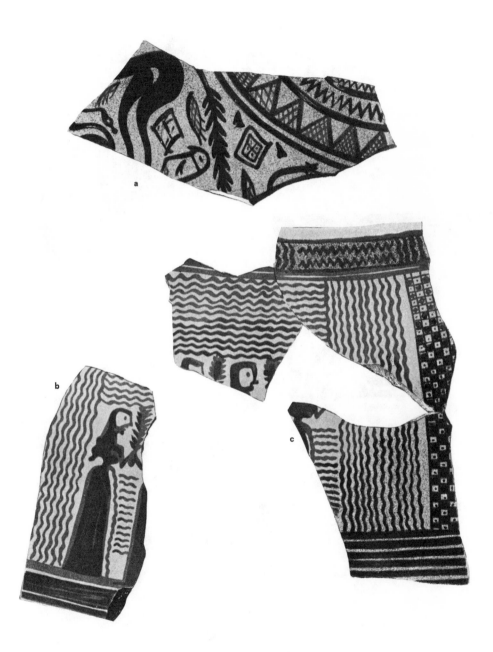

**PORTIONS OF VASES.**
**a** representing part of a Horse and other Ornaments; **b** and **c,** a Procession of Women holding Branches.

PLATE XVII.

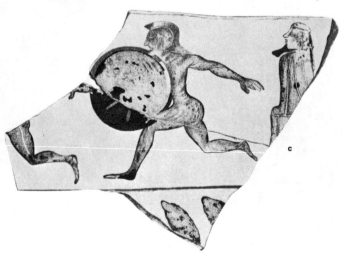

**PIECES OF LARGE VASES.**
**a** representing a Procession of Women holding Branches;
**b,** two Warriors; **c,** two Men running and a Woman standing.

PLATE XVIII.

PORTION OF A LARGE VASE WITH GEOMETRICAL PATTERNS,
A MAN, TWO HORSES, TWO FISHES, ETC.

PLATE XIX.

**THREE PIECES OF VASES.**
a representing a Horse; **b,** a row of Cranes and Horizontal Bands;
**c,** a vertically perforated breast-like excresence.

PLATE XX.

**FRAGMENTS OF VASES.**
a and b representing Geometrical Patterns; c, the upper portion
of a Stag; d, a Bird and portion of another.

PLATE XXI.

a, A fragment of a Vase, representing a Horse;
b, fragment with portion of a Horse's Head;
c, d, and e, a Gold Ornament; f, a Goblet;
g, a Whorl of Violet-coloured Stone with Ornaments.

PLATE XXII.

**FRAGMENTS OF VASES WITH VARIED ORNAMENTATION.**

PLATE XXIII.

**FRAGMENTS OF VASES WITH VARIED ORNAMENTATION.**
a and b, Fragments of Vases, the former representing a Man, the latter
two Birds; c, a Chair, d, a Bottle of Terra-cotta.

PLATE XXIV.

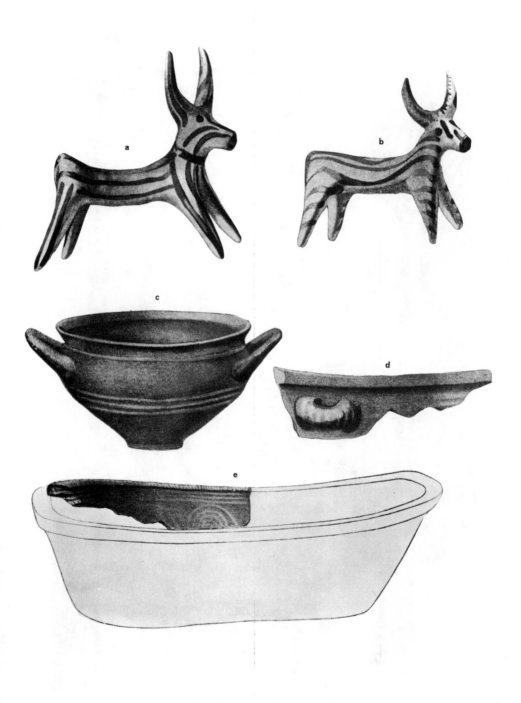

a and b are Hera Idols in the shape of Cows;
c, a Vase; d and e, fragment of a Bath of Terracotta.

PLATE XXV.

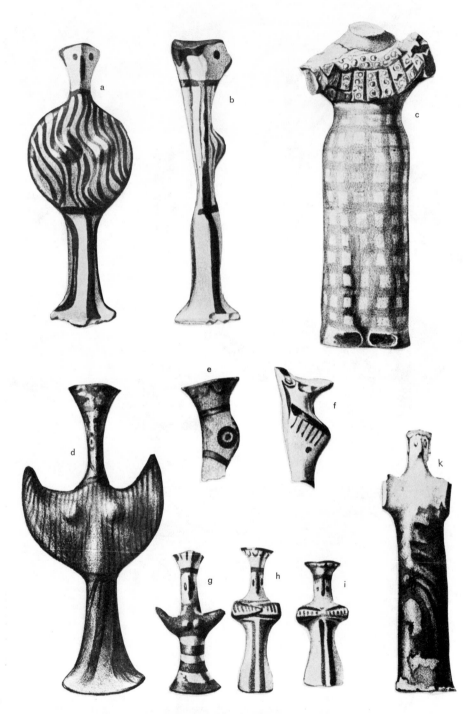

IDOLS OF TERRACOTTA OF VARIOUS SHAPES.

PLATE XXVI.

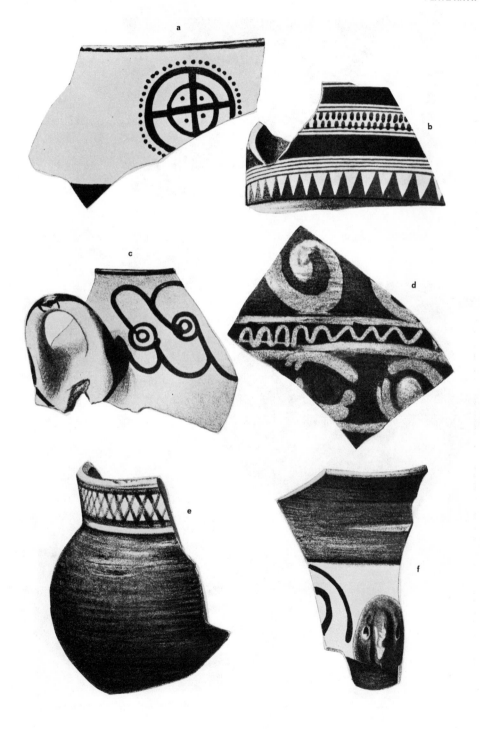

FRAGMENTS OF VASES WITH VARIED ORNAMENTATION.

PLATE XXVII.

a

b

d

c

POTTERY WITH VARIED ORNAMENTATION.